INDIAN CONQUISTADORS

INDIAN CONQUISTADORS

Indigenous Allies

in the Conquest of Mesoamerica

Edited by Laura E. Matthew and Michel R. Oudijk

UNIVERSITY OF OKLAHOMA PRESS : NORMAN

Also by Michel R. Oudijk:

Historiography of the Bènizàa: The Postclassic and Early Colonial Periods, 1000–1600 A.D. (Leiden, The Netherlands, 2000)

(with Maarten Evert Reinoud Gerard Nicolaas and Peter Kröfges) *The Shadow of Monte Alban: Politics and Historiography in Postclassic Oaxaca, Mexico* (Leiden, The Netherlands, 1998)

323.1197
I39
2007

Library of Congress Cataloging-in-Publication Data

Indian conquistadors : indigenous allies in the conquest of Mesoamerica / edited by Laura E. Matthew and Michel R. Oudijk.
    p. cm.
  Includes bibliographical references.
  ISBN 978-0-8061-3854-1 (hardcover : alk. paper) 1. New Spain—History, Military—16th century. 2. Indians of Mexico—Government relations. 3. Indians of Central America—Government relations. I. Matthew, Laura E. II. Oudijk, Michel R.
  F1231.I53 2007
  323.1197—dc22

                         2007012428

The paper in this book meets the guidelines for permanence and durability of the Committee on Production Guidelines for Book Longevity of the Council on Library Resources. ∞

1 2 3 4 5 6 7 8 9 10

Contents

Figures

Maps

TABLES

ACKNOWLEDGMENTS

This volume began with discussions between the various contributors dating as far back as 1998. At conferences and through e-mail, we pondered the thematic overlaps between our various Mesoamerican projects and the possibilities of a comparative project. A panel organized by Yanna Yannakakis and Laura Matthew at the 2002 Southern History Association conference in Baltimore, Maryland, called "Indios Conquistadores: Negotiating Power and Collective Identity in Colonial Mexico and Guatemala" jump-started the process, which was then slowed by several cross-continent and transatlantic moves by both the editors. We would therefore like to thank first and foremost the authors of this volume's chapters, who gave so willingly of their time and talent and waited patiently for the results.

A special acknowledgment is due to the keepers of the many colonial- and precolonial-era documents utilized in these studies: national and regional archivists, museum directors, and local officials in small towns across Mesoamerica. Without their devoted labor to safeguard such materials and to make them accessible to scholars, none of these studies would have been possible. We also acknowledge with gratitude the funding agencies that supported our collective work.

We also particularly thank Robin Gold of Forbes Mill Press and John Chuchiak for the extraordinary maps; Susan Schroeder for guidance and comments on all the chapters in the volume's early stages; the anonymous reviewers at University of Oklahoma Press for their insightful suggestions and careful reading; and Alessandra Jacobi and the production team at OUP for making this a better book than it was.

Indian Conquistadors

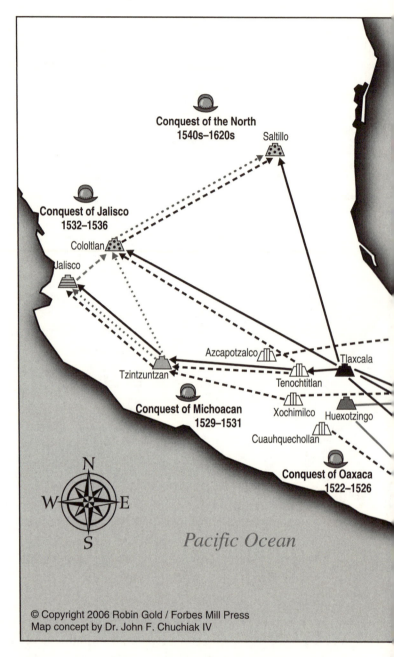

Conquest of the North
1540s–1620s
Saltillo

Conquest of Jalisco
1532–1536
Cololtlan
Jalisco

Azcapotzalco
Tlaxcala

Tzintzuntzan
Tenochtitlan

Conquest of Michoacan
1529–1531
Xochimilco
Huexotzingo

Cuauhquechollan

Conquest of Oaxaca
1522–1526

N
W   E
S

Pacific Ocean

Map 1. Indios conquistadores in Spanish expeditions of
conquest in New Spain, 1519–1620

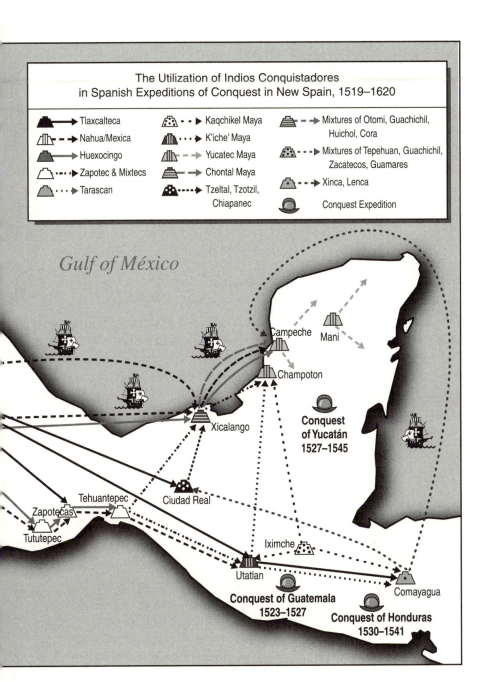

The Utilization of Indios Conquistadores
in Spanish Expeditions of Conquest in New Spain, 1519–1620

Tlaxcalteca

Nahua/Mexica

Huexocingo

Zapotec & Mixtecs

Tarascan

Kaqchikel Maya

K'iche' Maya

Yucatec Maya

Chontal Maya

Tzeltal, Tzotzil, Chiapanec

Mixtures of Otomi, Guachichil, Huichol, Cora

Mixtures of Tepehuan, Guachichil, Zacatecos, Guamares

Xinca, Lenca

Conquest Expedition

Gulf of México

Campeche

Mani

Champoton

Xicalango

Conquest
of Yucatán
1527–1545

Tehuantepec

Ciudad Real

Zapotecas

Tututepec

Iximche

Utatlan

Comayagua

Conquest of Guatemala
1523–1527

Conquest of Honduras
1530–1541

Introduction

The Genre of Conquest Studies

SUSAN SCHROEDER

W̲e are just a few years shy of the quincentennial commemoration of the alleged conquest of Mexico by Hernando Cortés in 1521. It will be interesting to see how Mexico and Spain choose to observe the occasion. I would like to begin with the question, how do we view the conquest today? and then propose an answer by placing the ideology of conquest in the context of its manifestation in the historiography. I see three familiar trends, or dimensions, in conquest studies: the epic Spanish conquest, the spiritual conquest, and the conquest as loser history, or a nonevent. The essays in this volume represent of a new, fourth trend: the Indians as the conquerors.

THE FIRST TREND: THE EPIC SPANISH CONQUEST

What good can come from these military campaigns that would, in the eyes of God, who evaluates all things with unutterable love, compensate for so many evils, so many injuries, and so many unaccustomed misfortunes?

FRAY BARTOLOMÉ DE LAS CASAS,
IN DEFENSE OF THE INDIANS

The history of the Conquest is necessarily that of the great man who achieved it.

WILLIAM HICKLING PRESCOTT,
HISTORY OF THE CONQUEST OF MEXICO

I propose a brief overview that is limited to English-language publications of first importance. That said, however, one cannot begin to consider the literature of conquest without giving credit to the earliest and most valuable sources on the initial contacts between Native Americans and Spaniards: the letters of conquest written by Cortés from America to Emperor Charles V (c. 1519–26), the history of Cortés's accomplishments as written in Spain by his priest and secretary Francisco López de Gómara (1552), and the reminiscent firsthand report from Guatemala by one of the men in Cortés's company, Bernal Díaz del Castillo (1568). There were, of course, other accounts, but none have proved as personal, expressionistic, or lasting as these truly remarkable works. They were first published in Spanish, but all were translated to English in the twentieth century and made available to a wide readership.[1] In Europe in the sixteenth, seventeenth, and eighteenth centuries, the Cortés histories, among others, were used variously and ultimately politically to discredit Spain and her American colonies. Not surprisingly, many of the citizens of New Spain used these same, now classic conquest histories as models for their own conquest-motivated cause for independence from Spain (1810–21).[2]

Taking it farther, politicians and other opportunists in the United States capitalized on the anti-Spanish conquest propaganda in Europe and used it to their own advantage as they advocated war against Mexico, which was launched in 1846. Contemporaneously, William Hickling Prescott (1796–1859) published his grand *History of the Conquest of Mexico* in 1843 and deserves recognition for being the first to make the history of the conquest available to the English-speaking audience of the United States. The book was acclaimed a masterpiece, and Prescott a genius of the epic narrative. It was indeed an epic history; the Modern Library edition of 2001 is 920 pages. Yet Prescott was as much a literary author as a historian, a romantic who considered himself a philosophical historian.[3] Analysis of his sources, it seems, was not an issue; nor was there much, if any, interest in truth or pattern.[4] Having been blinded in one eye during a dining room food fight while a student at Harvard University and then losing partial sight in his other eye while traveling abroad, Prescott at least had the financial resources to arrange for transcriptions and copies to be made of manuscript conquest accounts that were housed in repositories in Europe and Mexico and to hire secretaries to read all of them to him. Following the lore and history recorded by López de Gómara and the consummate conqueror himself, Cortés, Prescott subscribed to the Great Man theory of history that was fashionable in his circle. Ostensibly uncritical of his sources and oblivious to the indigenous perspective, Prescott wrote overwhelmingly from the Spaniards' point of view. Moreover, Prescott was a man of his time and place, and we are not necessarily surprised to see the Nahua of Mexico Tenochtitlan derogatorily described as barbarians, wretches, and a fierce and brutal race.[5] Although Prescott's history enjoyed tremendous critical and popular success, it also created improbable stereotypes of both the Spaniards and the Nahua that remained fixed in the minds of U.S. readers for many generations.

THE SECOND TREND: THE SPIRITUAL CONQUEST

Amongst those who receive the sacrament of penance, remarkable things have occurred and still occur every day, and most of them— nearly all, in fact—are well known to the confessors; and by these things they know the great mercy and goodness of God, who thus brings sinners to true repentance.

TORIBIO MOTOLINÍA,
HISTORY OF THE INDIANS OF NEW SPAIN

Although I think that it will not be held against me to speak of my opinions about why these heathen customs and superstitions have remained and have continued for so long in these natives after baptism, and even some [now exist] that were not permitted to them in their heathen state.

HERNANDO RUIZ DE ALARCÓN, *TREATISE*

Ninety years after Prescott published his opus, Robert Ricard began to champion a "spiritual conquest" exalting the mendicant clergy and their essentially exclusive and near-faultless role in the evangelization of native

New Spain.[6] He particularizes the orders and privileges the Franciscans and their messianic mission as doubtless one of the most important contributions to the formation and development of New Spain. Cortés is still important: he paved the way by destroying idols and temples and implanting crosses instead, and then he invited the regulars. The Franciscans were subsequently almost as zealous as Cortés had been as they campaigned for Christian souls, for they came to believe that the Indians were obviously God's gift to them and their means to save the Roman Church. According to their own accounts, they were largely successful, and Ricard too thought that the early activities of the religious in New Spain profoundly influenced the course of Mexican history. Many of the friars' writings were published, and when we read them uncritically, we are taken with the friars' devotion, piety, and optimism. But Ricard depended too much on these reports and ultimately concluded that if blame were to be placed for the natives' incomplete conversion to Catholicism, which was eventually apparent, it should fall on the Church for its failure to permit ordination of the Indians. It was for this reason alone, he felt, that a national Mexican Church was never realized.

In general, Ricard's book went unchallenged, and it was not until the last twenty years or so that we began to seriously examine his spiritual conquest hypothesis. In fact, Louise M. Burkhart's work reveals that more likely it was the religious who were conquered as they transformed medieval Catholicism to accommodate the Native American worldview and practice. Burkhart uses Nahuatl philology to demonstrate that the friars learned, adapted, and used the local languages and traditions to proselytize.[7] Contrary to the mendicants' and Ricard's understanding, it turns out that what the natives embraced of Christianity was often what was already known and practiced. The Franciscans' open-air colonial churches and sermonizing were well suited to precontact temples and religious theater. New lyrics and instruments were introduced, but otherwise music and dance continued to be important. Christian confraternities only served to reinforce community identity and solidarity, and even the language and worship of Catholic theology often conformed to the indigenous worldview and thus was seldom orthodox.

Many indigenous peoples converted to Christianity, though, and became stalwart believers. One such person is the seventeenth-century Nahua historian Chimalpahin, who by all the evidence was an exemplary Christian. He was quite taken with Christian pomp and circumstance, and among the pages of his annals of Mexico City spanning the time he lived there (1593–ca. 1624), are meticulous descriptions of the vestments of a local bishop and of the many processions in celebration of certain feast days, as well as numerous details about the activities of Franciscans and Nahua at their Chapel of San Josef at the Franciscan church in the capital. He follows the old indigenous year count, juxtaposes it to Gregorian calendar reckoning, and periodically marks time with notes regarding just how many years it has been since our lord Jesus Christ was born. As if there were no contradiction, he also includes straightforward histories of life in ancient times with all its wars of conquest, human sacrifice, and cannibalism.[8]

I do not intend to disparage the cultural and spiritual contributions of the regular clergy in early Mexico, for many wrote their own epic ethnographies, which have proved invaluable sources of information about indigenous life and history.[9] However, in all these works, as before, the Spanish and spiritual conquests are taken for granted.

THE THIRD TREND: LOSER HISTORY, OR THE CONQUEST OF MEXICO AS A NONEVENT

O what great good fortune for the Indians is the coming of the Spaniards.
FRANCISCO CERVANTES DE SALAZAR, *MÉXICO EN 1554*

The year Eleven House, 1529. At this time smallpox prevailed; there were blisters. And also there were comets.
DON GABRIEL DE AYALA, TEXCOCO,
RECORDED BY CHIMALPAHIN

The Mexican historian Bernardo García Martínez, who aptly reduced all of Prescott to "the great march and downfall of a great city," believes that we cannot separate the political and spiritual conquests; nor does he find destruction of the indigenous world.[10] Hence, an examination of the authors and their motivations for writing the conquest histories is in order. In my own work on Hernando Cortés, Bernal Díaz del Castillo, Francisco López de Gómara, Fray Bernardino de Sahagún, Cristóbal del Castillo, and even Diego Muñoz Camargo, I found that in many ways all these authors can be considered losers, for all felt they had lost out on what they believed were deserved recognition and reward and on their fair share of the distribution of the spoils of the conquest.[11] Writing a history would perhaps furnish one more opportunity to achieve the coveted compensation or, more likely, serve to assuage the disappointments. Consider Cortés and Díaz del Castillo, who were losers in both Spain and New Spain. For comparison, in the settling of the frontiers of northern North America one whose fame and fortune were established stayed in New York or Philadelphia. The same held true for Andalusia and Extremadura. Both men were obviously dispensable to their home communities and sought to improve their circumstances in America.

Cortés may have had advantages over most of his Spanish colleagues, especially in terms of his keen intelligence, cunning, and charismatic personal style. But in other matters Cortés was simply the first among other ne'er-do-well Spaniards who sought a better life in the Americas. Steve J. Stern refers to these undertakings as the "utopia of social precedence," which was compressed into three achievements: escape from stifling subordination and constraint in an old society, rise to a new position of command and authority over human dependents and clients in a new society, and acquisition of a recognized claim to high honor or service that legitimated reward and social superiority.[12] Cortés said as much when he prodded his men, "We shall win the greatest honor and glory that were ever won up to this time."[13]

But Cortés, for all his accomplishments in bringing about the destruction of the Mexica capital of Mexico Tenochtitlan, was never acknowledged or compensated as he felt he should have been. He died in Spain in 1547 with all his letters, petitions, and lawsuits, never to be appointed viceroy in the very place he himself had named, New Spain. Díaz del Castillo was a double loser as well. He ended up with an *encomienda* in faraway Guatemala instead of one of the great indigenous states close to the capital; and then, when he was an old man, he was threatened with the loss of his encomienda. He wrote his history as a veteran of the battles of conquest to exult the cause of the conquerors and save his estate.[14]

Francisco López de Gómara, writing exuberant histories in admiration of the great Spanish conquests in both North and South America, could not say enough about Cortés and his fellow Spaniards. Indeed, he went so far as to state, "The greatest act after the creation of the world, with the exception of the birth of the creator, Jesus Christ, is the discovery of the Indies."[15] His *Historia de las indias* was first published in Zaragoza in 1552, with six more editions in Spain by 1556.[16] But López de Gómara's history had been brought to the attention of Prince Philip, who suppressed its publication in Castile in 1553 and mandated severe penalties for anyone caught reading the book, even in the American colonies. For López de Gómara, everything was compounded when the Crown later confiscated all of his papers.

The Franciscans were also losers, and we should keep in mind that even Sahagún had a personal agenda when he enlisted the assistance of Nahua informants to write *The Conquest of Mexico*, book 12 of his *Historia general*. First, as staunch supporters of Cortés (who was being vilified by his enemies), the Franciscans wanted him to be recognized as the initiator of Christianity in New Spain. There is merit in this claim, for Cortés had done much to promote their evangelical enterprise. Yet, Cortés, his colleagues, his heirs, and the Franciscans too were perceived by the Crown as potential threats to the king's sovereignty in New Spain.

Second, the mendicant mission itself had lost the king's favor, and secularization was imminent. To glorify the political and spiritual conquests, Sahagún turned to the indigenous perspective. He brought in his aides, former Nahua students at the Franciscans' Colegio de Santa Cruz at Santiago Tlatelolco. For two centuries the Mexica Tlatelolca had shared the island with the Mexica Tenochca, better known as the peoples of the dominant ethnic state of the triumvirate Aztec or Mexica Empire. The Mexica Tlatelolca loathed the Tenochca, and hence we have for the Spanish conquest of Mexico a history of defeat and destruction blamed on the infamous Mexica Tenochca, who it just so happens had conquered the Tlatelolca in 1473.[17] As longtime losers, the Tlatelolca took revenge by blaming the fall of the great Mexica capital on the ineptitude of the Tenochca.[18] It is uncertain if Sahagún was even aware of the untoward ethnic enmity and bias that was implicit in his conquest history.

Briefly, Cristóbal del Castillo, as either a loser Nahua or a loser mestizo, wrote his Nahuatl history at the end of the sixteenth century in praise of the Spanish Crown and Catholicism along with nostalgia for the good old days.[19] Mostly, though, he was upset because he was old, impoverished, and unappreciated, for he too had apparently failed to receive any of the benefits of the conquest. He signed himself, "Auh ca in nehuatl ca nicnotlacatzintli" (I am a poor, humble person).[20] And Muñoz Camargo, if we look closely, was worried about the Tlaxcalteca as possible losers and wrote his Spanish conquest account to reiterate and even illustrate the all-important role of his fellow Tlaxcalteca patriots and ensure their promised privileges.[21] In 1584 Muñoz Camargo traveled to Spain to deliver his manuscript to the king personally.

The Spaniards invariably portrayed the conquest as Armageddon with little consideration for the native peoples who survived their invasions and onslaughts.[22] But war and conquest, not peace, were processual in Mesoamerica, and the Nahua, especially, wrote about them at length. Their pictorial and alphabetic annals are poignant, graphic reminders of centuries of warfare. Pictorially, the palace of the indigenous ruler in a particular ethnic state is depicted with the roof toppled and aflame and a sign for a shield and arrow as a Nahuatl metaphor for the destruction of the polity. In their alphabetical literature, there was a special Nahuatl vocabulary—the transitive verb *pehua* (to conquer someone), and the intransitive verbs *polihui* (to disappear, be destroyed, be defeated) and *yauh* (to go [out of existence])—to describe conquest and subjugation, whether it was conquest by other groups, by the Mexica decades earlier, or by the Spaniards in the sixteenth century. In English translation, the Nahuatl terms seem to connote profound loss of population and property.

Nahua historian Chimalpahin writes, "ypan in pehualloque yn chalca" (in this year [1465] the Chalca were conquered), and according to perceptions of the Chalca the golden age of their great society came to an end at that time.[23] Elsewhere, he notes, "auh ynic tepeuh Mexico yn capitan general Hernando Cortés, . . . ynic moyahuac Mexicayotl Tenochcayotl" (when Captain General Hernando Cortés conquered Mexico, . . . the Mexico Tenochtitlan entity [or state] went out of existence).[24] The Punic Wars and the leveling and utter destruction of Carthage (146 B.C.) immediately come to mind. But in Nahuatl, only political sovereignty was lost. In Chalco all the rulers went into exile but left their heirs to eventually succeed them. In Mexico Tenochtitlan, the king certainly died, but the four-part sociopolitical structure of governance was maintained with traditional nobles as Spanish-styled elected officials in control much as they had before. Analyzing the Nahuatl conquest terminology in greater context, a Nahua state can be "conquered," even "destroyed," but as long as the traditional royal lineage (*tlatocatlacamecayotl*) and the rulership (*tlatocayotl*) were intact and operating, the society and polity continued.

Many Nahuatl alphabetic annals are extant. Typically, each set is a chronology of key events or episodes that occurred in a particular polity, and some trace back several hundred years. Most are transcriptions of pictorial annals that document a people's migrations, wars of conquest, environmental and celestial phenomena, the ritual tying up of the years every fifty-two years, the births and deaths of rulers, and kings' successors and sometimes genealogies, essentially everything that was important in the history of the state. Most revealing is that many annals contain no record of the conquest, or, at best, the Spaniards are mentioned but only as if they were any other indigenous group in Mesoamerica. Many annals continue the reporting of events and local interests beyond 1521 and well through the sixteenth century or fail to include the year altogether—a true nonevent. It is worth noting that *conquista* as a loanword has yet to appear in Nahuatl annals.

THE FOURTH TREND: THE INDIANS AS CONQUERORS

The ruler was known as the lord of men. His charge was war. Hence, he determined, disposed, and arranged how war would be made.
FRAY BERNARDINO DE SAHAGÚN, *GENERAL HISTORY OF THE THINGS OF NEW SPAIN*, BOOK 8

And they were rewarded according to their merits; the ruler accorded favors to all—costly capes, breech clouts, chocolate, food, and devices, and labrets and earplugs. Even more did the ruler accord favors to the princes if they had taken captives. He gave them the offices of stewards, and all wealth without price—honor, fame, renown.
FRAY BERNARDINO DE SAHAGÚN, *GENERAL HISTORY OF THE THINGS OF NEW SPAIN*, BOOK 8

It is interesting that while the term *conquista* is absent from indigenous-authored histories, *conquistador* appears with some frequency. Chimalpahin states:

Auh yehuatl ipan in yn omoteneuh tlacatl moteucçomatzin xocoy-otl yhcuac tlatocati yn tenochtitlan ypan acico in hernando cortes yn capitan hualmochiuhtia yn ixquichtin quinhualhuicac Españoles in çatepan nican oquimotocayotico conquistadores.

[In the time when the said lord Moctezuma Xocoyotl was ruling in Tenochtitlan, Hernando Cortés arrived; he was captain of all the Spaniards that he brought with him, who afterward were called conquistadors here.][25]

Shortly thereafter, several native peoples from central New Spain seemed to appropriate the term for themselves. Of course, these were the Indians who joined forces with the Spaniards on expeditions of conquest subsequent to the fall of Mexico Tenochtitlan. Among the first of the expeditions to set out was that of Pedro de Alvarado (1524), who reportedly enjoyed the support of some six thousand native allies for his conquest of Guatemala. But Guatemala was not the only destination in New Spain for the *indios conquistadores*; there are reports of native groups traveling as far south as El Salvador and as far north as Santa Fe, New Mexico. Charles Gibson speculates that the Tlaxcalteca may have traveled to Florida in 1559 and to Havana and Santo Domingo in 1583.[26] The Tlaxcalteca, of course, are the best known of the indios conquistadores, for theirs was the first major polity to ally with Cortés in significant numbers. However, on most occasions, and as was certainly the case in the course of Cortés's great march to Mexico Tenochtitlan, the Tlaxcalteca are but one of several native groups who were recruited or forced or who volunteered to go to battle in foreign territories.

Traditionally, the Nahua peoples of central Mexico were fiercely loyal and patriotic to their home polities and lamented, even despised, the loss of local sovereignty upon conquest by outsiders, such as the Mexica. Once subjugated, though, they were obligated to participate in the imperial wars. Each ethnic group participated as a separate, corporate entity with designated duties, insignia, and positions as they marched into battle.[27] Survivors returned to their home communities, presumably with some portion of the booty.[28]

In the precontact era, warriors and subjugated peoples were constrained to go to war. But after the Spaniards brought down Mexico Tenochtitlan, we must question the push and pull factors that led large groups of Indians to leave their homes, often forever, to either wage war or establish colonies in distant lands. Thousands are known to have participated at the Spaniards' bidding over the course of the sixteenth century. The sources indicate that there were four quite distinct categories of indios conquistadores at this time: the individuals and groups who were forced, often in chains, to accompany Spaniards and battle other native peoples; the groups who volunteered to assist a conqueror or viceroy and then returned home; the groups who departed as warriors, conquerors, and auxiliaries and became permanent colonists; and the groups who eschewed warfare but went to colonize and by their good example lure natives in unsettled areas to follow their ways. For some groups, the forced marches and battles were extraordinarily difficult, even deadly. But for others, what were the enticements, and how could home communities afford to lose their most able-bodied citizens? Was it the "emerald arrowheads" in the north promised by Alvar Núñez Cabeza de Vaca?[29] Or might they have been losers, just like Cortés and his followers, whose only opportunity for prestige and privilege was far away from home? For example, according to Muñoz Camargo, King Xicotencatl (el Viejo) of Tizatlan, Tlaxcala, had more than five hundred wives and concubines and, thus, very many children.[30] Because only one son was eligible to succeed him in office, what possibilities were there for the hundreds of aspiring noble sons and sons-in-law?[31] In the past, the marriage of sons and daughters to nobles in distant polities had served imperial pretensions.

The sources seldom reveal the exact motivations of the conquistadores, but the chapters in this volume are rich in information about their lives in the course of battle or their settlements in foreign lands. For example, Ida Altman (chapter 5) contrasts the dreadful conditions of natives conscripted and brutalized by Nuño de Guzmán on his rampage (1530–31) across western New Spain with that of viceroy Don Antonio de Mendoza, who took willing allies (it seems) on his campaign in the north just a decade later (1541–42), while Stephanie Wood's essay about the Cholulteca and the Mapa de Cuauhtlantzinco (chapter 8) is suggestive of the category of indios conquistadores who returned home after going to battle but, according to their history and lore, carried on a spiritual conquest of sorts among other, more local, Nahua.

An excellent primary source is the Nahuatl account dictated by king Don Francisco de Sandoval Acacitli of Tlalmanalco to an aide as they traveled to Mexico City in response to a call to arms by viceroy Don Antonio de Mendoza.[32] Acacitli offered his services along with a contingent of fellow Chalca and some warriors from Xochimilco. They all went voluntarily and in full battle array—armor, shields, swords, and their respective insignia and devices. Two of Acacitli's sons were in the company. They departed on September 29, 1541, and the scribe furnishes what appears to be a day-by-day report of the route, terrain, stopovers, and length of each stay. Although not apparently written in traditional style, the travel and battle narratives are reminiscent of the migration accounts in Nahuatl alphabetic annals. Speeches and dialogue are also fairly standard in native annals, so we are not surprised to find conversations recorded between Acacitli and the viceroy, "Así es, muy buena gente es la de Chalco." This, of course, reflects an aspect of the expected ethnopatriotism in favor of the Chalca, for the conversations seem to be exclusive of anyone else on the expedition. On engagement with enemy Indians, the indios conquistadores destroyed crops and burned huts and temples, and their *flecheros* used their traditional bows and arrows as well as other weapons to capture and kill their enemies. According to Acacitli, in this undertaking, frequently referred to as the Mixton War (1541–42), the conquistadores were a ranked coalition of four groups: by ethnonym the Tlaxcalteca, Huexotzinga, and Quauhquecholteca; the Mexica and Xilotepeca; the Acolhua (Texcoca); and the peoples of Michoacan and Mextitlan and the Chalca. Indeed, Philip Wayne Powell cites a total of "30,000 Aztec and Tlaxcalan auxiliaries."[33] The Chalca were reportedly in charge of the artillery, munitions, and sheep. Throughout the narrative the battle groups maintain their ethnic identities, with Acacitli periodically reminding us that the Chalca were always the most formidable and available.

Even as early as 1541, Acacitli was quite familiar with the Roman liturgical calendar and noted the passing of the days following what must be the Julian calendar. Perhaps most interesting is that in the midst of battle everyone stopped to celebrate Christmas Eve. A banquet of food, chocolate, flowers, and incense was brought out for the conquistadores, and fodder was provided for the horses. In addition, following ancient warfare practices, there was celebratory dancing. On the first night the Amaquemeque of Chalco danced, and on the third night Acacitli sang and danced.[34] Then, each ethnic group danced in full battle regalia.

But things did not continue to go so well, and soon there was a shortage of food and potable water, and sickness prevailed. Acacitli was taken seriously ill, but he reports that he refused to leave the viceroy. Other groups deserted, however, and Acacitli notes that the Tlaxcalteca were among the first to depart. Viceroy Mendoza praised those who stayed for their dedication, and when they were ultimately victorious he proffered his gratitude and promised to remember all that they had contributed. The expedition appears to have lasted from September to close to Easter of the following year.[35] On their return to Tlalmanalco, Acacitli and his entourage received a grand reception, with a procession through decorative arches and everyone lining the street to greet them. Doubtless due to the successful outcome of the war, individuals, families, and groups from all over central Mexico began to make their way north to find work as warriors, miners, and in any number of other undertakings.

Obviously, Acacitli and his men garnered a great deal of prestige for having supported the viceroy. Surely he was among the *teteuctin* (lords) who were granted the privilege of riding a horse, wearing Spanish clothing, and carrying a sword and dagger. Earlier, the Chalca had been quick to offer women, gold, and their service to Cortés as he made his way to Mexico Tenochtitlan. Moreover, Cortés had maintained a relationship with some of the Chalca kings, even serving as *compadre* on the baptism of one of their sons.[36] Acacitli showed great foresight and wisdom in keeping a journal documenting the Chalca's invaluable services on behalf of the viceroy.

The third category of indios conquistadores, those who signed on with the Spaniards for foreign wars of conquest and then settled permanently among the newly subjugated peoples, can be described as *naborías*. They left because of death and destruction in their home communities or just because they hoped to profit from a close relationship with a Spaniard. In these instances, the spoils of conquest included land, privileges, and exemption from encomienda service. The chapters in this volume by Florine Asselbergs (chapter 2), Laura Matthew (chapter 3), Robinson Herrera (chapter 4), and Yanna Yannakakis (chapter 7) furnish a rich array of histories about the various groups of men and women who served with the Spaniards in the conquest of Guatemala and Oaxaca and then stayed on.

In both regions the conquistadores strove to maintain their ethnic identities and to optimize their distinctive role as conquistadores. Like Acacitli, they employed a variety of written devices such as *mapas, lienzos, probanzas*, and letters to document all that they had contributed. These reports were submitted as appeals to local and Crown authorities to secure their privileges, and in many cases they were successful for many years. Asselbergs's study of the Lienzo de Quauhquechollan (chapter 2) brings to light the great value of lienzos. In alphabetic form, the letter from the neighboring native *cabildo* of Huexotzingo to the king of Spain, generated at the same time, says much the same thing.[37] The Lienzo de Quauhquechollan reiterates that the Quauhquecholteca were identical to all the other ethnic states that allied with Cortés; they were using whatever means necessary to maintain the integrity of their polity, and that meant demonstrating their crucial role as allies of the Spaniards.

This lienzo, however, portrays a double conquest, for the Quauhquecholteca also accompanied the Alvarado brothers in their conquests at Guatemala. It is likely that this extraordinary document was typical of the canvas art that was hung as tapestry in the palaces of native rulers as glorious reminders of victorious battles; except that all these ancient precious works are lost. One need only recall the walls in the galleries of El Escorial built by Philip II, very likely the man to whom the lienzo was addressed, to appreciate the universal appeal of such commemorative documents. Moreover, the lienzo is telling of classic ethnopatriotism—with the *altepetl* glyph, a token Hapsburg medallion, and the standard pictorial literary devices necessary to relate such an essential story.

Although proud of their role as conquistadores, not all were distinguished as such. Rather, in Guatemala, as Matthew reveals (chapter 3), most of the natives who had fought with Alvarado were labeled "indios mexicanos," surely an attempt to distinguish the newcomers from the resident Maya peoples. The Spaniards referred to Nahuatl, the language that most of the indios conquistadores spoke, as "Mexicano," and largely it served, though Mixtec and Zapotec speakers were also among the conquistador corps. The conquistadores settled in their own communities on the outskirts of Santiago and used the same label to identify themselves generally for political and economic purposes while retaining considerable ethnic autonomy.

It is likely that this first settlement represented the Mesoamerican canonical eight, with a special Spanish-generated sector of elites (the *reservados*) and a group from Tehuantepec who formed a not very Nahua total of ten. They enjoyed a quasi-elite status, not as Spaniards, but with privileges that the colonial Guatemalan Maya did not share.[38] As militia they came to participate in local political and religious affairs, and I wonder if they continued to wear traditional altepetl insignia on uniforms and banners when they put themselves on public display. They especially participated in church festival celebrations, most notably the Fiesta del Volcán, which purportedly was a serial reenactment of conquest and their own defeat. Repatriation was not a concern, although apparently some contact was maintained with the home community, and additional recruits arrived periodically. Moreover, the indios mexicanos of Santiago continued to participate in campaigns of conquest near and far across present-day Central America.

Yannakakis (chapter 7) furnishes another exemplary study of colonizing Indians and their survival due to common identity. In this case the Tlaxcalteca served as mercenaries for the Spaniards in Villa Alta, Oaxaca, and it was the Zapoteca who were subjugated. In every instance the indios conquistadores of Oaxaca are classic examples of native naborías. Naturally, these natives were quicker to acculturate, and many were employed as interpreters, school teachers, and political intermediaries for both Spaniards and Zapoteca. They never assimilated in Spanish society, and as was the case with the Mexicano militia in Guatemala their social status was above that of local Zapoteca but always apart and subordinate to the Spaniards.

Yet Analco, their town, seems to have been an eclectic, inclusive community of Indians, with mestizos and other indigenous peoples residing there and marrying in. This contrasts with the Tlaxcalteca of the north, for example, who, however idealized, kept themselves endogamous. The Oaxaca indios conquistadores appear to have been far more worldly and opportunistic. For centuries, as the Spaniards' allies they successfully defended their prerogatives in the courts. This association was also to be their undoing, ultimately, for their activities as spies and *gusanos* (traitors) endeared them to no one. Yannakakis also takes up the issue of race, and it is apt. However humble their circumstances, the Spaniards traditionally considered themselves superior and kept themselves apart from other social groups in New Spain. The Quauhquecholteca made a point of this graphically by skin-color representations on the lienzo. In this instance, the indios conquistadores of Oaxaca, no matter how great their loyalty to the Spaniards, which often forced them to engage in many despicable actions against other native peoples, were nonetheless unable to overcome the Spaniards' racial prejudice. Under Bourbon rule in the eighteenth century, things simply became worse.

Again, we must ask, What prompted these peoples to abandon their homeland and endure all the hardships of travel and war while serving under the Spaniards? We are inclined to believe—indeed, much of the literature agrees—that they went voluntarily, but many Nahua, especially the Quauhquecholteca and Xochimilca, were from the Alvarados' encomiendas, and they may not have had a choice. This supports what seems to be a glaring contradiction that John F. Chuchiak puts forth in chapter 6—that not all indios conquistadores were necessarily representative of a "coalition of the willing."[39] Chuchiak's focus is the conquest of Yucatan, which entailed a series of long, drawn out, not always victorious, battles against Yucatec Maya. The sheer numbers of coerced natives from regions as distant as Honduras who participated as warriors and auxiliaries confounds the heretofore general notion that hordes of Indians were eagerly rushing off to battles as Spanish partisans. Instead, we come to appreciate the very complexity of the Spanish invasions and their utter dependence on native peoples for their wars of conquest.

Although little has been said of the roles of women as indios conquistadores, Herrera (chapter 4) reminds us that women and children were certainly a part of any colonizing expedition. They served as consorts, cooks, and porters and then as founders of new communities once the battles for conquest were over. Most of these women are anonymous, and, again, we do not know if they were always willing participants. Malintzin (Doña Marina), Cortés's interpreter and companion, is famous for her contributions to the downfall of the Mexica.[40] Pedro de Alvarado, like his captain, fortuitously allied with a woman who greatly facilitated his conquest undertaking in Guatemala. In truth, there were two women, sisters, Doña Luisa and Doña Lucía, the daughters of King Xicotencatl of Tizatlan, Tlaxcala, and the mistresses of Pedro de Alvarado and his brother Jorge, respectively. Because of their indigenous royal affiliation, the women commanded great respect and loyalty from their fellow conquistador Tlaxcalteca, and Doña Luisa actually gave birth to Pedro's child during a siege against the Maya. This child, as one of Alvarado's surviving heirs, was in line for an encomienda on his death, and she and her mother enjoyed relatively high status in local Santiago society.

Many of the native conquistadores in Guatemala considered themselves elite, and on these earliest expeditions of conquest it may well be that they were among the surplus nobility in their hometowns. They were well familiar with the privileges of their esteemed royal ancestors, which included such benefits as plural wives, a full retinue of servants in attendance at court, and assigned tributaries for labor and goods. Under Spanish rule polygyny was forgone, but otherwise the conquistador nobles anticipated the traditional perquisites. For example, the privileges promised by Cortés to the Tlaxcalteca are legendary.[41] Gibson lists tribute exemptions, division of conquered land, and equal distribution of the spoils between Spanish and Tlaxcalteca warriors.[42] The evidence of such largesse, according to the Spaniards' records, is scant, and to make it all even more unlikely, there were numerous other Nahua groups who would have to be compensated in the same manner. Nonetheless, the Tlaxcalteca had recollections of some arrangement, and in the 1560s they began to agitate for exemption from tribute.

From the profusion of petitions and delegations to Madrid, we are inclined to think that they should have been obligation free, but Gibson has shown that the Tlaxcalteca, while enjoying certain exemptions, were nevertheless still encumbered with numerous onerous labor and tribute assignments. First, he notes, in particular, the years following the post-conquest exodus (1520s) when there was a period of relative tranquility and prosperity.[43] The Tlaxcalan Actas de Cabildo are largely representative of this period.[44] During this time (1560) the viceroy asked the cabildo for recruits to relocate in northern New Spain. The cabildo at first agreed but then reconsidered and refused the request.[45] Affairs in Tlaxcala were still manageable, it would seem. But Spaniards were steadily settling in Tlaxcala, and although the Tlaxcalteca waged legal battles to have them removed, they were seldom successful.[46] By the end of the sixteenth century the social and economic situation had worsened significantly, and when in 1590 the viceroy asked the Tlaxcalteca again for volunteers to colonize the north, the Tlaxcala cabildo sent along some fifteen hundred men, women, and children.[47]

The fourth category of indios conquistadores is, then, those who went to conquer enemy Indians by being model colonizers. The 1590–91 undertaking by the Tlaxcalteca mentioned earlier is very well known. Chimalpahin reports:

Lunes a 17. de junio. de 1591 años. yquac onpeuhque tlaxcalteca yancuic mexico chiuhcnauhtlan yn namicoto oncan papaquiltiloque yollaliloque yn ica tlaqualtzintli y nohuian altepetl ypan tlahtoque yhuan in mexico tlatilolco san Francisco teopixque quinmohuiquillique oncan teochihualloque nahuatiloque in chiuhcnauhtlan in vissurey. no oncan quinmonamiquillito yhuan no omentin yahque tlapitzque tlatzotzinque mexica ce san Pablo ychan ytoca augustin cano ynic ome ytoca domingo Sánchez san Juan ychan.

[Monday the 17th of June of the year 1591 was when the Tlaxcalteca left for New Mexico. At Chiucnauhtlan people went out to meet them and feted them and encouraged them by feeding them. The rulers of altepetl all around and the Franciscan friars in Mexico City and Tlatelolco accompanied them; there they were blessed and bid farewell for Chiucnauhtlan. The viceroy also went there to meet them. And also two Mexica musicians (a fife and a drummer) went; one is from San Pablo [Teopan Tenochtitlan], named Agustín Cano; the second is named Domingo Sánchez, from San Juan [Moyotlan Tenochtitlan].][48]

Diego Muñoz Camargo reportedly accompanied his fellow Tlaxcalteca to help them get settled.[49] They typically traveled four families to a wagon, along with almost everything that was necessary to start a new life: agricultural seeds and tools, plants, fruit trees, animals for food and labor, and all the things that were requisite to emulate Tlaxcala.[50] Chimalpahin adds that in August Agustín Cano returned to Mexico City along with some Chichimeca to collect more people.[51] Yet not all was in accord. Don Juan Buenaventura Zapata y Mendoza, a native of Tlaxcala who furnishes rich details about the order and timing of the departures from Tlaxcala in his Nahuatl annals, reported that there was considerable dissension among the Tlaxcalteca, and two rulers refused to participate. They went so far as to file lawsuits against the government. He also records the deaths of sixty Tlaxcalteca by enemy Indians shortly after their arrival at Chichimecatlalpan ("In the Land of the Chichimeca").[52]

With such fanfare a successful venture was almost assured. Indeed, that seems to have been the case; the Tlaxcalteca were settled in six "towns" where it was believed they could do the most good. Labor was needed for the silver mines, and although the conquistador-colonizers were not obligated to work in the mines, it was hoped that the Indians in whose territory they now lived would be drawn in. The colonists were also expected to cultivate crops that would, in part, supply the labor force at the mines.

These Tlaxcalteca conquistadores were doubtless aware of the travails of their predecessors, yet they were ready for the challenges and promised opportunities. At home, over the years their cabildo representatives had been able to negotiate certain privileges: for example, the award of the title La Muy Noble y Leal Ciudad de Tlaxcala, the grant of coats of arms to nobles, the right of some nobles to adopt Spanish dress and bear arms, the confirmation of a traditional indigenous form of government and market, and limits to labor obligations in Puebla and the amounts of tribute to be delivered to Mexico City. As might be anticipated, the model colonizer-conquistadores had their own expectations of just rewards. Following precedents for establishing other towns, all privileges enjoyed by the home community would be granted to the colonists; the colonists and their descendants would be considered *hidalgos,* with exemptions from tribute and personal service; food would be provided for two years; they would live separately from Spaniards; they could ride horses and carry weapons; and so forth.[53] For many years they retained their four-part system of governance, with the descendants of traditional rulers holding sway in each community.

As the Spaniards continued to explore for silver and thus penetrate new territories, satellite communities sprang from the Tlaxcalteca colonies and individuals and groups carried on what seem to be never-ending battles of conquest on New Spain's northern and western frontiers. Bret Blosser (chapter 9) furnishes ample details about the vital role indigenous *flecheros* (archers) played in subduing the north. In all instances, it appears, these indios conquistadores were willing participants, even mercenaries, for most of the colonial period. Blosser's is a vivid military history of the ubiquity of the flecheros and their close association with Spaniards, who for nearly two centuries were dependent on their readiness and fortitude. These indios conquistadores largely refashioned themselves as indispensable commodities to the Spaniards for the pacification of the frontier.

To show the near singular role of native peoples in the Spanish conquest is the purpose of Michel R. Oudijk and Matthew Restall's chapter 1. The old stereotype of abject and muted Indians is permanently erased and the canon debunked. From them we learn especially of the great importance and number of native allies and how Cortés would have been stopped in his tracks in Cempoala without them (and possibly earlier, without Malintzin's extraordinary diplomatic and linguist skills as interlocutor). Now we know more about indigenous agency and the value of allies who knew and shared established communication networks, whether as spymasters or the course of the roadways themselves. There is also strong evidence of cultural continuity in the form of ethnopatriotism and remarkable strategies for community survival up to the end of the colonial period. This was not a Spanish conquest or a spiritual one, and the indios conquistadores only partially fit my profile of loser history and the conquest as a nonevent. War and conquest were fundamental to Mesoamerican culture. That they continued, along with so many other things, into the colonial era should come as no surprise.

In assessing the Chichimeca War (1550–90), Powell offers the astonishing observation that the Spaniards made so many concessions and accommodations that in most ways the Chichimeca seem to have won the war.[54] On the other hand, Ramón A. Gutiérrez and Richard C. Trexler, who have studied indigenous dances and theaters of conquest, take them at face value and believe that the Indians enjoyed making a big show of their defeat.[55] Consider once again the indios mexicanos and their performance in the Fiesta del Volcán in Guatemala. Celebrated by more than one thousand Kaqchikel wearing traditional dress, the spectacle served the purpose of the Spaniards by reminding everyone of their success as conquerors; it served the indios mexicanos by enhancing their status as privileged natives; and it served the Kaqchikel, who surely used the occasion to celebrate their own ethnicity and patriotism and the fact that it was their homeland, which certainly could not be said for the Spaniards or the indios mexicanos. But were they really celebrating their own subjugation? Max Harris does not think so: he proposes that there was a subtext, or ulterior motive, being danced by groups such as the Kaqchikel or the Pueblo peoples that was more about reconquest and continuity than it was about dominance by outsiders.[56] According to Matthew Restall, "The trick of turning calamity into continuity effectively weakens the impact of the Conquest by denying its uniqueness and its inexplicability; more than this, it also seems to deny that the Conquest, as the Spaniards saw it, ever occurred."[57]

NOTES

1. Cortés, *Letters from Mexico*; López de Gómara, *Cortés*; Díaz del Castillo, *Discovery and Conquest of Mexico*. Díaz del Castillo concluded his first draft in 1568, but the final version was not published until 1632.

2. See, e.g., any of the many publications by Carlos María de Bustamante, including, *Necesidad de la unión* and *Historia de las conquistas*. Note that Bustamante has Chimalpahin's name wrong, and it is still uncertain as to whether Chimalpahin translated the manuscript to Nahuatl. See Chimalpahin Quauhtlehuanitzin, *Codex Chimalpahin*, vol. 6. For an excellent study of New Spain's creole response to challenges from Europe, see Cañizares-Esguerra, *How to Write*.

3. See the preface to the Modern Language 2001 edition of Prescott's *History* for additional information about Prescott's intellectual formation and ambitions, v–vii.

4. See James Lockhart's introduction to Prescott, *History*, xxv–xxxiv.

5. Prescott, *History*, 64, 108, 744, 797, 814, 913.

6. Ricard, *Spiritual Conquest of Mexico*.

7. Burkhart, *Slippery Earth* and *Holy Wednesday.*

8. Chimalpahin Quauhtlehuanitzin, *Codex Chimalpahin*, vols. 1–3.

9. For just two examples see, Sahagún, *Florentine Codex*, and Durán, *History of the Indies.*

10. García Martínez, "Conquest of Mexico Revisited."

11. See Schroeder, "Loser History." For those who may take issue with my use of the term "loser," saying that it is pejorative slang most typical of the United States and, even worse, Hollywood, in English the word dates back at least to 1349 and of course appears in the works of William Shakespeare, e.g., *Hamlet* (1602) and other plays, with essentially the same meaning that I intend here: someone who is a destroyer yet still not a winner along with all that might be attributed to its Hollywood incarnation. Also see *Oxford English Dictionary*, (Oxford: Clarendon Press, 1978), 6:452. In Spain, wealth in addition to noble lineage was a crucial indicator of high social standing. Service in the military (preferably along with an advantageous marriage) was a means to gain wealth and possibly improve one's status. However, very few of the men and women who set out to conquer or even explore North America had an affiliation with the military.

12. Stern, "Paradigms of Conquest," 1–34.

13. López de Gómara, *Cortés*, 113–14.

14. Adorno, "Discourses on Colonialism."

15. Cited in Závala, *La filosofía política*, 17 (my translation and paraphrase).

16. López de Gómara, *Historia de las indias*. The second part of this work is *La crónica de la Nueva España*, also known as *La conquista de México.*

17. Chimalpahin Quauhtlehuanitzin, *Codex Chimalpahin*, 1:136–39.

18. See Lockhart, *We People Here.*

19. Cristóbal del Castillo's ethnicity is uncertain. Although he wrote in Nahuatl, some scholars believe that he was a mestizo. See his *Historia.*

20. Castillo, *Historia*, 164.

21. Muñoz Camargo, *Historia de Tlaxcala*. For reproductions of many of the paintings that were made to illustrate the roles of the Tlaxcalteca as allies, see Acuña, *Relaciónes geográficas.*

22. It is little known that nearly 60 percent of the Spanish conquerors died during the siege at Mexico Tenochtitlan. Bernard Grunberg estimates an eventual total of twenty-one hundred conquerors fought to bring down the capital. "Origins of the Conquistadores," 261.

23. Bibliothèque Nationale de France, Paris, Fonds Mexicain (hereafter, BnF, FM), f. 170.

24. BnF, FM, 74, f. 190v.

25. BnF, FM, 74, f. 249v.

26. Gibson, *Tlaxcala*, 159.

27. Bernardino de Sahagún describes in great detail the rank and file of warriors headed for battle. See *Florentine Codex*, book 8, *Kings and Lords*, 52–54.

28. Hassig, *Aztec Warfare*, is an excellent source of information about precontact military practice.

29. Núñez Cabeza de Vaca, *Castaways*, 104.

30. Muñoz Camargo, *Historia*, 115.

31. In Texcoco, King Neçahualpilli (1472–1515) was said to have more than two thousand wives and concubines and some 144 children. His father, King Neçahualcoyotl (1418–72), reportedly had sixty sons and fifty-seven daughters. See Berdan, *Aztecs of Central Mexico*, 68.

32. Using the reverential *-tzin*, Chimalpahin identifies him as Don Francisco de Sandoval Acacitzin, Tlatquic teuctli, of Itzcahuacan Tlacochcalco (Tlalmanalco) (1521–54). See Schroeder, *Chimalpahin*, 92, 98. Chimalpahin notes that Cortés was in attendance when Acacitzin was baptized and installed in office. For a Spanish translation of the Nahuatl account, see Francisco de Sandoval Acazitli [*sic*], British and Foreign Bible Society, Cambridge University Library, MS 374, vol. 2, ff. 153–59v, and "Relación de la jornada." The Nahuatl was translated to Spanish in 1641. See Altman, chapter 5, this volume, for greater detail about Acacitli's journal.

33. Philip Wayne Powell, *Mexico's Miguel Caldera*, 7.

34. See Sahagún, *Florentine Codex*, book 8, *Kings and Lords*, 55: "the ruler was greatly concerned with the dance, the rejoicing, in order to hearten and console all the rulers, the noblemen, the lords, the brave warriors, and all the common folk and vassals."

35. Acacitli lists the days, not months or the change of the calendar year.

36. BnF, FM, 74, 256v.

37. Council of Huexotzingo, "Letter to the King."

38. For more information about the indios conquistadores in Guatemala, see Matthew, "Neither and Both." See also Matthew, "Marching as a Group Apart."

39. A phrase used repeatedly by President George W. Bush to describe supposed international participants in the war in Iraq. See Michael Moore's *Fahrenheit 911* (2004). See also Ida Altman's discussion of indigenous conscripts in chapter 5, this volume.

40. See Karttunen, "Rethinking Malinche."

41. It has yet to be determined if Cortés actually promised all that the Tlaxcalteca claimed. Nevertheless, his alleged promises became legend, for even in 1753 it was believed that "the Indians who enjoy esteem are the *caciques*, nobles, and the Tlaxcaltecas who so much aided Cortés during the conquest." See Katzew, *Casta Painting*, 42.

42. Gibson, *Tlaxcala*, 159–60.

43. Ibid., 158–67.

44. See Lockhart, Berdan, and Anderson, *Tlaxcalan Actas*, and Celestino Solis, Valencia R., and Medina Lima, *Actas de cabildo*.

45. Lockhart, Berdan, and Anderson, *Tlaxcalan Actas*, 60, 106–8.

46. Szewczyk, "New Elements."

47. Gibson, *Tlaxcala*, 181–89.

48. Chimalpahin Quauhtlehuanitzin, *Codex Chimalpahin*, vol. 3.

49. Powell, *Mexico's Miguel Caldera*, 153.

50. Martínez Saldaña, *La diáspora tlaxcalteca*, 77–78. See also Muñoz Camargo, *Suma y epíloga*, and Martínez Baracs, "Colonizaciones tlaxcaltecas."

51. Chimalpahin Quauhtlehuanitzin, *Codex Chimalpahin*, 3:37. It should be noted that Chimalpahin makes no further mention of the Tlaxcalteca in the north. However, from time to time he notes that the friars returned to get more friars and more people, especially artisans, such as blacksmiths. He also tells about the great difficulties the Franciscans were having with the governor of New Mexico (possibly Don Juan de Oñate), who reportedly was very abusive.

52. Buenaventura Zapata y Mendoza, *Historia cronológica*, 179–85.

53. See Gibson, *Tlaxcala*, 184, for a full list and more details about their privileges.

54. Powell, *Mexico's Miguel Caldera*, 157.

55. Gutiérrez, *When Jesus Came*, 47–48, and Trexler, "We Think, They Act."

56. Harris, *Aztecs, Moors, and Christians*.

57. Restall, *Maya Conquistador*, 43.

CHAPTER ONE

MESOAMERICAN CONQUISTADORS IN THE SIXTEENTH CENTURY

MICHEL R. OUDIJK AND MATTHEW RESTALL

Y en esto que escribe es por sublimar a Cortés y abatir a nosotros los que con él pasamos, y sepan que hemos tenido por cierto los conquistadores verdaderos que esto vemos escrito, . . . porque en todas las batallas o reencuentros éramos los que sosteníamos a Cortés, y ahora nos aniquila en lo que dice este coronista.

[And it seems to me now that he [Francisco López de Gómara] wrote this in order to raise up [Hernando] Cortés and knock down those of us who were with him, seeing as we have been taken as surely being the true conquistadors, . . . for in all the battles it was us who sustained Cortés, and now he obliterates us in what he writes this chronicler.]

BERNAL DÍAZ DEL CASTILLO, *HISTORIA VERDADERA DE LA CONQUISTA DE LA NUEVA ESPAÑA*

In the seventh painting of the Kislak Conquest of Mexico series, created around the 1680s, the fall of Tenochtitlan is depicted as an epic battle between Spanish troops and Mexica defenders (see fig. 1.1). Titled *Conqvista de México por Cortés*, the image promotes the roles of the Spanish leader and his principal captains (three of whom are named in the key), emphasizes the military prowess of the conquerors, eclipses the presence of black soldiers completely, and marginalizes the part played by the Tlaxcalteca and other native allies of the invaders. The Tlaxcalteca are not omitted altogether from the picture, but they are shown as merely bringing up the rearguard (dressed in white, on the causeways at the top or in the background of the painting), arriving behind the Spaniards, when most, if not all, the fighting had been done (Pedro de Alvarado has already "raised His Majesty's flag" atop "the pyramid of Guichilobos").[1]

The Kislak series most immediately reflects (and may have been directly influenced by) the interpretations and emphases of the *Historia de la conquista de México* published by Antonio de Solís y Rivadeneira in 1684. Solís's account, however, drew upon earlier narratives, and in a larger sense both the Solís text and the Kislak images represent a perspective on the conquests of Mexico and Peru that was rooted in the accounts of the Spanish invaders themselves, reinforced during the centuries of colonial rule, reified by William Prescott's nineteenth-century epics (still in print), and perpetuated in various ways through the twentieth century. This perspective tends to begin by posing the question, How were such amazing feats possible?

The question has been repeated by chroniclers and historians from the early sixteenth century to the present.[2] It has functioned well as an irresistible hook that pulls the reader into the story while at the same time setting up that story as an elaborate answer or explanation for the conquest. That explanation (with respect primarily to central Mexico but to some extent to Mesoamerica) has variously stressed the genius of Hernando Cortés, the superiority of Spanish military resources, the providential intervention of God, the political and moral decadence of the Mexica empire at the time of the invasion, the structural weakness of that empire and the disunity of Mesoamerican peoples, the impact of epidemic disease, and the failings of Moctezuma and his alleged belief that Cortés was the returning deity of Quetzalcoatl. Not surprisingly, in the twentieth century religious explanations (the conquest as miracle) faded in popularity in favor of more secular ones (relative military technologies), while an emphasis on "great men" was largely replaced by one on structures and patterns. For example, in the recent *Seven Myths of the Spanish Conquest*, Matthew Restall argues that Spanish conquests in the Americas can mostly be explained by a combination of three factors working together—epidemic disease, native disunity or micropatriotism, and metal weapons (but not necessarily guns and horses).[3]

FIGURE 1.1.
*Conqvista de México por Cortés, painting 7 in the Kislak Conquest of Mexico series,
ca. 1680s. Reproduced courtesy of the Jay I. Kislak Collection, Rare Book and Special
Collections, Library of Congress, Washington DC.*

The traditional conquistador-based view of the conquest is not as
entrenched as it once was. On the one hand, *Seven Myths of the Spanish
Conquest* presented these "myths" (meaning misconceptions and well-
entrenched erroneous perceptions) as so deeply rooted as to persist in some
form or another to this day. On the other hand, that book was also made
possible by increasing numbers of revisionist voices and presentations of
myth-debunking evidence—a development notably reflected in the present volume. Indeed, the aspect of the revisionist view of the conquest that
has arguably become most widely known and accepted is the existence of
native allies.[4] The most obvious example is the undisputed fact that Tlaxcala
provided large numbers of warriors to assist the Spaniards in their siege
and destruction of Tenochtitlan; in fact, this is no longer a revisionist observation at all, as no historian today would argue that the marginalization
of Tlaxcalteca in the Kislak paintings accurately reflects their role in the
destruction of the Mexica empire. However, what is far less well known
is the full extent and nature of native support and influence during the

decades of Spanish military activity in Mesoamerica, beginning in 1519 and stretching through the sixteenth century.

In this chapter, we will discuss native roles in four categories, moving from the better known toward a more novel suggestion regarding conquest patterns and possibilities. These four categories are, first, the numbers of native auxiliaries; second, the ubiquity of native allies beyond the best-known examples from the Spanish-Mexica war of 1519–21; third, the crucial role of noncombatant auxiliaries, such as guides, spies, interpreters, porters, cooks, and so on; and fourth, the possibility that the Spanish conquest imitated preconquest patterns of imperial expansion in Mesoamerica, so that it became modeled to some extent on the conquests that created the Mexica empire. Our sources are a combination of secondary sources and primary archival ones, mostly petitions sent to Spain by sixteenth-century Mesoamerican conquistadors.

A GREAT QUANTITY OF INDIAN FRIENDS

E vio que al tiempo que vinieron a ayudar a la conquista della mucha cantidad de yndios amigos naturales de taxcala e mexicanos y naturales de chulula e çapotecas e mistecas e yopes e de guacachula todos amygos de los españoles los quales despues de venidos a esta tierra bio este testigo que en serviçio de dios nuestro señor y de su mag[estad] se hallaron en todas las vatallas e rrecuentros . . . y servieron muy bien con sus personas e armas padesçiendo mucho cansançio e hanbres e nesçeçidades y muchas heridas muchos años hasta que se conquisto e paçifico la tierra y se puso so el dominio de su mag[estad].

[And he saw that at that time there came to help in the conquest a great quantity of Indian friends, natives of Tlaxcala, and Mexicans and natives of Cholula and Zapoteca and Mixteca and Yope and from Cuauhquecholan, all friends of the Spaniards, who after coming to this land—this witness saw—in the service of God our Lord and of Your Majesty, were at all the battles and encounters . . . and served very well with their persons and their arms, suffering much exhaustion and hunger and deprivation and many wounds over many years until the land was conquered and pacified and placed under the dominion of Your Majesty.

PEDRO GONZÁLES NÁJERA, 1573

In styling the Spanish-Mexica war as "The Conquest of Mexico" or "The Spanish Conquest," albeit one made possible by native "allies" or with native "assistance," one runs the risk of recasting the war with native allies still in a supporting role. Such language cannot be avoided altogether. Nor should the role of the Spaniards as initiators and ultimate beneficiaries of the war be forgotten. Yet a highlighting of the demographic balance within allied forces—the sheer numbers of native warriors fighting against the Mexica in 1519–21 and against other polities in subsequent years—helps to illuminate the important ways in which the nominal subordination of native forces to Spanish leadership was tempered by the utter dependence of Spaniards on the native warriors who consistently outnumbered them.

Even before the Spanish-Mexica war had begun, when the invaders were still in the Cempoala region, Cortés and his company were outnumbered five to one by an allied native force of two thousand soldiers. From this point on, the ratio became more and more profound, as rulers of towns through which the Spanish-native caravan—whom we shall call "the allies"—would pass donated soldiers to take part in the campaign. The calculation of numbers is admittedly an imprecise science, as total numbers are seldom given, and Spanish accounts often omit mention of native allies. For example, in his first letter to Cortés during his campaign in Guatemala, Pedro de Alvarado makes no mention of the Mexica, Tlaxcalteca, and other natives accompanying him. Yet we know from many other sources that they existed, and in his second letter Alvarado lets slip, in parentheses, that his forces comprised 250 Spaniards "and about five or six thousand friendly Indians."[5]

Calculations of numbers are also complicated by the fact that armies are often described in terms of captains. Thus Cempoala gave forty captains, while Xalacingo gave twenty. Evidence from Alvarado's Guatemala campaign suggests that these captains were in charge of units that the Spaniards termed *cuadrillas*, squadrons that consisted of people from the community (or barrio within a town) of origin of each particular captain.[6] Such cuadrillas consisted of either two hundred or four hundred soldiers, which means that calculations of total warriors can be off by a factor of two.[7] Nevertheless, even if we take the lower figure of two hundred to a cuadrilla, Cempoala's contribution to the allies was an impressive eight thousand men. Furthermore, these numbers were dwarfed by Tlaxcala's contribution, once that city entered the new alliance. According to Bernal

Díaz del Castillo, Xicotencatl, the principal ruler of Tlaxcala, insisted that ten thousand soldiers should accompany the Spaniards to Cholula. Later, during the siege of Tenochtitlan, the number of Spaniards had grown to some five hundred men, while at least twenty-four thousand indigenous allies took part. These numbers could have been higher still; there are references to as many as forty thousand indigenous soldiers taking part in a campaign to Iztapalapa.[8]

Armies of "Indian friends" were less likely to number in the tens of thousands after 1521, due to the death toll of the Spanish-Mexica war and the impact of waves of epidemic disease beginning in 1520. But it was still common for Spaniards embarking on campaigns throughout Mesoamerica to be accompanied by thousands of Nahua from central Mexico and other native warriors. As the next section briefly discusses (and subsequent chapters in this volume demonstrate in detail), this was true for decades—through the founding of a Spanish colony in Yucatan in the early 1540s.

IN EVERY ONE OF THESE PROVINCES AND CITIES

E despues de conquistada e ganada esta tierra los d[ic]hos yndios conquistadores de la nueva españa muchos dellos se quedaron poblados en la çiudad bieja de almolonga ques çerca de guatimala donde agora estan y biven ellos e sus hijos y desçendientes y asimismo este testigo sabe e bio que muchos españoles capitanes salieron desta çiudad de guatimala con mucha gente a conquistar e poblar las provinçias de cuzcatlan que agora se llama entre españoles san salvador e la provinçia de honduras e la provinçia de la verapaz e la de chiapa con los quales d[ic]hos capitanes este testigo vio que ffueron muchos yndios de los d[ic]hos conquistadores mexicanos y taxcaltecas e çapotecas e chulutecas e mistecas e otras naçiones.

[And these Indian conquistadors of New Spain, having conquered and won this land, stayed in large numbers to settle the old city of Almolonga, which is near to Guatemala [Antigua]; where they and their children and descendents now are and live and . . . many Spanish captains went out from this city of Guatemala with many people to conquer and settle the provinces of Cuzcatlan, which the Spaniards now call San Salvador, and the province of Honduras and the province of Verapaz and that of Chiapa; and this witness saw that with those captains went many Indians from among those Mexica, Tlaxcalteca,

Zapoteca, Cholulteca, and Mixteca conquistadors, and those of other nations.]

GONZALO ORTÍZ, 1564

The high numbers cited in some sources on the Spanish-Mexica war of 1519–21 also crop up regularly in the many indigenous requests and claims that were sent to the Audiencia Real and to the emperor during the sixteenth century—petitions relating in part to 1519–21 but primarily to the decades of conquest wars that followed the fall of Tenochtitlan. All Spaniards participating in the process of exploration, discovery, conquest, and colonization in the Americas were required to submit reports to royal officials—addressed directly to the king—detailing what they had found and done. These reports sometimes took the form of *cartas* (letters), *relaciones* (accounts), or other related genres, but most commonly they conformed to the genre of the *probanza de mérito* (proof of merit). The rewarding of titles of office and other benefits of conquest was contingent upon the submission of these reports, but they were also the principal means whereby any participant in any Spanish conquest might acquire (or have restored) official reward, privilege, or benefit. Thus while most probanzas were submitted by Spaniards and requested the granting of pensions, *encomiendas*, and offices of colonial rule, black conquistadors also petitioned for such rewards as royal pensions, tribute exemption, and the right to a house-plot in the *traza*, or central zone, of a colonial city.[9]

Likewise, native elites or entire native communities (represented by their municipal councils or *cabildos*) also submitted petitions, whose style and form tended to be a hybrid blend of the Spanish probanza and the Mesoamerican petition.[10] In particular during the second half of the sixteenth century, various indigenous groups sent letters claiming rights and privileges based on their participation in the conquest. In addition to styling themselves as conquistadors, these native petitioners often cited the numbers of people that were involved in conquest campaigns.[11] Although such numbers may have been exaggerated for obvious reasons, when compared to the numbers given in Spanish sources they give us a good sense of how many indigenous troops actually took part in certain campaigns. A document from Xochimilco, for example, claims that twelve thousand Xochimilca took part in the siege of Tenochtitlan and that another twenty-five hundred accompanied Pedro de Alvarado to Guatemala and Honduras.

A 1547 letter from Tlaxcala refers to a thousand men going on this same Guatemalan campaign, but in a 1567 letter a number of twenty thousand Tlaxcalteca is given for all the soldiers provided by Tlaxcala for Spanish conquests throughout Mesoamerica. Don Juan Cortés, the indigenous ruler of Tehuantepec, supposedly sent two thousand men with Pedro de Alvarado for the conquest of Chiapas and Guatemala, while Pedro Gonzalez Nájera, a Spanish resident of Guatemala City and conquistador of the region, claims that seven thousand indigenous allies took part in the conquests. Finally, Jorge de Alvarado brought some five to six thousand native auxiliaries to Guatemala in 1527.[12]

Mesoamerican conquistadors spoke of the sufferings of war as much as their Spanish counterparts did, and the casualties of some of these campaigns seem to support assertions that victories often came at heavy native costs. On one expedition to San Salvador, for example, a campaign lasting about one hundred days, 300 indigenous soldiers left, but only 140 came back. Other testimonies of the campaigns to southern Mesoamerica are vague as to the number of people that died, but all agree that many did. On some expeditions, survivors settled as colonists; for example, in a letter to the king the authorities of Xochimilco claim that more than 1,100 warriors left on campaigns to Panuco, Guatemala, Honduras, and Jalisco, but not a single one of these men came back.[13]

There is some evidence that the indigenous contribution went much further than cooperation and alliance. In 1584 Don Joachin de San Francisco, *cacique* of Tepexi de la Seda in present-day Puebla, demanded to be exempted from paying tribute due to the merits and services of his grandfather, Don Gonzalo Matzatzin Moctezuma.[14] In an astonishing testimony, backed-up by the statement of some thirty witnesses, Don Joachin claimed that when Hernando Cortés was in Tlaxcala his grandfather had sent ambassadors with rich gifts in order to vow loyalty to the new emperor. Such a ceremony was repeated much later (after the so-called Noche Triste) when Cortés and his troops had conquered Tepeaca (from where Cortés had come to Tepexi). On this occasion Matzatzin received a lance and sword, and he agreed to conquer the "province of the Mixteca and Oaxaca" for which he received in the name of the king of Spain the title of captain. While Cortés returned to the north on his way to reconquer and punish Tenochtitlan for its uprising, Matzatzin turned south and—before the Mexica capital itself had finally fallen—conquered as many as twenty towns in the Mixteca Baja and Alta.

It is tempting to dismiss this document as fraudulent in its claims, at least in the alleged timing of these conquests if not the very role played by warriors from Tepexi. This would hardly be the only colonial Mesoamerican source to exaggerate or invent native roles in the conquest.[15] Furthermore, neither Cortés, Díaz del Castillo, nor any other chronicler refers to the Tepexi alliance or to Matzatzin's conquests. However, a strong argument can be made for the veracity of Don Gonzalo's version of events. The pictorial Lienzo de Tlaxcala shows the same sequence of events as described by Don Joachin and his witnesses: the Noche Triste, the arrival in Tlaxcala, the conquests of various towns in southern Puebla (including Tepexi), and the conquest of Tenochtitlan.[16] Furthermore, Cortés (and to a lesser extent, Díaz del Castillo) had much to gain from not mentioning the Tepexi alliance. First, in his letters to the king, Cortés wanted to show that he alone had directed the conquest, despite the opposition of formidable forces. Second, and probably more important, when he received Cortés and his men, Matzatzin gave rich presents of gold, silver, and precious stones to show his friendship and loyalty. If Cortés or Díaz del Castillo had mentioned these, the king would have demanded his share—the royal fifth. Of course, many gifts were reported and much was remitted to Spain, but enough was held back in order to make the enterprise more profitable. Furthermore, testimonies by the witnesses, many of whom were from the conquered towns, lend considerable credibility to the Tepexi document. In addition, on July 8, 1588, Don Joachin received the *merced* (grant) that exempted him from paying tribute.[17] Of course, six of the conquered towns are also known to have been part of tributary provinces of the Triple Alliance that underpinned the Mexica empire.[18] However, this still leaves fourteen towns that could have been conquered by Matzatzin. This may explain the manner in which these conquests took place. According to several witnesses, some towns were subdued through "lagoons of good words," while others were subdued through war.[19] If some of these towns were already subject to the Triple Alliance (whose emperor was a relative of Matzatzin), they may have been more willing to accept these new "conquests."

Finally, a further dimension of the use of native allies by Spaniards in Mesoamerica—and one that has received little scholarly attention—is the taking of native warriors on Spanish campaigns outside Mesoamerica. As one Spanish conquest tended to act as a springboard for another, and Spaniards discovered Peru a decade after they found Mesoamerica, it is not surprising that a number of Mesoamerican warriors ended up fighting in the Andes. Such soldiers did not participate in the initial Pizarro-Almagro invasion of Peru, as that was launched from Panama (with native men and women brought from no further north than Nicaragua). But Pedro de Alvarado brought Nahua and Maya, in addition to Nicaraguan natives, into the northern Andes in 1534. According to Pedro de Cieza de León, many of these native warriors and servants "died either because of the sea or from the great hardship they suffered on land." Evidently some fought against Andeans, as the chronicler-conquistador also claims that Alvarado himself "reported to me that the Indians whom they had brought from Guatemala ate countless native people of these villages . . . and afterwards most of them froze in the cold and starved to death." Cieza de León suggests that these ignominious deaths—Andeans eaten by Maya, Maya freezing in the high Andean mountain passes—are divine retribution for "their detestable sins." Local Andeans, he alleges, practiced sodomy, and Guatemalan natives were cannibals—"sins so enormous that they deserved to suffer what they suffered; indeed, God permitted it."[20]

The Maya brought by Alvarado to the Andes were surely not the only Mesoamericans to die on Spanish ships in the Pacific Ocean. A 1624 request for a pension by a Spanish veteran of the wars of conquest in the Philippines claimed that in a 1603 campaign against "bloodthirsty Chinese [chinos]" (meaning Philippine natives), the Spanish force included "some Japanese and Indians." That these "Indians" may have been Mesoamericans is strongly suggested by a petition, preserved in the same volume in the imperial archives in Seville, from the cabildo of Tlaxcala. Addressed to the king in 1630, the petition complained that the city had received many grievances from the officers (gente de guerra) that were sent to the Philippines and Havana or that were used for the defense of New Spain.[21] Significantly, the cabildo's gripe was with the conduct of Spanish officers and the abuse suffered by native soldiers, but the town councilors did not protest the practice of recruiting Tlaxcalteca men to serve the empire abroad, even as far away as the other side of the Pacific Ocean. A century after the Spanish-Mexica war, it had long become an accepted fact of life that Mesoamerican soldiers fought near and far in the service of His Majesty. It has recently become increasingly clear to historians that black and free colored soldiers were a ubiquitous presence on Spanish campaigns of conquest and networks of colonial defense; what should not be forgotten is the fact that native Mesoamericans also played significant roles that were almost as wide-ranging, both geographically and chronologically.[22]

TREPIDATION IN THEIR HEARTS AND BAGS ON THEIR BACKS

Mexicalcinco (who afterwards took the name of Cristóbal) revealed to Cortés the conspiracy of Cuauhtémoc, and showed him a paper with the glyphs and names of the lords who were plotting his death. Cortés praised Mexicalcinco and promised him great rewards.

FRANCISCO LÓPEZ DE GÓMARA, *CORTÉS*

Çelutapech was killed by the Cehach men. . . . For this reason, the Castilian men went on with trepidation in their hearts, but as they killed five or six of the [Cehach] soldiers upon arriving in Cehach, it was Cehach men who cleared the way through to Tayasal [Ta Ytza].

TITLE OF ACALAN-TIXCHEL, 1604

On the European side of the Atlantic, Spanish and other continental soldiers were increasingly part of complex, large, and (sometimes well-) organized armies dependent on a vast supply and support network. However, these changes, which were part of what historians have dubbed the Military Revolution, were of little relevance to sixteenth-century Spanish conquests in the Americas (although they contributed to subsequent mythology about the conquest). Spanish invaders in Mesoamerica were not soldiers in a formally structured army but armed members of companies of exploration, conquest, and—if successful—settlement.[23] These men hoped that military activities would give way as soon as possible to the business of settlement, permitting Spanish merchants to follow conquistadors into a foundling colony, bringing with them supplies, slaves, correspondence, and perhaps, in time, family members. Meanwhile, would-be Spanish settlers were dependent on native networks of supply and support. Warriors were thus not the only natives who contributed to allied forces in Mesoamerica; there were also porters, cooks, guides, spies, and interpreters, who often played roles as crucial to Spanish survival as those played by armed native allies.

Large numbers of porters (or *tameme*, as Nahuatl speakers called them) were of the utmost importance for the success of any military undertaking in Mesoamerica. After all, beasts of burden were unknown in Mesoamerica, and Spaniards brought with them relatively few horses in the early years of the conquest, so that without these tameme the conquistadors had to carry everything themselves. After the ruler of Cempoala had provided the Spaniards with four hundred tameme, Díaz del Castillo almost sighed with relief: "when we saw so many Indian porters we were very pleased, because before we always had to take our bags on our own backs."[24] Díaz del Castillo makes it clear that from then on they always demanded tameme, although the demand was unnecessary since it was a preconquest obligation for a ruler to provide allied lords with carriers. The sources on campaigns throughout Mesoamerica give many references to the tameme given to conquistadors; even a low-ranking Spanish conqueror who could not afford a horse had two indigenous porters. Indeed, one of the main complaints of the *conquistadores amigos* in the second half of the sixteenth century was precisely that their communities had provided large numbers of tameme carrying supplies, arms, and food for the Spaniards, without adequate recognition or reward. This same complaint is depicted in the painted *lienzos* from Analco and Quauhquechollan.[25] Of course, not only natives officially designated as tameme would have served as carriers. On various occasions indigenous conquistadors would have had to carry wounded Spaniards from the battlefield to safe havens, and, at times, when tameme were relatively few in number, warriors would have carried the sick and wounded during the march.[26]

The importance of food supply is obvious, yet the native role is often ignored or understated. From the very onset of the Spanish invasion of Mesoamerica, every time Spaniards stepped foot on shore they needed to gather or acquire food. The problem during this early stage of the invasion was that many of the villages they encountered along the coast were either abandoned or openly hostile. On the island of Cozumel, Pedro de Alvarado simply took food from a village that had just been abandoned; he was allegedly reprimanded for this by Cortés and shortly after made an agreement with the local rulers to provide his men with the necessary resources. Díaz del Castillo often mentions the food that was provided by local rulers as well as the times they were without food.[27] From the moment the Spaniards reached Cempoala, where the local ruler invited them to stay and where they began the march toward Tenochtitlan, food was given by native amigos. References to this fundamental service are also common in other documents that concern Spanish-indigenous relations.[28]

One of the most important Yucatec Maya sources on the conquest, the primordial *título*, or Title of Calkini, features a detailed description of a ritual presentation of a large quantity of food by Calkini's rulers to a combined Spanish-Nahua invasion force. The event became an important part of the local memory of the conquest, and it must have made considerable impact on the hungry invaders too; the Maya text describes how the Nahua rushed to collect the "turkeys, corn, and honey . . . grabbing it all," with their captain admonishing them for not being more orderly.[29] In cases such as this, local rulers provided food from their own territories and consequently experienced problems feeding the conquistadors and their allies once they had moved outside of them. This situation was worsened by the tactics of the opposing side, who would hide food and other resources before hiding themselves in the mountains, leaving behind empty villages and barren lands.[30] Thus, in Guatemala, indigenous auxiliaries from central Mexico and Oaxaca "often suffered the travails of hunger."[31] During the Cortés-led expedition to Honduras in 1525–26, the strain that was placed on the resources of the Chontal Maya kingdom of Acalan-Tixchel was so great that in the middle of the expedition's sojourn there, a combined Spanish-Maya force went off for several days to plunder neighboring polities for food and slaves—some of whom became part of the allied expedition's porter corps.[32]

Another important aspect of indigenous participation in the conquest is the role of native guides, spies, and messengers, upon whom the Spaniards were almost completely dependent whenever entering territory that was unexplored or poorly known to them. En route to Tenochtitlan native guides warned the invaders on various occasions that there were large armies awaiting them on the road ahead. During subsequent campaigns to Guatemala and Honduras these guides would "go always in front discovering land and, if it would not have been for them, [the Spaniards] would have perished many times because the enemy Indians had placed ambushes for them and many pits from which one who fell in could not escape."[33] The path ahead often needed to be cleared or widened so that the expedition could pass, forcing guides to double up as laborers. This was particularly the case in southern Mesoamerica; sources often mention that the indigenous allies had to "open up the road," for the terrain was not only rough but post-1521 Spanish expeditions were often vast, with hundreds of Spaniards and Africans and thousands of native warriors and porters.

Guiding and clearing roads was certainly not a job without its risks, for any Mesoamerican on the allied side who was taken prisoner was likely to be ritually executed or sacrificed, as indigenous conquistadors make clear in their testimonies.[34] The Cortés-led crossing of northern Guatemala in 1525 offers an example of how Spaniards used local men to traverse unknown and hostile territory. In order to get from Acalan-Tixchel to the next large Maya kingdom, that of the Itza, the expedition had to cross rivers and forests, as well as the smaller Cehach Maya kingdom. To accomplish this, they used large numbers of Chontal Maya to build a bridge, which took four days, and "to clear the way as far as Cehach." One of the Maya captains in charge of this operation, Çelutapech, was killed by Cehach warriors in an attack that unnerved the Spaniards. But once some Cehach Maya had been killed, the allied expedition was able to coerce the Cehach to then clear the way to the Itza capital (see the quote at the opening of this section); the Cehach motive for speeding the expedition through their territory is obvious.[35]

As a group, messengers were also frequently referred to in conquest sources, and they too seemed to have feared for their lives while working for allied expeditions, at least according to Díaz del Castillo.[36] Moctezuma Xocoyotl had a system of messengers working throughout the region under his control and maybe beyond. As soon as the Spaniards set foot on shore, reports were sent to the Mexica ruler. This well-established system was soon appropriated by the Spaniards as a means of communicating both with enemy groups and among the conquistadors and allies themselves. This flow of information was crucial during the conquest period. Conquistadors often mention messages being continuously sent, although they seldom give much indication of exactly how this system worked. From one Spaniard, Gonzalo de Caravajal, we know that the system of native messengers covered much of Mesoamerica; he mentions, for example, that every month messengers came from Mexico City to the province of Yucatan.[37]

A final group of noncombatant Mesoamericans who aided the Spaniards in crucial ways have been given more attention in conquest accounts than porters and spies—going all the way back to Díaz del Castillo—but in a somewhat distorted way. These are interpreters who have come to be symbolized by Doña Marina, or Malinche, whose history and historiography are lengthy and complex. Malinche has become legendary in a way that reveals more about postconquest (especially postcolonial) Mexican history than it does about the role of interpreters in the conquest. The important point here is that there were many native interpreters during the sixteenth century, and in the century's early decades most of them seem to have taken on the task with considerable reluctance. There would later be a generation of bilingual, even bicultural, Mesoamerican elites who would act as formal interpreters and cultural brokers (like Gaspar Antonio Chi), but in the interim, in the words of Frances Karttunen, "for individuals pressed into service, the requirements of survival were flexibility, youth, sharp intellect, and sheer good luck." Like spying and carrying messages, interpreting was risky business.[38]

Among the sources quoted earlier, there are Spaniards described as suffering trepidation and heavy burdens along the road; yet it is clear from the full array of sources that during the conquest it was primarily Mesoamericans, coerced or obliged in some way or another, who carried bags, cleared roads, took messages, and provided and cooked food.

PRECEDENTED EXPANSION

Cities were often attacked sequentially, with the resources, intelligence, and, sometimes, the soldiers of the latest conquest aided in the next one. . . . The Aztecs' unprecedented expansion took them to regions where they had no traditional enemies but where they were sometimes able to exploit local antagonisms by siding opportunistically with one adversary against another. They also waged campaigns of intimidation against cities they did not attack directly. Emmissaries went to such cities to ask that they become subjects of the Aztec king—usually on reasonably favorable terms. Both the proximity of a large, trained, and obviously successful army and the object lessons burning around them led many cities to capitulate peacefully.

ROSS HASSIG, *AZTEC WARFARE*

The strategies of expansion and mechanisms of conquest employed by Spaniards in sixteenth-century Mesoamerica have traditionally been explained in terms of the genius of Cortés and the precedents he set (as discussed earlier). More recently, historians have emphasized patterns of conquest rooted in the Castilian experience in Spain, the Canaries, and the Caribbean in the decades, even centuries, before the invasion of Mexico. Restall recently argued that these patterns amounted to a series of standard conquest procedures followed by Spanish conquistadors before and after Cortés and well evidenced throughout the Americas. None of these procedures was, according to this argument, rooted specifically in preconquest indigenous procedures or patterns of conquest.[39] However, our suggestion here is that the history of Spanish conquests in Mesoamerica is marked by strategies and mechanisms that imitated those used in pre-conquest Mesoamerica—an imitation stemming from and symptomizing the extensive role played by native allies in these conquests. Specific strategies included the forging of multicity alliances, the pursuit of sequential conquests, the heavy use of trade routes, and the granting of lordships and lands as a way of coercing or motivating native communities into joining alliances.

This interpretation is not without problems. One could argue that these strategies were used equally in western European traditions of warfare and alliance building. Yet the question is less, What was customary in Europe at the time? but more, What did the indigenous population accept? Based on their experience and traditions the Spaniards hoped to implement many things as soon as they reached Mesoamerican soil, but they were not likely to succeed if the local populations were not willing to cooperate—at least in the initial conquest years when the Spaniards did not have the same means of colonial coercion developed later. Furthermore, in the larger colonial context, the entire framework of Spanish settlement and economic exploitation in the Americas was based on responses to Native American resources—as illustrated by what James Lockhart has called the "trunk lines and feeder lines" of colonial development.[40]

In the remainder of this chapter, the presentation of our argument regarding Spanish-Mesoamerican patterns of conquest will cover four topics: alliances, sequential conquests (or the stepping-stone pattern), trade routes, and lordships and land grants.

Alliances

Colonial coercion was rooted in a system of administration and rule that depended upon the collaboration of local elites. A popular theme since the sixteenth century has been the supposed reputation of the Spaniards as invincible warriors, even gods—but conquest-era evidence suggests that this was a postconquest myth, that tales of apotheosized invaders were apocryphal.[41] The real story lies in how local elites drew on Mesoamerican traditions of alliance formation to deal with the Spanish invasion.

According to Ross Hassig, "multi-city alliances were composed of allied city-states or multi-city states drawn together by mutually perceived interests, including security from external military threats, and they could thus be of considerable size." The members of such alliances were not centrally controlled, nor did they share "a common ethnic identity." But, being "less bound by geographical limitations," they essentially functioned as "special-purpose institutions, arising from perceived needs and persisting as long as needs were satisfied."[42]

It is no coincidence that Hassig's description of preconquest political organization and imperial strategy—and opposition to it—in central Mexico could just as accurately apply to Spanish strategies in Mesoamerica after 1519. In that year, the so-called Fat Cacique of Cempoala responded to the arrival of Hernando Cortés and his men in his town by proposing an alliance with Tlaxcala, Huexotzingo, and other city-states for the purpose of conquering Tenochtitlan.[43] Throughout preconquest times, such multicity alliances were created both for defensive and aggressive purposes, evolving as political mechanisms fundamental to Mesoamerican city-state cultures.[44] The so-called Triple Alliance—a sort of confederation between Tenochtitlan, Texcoco, and Tlacopan—was developed and used by the Mexica as a conquest machine that served to incorporate much of Mesoamerica into their empire by the time of the Spanish invasion. The Triple Alliance had succeeded another confederation between Azcapotzalco, Culhuacan, and Coatlinchan, which in turn was preceded by the alliance of Culhuacan, Tula, and Otumba.[45] The founding ideology of such alliances was often a rallying cry against the tyrannical rule of the existing power; this was the case with the creation of the Triple Alliance and with the alliance proposed by the Fat Cacique a century later. This kind of appeal across political boundaries could also be used against Spanish interests, of course, and thus helps to explain hindrances to Spanish expansion in regions such as Yucatan as much as it helps explain success in other regions.

One important dimension to alliance building in Mesoamerica both before and during the Spanish invasion was the exchange of women for marriage.[46] The Mixteca codices, for example, feature complex genealogies showing how each ruling house was related to others through marital exchanges. Central Mexican sources like the *Crónica mexicayotl*, the *Anales de Cuauhtitlan*, and the writings of Diego Durán do not show lineages as long, but they do give the history of ruling houses and their intermarital relationships. The longer a relationship or alliance between two houses lasted, the more intermarriages would take place and, therefore, the stronger and closer the relationship would become. This pattern of intermarriage continued through the early colonial period.[47] It is exactly this pattern that we frequently see mentioned in the sources with respect to the Spaniards. Both in Cempoala and in Tlaxcala the Spaniards received daughters of the rulers to *hacer generación*, "to make generations" or "to engender."[48] The most famous case is probably that of Doña Isabel Moctezuma, daughter of Moctezuma Xocoyotl, who was married to three preconquest rulers—her uncle Altixcatzin, Cuitlahuac, and Cuauhtemoc (the latter two being emperors in Tenochtitlan during the Spanish-Mexica war). After the conquest, she was briefly part of Cortés's household, giving birth to his daughter but never marrying him. She did, however, marry three other Spaniards in succession—Alonso de Grado, Pedro Gallego, and finally Juan Cano.[49] From the native perspective, male rulers—or in Doña Isabel's case, a noblewoman, as we must surely recognize the agency of Doña Isabel herself in her marital history—sought to build permanent blood-based alliances with prominent Spaniards.

As illustrated by the Mixteca codices, this political system of alliance building was not just typical for central Mexico. Throughout the postclassic period (A.D. 1000–1521), lords in the Mixteca Alta continuously shifted and adjusted alliances, creating a complex and vibrant web of political ties. Between the mid-fourteenth century and 1450 many city-states from the Valley of Oaxaca and the Mixteca Alta constituted a confederacy, which was used to invade the Isthmus of Tehuantepec to control the trade route to Xoconosco and Coatzacualco.[50] Coixtlahuaca was probably "confederated" with, among others, Cholula, Huexotzingo, and Tlaxcala.[51] Once this alliance failed, it meant the incorporation of Coixtlahuaca into the Triple Alliance's tributary empire.

When Cortés and his men met the so-called Fat Cacique—who offered them food and shelter and suggested the alliance against Moctezuma—the Spaniards were well disposed to listen carefully (as much as language barriers permitted) to the possibilities the Cempoala lord presented to them. During the preceding months, the Spaniards had frequently encountered deserted towns and villages or had suffered attacks from indigenous warriors that had injured many Spaniards and their horses.[52] On top of this, they learned that the Cempoala polity, while keen to rebel against Moctezuma in alliance with Cortés, had a history of being repeatedly conquered by an empire of considerable size and strength (Cempoala was conquered for the first time by Moctezuma Ilhuicamina, who ruled 1440–68, and then again by both Axayacatl and Moctezuma Xocoyotl).[53]

Even if we accept Díaz del Castillo's claim that there was no clear agreement between Cortés and the Fat Cacique, from his own account it is clear that Cempoala was the place where Cortés and his men became involved in Mesoamerican sociopolitical patterns often without knowing it themselves. For example, it was not Cortés but the lords and guides from Cempoala who decided that the road to Tenochtitlan had to go through Tlaxcala. Even after the Spaniards and their allies had been received as friends by Olintetl—who was ruler of Iztacamaxtitlan, subject to Moctezuma, and who advised the Spaniards to go through Cholula on their way to Tenochtitlan—Cortés still followed the advice of the Cempoala lords and continued on to Tlaxcala. Cholula was yet another subject city of the Mexica empire and probably a place where Cortés and his men would have found considerable, if not decisive, resistance. But Tlaxcala was potentially an ally against the powerful Triple Alliance. There is no direct evidence that this was the rationale behind the advice of the Cempoala ruler, but it is clear that neither Cortés alone nor his fellow Spanish captains made such decisions without relying heavily on the expertise and arguments presented by allied Mesoamerican lords—not just in the case of the march to Tenochtitlan, but throughout the Spanish campaigns in Mesoamerica from 1519 on.

Sequential Conquests

Again, Hassig's description of Nahua patterns provides us with a model that can be applied to Spanish activities in the sixteenth century. In the passage quoted earlier, Hassig describes the sequential strategy of Mexica expansion; like the Spaniards after that, the Mexica used each newly conquered location—including its resources and personnel—as a springboard for the next. Added to this technique were the strategies of exploiting "local antagonisms" and waging "campaigns of intimidation" in which communities were invited to capitulate peacefully but reminded at the same time of "the object lessons burning around them."[54] This stepping-stone pattern is so equally applicable to the Spanish-allied conquests in Mesoamerica that most of the phrases used by Hassig could be applied to the Spanish conquest unaltered.

One of the most obvious examples is, of course, that of Tlaxcala. Whereas the Tlaxcalteca are often depicted as voluntarily aligning themselves with the Spaniards, this was initially not the case. On three different occasions Cortés and his men were faced with fierce resistance from the largest army that Tlaxcala could field. Having opposed the Triple Alliance for decades, the Tlaxcalteca were not ready to simply surrender their independence to these new invaders. Furthermore, whereas the Fat Cacique may have seen opportunities in an alliance with the Spaniards after they had been victorious in a couple of battles on the Gulf coast, the Tlaxcalteca were not especially impressed by the surrender of these relatively small polities. After all, along with Tenochtitlan and Texcoco, Tlaxcala was one of the largest and most powerful political entities in central Mexico. However, things had changed considerably after the three battles. Unable to beat the Spaniards, Tlaxcala was forced to consider an alliance with them. This failure to defeat the Spaniards was turned into a potential positive; it meant that the Spaniards might be able to help Tlaxcala beat the Mexica, thereby opening the door to Tlaxcalteca imperial expansion (an expansion, it turned out, that would take place with Tlaxcalteca warriors but with somewhat different imperial ramifications). And if the alliance proved to be unsuccessful or unworkable, Tlaxcala might still continue to oppose the Triple Alliance as before.

Although some Tlaxcalteca factions were ready to continue fighting against the Spaniards (and arguably, eventually they would have defeated them and forced the survivors back to the coast), an alliance was forged, and it became the turning point in the 1519–21 war. The Tlaxcalteca who had initially fought against the Spanish invaders now became part of a large army of Spanish-indigenous allies. As with the Cempoala before them, the Tlaxcalteca warriors were incorporated into this army but would continue to be semiautonomous sections. Each section had its own captain, its own banner, and its own internal organization and as such represented its own community or barrio. As discussed earlier (and in subsequent chapters in this volume), this pattern was repeated across Mesoamerica in the ensuing decades: after the fall of Tenochtitlan, Mexica soldiers took part in the campaigns to Guatemala and Honduras; other Nahua went to Yucatan, while those from Chiapas went as far as Cuzcatlan; in Guatemala itself we see that K'iche', Achi, and other Maya troops took part in the campaigns to Honduras and El Salvador; and so on.[55]

One fascinating case, recorded in the sources from Tepexi de la Seda, illustrates the ordinary pattern but with the addition of some extraordinary details. Various lesser-ranked noblemen from towns all over the local region were in Tepexi to perform personal service to the *tlatoani* (hereditary ruler) and ritually recognize his lordship when news came that Cortés and his Spanish-allied forces were en route to conquer the region. The whole ceremony was suspended, and the occasion turned into a local summit to discuss the impending invasion. The tlatoani of Tepexi, Don Gonzalo Matzatzin Moctezuma, decided not to fight the Spaniards and their allies but rather strike the deal discussed earlier. The noblemen of the subject towns, who had been gathered in Tepexi when this decision was made, took part in the subsequent campaign to southern Puebla and the Mixteca. The twist in the tale, however, is that they took part in the (allegedly) violent conquests of their own towns. In fact, the majority of the towns Matzatzin conquered were already paying tribute and personal service to him. Why, then, did he conquer them again? Was he tricking the Mexica? Or was he tricking the Spaniards? Although the Tepexi source cannot answer these questions definitively, we suggest that Matzatzin (or his father, Xochiztin or Tozancoztli) took part in the conquest of the Mixteca under Ahuizotl or Moctezuma Xocoyotl.[56] In return for this participation, he had received the right to tribute and personal service from some of the neighborhoods, or *parcialidades*, in the Mixteca and Chochona towns. The bulk of the tribute, of course, would have gone to the Triple Alliance. Then, in 1520, with the arrival of the Spaniards, Matzatzin saw the opportunity to improve this settlement by reconquering, or perhaps conquering, the towns that were subject to the Triple Alliance, allowing him to receive all their tribute, rather than just a part of it. The trick, therefore, was played against both the Mexica (specifically his grandfather, Moctezuma) and the Spaniards—an impressive manipulation of the complex power politics of early-sixteenth-century Mesoamerica.

Furthermore, we should not forget the ambivalent nature of alliances and the possibilities for historiographical manipulation. After a peaceful agreement is reached, both sides can claim victory because nobody is clearly conquered. We see this in the Tlaxcalteca-Spanish alliance, but it clearly occurred in preconquest times too. According to a number of Mexica sources, Tehuantepec was conquered by Ahuitzotl, but sources are divided on whether Tehuantepec paid tribute or not. A subsequent marriage between Cocijoeza, the Zapoteca ruler of Tehuantepec, and a daughter of Moctezuma Xocoyotl sealed the peace between these two kingdoms. Oaxacan sources, however, emphasize that Cocijoeza and Moctezuma fought a long exhaustive battle, which the latter ended with a peace proposal that was sealed by this marriage. Obviously, these Oaxacan sources deny that the Zapoteca were obliged to pay tribute to Tenochtitlan. In short, an agreement between two lords was interpreted in two different ways by their respective historians, each giving the benefit of the doubt to their own group.[57]

Thus, although the Mesoamerican stepping-stone pattern of sequential conquests was most obviously used by Cortés and his fellow captains both against the Mexica and in the post-1521 campaigns, there were other preconquest patterns behind this one—as suggested by Matzatzin initiating a military campaign in the name of the king of Spain against his own subject towns. These other patterns or mechanisms of conquest were related to that of sequential conquests and likewise persisted during the sixteenth century.

Trade Routes

When the Spaniards arrived in Mesoamerica, this culture area consisted of a multitude of city-states interconnected through a complex web of social, political, and economic relationships. In the late postclassic period (1200–1521) this expressed itself in what is known as the Mixteca-Puebla style or the postclassic international style.[58] This style developed as a result of centuries of continuous exchange of information and material between the Mesoamerican city-states. According to Michael E. Smith and Frances Berdan, these city-states can be divided into different, partly overlapping, zones: the core zones, the affluent production zones, and the resource-extraction zones.[59] Trade, gift exchange, and tribute payments took place both within and between these zones.

Considering that during their military campaigns the Spaniards were to a large extent led by local lords and guides, we can presume that they followed existing routes. Logically, the routes of conquest would consequently follow the prehispanic trade routes. A simple comparison of the zones proposed by Smith and Berdan with the routes of the early conquest expeditions reveals that this was indeed what happened, as illustrated by map 2. The circles are Smith and Berdan's "Affluent Production and Resource-Extraction Zones"; the lines are the various early campaigns of conquests, from 1521 to 1545. The campaigns in the near north and west were (from north to south) by Nuño de Guzmán (1529–36), Francisco Cortés de Buenaventura (1524), and Cristóbal de Olid (1522). Into Oaxaca, Xoconosco, and Guatemala went Francisco Orozco (1521), Luis Marín (1521–24), and Pedro de Alvarado (1523), while Gonzalo de Sandoval invaded Coatzacualco (1521). In the Yucatan peninsula, there were three Montejo campaigns—those led by Francisco de Montejo the elder in 1527–29 and 1529–35 and that led by his son in 1535–45. The correlation between the two patterns is striking, albeit approximate. Nor does it include every trade route or related zone or the route of every expedition. For example, Cortés and Díaz del Castillo tell us that Pedro de Alvarado went to Tututepec, Oaxaca, to put down a rebellion without giving us any information about the route he took. The same is true for Zacatula, which was a known tributary city-state of the Triple Alliance, but no information exists about how this tribute got to central Mexico.[60]

However, some of the trade routes are well documented. The route from Tenochtitlan to Guatemala is one of them; it passed through Chalco, Cholula, Izucar, Acatlan, Huajuapan, Coixtlahuaca, Nochixtlan, Huajolotitlan, Zaachila/Cuilapan, Tlacolula, Mitla, Nexapa, Tehuantepec, Tonala, Xoconusco, Zapotitlan, Quetzaltenango, and the Guatemalan highlands. Of course, there were alternative paths at several points along the way. For example, after Cholula one could go to Tecamachalco, Tehuacan, Teotitlan, and Cuicatlan to hook up again in Huajolotitlan. Or if one wanted to avoid Cholula the route would pass through Amecameca and Cuautla before arriving in Izucar. Furthermore, at several points one could take routes to other places. Teotitlan was an important crossroads toward Tuxtepec via Huauhtla in the Mazatec mountains. In Tlacolula there was a path north through the Sierra Zapoteca connecting again with Tuxtepec, or one could go a bit further to Mitla and turn north to Coatzacualco. Alternatively, one could go to Coatzacualco via Tehuantepec. From Coatzacualco the route goes to Xicalango and Tixchel from where the Yucatan Peninsula can be crossed to Caye Coco and Santa Rita in northern Belize. Or one could continue along the coast via Champoton to the city-states of northern Yucatan like Mayapan or Chikinchel.[61]

Comparing the trade route to Guatemala with that followed by the conquistadors it becomes clear that they are indeed the same. The last part of the route is confirmed both by Díaz del Castillo and López de Gómara in their descriptions of the 1523 campaign of Pedro de Alvarado to Guatemala; it went through Tehuantepec, Xoconosco, Zapotitlan, Quetzaltenango, Utatlan.[62] Although no historical sources exist that confirm the exact route of the conquistadors from the Valley of Oaxaca to the Isthmus of Tehuantepec, the only practical way is through the Nexapa Valley. Furthermore, in the Valley of Oaxaca itself there is hardly any alternative between Huajolotitlan and Mitla.

Finally, the route of the conquistadors through Puebla and the Mixteca is amply demonstrated in the document by Don Joachin Moctezuma of

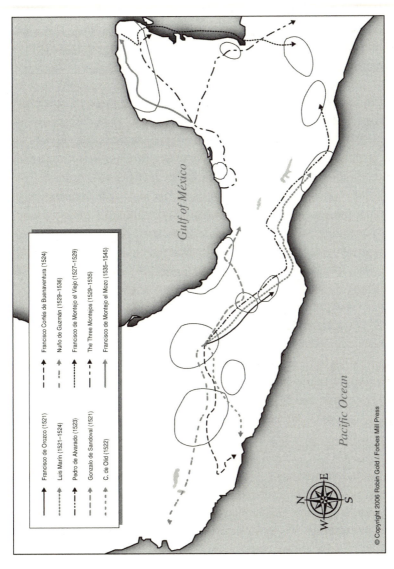

Map 2. The correlation between preconquest trade routes and conquest expedition routes

Legend:

- Francisco de Orozco (1521)
- Luis Marín (1521–1524)
- Pedro de Alvarado (1523)
- Gonzalo de Sandoval (1521)
- C. de Olid (1522)
- Francisco Cortés de Buenaventura (1524)
- Nuño de Guzmán (1529–1536)
- Francisco de Montejo el Viejo (1527–1529)
- The Three Montejos (1529–1535)
- Francisco de Montejo el Mozo (1535–1545)

Gulf of Mexico

Pacific Ocean

Tepexi de la Seda; almost certainly, the Spaniards later used the very same routes that were "pacified" by Don Gonzalo Matzatzin Moctezuma. According to the *interrogatorio* and related testimonies, Matzatzin's campaign can be divided into two parts: first his army went southwest of Tepexi, conquering until it reached the Valley of Oaxaca; then it turned back north conquering more towns. The towns of the first part are somewhat confusing, as there does not seem to be a clear pattern in their distribution: Chinantla, Igualtepec, Tlanchinola, Acatlan, Ecatepec, and Huajolotitlan.[63] Apart from Acatlan and Huajolotitlan, the motivation for the conquest of these towns seems to be related to the control over centers of extraction of raw materials since they are not situated on any particular trade route. However, Tlachinola was the headtown of a gold-producing province, while Igualtepec, Acatlan, and Chinantla were salt-producing centers.[64] Although the witnesses seem to say that Huajolotitlan is the town of that name situated at the entrance of the Valley of Oaxaca, the context of the other conquests make clear that this is simply impossible. At no time did the army of Matzatzin reach that far south, and it is therefore at this time not clear how to explain these claims. The identification of the town as Huajolotitlan in the state of Puebla is strengthened if we consider the subsequent conquests of Chila, Teotitlan, Te[qui]cistepec, Tecomauacan, Acatepec, Quiotepec, Zapotitlan, Cuicatlan, Tehuacan, Coixtlahuaca, Chiapulco, Texupan, Coxcatlan, Tamazulapa, and Teposcolula.

It is immediately clear from the layout of these towns (see map 3) that Matzatzin was taking over the two main trade routes between the Valley of Mexico and southern Mesoamerica. Furthermore, he secured the crossroads to Tuxtepec and the Mixteca coast when he took Teotitlan and Teposcolula. Whereas at first his conquests appear to be an opportunistic attempt to gain more power, this analysis of the geography of his expedition shows that Matzatzin was orchestrating a calculated military campaign to control one of the economic lifelines of Mesoamerica and an important resource-extraction zone. The conquests show the existence and importance of trade routes connecting central Mexico to the Gulf coast, from where Yucatan could be reached, or to the Oaxaca region, which leads to Xoconosco and Guatemala. In taking over southern Puebla and the Mixteca, Matzatzin not only enriched and empowered himself but also paved the way for later Spanish intrusions into the Valley of Oaxaca, the Tututepec province, and southern Mesoamerica. This explains why none of the conquistadors or chroniclers mention any military conquest in these two particular regions;

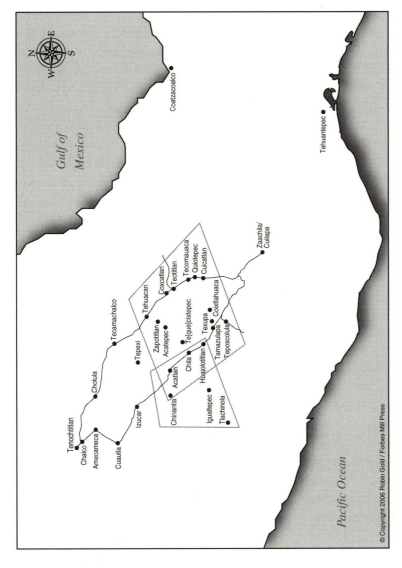

Map 3. The correlation between trade routes and Matzatzin of Tepexi's conquest routes of 1520

Matzatzin had already effectively incorporated these towns into what was becoming New Spain.[65] Further examples could be added, and indeed one has already been implied with the discussion of the Cortés-led expedition to Honduras in 1525–26, which clearly traveled for most of the way along existing paths. Some of these paths, such as the route through the Chontal Maya capital of Itzamkanac and into the Itza Maya kingdom may have been many centuries old, possibly those also used by expeditions from classic period Teotihuacan to Tikal (located within sixteenth-century Itza borders, just north of the capital, Tah Itza or Tayasal).[66]

Lordships and Land Grants

One of the intriguing aspects of the conquest period is the question of motivation. What motivated indigenous troops to participate in the Spanish undertaking? The most common explanation has been the wish to free themselves from the Mexica military and tributary control, but this can explain only part of the story. As detailed earlier, indigenous participation did not stop after the destruction of Tenochtitlan but continued for many decades; as the conquest continuously developed and changed, the motives for native participation must have developed and changed with it. Of course, right from the start the Fat Cacique complained about the tribute and service he had to give to Moctezuma and the people he had to hand over for sacrifice to the Mexica gods. But it is curious that when Cortés ordered a campaign against neighboring Tizapancingo, Cempoala brought together a large army of two thousand soldiers to accompany the Spanish troops. According to the Fat Cacique Tizapancingo was full of Mexica warriors who were destroying Cempoala's fields and subject towns as well as assaulting its people. However, when Cortés's army and their newly found allies arrived in Tizapancingo it turned out that the Fat Cacique was using the Spaniards to settle old debts with their neighbor.[67] This example is a cautionary tale, suggesting that there were various levels of decision making at different moments, based on different kind of motives.

The motives for participation by native groups often seem to have been opportunistic and short-term. What, therefore, did local rulers imagine would happen in the long run? This is a difficult question to answer since we lack indigenous sources from the 1520s that could illuminate such expectations.[68] We can, however, determine preconquest practice in relation to conquest and its aftermath, and we can analyze the letters of indigenous rulers to the emperor or the Audiencia, mentioned earlier, as the claims that they make and the frustrations they express may be considered to be indications of unfulfilled expectations. Of course, these letters might be viewed as inflated reports by indigenous groups who knew how to manipulate the Spanish legal system. But if we can show a continuity of conquest practices from preconquest to early colonial decades and show that the claims these indigenous conquistadors made were actually based on this practice, then we must accept that such letters were more than mere manipulations and exaggerations.

A typical aspect of conquest practice prior to the Spanish invasion was the division of land by a warlord, a religious leader, or a supreme ruler among his captains. These captains were probably leaders of cohesive groups based on some kind of relationship (consanguinity, ethnicity, geography, etc.). A clear example of this pattern is described by the central Mexican chronicler Ixtlilxochitl in relation to the early Nahua conquests by Xolotl. Having sent his four captains in the four cardinal directions to seize the territory, Xolotl then divided it among his lords and assigned people to serve them.[69]

But in other regions too, like the Isthmus of Tehuantepec, we find further examples. We know that around A.D. 1375 Cosijoeza I founded various villages as strongholds along the trade route to Xoconosco.[70] In the mid-fifteenth century these foundations were followed by a large-scale military invasion and migration in which Cocijopii led forces to the isthmus. New towns were established, and the warlords received the Title of Pichana, or Xoana—comparable to the central Mexican Title of Teuctli. From that moment on, these Xoanas periodically had to pledge loyalty to their lord, who in return gave them recognition. The lienzos of Guevea, Santo Domingo Petapa, and Huilotepec contain representations of ceremonies in which the authorities of these villages received the Titles of Xoana, based on the simple fact that their ancestors had been captains in the conquest of the region, following which events the supreme lord and leader of the campaign had divided the land among these captains. In other words, the ritual is a reenactment of conquest.

The division of land in return for military support is a well-known Mesoamerican theme, as shown in the "contract" the Tolteca-Chichimeca made with the Chichimeca in order to defeat the allied lords of Cholula. Once the Tolteca-Chichimeca won the war, they gave these mercenaries the title of *teuhctli*, as well as land and people to work it.[71] But we can find

examples in just about any central Mexican source.[72] This very same phenomenon took place years later when various city-states supported the
Spanish conquistadors. In 1571 various indigenous groups living in
Guatemala but originally from central Mexico, Puebla, and Oaxaca claimed
from the Spanish Crown the right to land and tribute based on the participation of their ancestors in the conquest of the region.[73]

Similar claims were put forward by the authorities of Tlaxcala, who on
several occasions made clear that Cortés had made a verbal promise to
reward the city with a land grant in return for their help in the conquest.[74]
Whether true or not, the promise was used as a means to claim privileges
and rights and as such fits perfectly within the Mesoamerican scheme of
participation in conquest and alliance.

Of course, the Spaniards also claimed similar rights and privileges from
the Crown as a reward for their part in the conquest, and as such they also
followed an old tradition which goes back into the Middle Ages. However,
the existence of this Spanish tradition does not explain indigenous
Mesoamerican participation in the conquest. It is evident that indigenous
troops took part in the Spanish-allied conquest because they took for
granted that they would receive what until then was usually granted after
such campaigns. But, when the Spaniards did not respond in the same way
as the preconquest lords used to do, indigenous nobles began submitting
judicial claims. These petitions reveal a growing desperation as the early
colonial period wore on. Eventually, these kinds of claims by indigenous
nobles and their descendants faded away as they became aware that the
system no longer worked in the same way. Preconquest society had
changed into colonial society.

CONCLUSION

The discovery of increasing numbers of documents detailing the extensive roles of indigenous allies in the Spanish conquest has made a reeval-
uation of the conquest period necessary. Whereas our view of this period
was and still is based on sources produced within the European historiographical tradition, these recently emerged sources make it clear that an
indigenous historiographical tradition existed too (albeit one recorded and
preserved within the formats of the colonial system). The views expressed
in the native tradition are often diametrically opposed to the claims of the

Spanish one. Whereas Spanish historical sources portray the conquest of Mesoamerica as a controlled and conscious military campaign led by heroes like Hernando Cortés and Pedro de Alvarado, the indigenous sources describe a far more complex process of alliances and negotiations among various groups. Moreover, the conquest is described as a continuation of precolonial processes of conquest and domination.

In order to reach a balanced view on the conquest period it will be necessary to reconstruct and study the indigenous historiographical tradition thoroughly and as a whole. That is, we need to consider this corpus of documents as independent from those of the European tradition before we can begin an analysis and comparison of the two traditions.[75]

This chapter contributes to the initial stage of this complicated process of reconstructing the indigenous historiographical tradition on the conquest of Mesoamerica. We have offered a preliminary discussion of some of the sources through the creation of four categories of analysis. The first two categories or topics—on "friendly Indian" numbers and the role of indigenous allies after the fall of the Mexica empire—presented an indigenous vision of the conquest of Mesoamerica as a series of events decided and determined by the many indigenous troops and "captains" that made it possible. Although Spanish captains were often in primary leadership positions, this was not always the case, as demonstrated by the conquests of Don Gonzalo Matzatzin Moctezuma of Tepexi de la Seda. The third category detailed nonmilitary participation in the conquest by natives in ways that are less obvious but often just as decisive. In other words, noncombatant indigenous participation—from spies to interpreters and from porters to cooks—was as important as combatant participation. More surprising, however, was the importance of the continuation of precolonial patterns and mechanisms during the conquest period. This fourth analytical category argued that there was a correspondence between prehispanic trade routes and conquest routes and that motivations for conquest participation and the maintenance of multicity alliances were both continuations of precolonial practices and patterns.

All this suggests that there is another story to be told, one that we will eventually be able to tell in considerable detail. We know the half that was written by the Spanish conquistadors and their compatriots, but there is still another half that needs to be unlocked—the other side of the conquest of Mesoamerica.

NOTES

1. The unsigned paintings, formerly known as the Strickland series, were acquired by the Jay I. Kislak Foundation in 1999 and were loaned in 2003 to the University of Miami's Lowe Art Museum; see the catalog for the exhibit, Jackson and Brienen, *Visions of Empire*. They are now housed at the Library of Congress in Washington, D.C. The series is oil on canvas, and the seventh painting is 48 x 78 inches. The second painting is reproduced and discussed briefly in Restall, *Seven Myths*, 30–31.

2. For examples, see Restall, *Seven Myths*, 3.

3. Restall, *Seven Myths*, 140–44.

4. Partly for this reason, the discussion of native allies is presented in *Seven Myths* (44–63) in the larger context of the assistance that Spaniards received both from native and African soldiers; on the latter, also see Restall, "Black Conquistadors."

5. Alvarado, *Account of the Conquest*, 80. An example of evidence of such allies outside Alvarado's own reports is the proceedings surrounding the 1564 petition by the descendants of such allies for tribute exemption, in Archivo General de Indias, Seville (hereafter, AGI), Justicia 291, 1.

6. "Al tiempo que el d[ic]ho don pedro de alvarado passo con los d[ic]hos españoles e yndios capitanes de suso declarados vido que trayan consigo muchos yndios de sus tierras que dezian que heran sus deudos e maçeguales y quel t[iem]po que este testigo anduvo en la guerra vido que los d[ic]hos capitanes hizieron su cuadrillas cada uno por su orden." AGI Justicia 291, 1, f. 96v.

7. See Hassig, *Aztec Warfare*, 56.

8. Díaz del Castillo, *Historia verdadera*, chaps. 81 and 150; Cortés, *Letters from Mexico*, 211.

9. See Restall, *Seven Myths*, 11–18, 37, for further discussion of the probanza genre and its role in the development of "myths" of the conquest. Examples of probanzas by black conquistadors are in AGI México 204 and 2999, 2. Also see Restall, *Seven Myths*, 54–63.

10. See Restall, "Heirs to the Hieroglyphs," 239–67.

11. See Restall, *Maya Conquistador*; Wood, *Transcending Conquest*; Sousa and Terraciano, "Original Conquest."

12. AGI Patronato 245; AGI Guatemala 52, ff. 77r–78r; AGI México 94, 9; AGI Escribanía 160b, 1, f. 285r; AGI Justicia 291, 1, f. 239r. On the campaign of Jorge de Alvarado, see Asselbergs, chapter 2, and Herrera, chapter 4, this volume; also see Asselbergs, *Conquered Conquistadors*.

13. AGI Justicia, 291, 1, f. 88v; AGI Patronato 184, 50, published in Pérez-Rocha and Tena, *La nobleza indígena*, 281–86. Some of these conquistadors not coming back to their original communities may also be due to settlement in the conquered regions rather than death in battle. (We thank the referent for this suggestion.)

14. Don Joachin claimed that his grandfather, Don Gonzalo, was a grandson of Moctezuma Xocoyotl through his mother, Doña Maria, who supposedly was a

daughter of the Mexica ruler. For historical and chronological reasons it seems more likely that Don Gonzalo was a great-grandson of Moctezuma Ilhuicamina (1440–68) as is confirmed information from Alvarado Tezozomoc, *Crónica mexicayotl*, 200; Chimalpahin Quauhtlehuanitzin, *Codex Chimalpahin*, 1:132–33; and several witnesses (AGI Patronato 245, R. 10:4v, 12r, 14r, 17r, 19v). Klaus Jäcklein accepted Don Joachin's claim that his grandfather was a grandson of Moctezuma Xocoyotl. *Los popolocas de Tepexi*.

15. E.g., see the competing Mixteca and Nahua accounts from the Valley of Oaxaca (Sousa and Terraciano, "Original Conquest") and the creative borrowing that may have contributed to the narrative in the Mapa de Cuauhtlantzinco (Wood, *Transcending Conquest*, 77–106).

16. For a discussion of the concept of conquest in Mesoamerica, see Oudijk, "La Toma de Posesión." See also Acuña, *Relaciones geográficas*, plates 60–66.

17. AGI México 110.

18. See Berdan et al., *Aztec Imperial Strategies*; Berdan and Anawalt, *Essential Codex Mendoza*, 102–103.

19. "Por buenas palabras a lagunas y a otros por guerra." AGI Patronato 245, R. 10, ff. 10r.

20. Cieza de León, *Discovery and Conquest*, 295, 302.

21. AGI México 274, 1, f.10r (1624); no n., f. 1r (1630).

22. For more details and examples of Mesoamericans and other native soldiers serving as militiamen in the Spanish colonies, particularly in Mexico after about 1550, see the sections "The Role of Native Militias" and "Native Militiamen on the Frontier: Sonora in the 1790s" in Vinson and Restall, "Black Soldiers, Native Soldiers," 15–52.

23. On the Military Revolution, see Parker, *Military Revolution*; on its relevance to the Spanish conquest and misperceptions of it, see Restall, *Seven Myths*, 28–33, 143.

24. "Desde que vimos tant indio de carga nos holgamos, porque antes siempre traíamos a cuestas nuestras mochilas." Díaz del Castillo, *Historia verdadera*, chap. 45.

25. See Asselbergs, chapter 2, and Yannakakis, chapter 7, this volume.

26. AGI Justicia 291, 1, ff. 63r, 89r, 94r, 113v–114r, 124r.

27. Díaz del Castillo, *Historia verdadera*, chaps. 44, 45, 51, and 68.

28. AGI Guatemala 52, ff. 77r–78r (1547); AGI Patronato 2, 2; AGI Justicia 291, 1, ff. 69v, 97r, 171r–v, 174r; AGI Escribanía 160b, ff. 186–89; Muñoz Camargo, *Historia de Tlaxcala* (ed. Vasquez), book 2, chap. 4: 194–209.

29. The complete título is published in translation in Restall, *Maya Conquistador*, 86–103, quote on 87.

30. "Porque los naturales rrebeldes avian alçado los bastimentos e los escondian y no hallavan de comer." AGI Justicia 291, 1, f. 149r.

31. "Y vido que padesçieron muchos trabajos de hambre." AGI Justicia 291, 1, f. 93v and further.

32. Restall, *Seven Myths*, 149. The chief source on this raid is Díaz del Castillo; see *Historia verdadera*, f. 200r of the original 1632 edition (copy in John Carter Brown Library [JCBL], Brown University, Providence, Rhode Island).

33. "Yvan siempre delante descubriendo tierra e sino fuera por hellos pereçieran muchas vezes porque los yndios henemygos les thenyan puestas çeladas y muchos hoyos hechos donde el que caya no podia escapar lo qual descubrian los d[ic]hos yndios." AGI Justicia 291, 1, f. 98r. The Lienzo de Quauhquechollan seems to portray a variant of these pits; see Asselberg, "La conquista de Guatemala."

34. See, e.g., AGI Justicia 291, 1, ff. 39v, 76r, 82v, 106v.

35. The Chontal Maya text, the Title of Acalan-Tixchel, ff. 72v–73r, translated in Restall, *Maya Conquistador*, 64.

36. Díaz del Castillo, *Historia verdadera*, chap. 62.

37. AGI Justicia 291, 1, f. 17r.

38. Karttunen, "Interpreters," 215. On Chi, Malinche, and other native interpreters, see Karttunen, *Between Worlds*; Restall, *Maya Conquistador*, 144–52; Restall, "Gaspar Antonio Chi"; and Restall, *Seven Myths*, 23–24, 82–88, 91, 93.

39. Restall, *Seven Myths*, 18–26.

40. Presented variously by Lockhart; see, e.g., "Trunk Lines and Feeder Lines."

41. Restall, *Seven Myths*, 108–20. With respect to central Mexico, this misconception or myth was based largely on the use of the Nahuatl term *teotl* as a reference to the Spanish invaders. Díaz del Castillo explained that the term related to "the idols, or their gods, or bad things." *Historia verdadera*, chap. 61, esp. p. 104 (ed. Ramírez Cabañas). Nahua were probably referring to the latter of these semantically related concepts when they called the Spaniards *teules*. The apparently contradictory nature of these concepts is rooted in the Mesoamerican belief system and the characteristic of sacred entities as being loaded with *mana* (power). (See López Austin, *Los mitos del Tlacuache*, chaps. 10–12, for a discussion of the nature of Mesoamerican gods.) That the Nahua meant "bad things" rather than simply "gods" is confirmed by one of Cortés's actions early on in the conquest. In order to impress the Mexica garrison in Tizapancingo he sent out Heredia "El Viejo," a conquistador with "a nasty look in his face, a long beard, his face partly slashed away, blind in one eye, and limping with one leg" ("tenía mala catadura en la cara, y la barba grande y la cara medio acuchillada, y un ojo tuerto, y cojo de una pierna"). Díaz del Castillo, *Historia verdadera* (ed. Ramírez Cabañas), 83. Furthermore, Cortés told him to shoot his rifle like a madman. That these tactics worked is clear from some descriptions in indigenous sources expressing an awe and fearful respect for certain Spaniards; see, e.g., the second page of Lima, *Libro*, or see the descriptions in AGI Patronato 245, R. 10. However, this did not keep Mesoamerican soldiers from fighting and killing the Spaniards or their horses. On the contrary, Spaniards may have been seen as the *ixiptlatli* of the *teteuh*; i.e., they were representatives or impersonators of the teteuh and as such had to be treated with respect but could be killed. In fact, in Mesoamerican ritual life the role of the ixiptlatli is to be killed, as various sources attest; Hvidtfeldt, *Teotl and Ixiptlatli*, on the concept of ixiptlatli and particularly Sahagún, *Historia general*, on Mexica rituals. The issue of the

Spaniards as teteuh (or ixiptlatli) strongly suggests that both sides were looking for meeting points or familiar features in the other's culture, seeking to bring these together to form a basis on which they could communicate and work together—the beginnings of syncretism. See Oudijk, "La Toma de Posesión," 95–131, esp. note 8 for a discussion of the process of syncretism and Mesoamerican colonial traditions.

42. Hassig, *Aztec Warfare*, 23.

43. López de Gómara, *La conquista de México*, 104–107. Note that Díaz del Castillo denies that such an alliance was proposed at this stage: "Aquí es donde dice el cronista [*sic*] Gómara que estuvo Cortés muchos días en Cempoal, y que se concertó la rebelión y liga contra Montezuma: no le informaron bien, porque, como he dicho, otro día por la mañana salimos de allí." *Historia verdadera* (ed. Ramírez Cabañas), 77. According to Díaz del Castillo, the rebellion against Moctezuma began at the instigation of Cortés, when the Spanish leader pressed Cempoala into taking Moctezuma's tribute collectors prisoner and refusing to pay tribute to anyone but the king of Spain. Ibid., 79–81.

44. Hansen, *Thirty City-State Cultures*, and Hansen, *Six City-State Cultures*. See these two volumes for contributions on the Maya, Mixteca, Mexica, and Zapoteca city-state cultures by Nikolai Grube, Michael Lind, Michael Smith, and Michel R. Oudijk, respectively.

45. Chimalpain Quauhtlehuanitzin, *Memorial Breve*, chaps. 7 and 15.

46. See Herrera, chapter 4, this volume, for further discussion of this mechanism during the conquest.

47. Oudijk, *Historiography*; Pérez-Rocha and Tena, *La nobleza indígena*; S. Gillespie, *Aztec Kings*.

48. See Díaz del Castillo, *Historia verdadera*, chaps. 51 and 76. "Generation" is probably not meant to be understood as the relation from father to son but rather in the sense of lineage. Both in Nahuatl and Zapotec "lineage" and "generation" are one and the same word: *tlacamecayotl* and *tija*, respectively.

49. AGI *México* 762 (1629); see Pérez-Rocha and Tena, *La nobleza indígena*, and Pérez-Rocha, *Privilegios en lucha*, for a discussion of Doña Isabel and the transcription of some documents related to legal battles for privileges. Also see Chipman, *Moctezuma's Children*.

50. Oudijk, *Historiography*, and Oudijk, "Zapotec City-State."

51. Pohl, "Royal Marriage."

52. In Cozumel they found empty villages as the population had fled to the mountains. This meant the Spaniards ran out of food and water. At a village on the Rio Grijalva they received some food under threat of war. The next day a battle took place and they deserted their village, only to be followed by more days of battle. Cortés, *Cartas de relación*, first letter; Díaz del Castillo, *Historia verdadera*, chaps. 25–44.

53. Durán, *Historia de las indias*, chaps. 19–20; Alvarado Tezozomoc, *Crónica mexicana*, chaps. 49–50; Díaz del Castillo, *Historia verdadera*, chaps. 45–47. See also Hassig, *Aztec Warfare*, 328n48; Berdan et al., *Aztec Imperial Strategies*, 286–87.

54. Hassig, *Aztec Warfare*, 21.

55. AGI Justicia 291. The whole document shows this pattern but see particularly ff. 86r–91v, 118v, 127v, 131r–v, 148r; also see earlier AGI citations.

56. See Berdan and Anawalt, *Essential Codex Mendoza*, 22–25, for a discussion of the conquests by these Mexica rulers.

57. See Oudijk, *Historiography*, chap. 2, for a full discussion. But even conquests are ambivalent as different kinds occur: "e que alg[un]os dellos ffueron conquistados y allanados por fuerça de armas y otros por rruegos y amonestaçiones." AGI Patronato, 245, R. 10, f. 294. See Oudijk, "La toma de posesión," for a discussion of the concept of conquest in Mesoamerica.

58. Nicholson and Quiñones Keber, *Mixteca Puebla*; Smith and Berdan, *Postclassic Mesoamerican World*.

59. Smith and Berdan, "Spatial Structure."

60. See Berdan et al., *Aztec Imperial Strategies*, 277–78.

61. Lee and Navarrete, *Mesoamerican Communication Routes*; Smith and Berdan, *Postclassic Mesoamerican World*, chaps. 22, 31, 33–35; Gutiérrez Mendoza et al., "Least Cost Path Analysis"; Oudijk, *Historiography*, chap. 2.

62. López de Gómara, *La conquista de México*, 338–41; Díaz del Castillo, *Historia verdadera*, chap. 164.

63. Chinantla is a bit confusing, as it is normally associated with the Chinantec region in northern Oaxaca. However, within this context it seems to be referring to the name of the town right next to the important town of Piaztla. See Gerhard, *Geografía histórica*, 44. A similar thing can be said of Tlachinola, which is or became a barrio of Tlapa and is sometimes even used an alternative name for Tlapa. Ibid, 333; Carrasco, *Tenochca Empire*, 276–79. We have not been able to identify the town of Ecatepec. See also Jäcklein, *Los popolocas de Tepexi*, for an identification of these towns.

64. See Berdan and Anawalt, *Essential Codex Mendoza*, ff. 39r, for the Tlapa province and Berdan et al, *Aztec Imperial Strategies*, 273, 284, for a discussion of those of Chiauhtlan and Acatlan.

65. When the Spaniards were in Tepeaca after the so-called Noche Triste, Cortés received ambassadors from Coixtlahuaca and eight other towns of that region who promised loyalty to the king of Spain. Cortés, *Cartas de relación*, 94; López de Gómara, *La conquista de México*, 263–64.

66. Restall, *Maya Conquistador*, 62–65; Izquierdo, *Acalán y la Chontalpa*; Piña Chan, "Commerce."

67. Díaz del Castillo, *Historia verdadera*, chaps. 49 and 51.

68. See Gruzinski, *Conquest of Mexico*, for an analysis of the adaptations and changes of the indigenous cosmovision and psyche as a consequence of the arrival of the Spaniards and the establishment of colonial society.

69. Fernando de Alva Ixtlilxochitl, *Obras históricas*, 1:296.

70. AGI Escribanía de Cámara 160b; Oudijk, *Historiography*, 2000.

71. See Kirchhoff, Odena Güemes, and Reyes García, *Historia tolteca-chichimeca*, 158–87, 161–282.

72. See, e.g., Durán, *Historia de las indias*, 129–30; Ixtlilxochitl, *Obras históricas*, 1:295–96.

73. AGI Justicia 291, f. 505v.

74. AGI Mexico 94, exp. 33.

75. This is a similar methodological challenge to that faced by historical archaeology; in the words of Michael E. Smith, "the archaeological and ethnohistorical records should be analyzed independently to yield their own separate conclusions before correlation is attempted. When the two records are compared, one should not confuse any resulting composite models with the independent primary data sets." "Expansion of the Aztec Empire," 88. Also see Charlton, "Archaeology, Ethnohistory, and Ethnology"; Trigger, *History*; Malina and Vasicek, *Archaeology Yesterday and Today*; Small, *Methods in the Mediterranean*; Andrén, *Between Artifacts and Texts*; Moreland, *Archaeology and Text*.

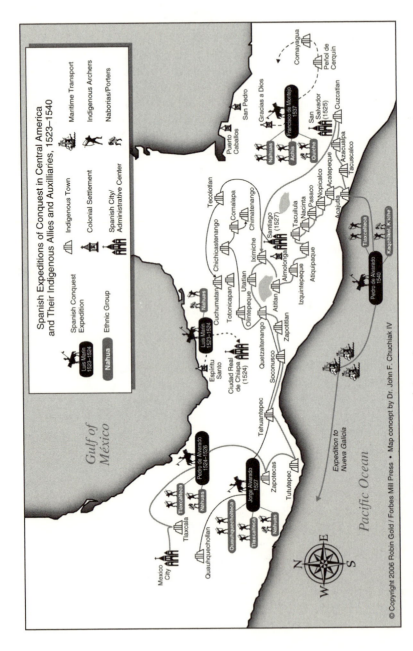

Map 4. Conquest expeditions in Central America

CHAPTER TWO

The Conquest in Images

Stories of Tlaxcalteca and Quauhquecholteca Conquistadors

FLORINE G. L. ASSELBERGS

The indigenous record of the conquest of Mesoamerica consists not only of alphabetical records; there are also a number of early colonial Nahua *lienzos* that shed light on this turning point in history. The creation of colonial pictorials continued a prehispanic historical tradition in which information and claims were recorded and communicated through narrative pictography. The Nahua script, as part of this tradition, made use of a repertoire of images (pictographs, logograms, and ideograms) to log historical events, genealogies of ruling lineages, tribute lists, geographical descriptions, and religious information.[1] Native pictorial records reflect the indigenous vision of historical events, concepts, and ideas, but also, even more interestingly, they display this indigenous vision by means of a medium the indigenous peoples themselves developed, felt comfortable with, and knew how to use to its fullest extent.[2]

This chapter will focus on three pictorials from Mexico and Guatemala that narrate indigenous conquest stories under the Spanish banner. Probably the most famous is the Lienzo de Tlaxcala from Tlaxcala, Mexico, which describes the Spanish-Tlaxcalteca alliance and presents impressive lists of Spanish conquests in which Tlaxcalteca conquistadors participated. Although the original Lienzo de Tlaxcala is lost, this document is known through surviving descriptions and various copies. Another Tlaxcalteca conquest story is the Lienzo de Analco, which pertains to the municipality of Nuestra Señora de los Remedios Analco, presently part of San Ildefonso Villa Alta, Oaxaca. This document relates to the role of Tlaxcalteca conquistadors in the area of Villa Alta, where they founded a satellite colony: Analco. A third pictorial story of indigenous conquistadors is the Lienzo de Quauhquechollan from San Martín Huaquechula, situated about seventy kilometers to the southwest of Tlaxcala. This final document describes the alliance of the Spaniards with the Quauhquecholteca and the role of Quauhquecholteca conquistadors in the period of the Spanish conquest.

There is little doubt that there were once other lienzos made by indigenous conquistadors who fought under the Spanish banner. A concrete reference to a similar but lost painting can be found in the Título de Caciques, a document composed by a group of K'iche' lords from Totonicapan, Guatemala, in 1544. This manuscript refers to a group of central Mexican conquistadors who had arrived with the Spanish and who had settled in San Miguel Totonicapan. Reportedly, these conquistadors came from Tlaxcala, Cholula, Uzmatla, and Ayutla and had "their titles together with a map and a lienzo of San Juan Bautista." The text states that the indigenous conquistadors "are in the map." This *mapa* was most probably a conquest pictorial; the "lienzo" may have been another pictorial or perhaps an alphabetic text. The títulos were written in Nahuatl ("en lengua mexicana") and relate that "they [the central Mexican conquistadors] came with their arrows and shields in order to defend the law of God." Possibly, these títulos are still in the town of Totonicapan.[3] Since the pictorial is lost, however, it could not be included in this study.

The Lienzo de Tlaxcala, the Lienzo de Quauhquechollan, and the Lienzo de Analco were all painted in the decades following the conquest. Also, all three documents are composed in Nahua pictorial writing style, the writing tradition of the homelands of the conquistadors who painted them: Tlaxcala and Quauhquechollan, both Nahua communities located in central Mexico. In this chapter I will provide brief descriptions of each of these three early conquest accounts. I will discuss them in relation to one another with special attention to their formats, rhetoric, and the way in which the indigenous conquistadors presented their accounts.

THE CONQUEST PICTORIALS

The Lienzo de Tlaxcala was painted around 1550 in Tlaxcala, Mexico. This document is now lost, but before it disappeared it was described by

Don Nicolás Faustino Mazihcatzin y Calmecahua, a municipal official of Tlaxcala who wrote in or before 1787, and it was copied repeatedly.

According to Mazihcatzin, the document was a *mapa historiographo* painted on the request of viceroy Don Luis de Velasco and under the supervision of the Tlaxcalteca *cabildo*. Mazihcatzin reported three originals: one for the king of Spain (Charles V), a second for the viceroy in Mexico City (Velasco himself), and a third for the town hall or archives of Tlaxcala. Only the last was seen and described by Mazihcatzin.[4] Not long after the municipal official wrote about the document, it was transferred to Mexico City to be copied by the Comisión Científica Francesa. When Tlaxcala requested its return in 1867, it could not be found. The Italian voyager Beltrami, who had been in Tlaxcala in 1825, reported a "map" painted on cotton cloth and kept by the cabildo of Tlaxcala. This was probably the same Lienzo de Tlaxcala.[5] Presently, none of the originals are known, and it is unclear if they were identical or not.

Fortunately, the lost Lienzo de Tlaxcala was copied repeatedly. In their 1975 census, John B. Glass and Donald Robertson reported ten copies and several "falsifications." More recently, yet other copies have been identified.[6] The three best-known copies are a large painting made by Juan Manuel Yllañes in 1773, lithographs made by Genaro López in the nineteenth century (also known as the Serrano copy), and a document known as the Glasgow manuscript. Although the surviving copies vary in form and content, most have similar outlines: they start with the Spanish-Tlaxcalteca alliance as established in 1519; they comment on the most important people, places, and events related to this alliance; and subsequently they describe the military achievements of the Tlaxcalteca under the Spanish banner.

From Mazihcatzin's description of the sixteenth-century Lienzo de Tlaxcala and from the layouts of its copies, it can be deduced that the original document had an initial scene at the top presenting the place glyph of Tlaxcala, the Spanish viceroys, the members of the Royal Audiencia in Mexico City, and the indigenous *caciques* and captains of the four principal districts of Tlaxcala. This scene referred to the Spanish-Tlaxcalteca alliance and also to the conversion of the Tlaxcalteca lords to Christianity. The rest of the painting consisted of at least eighty-seven quadrants, each of which showed persons, places, and events related to the subjection of Tlaxcala to Spanish rule and to the conquest of many places throughout Mesoamerica. Each extant copy has its own emphasis and its own reach, the most elaborate being the Glasgow manuscript that leads the viewer through battles in places as far as modern-day Nicaragua.[7]

There are other Tlaxcalteca documents that refer to the Spanish-Tlaxcalteca alliance. One is the so-called Texas manuscript, a pictographic text of four pages painted on the two sides of a folded folio of maguey paper. This document illustrates the establishment of the alliance between the Spaniards and the Tlaxcalteca: it shows Cortés seated next to the Tlaxcalteca lord Xicotencatl in his palace in Tiçatla, while all the lords of Tlaxcala offer to him luxurious gifts and some of their daughters.[8] Furthermore, in his *Descripción de la ciudad y provincia de Tlaxcala*, the chronicler Diego Muñoz Camargo refers to paintings in one of the rooms of Xicotencatl's palace in Tiçatla, which depicted "the arrival of Cortés and his Spaniards, and the good welcome that was given him, and the conquest of Mexico."[9] The chronicler also mentions that by 1560 the walls of the ruling houses of Tlaxcala were decorated with later paintings about Cortés' arrival "and the reception and gift that Tlaxcala gave him, and the peace it gave him in this entire province . . . and of the exploits that they and the Spaniards made in the pacification of all of this land."[10] Unfortunately, these conquest pictorials are now lost, and it is unknown whether they were images painted directly on the walls or whether they were painted on cloth that was later mounted on the walls.

The Lienzo de Analco (see fig. 7.1 in this volume) is also a Tlaxcalteca conquest narrative; however, this pictorial, painted on a cotton cloth measuring 245 x 180 centimeters, depicts Tlaxcalteca conquistadors in alliance with Spaniards during the conquest of the Sierra Norte, Oaxaca. In 1526 Tlaxcalteca conquistadors settled in this area and founded a barrio named Analco in the town Villa Alta. The document shows stylized plans of both Villa Alta and Analco and an accurate geographic landscape of the surrounding area made up of towns, mountains, roads, rivers, vegetation, and market places.[11] Scattered over this landscape are images of captains and warriors, battles between the Spanish-Tlaxcalteca army and the local population, Mixe invasions into the area, the use of indigenous people as *tameme* and workers, and scenes of punishment.[12] The scenes of punishment probably represent those executed by Luis de Berrio, the first *alcalde mayor* of Villa Alta, who was reputed to have ruthlessly hanged, burned, and thrown to the dogs anyone who did not obey his orders.[13]

The Lienzo de Analco does not depict Tlaxcala. The identification of the indigenous conquistadors that appear in this document as Tlaxcalteca is primarily based on the fact that the document pertained to Analco, which was founded and inhabited by Tlaxcalteca, and on the fact that the latter indeed played an important role in the pacification of the area depicted in the document.[14] It can therefore also be presumed that the Lienzo de Analco was painted in Analco, not in Tlaxcala. This is confirmed by the accuracy with which the geographic landscape is depicted; clearly, the *tlacuiloque* were very familiar with the area. The Lienzo de Analco must have been created after 1526, when Analco was founded, and before 1550, as in that year an important church, wall, and two bridges were built, none of which is depicted. Also, the document focuses only on the conquest period itself (1527–31) and represents no events of a later time.[15]

The scenes in the Lienzo de Analco are positioned in a variety of directions, and there is no top side or bottom side that can be determined. It can therefore be presumed that the document was meant to be laid out on the floor to be read. The readers would then stand and walk around it, making this diverse orientation a logical one. This process transformed the document into a physical microversion of the landscape of the narrative.

By the middle of the twentieth century, when the Lienzo de Analco was first mentioned in Western literature, it was still in Analco and accompanied by a pile of alphabetical documents written in Spanish and Nahuatl (possibly títulos).[16] The contents and present-day location of these alphabetic texts are unknown.[17] Presently, the Lienzo de Analco is in the collection of the Biblioteca Nacional de Antropología e Historia in Mexico City. Reportedly, there existed at least one copy of this document; however, the present whereabouts of this copy are unknown.[18]

The Lienzo de Quauhquechollan (see fig. 2.1) tells the experiences and military achievements of another group of indigenous conquistadors: the Quauhquecholteca from Quauhquechollan, Puebla, Mexico. This conquest narrative is painted on a cotton cloth of almost twice the size of the Lienzo de Analco: it measures 235 x 325 centimeters.[19] Originally, the cloth was even larger, but it has been cut off at the right side.

The narrative of the Lienzo de Quauhquechollan starts with the alliance between the Spaniards and the Quauhquecholteca in 1520, and then it describes the 1527–30 conquering campaign to Guatemala under Jorge de Alvarado's banner. It depicts the military base camp of Jorge de Alvarado and his allies in Chimaltenango (central Guatemala), from which site his army waged war against the Kaqchikel. It also depicts the city of Santiago at Almolonga, founded by Jorge in 1527, where the Quauhquecholteca later settled and founded a barrio named Quahquechula. From this site Jorge and the Quauhquecholteca started other campaigns leading into Verapaz and

FIGURE 2.1.
*Lienzo de Quauhquechollan. Photography by Bob Schalkwijk (2001). Reproduced
courtesy of the Museo Casa de Alfeñique, Puebla, Mexico.*

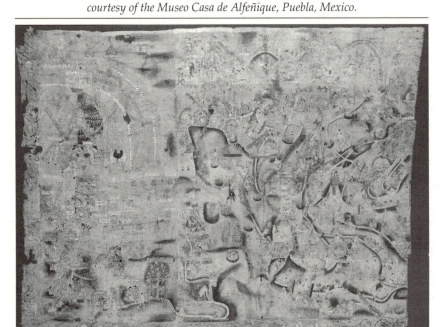

the Cuchumatanes. Just like in the Lienzo de Analco, the Quauhquecholteca
conquest story is positioned in an accurate geographical landscape.

The exact provenance of the Lienzo de Quauhquechollan is unknown.
By the end of the nineteenth century, when the document was first mentioned in the literature, it was in Puebla, Mexico.[20] The contents of the narrative and the accuracy of the landscape depicted, however, suggest a
creation in Guatemala, most likely in the Quauhquecholteca barrio
Quahquechula in the city of Santiago at Almolonga. If indeed made in
Guatemala, one can presume the document was made at least in two-fold,
with one copy remaining in Guatemala and the other being sent to
Quauhquechollan (the latter being the copy known to us today). The possibility of a creation of the lienzo in Quauhquechollan itself, however, cannot be excluded. The Lienzo de Quauhquechollan records only events before
1530, and it can be presumed that it was painted in the decades following
the conquest, probably in the 1530s or 1540s.[21] The original Lienzo de
Quauhquechollan is presently kept in the Museo de la Casa del Alfeñique

in Puebla, Mexico. There exist two copies, which are both in the collection of the Biblioteca Nacional de Antropología e Historia in Mexico City.

During her research in the Archivo General de Indias in Sevilla, Spain, Wendy Kramer encountered a document dated 1571 in which the Spaniard Juan Fernández Nájera declared that he had seen "a painted piece of cloth, which some Indians brought to this city [Santiago de Guatemala] and in which they pointed out the conquistadors and the journeys they had made, for those who had stood out most and served best in the said conquests." The Spaniard added that this painting included images of Diego Sánchez de Santiago, one of the first conquistadors of the area.[22] This cloth document may well have been the very Lienzo de Quauhquechollan, which would confirm a creation and early use of this document in Guatemala. It is also possible, however, that the Spaniard referred to a comparable document that is now lost.

The Tlaxcalteca barrio Analco in the town Villa Alta, the Quauhquecholteca barrio Quahquechula in the city of Santiago at Almolonga, and the settlement of central Mexican conquistadors in Totonicapan are but three examples of a series of satellite colonies founded by central Mexican conquistadors all over Mesoamerica. These barrios were usually named after the barrio, *altepetl* (city-state), or confederation of altepetl where the founders came from. The inhabitants tended to remain rather closed groups, keeping the customs and traditions of their homeland in use, and they enjoyed certain privileges in return for their community's contribution to the Spanish conquest (see other chapters in this volume). It is likely that, just like the indigenous conquistadors who settled in Villa Alta, the city of Santiago at Almolonga, and Totonicapan, most other communities of indigenous conquistadors also maintained their own historical record, including lienzos, maps, or other pictorials created according to the traditions of their homeland.

THE SPANISH-INDIGENOUS ALLIANCES AS REPRESENTED BY THE TLAXCALTECA AND QUAUHQUECHOLTECA

The Tlaxcalteca and Quauhquecholteca conquest pictorials communicate comparable stories. The Lienzo de Tlaxcala and the Lienzo de Analco depict the Tlaxcalteca in alliance with the Spaniards and their military achievements and experiences in the initial period of the conquest. The Lienzo de Quauhquechollan does the same for the Quauhquecholteca.

The Lienzo de Quauhquechollan and the different versions of the Lienzo de Tlaxcala show the establishment of alliances with the Spaniards in their initial scenes. The contents of these first scenes show tellingly the way in which the alliances were regarded by the Tlaxcalteca and Quauhquecholteca and how the lords of these communities chose to represent and communicate these events both to their own people and to the Spaniards. This point of view is expressed consistently throughout the remainder of both documents.

A first message conveyed by pictorials is that the Tlaxcalteca and Quauhquecholteca received the Spaniards kindly. The tlacuiloque painted the indigenous lords in a friendly meeting with the Spaniards, embracing them and presenting gifts and without any sign of hostility. From the alphabetical record it is known that the Quauhquecholteca indeed never fought against the Spaniards. Quauhquechollan was one of the towns previously subjected to Tenochtitlan, and when the Spaniards arrived, the Quauhquecholteca allied with them almost immediately to free themselves from the Mexica.[23] The Tlaxcalteca, however, had remained independent from Tenochtitlan and in fact had initially waged war upon the Spaniards. Only later, after at least three hostile confrontations, did they decide to establish an alliance.[24] These initial clashes are not recorded in any of the Tlaxcalteca pictorials. They are ignored in the narratives as if to suggest that they never took place. The Tlaxcalteca obviously wanted to stress their loyalty to the Spaniards. Regardless of the fact that military confrontations did take place, they recorded themselves as having been faithful allies right from the very beginning, in order to present an unambiguous story that would best serve their interests.

A second message expressed by the Quauhquecholteca and Tlaxcalteca tlacuiloque is that their lords' alliances with the Spaniards were perceived as equal and not as alliances compelled by the Spaniards' domination. The Tlaxcalteca and Quauhquecholteca communities were subjected to the Spanish Crown, it was true, but not in a way that was humiliating. Instead, the alliances with the Spaniards were perceived to be a gathering of forces and as the establishment of a new power. To demonstrate these alliances, the tlacuiloque sought ways to show the connections between themselves and the world of the Spaniards. They came up with a variety of modifications of pictographic conventions that enabled them to make these connections without giving up their own identities. The captains and soldiers are depicted in the pictorials with Spanish swords, for example, but also with their own indigenous war costumes and emblems. The Quauhquecholteca tlacuiloque even portrayed both the Spaniards and Quauhquecholteca with the same white skin color, while their enemies are provided with brown and red skin. Such indicators served to show that these communities had now become Spanish allies, without giving up their own identity and heroic past but by adapting them to the new situation. In this way, the documents served as means for these communities to assert their claims to status and privileges, by reaffirming their independence, identity, and equality.

A third message communicated by the pictorials is the distinction between the indigenous conquistadors who fought with the Spaniards and nonallied indigenous peoples. In comparison to the Tlaxcalteca and Quauhquecholteca, the other indigenous peoples depicted in the pictorials are scantily clothed and use a much more limited variety of weapons. In contrast to the allies' swords, backracks (emblems fastened to a wooden or bamboo ladderlike frame and strapped to the back), insignia, and elaborate costumes, their opponents normally wear a simple cotton warrior costume, are barefoot, and carry ordinary shields, bows and arrows, spears, or axes. This distinction in presentation does not correspond to how they dressed in real life. To the contrary, from the Spanish chronicles it is known that the enemies encountered by the indigenous conquistadors used the more elaborate warrior costumes and insignias as well. Bernal Díaz del Castillo wrote about the battle at Tecpan Atitlan in Guatemala, for example, that their enemies came out "with great lances and good bows and arrows and many other arms and corselets, sounding their drums, and with ensigns and plumes."[25] And the K'iche' lords were celebrated by Pedro de Alvarado for their impressive headdresses of quetzal feathers.[26] Both the Lienzo de Tlaxcala and the Lienzo de Quauhquechollan, however, show little of the plumes and insignia used by the indigenous enemies.

All these elements are purely rhetorical devices used by the composers to enhance their identity and to make a critical point: the Tlaxcalteca and Quauhquecholteca were conquistadors, related now to the world of the new lords and in possession of a position distinct and separate from the other conquered peoples. And this was how they expected to be recognized by others.

After the establishment of the alliances, both the Quauhquecholteca and Tlaxcalteca sent captains, soldiers, and retinue with the Spaniards to help them overthrow the Triple Alliance. They also assisted them in later conquests to the north and down into Central America. The Spanish-

Tlaxcalteca alliance is fairly well documented in the literature. An endur-ing alliance had evolved between the Spaniards and Tlaxcalteca that lasted well into the eighteenth century and proved mutually advantageous for both. The Tlaxcalteca, for their part, enjoyed a series of privileges allow-ing them to hold on to a relatively independent position (both politically and economically) in comparison to that of many other conquered indige-nous peoples. The Spaniards, in turn, were provided with a large and reli-able corps of loyal allies in their conquering campaigns.[27]

The Spanish-Quauhquecholteca alliance is unfortunately much less doc-umented. From Cortés's letters we know that the Quauhquecholteca declared their loyalty to the Spanish Crown in 1520, not long after the Spanish-Tlaxcalteca alliance had been established. The Quauhquecholteca also assisted in the subjection of the Mexica to Spanish rule. Subsequently, they set out among others to the Chichimec region in the north, and later, in 1527, they traveled to Guatemala to fight under Jorge de Alvarado's banner.[28]

THE HABSBURG COAT OF ARMS

The initial scenes of the Lienzo de Tlaxcala and the Lienzo de Quauhquechollan show among others the famous Habsburg coat of arms (see fig. 2.2). The use of this coat of arms was one of the privileges most commonly granted to indigenous communities who had provided mili-tary services to the Spaniards.[29] There was a popular tradition in fifteenth- and sixteenth-century Europe of using heraldic shields: many European towns and also families had their own coats of arms. Mesoamerican communities maintained a comparable tradition with the use of special warrior costumes, war shields, and backracks, and with the pictorial representations of community names. Both traditions seem to have been mutually appreciated, and with the conquest, the insignias of the indige-nous towns and lords were occasionally modified to include the newly introduced Spanish weapons.[30] When the use of the Habsburg eagle was granted to an indigenous community, it was also adapted and elaborated with the particular indigenous elements of the community to which it was given. This resulted in a new and unique series of emblems fit for the colo-nial world.

The use of the Habsburg coat of arms was granted to the Tlaxcalteca in 1535 by Charles V.[31] In the Yllañes copy of the Lienzo de Tlaxcala, this emblem consists of a double-headed eagle with a European-shaped illustrated shield inside, a crown on top, and the two columns of Hercules at its sides with

FIGURE 2.2.
The Habsburg coat of arms incorporated into the glyph for Quauhquechollan in the
Lienzo de Quauhquechollan.

the words "Plus Ultra," which Charles V had added to this coat of arms. This image is largely similar to how it appears in Spanish imagery, but in this case the eagle is positioned on top of a mountain, the indigenous pictorial convention for place. Within this mountain are depicted a temple and the Virgin Mary. Around this emblem are images of the four polities that ruled the altepetl, the lords and different insignia related to each of these polities, and an extensive overview of the rulers of Tlaxcala and the viceroys of New Spain. The emblem in combination with the elements around it reflect the mutual recognition of power and tradition, and simultaneously a merging of identities: they refer to the fact that a new elite had come into being, based on both local prehispanic traditions and the power of the newcomers. Serge Gruzinski points at this meeting of two symbolisms of power among others by associating the Habsburg eagle with the heron of Mazihcatzin of Ocotelulco, both depicted in this scene.[32]

The initial scene of the Lienzo de Quauhquechollan shows the Habsburg eagle with other characteristics. Instead of two columns along the sides, the eagle holds a sword in each claw. One is an indigenous sword and the other a Spanish one, referring to the combination of the Spanish and Quauhquecholteca military forces. This eagle is also positioned on top of a mountain. Within the mountain is a largely faded image in front of a white pyramid.[33] The indigenous name Quauhquechollan includes the Nahuatl word for eagle (*quauh-*), and the eagle was an essential element in the original indigenous place glyph of the town.[34] The Quauhquecholteca Habsburg eagle emblem was thus an appropriated image that referred to the glorious history and lineages of Quauhquechollan and in the meantime also served as a privileged insignia by relating Quauhquechollan to the Spanish Crown. The fact that the Habsburg eagle is depicted in the Lienzo de Quauhquechollan indicates that the use of this coat of arms was also granted to this community, or at least the tlacuiloque claimed so.[35]

The Habsburg coats of arms represented in the Lienzo de Tlaxcala and the Lienzo de Quauhquechollan are typical examples of the mixture of indigenous and Spanish cosmovision as a result of the conquest. The complexity of these newly created images should not be underestimated. The adapted Habsburg coats of arms not only refer to the relation of the caciques of Tlaxcala and Quauhquechollan with the Spanish kings but also to the heroic role of the Tlaxcalteca and Quauhquecholteca in the Spanish conquest. Moreover, the fact that the eagle is one of the most powerful *nahuales* (spirit powers) in Mesoamerican cosmovision no doubt also encouraged the adaptation of this image. The emblems thus consist of different layers of information that communicate a variety of messages.

A VISUAL IMAGE OF THE INDIGENOUS CONQUISTADORS

The conquest pictorials provide unique visual information on the warrior dress, emblems, and weapons used by the indigenous conquistadors. The various versions of the Lienzo de Tlaxcala and the Lienzo de Quauhquechollan show the indigenous captains in full warrior gear, with a large variety of prestigious backracks, shields with colorful designs, and a variety of weapons (see fig. 2.3).

Backracks (also referred to as back devices) were an essential element in indigenous warfare. They served both as emblems and as visual means to keep the different units together during battle. When sound devices

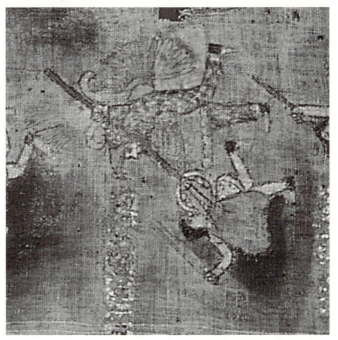

FIGURE 2.3.
Quauhquecholteca warriors fighting against other peoples in Mexico (left) and in Guatemala (right). The Quauhquecholteca wear full warrior regalia and are shown in a higher position than their opponents, signifying victory in battle. From the Lienzo de Quauhquechollan.

and musical instruments such as drums and trumpets were no longer audible, for example, these insignia provided a highly visible sign indicating where and when a unit was advancing or retreating. Some of the painted warriors wore animal costumes with masks instead of backracks, such as eagle and coyote costumes that covered the whole body while the wearer looked out of the animal's opened jaw.[36]

The war shields were normally made of hide or plaited palm leaves, with a feather-work design and a feather fringe at the bottom. Bernardino de Sahagún's team made drawings of how these feather-work shields were manufactured. Normally, each backrack was related to a specific suit of armor and had a set design on the shield.[37]

Both the Lienzo de Tlaxcala and the Lienzo de Quauhquechollan show a considerable repertoire of indigenous war costumes, backracks, and war shields, including a large variety of quetzal feather emblems, human masks, backracks consisting of holders with different numbers of banners, a claw back device, a quetzal bird, a heron, a wolf head, a winding umbilical chord, and a bundle. Some insignia appear in both documents. There is also an overlap with insignia depicted in other pictorials, such as the Codex Mendoza, Codex Florentino, Codex Durán, Codex Telleriano-Remensis, and Mapa de Popotla. The insignia depicted in the conquest pictorials identify the altepetl, cabecera, barrio, and lineage of the indigenous conquistadors that appear in the documents.[38]

As opposed to the Lienzo de Tlaxcala and the Lienzo de Quauhquechollan, the Lienzo de Analco hardly shows any identification of the Tlaxcalteca conquistadors it depicts. It does show some captains wearing jaguar costumes, but the majority of the Tlaxcalteca are dressed in an indigenous cotton warrior costume, without carrying any specific insignia.

The Lienzo de Tlaxcala, the Lienzo de Quauhquechollan, and the Lienzo de Analco show a variety of weapons used by the Quauhquecholteca and Tlaxcalteca conquistadors. Depicted are bows and arrows, spears and lances, indigenous swords, Spanish swords, and axes. The indigenous sword, or *macuahuitl* in Nahuatl, is the most frequently depicted weapon. This was a weapon made of wood, usually oak, with obsidian or flint blades fitted and glued in grooves along the edges, generally measuring three to four inches wide and a little over three and a half feet long.[39] Most Tlaxcalteca and Quauhquecholteca have a macuahuitl or a Spanish sword in one hand and a shield in the other. The Tlaxcalteca depicted in the Lienzo de Analco mostly use lances, Spanish swords, and bows and arrows.

The use of Spanish swords was a privilege granted to the indigenous conquistadors, as was the permission to ride a horse. These privileges were normally granted with special permission by *cédula* (royal order) and usually
only during the period of the conquest.[40] We know that the Tlaxcalteca were
allowed to bear certain European arms in return for their aid in overthrow-
ing the Mexica empire.[41] The fact that the Quauhquecholteca are depicted
with Spanish swords as well indicates they were granted the same privilege.
The use of such Spanish elements by the indigenous caciques was not only
a practical thing, but it also served to identify them with their new lords and
to legitimize their position in the new colonial system. As mentioned earlier,
depicting the Tlaxcalteca and Quauhquecholteca with Spanish elements was
part of their presentation as related to the world of the Spaniards and to distinguish themselves from the nonallied indigenous peoples.

THE LIENZO DE TLAXCALA, THE LIENZO DE ANALCO AND
THE LIENZO DE QUAUHQUECHOLLAN COMPARED

The Lienzo de Tlaxcala, the Lienzo de Analco, and the Lienzo de
Quauhquechollan have the theme of conquest in common, and they share
to a large extent a similar message. Yet there are also a number of differences, which are as significant as the similarities. The lienzos are the individual stories of distinct communities, each of which had its own unique
history and its own specific concerns that determined the contents, layout, and rhetoric of the narratives. And obviously, each document was
created in its own unique circumstances, for its own specific public, and
with its own purpose.

The Lienzo de Tlaxcala, the Lienzo de Analco, and the Lienzo de
Quauhquechollan depict not only scenes of alliance and battles but also
other aspects of the conquest. One example is the use of indigenous allies
as tameme. The indigenous communities provided their new allies not only
with manpower for battle but also with large numbers of bearers for both
objects and persons (see also Oudijk and Restall, chapter 1, this volume).
The Lienzo de Tlaxcala shows men carrying packages, anchors, a cannon,
and a Spaniard; the Lienzo de Analco shows men carrying packages; and
the Lienzo de Quauhquechollan shows women carrying warrior gear
(headdresses, shields, insignia) and men carrying backpacks filled with
round objects or other packages. The indigenous tameme carried among
other things parts of boats overland from one coast to the other, including

anchors that weighed, according to Bartolomé de las Casas, up to seventy or eighty pounds each. The Dominican friar also testified that when he was in Guatemala in the late 1520s, he saw indigenous allies loaded with artillery, suffering along the roads. He added that many died under the heavy weight or during the reconstruction of the boats on the other coast.[42]

Another aspect of the conquest that is portrayed in the conquest pictorials is the often cruel punishment of indigenous peoples. The Lienzo de Quauhquechollan, the Lienzo de Analco, and some of the versions of the Lienzo de Tlaxcala all depict the burning and hanging of people. The Lienzo de Analco and the Lienzo de Quauhquechollan also depict the punishment of throwing people to dogs that tore their victims to pieces and ate them. This was a European practice that had also become common throughout the Americas during the conquest era.[43] Luis de Berrio, the first alcalde mayor of Villa Alta, was notorious for having thrown indigenous people to the dogs.[44] Jorge de Alvarado reportedly also used this way of punishment, for instance when suppressing rebellions in the western highlands around Sacapulas and Uspantan.[45]

Furthermore, the conquest pictorials depict the way in which nonallied indigenous peoples defended themselves. All three pictorials depict fortified mountains. In the case of the Lienzo de Tlaxcala and the Lienzo de Quauhquechollan, these mountains are integrated into place glyphs. At several places in the Lienzo de Quauhquechollan one also finds depictions of fortifications on roads. In a civilization where transportation was based on foot travel, blocking a road was, of course, not effective for the purpose of barring traffic or stopping armies. In indigenous warfare road blockades served primarily a political purpose: they signaled the intention of cutting relations, resisting hostile passage or entry, and initiating a war. When a subjected town or independent city blocked its roads, it was regarded as an act of rebellion.[46]

With regard to religion, the Lienzo de Tlaxcala displays the most elaborate references to the conversion of the community to Christianity. The Yllañes copy shows a cross and an image of the Virgin of the Assumption, who was adopted by the Tlaxcalteca as patroness in 1521, in the initial scene.[47] The Glasgow manuscript shows these elements as well and even dedicates a page to depicting the burning of the prehispanic books and possessions of the indigenous priests.[48] The Lienzo de Analco, in turn, shows a church and some friars who perform rituals that are yet to be identified. The Lienzo de Quauhquechollan, however, does not show any churches; nor does it include any friars in its narrative. The almost suspicious absence of churches in this document, in sharp contrast to the presence of at least one and often several churches in almost every other colonial pictorial, might indicate that it was created before the building of notable churches started. In Guatemala the construction of churches started later than in Mexico. The lack of churches in this conquest pictorial therefore suggests either a very early date of creation or a creation in Guatemala.

A major difference between the Lienzo de Tlaxcala and the Lienzo de Quauhquechollan on the one hand and the Lienzo de Analco on the other is that the first two have a clear and prominent initial scene and the latter does not. The Lienzo de Analco does not even depict Tlaxcala, the hometown of the main actors. It seems that the composers of the Lienzo de Analco were exclusively concerned with the experiences and achievements of the Tlaxcalteca who had settled in Analco and not with those who had remained in Tlaxcala or those who participated in conquering campaigns elsewhere in the Americas. The fact that the Lienzo de Analco was found in Analco and not in Tlaxcala confirms this.

Another difference is that the Lienzo de Tlaxcala and the Lienzo de Quauhquechollan show only a few warriors in each conquest scene, while the Lienzo de Analco depicts large squadrons of marching Tlaxcalteca. The images of these Tlaxcalteca often overlap one another, which is a stylistic element borrowed from European painting that does not appear in either the Lienzo de Tlaxcala or in the Lienzo de Quauhquechollan. Both the general manner in which the warriors are represented (with hardly any insignia) and the style that, uniquely, contains overlapping figures indicate that the tlacuiloque of the Lienzo de Analco were more or otherwise influenced by European painting styles than those of the Lienzo de Tlaxcala and the Lienzo de Quauhquechollan.

The Lienzo de Tlaxcala is the only conquest pictorial with elaborate references to the sociopolitical divisions of the polities within the altepetl and their rulers. The Lienzo de Quauhquechollan, in turn, is the only document representing a migration story: the journey of the Quauhquecholteca from central Mexico to and through Guatemala. The various versions of the Lienzo de Tlaxcala show campaigns to and through Central America as well, but these campaigns are not represented as migrations. Instead, they are merely presented in broad overview without any indication as to whether certain places were more significant to the story than others. The Lienzo de Analco does not show a migration either. It barely even provides the names of the places where the battles and other events depicted took place.[49]

Finally, the Lienzo de Analco and the Lienzo de Quauhquechollan differ considerably from the Lienzo de Tlaxcala in their layout and use of space. The narratives of the Lienzo de Analco and the Lienzo de Quauhquechollan are set up in geographical landscapes showing roads, rivers, and place glyphs, with the roads serving as structuring tools to organize the narrative and to act as aids to memory for recitation. The conquests presented in the different versions of the Lienzo de Tlaxcala, in turn, are presented in squares. The presentation of information in squares was an indigenous way of organizing space, as is known from the Tonalamatl de Aubin (a possibly prehispanic calendrical screenfold from the same area), the Codex Telleriano-Remensis (which represents Mexica conquests in sequential images), and the Lienzo de Jucatacato from Michoacan. This was simply another choice of structuring a story and to create an aid to memory for recitation.

THE TLAXCALTECA AND QUAUHQUECHOLTECA IN SPANISH CAMPAIGNS TO THE SOUTH

The Lienzo de Tlaxcala and the Lienzo de Quauhquechollan are the only pictorials known that comment on the conquest of what is today Central America. The Glasgow manuscript shows Pedro de Alvarado's 1524 conquering campaign through Guatemala and El Salvador, and it reports the conquests of thirty-five other places in Central America.[50] Pedro de Alvarado was indeed always accompanied by large numbers of Tlaxcalteca conquistadors. Many others traveled to Guatemala with Jorge de Alvarado. The latter had returned to Mexico after the 1524 campaign, but in 1527, when his brother Pedro left for Spain, he set out for Guatemala again to take over the position of lieutenant governor. At the time, the Kaqchikel were in open and hostile rebellion, and the country was far from being conquered. Jorge brought a fresh army of approximately five to six thousand indigenous allies, including both Tlaxcalteca and Quauhquecholteca, to subject the area to Spanish rule.[51] This was one of the largest migrations of central Mexicans into Central America at any one time. Today there are still references to this migration in local oral traditions.[52]

The Tlaxcalteca occupied a special place with the Alvarado brothers during their campaigns to the south. This was not only due to their large numbers but also because of the personal relations that existed between the Tlaxcalteca nobility and the Spanish conquistadors. As discussed by Michel R. Oudijk and Matthew Restall (see chapter 1, this volume), the Nahua built alliances among others through the exchange of women for marriage, and the lords and principles of Tlaxcala had given at least five princesses to Cortés for this purpose.[53] This is also depicted in the Tlaxcalteca conquest pictorials. Cortés gave one of these princesses, a daughter of the Tlaxcalteca lord Xicotencatl, to Pedro de Alvarado. This girl was baptized Doña Luisa, and Pedro de Alvarado had two children with her. She accompanied him on nearly all his campaigns, even to Peru.[54] Díaz del Castillo wrote of Doña Luisa that "all of the major parts of Tlaxcala respected her and gave her presents and held her as their Lady."[55] Jorge de Alvarado, in turn, was joined with Doña Lucía Xicotencatl, a sister of Doña Luisa.[56] The presence of these princesses at the side of the Spanish conquistadors helped to secure the loyalty of the Tlaxcalteca units. It is not unthinkable that during both Pedro de Alvarado's 1524 campaign and Jorge de Alvarado's 1527 campaign, the Tlaxcalteca nobles who went along took care of part of the communication between the Spaniards and the indigenous units of the army, as they were the ones with whom the Spaniards were most involved.[57] The Tlaxcalteca nobility was favored by the Spaniards in the years following the conquest, and for a long time they received special privileges that others had not.[58]

The Lienzo de Quauhquechollan focuses solely on Jorge de Alvarado's 1527–30 campaigns of conquest through Guatemala, and the subjection of the Kaqchikel to Spanish rule. Jorge's military achievements of this period are poorly documented in the alphabetical sources, but fortunately the Lienzo de Quauhquechollan now provides valuable information, as it depicts a large number of battles that took place between 1527 and 1530.[59] Many of these wars were waged at Kaqchikel sites, but some also took place at K'iche' sites or sites to the north in Verapaz and the Cuchumatanes.

Since the Tlaxcalteca and Quauhquecholteca conquistadors were all speakers of Nahuatl, it is not surprising to find that the place glyphs in the Lienzo de Tlaxcala and the Lienzo de Quauhquechollan refer to the Nahuatl names of the towns represented. This applies also to the depictions of sites in Central America. Not only among themselves but also in their communication with the Spaniards, the Nahua allies translated the Maya names of Guatemalan towns into Nahuatl. These names were taken over by the latter, and many are still in use today. With a few exceptions, they are literal translations of the original Maya names.

One exception is the name Quetzaltenango. The original K'iche' name of this place is Xe Lajuj Noj, which refers to a calendric name and a mountain. The Nahuatl name Quetzaltenango, in turn, consists of the elements *quetzal-* (quetzal feathers), *tenam-* (wall), and *-co* (a locative). Reportedly, the central Mexican conquistadors created this name as a reference to the quetzal feathers that adorned the enemy K'iche' lords who awaited them there for battle.[60] The place glyphs for this site as represented in the Lienzo de Tlaxcala and the Lienzo de Quauhquechollan both consist of feathers and a wall and thus refer to the Nahuatl name and not to the K'iche' name. (See figs. 2.4–5).

Another exception is the place glyph for Iximche', or Cuauhtemallan. Iximche' is the original Kaqchikel name of this town, reportedly referring to a maize tree (*ixim*, "maize," *che'*, "tree") and also translated as "a bunch of trees."[61] The indigenous conquistadors referred to this site as Cuauhtemallan or Tecpan Cuauhtemallan (*cuauh-* being the root of *cuahu(i)*, Nahuatl for "tree"). The Lienzo de Tlaxcala represents this place not by means of a tree but by means of an eagle (*quauh-* in Nahuatl). The Tlaxcalteca painters may have chosen to use the eagle as a phonetic indication to avoid confusion. Depicting a tree might have made the reader insecure about which tree was meant and thus what word to use, while an eagle is rather unambiguous.[62]

It is precisely these exceptions that allow us to distinguish that the Quauhquecholteca and Tlaxcalteca tlacuiloque were, in their pictographic rendering of place names, referring to Nahuatl translations of the local names instead of transcribing local language place names into Nahua pictography. The glyphs of towns in present-day Guatemala presented in the Lienzo de Tlaxcala and the Lienzo de Quauhquechollan are unique to these documents. Although some places had been known by Nahuatl names in prehispanic times as well, most glyphs must have been newly invented by the Tlaxcalteca and Quauhquecholteca tlacuiloque in the decades following the conquest.

PICTORIAL FORMATS FOR CONQUEST NARRATIVES

The indigenous peoples initially experienced the Spanish conquests and the establishment alliances with the Spaniards as continuations of precolonial patterns of conquest and domination (see also Oudijk and Restall, chap-

FIGURE 2.4.
*Two variations of Quezaltenango's place glyph from the Lienzo de Quauhquechollan.
Drawings by the author.*

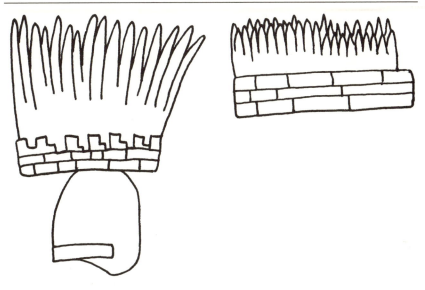

FIGURE 2.5.
*Quezaltenango's place glyph from the Glasgow manuscript of the Lienzo de Tlaxcala
(f. 290r). Drawing by the author.*

ter 1, this volume). This way of perceiving the Spanish conquest is clearly reflected in the Quauhquecholteca and Tlaxcalteca pictorial records. The narratives presented in these pictorials are of the colonial era, but the medium, format, function, and underlying principle of the narratives are primarily indigenous in design. The alliances with the Spaniards and the conquests achieved under the Spanish banner are not depicted any differently from prehispanic conquest narratives: prehispanic conventions are used, and the stories are ordered according to the same rules and principles. In other words, these alliances and conquests were understood within a prehispanic historical framework, and they were communicated as such.

In prehispanic Mesoamerican narratives, conquest and migration are prevalent themes, as they were central to a community's identity and justified the power and position of its ruling elite. Well-known examples of painted prehispanic Nahua conquest and migration stories are that of the Mexica, starting at Aztlan and ending with the founding of Tenochtitlan;[63] that of the Chichimeca who emerged from Chicomoztoc and settled in Cuauhtinchan;[64] and the migration of the Acolhua into the Valley of Mexico and the founding of Texcoco.[65] Similar conquest and migration stories can be found in the Mixteca historical screenfolds and in the Coixtlahuaca group of early colonial lienzos from the Valley of Coixtlahuaca, Oaxaca. Most of the conquest and migration stories presented in these documents follow a similar format. They generally start at the place of origin of the main actors. Then they show a series of places, usually represented sequentially, that were conquered or where other events relevant to the story take place. In the times that these documents were made, war was indispensable, as it was the primary means to obtain new lands. Finally, these stories conclude with a narration of how the main actors form a new settlement, often an altepetl or barrio. Often, references to the boundaries of the community in question are included, as is its ruling dynasty or its patron deity. This same format is used for the colonial Tlaxcalteca and Quauhquecholteca conquest pictorials.

A particularly good example is the striking similarity between the format and layout of the Lienzo de Quauhquechollan and that of the Mapa de Cuauhtinchan No. 2 from Cuauhtinchan, Puebla (see fig. 2.6). Cuauhtinchan was, just like Tlaxcala and Quauhquechollan, a powerful Nahua altepetl, situated some sixty kilometers to the northeast of Quauhquechollan. The Mapa de Cuauhtinchan No. 2 is painted on paper

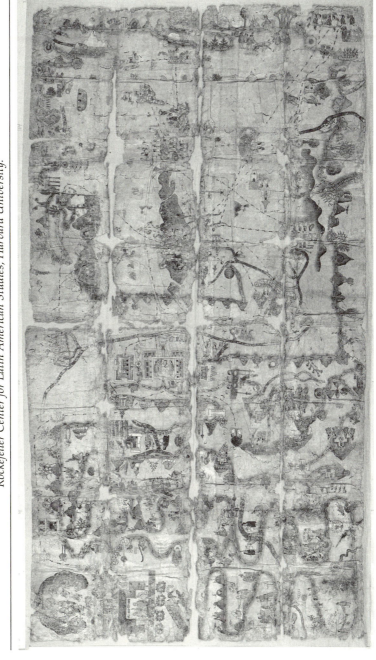

FIGURE 2.6.

Mapa de Cuauhtinchan No. 2. Photography by Jorge Pérez de Lara. Reproduced courtesy of the Cuauhtinchan Project at the David Rockefeller Center for Latin American Studies, Harvard University.

and shows a prehispanic conquest and migration story. In a landscape of roads and rivers is represented the migration of a group of Chichimeca from Chicomoztoc (the mythical place of origin of many indigenous communities) into Puebla and the founding of the altepetl Cuauhtinchan.[66] The events recorded in this manuscript took place between the twelfth and the fifteenth centuries, although seemingly some more recent date glyphs were added. The Mapa de Cuauhtinchan No. 2 was painted in the 1580s; however it is probably an adapted copy of a prehispanic document.

Both the Mapa de Cuauhtinchan No. 2 and the Lienzo de Quauhquechollan start with a large initial scene in the upper left corner showing the places of origin of the main actors (Chicomoztoc and Quauhquechollan, respectively) and a scene below each of these sites of origin that establishes the beginnings of the time periods in which the stories take place. The Mapa de Cuauhtinchan No. 2 shows a New Fire ceremony in this spot, indicating the beginning of a new year count. The Lienzo de Quauhquechollan, in turn, shows a meeting between the lords of Quauhquechollan and the Spaniards and the establishment of an alliance between the two. These scenes indicate the beginnings of new episodes in history and the beginnings of the narratives depicted.

The narratives presented in the two pictorials are both organized along a road with footprints or horses' hoof prints. These roads depart from the initial scenes, cross rivers, and pass by place glyphs where battles or other events take place. The main actors of the stories travel along these roads. In both documents this road first leads to the bottom left corner of the painting. It then turns to the right (from the point of view of the viewer) and proceeds part-way along the bottom edge of the document. Next the roads go up, split, and subsequently define the landscapes that fill up the right parts of each manuscript. Although the network of roads presented in the Lienzo de Quauhquechollan is more detailed and complex than that in the Mapa de Cuauhtinchan No. 2, in outline the two are largely the same.

Both pictorials show the destinations of the Chichimeca and Quauhquecholteca migrations in the center of the right part of each landscape, with the place glyphs depicted in particularly large size. The Mapa de Cuauhtinchan No. 2 shows the glyph for Cuauhtinchan in this spot. This is the place where the migrating Chichimeca settled and founded their altepetl. It is also the place where the document was painted. In the Lienzo de Quauhquechollan, Chimaltenango and the city of Santiago at Almolonga (both in central Guatemala) occupy the same position. Both of these sites were of special importance to the story of the Quauhquecholteca. As stated earlier, the Quauhquecholteca established a settlement in the city of Santiago at Almolonga, and the Lienzo de Quauhquechollan may very well have been painted at this site.

Both the Mapa de Cuauhtinchan No. 2 and the Lienzo de Quauhquechollan distinguish different subgroups among the migrating peoples. The Mapa de Cuauhtinchan No. 2 shows the seven houses representing the seven subgroups within Cuauhtinchan. The Lienzo de Quauhquechollan, in turn, makes a clear distinction between the captains of the different barrios of Quauhquechollan by depicting each of them with his insignia. This observation is important to achieve a better understanding of what the painters found important to record and what their message was meant to convey. They depicted not the concept of migrating Cuauhtinchan people or Quauhquecholteca in general but instead clearly indicate that there were specific subgroups, each of which fulfilled its own significant role in the stories.

Another aspect common to both the Mapa de Cuauhtinchan No. 2 and the Lienzo de Quauhquechollan is the importance of a leader to a migration story. This is also found in other Nahua migration pictorials: the Mexica who had migrated from Aztlan and founded Tenochtitlan were led by their patron deity Huitzilopochtli, and the Acolhua who migrated into the Basin of Mexico and founded Texcoco were led by their leader Xolotl.[67] The Mapa de Cuauhtinchan No. 2 presents Teuhctlecozauhqui as one of the leaders of the migrating Chichimeca. To the Quauhquecholteca, this important leader was Jorge de Alvarado, who is depicted repeatedly. Jorge de Alvarado was the one who had taken them from Quauhquechollan, the one who had brought them to Guatemala, and the one under whose banner they fought. In other words, Jorge de Alvarado was for the Quauhquecholteca what Huitzilopochtli was for the Mexica of Tenochtitlan, Teuhctlecozauhqui for the Chichimeca of Cuauhtinchan, and Xolotl for the Acolhua of Texcoco.

Also, the geographical character and orientation of the two documents show many similarities. When comparing the landscape depicted in the Mapa de Cuauhtinchan No. 2 to a modern geographical map, it can be concluded that in the left part of the pictorial it was primarily the narrative that determined the placement of elements in the map, while the landscape depicted in the central part of the right side shows many correlations to the actual geographical landscape. The distances between the places are not always presented accurately, but their relative positions largely correspond to how they are distributed on the ground.[68] The Lienzo de Quauhquechollan shows similar characteristics. The left part shows one road leading from Quauhquechollan to Olintepeque. The outlines of this route do correspond more or less to the outlines of the route traveled in the actual landscape, but it is primarily the story that is determinative. The places are shown in the order in which Jorge de Alvarado's army passed through them. The places in the right part of the document, on the other hand, are skillfully organized according to their geographical locations. Apart from the bell-shaped mountains that form the bases of the place glyphs, both documents also show other mountain glyphs, referring to mountainous landscapes. Furthermore, they both include references to trading or market places, the authority of certain people over others, the presence of women, and a ballcourt.

The remarkable similarities between the format of the Mapa de Cuauhtinchan No. 2 and that of the Lienzo de Quauhquechollan indicate that a prehispanic indigenous format and layout for conquest and migration stories and the same "sets of ingredients" were used to present the colonial conquest story of the Quauhquecholteca. Possibly, the lost Mapa de Totonicapan had similar layouts too.

The continuation of the use of precolonial formats can also be found on the level of individual scenes. The initial scene of the Yllañes copy of the Lienzo de Tlaxcala, for example, shows a combination of references to the sociopolitical structure of the altepetl, as mentioned earlier. This combination of elements is comparable to those included in the initial scene of the Mexica Codex Mendoza, which narrates the founding of Tenochtitlan.[69] Both scenes depict the place glyph of the community (Tlaxcala and Tenochtitlan, respectively), its rulers, a reference to religion (in the case of the Codex Mendoza this is a temple and a *tzompantli* [skull rack]), and the four districts of each altepetl. Both scenes communicate a similar message: the establishment of the new sociopolitical entity of Tenochtitlan and "colonial" Tlaxcala. The Lienzo de Quauhquechollan and the Lienzo de Tlaxcala show comparable scenes as well. The layout of the scene representing the meeting between the lords of Quauhquechollan and Cortés, for example, is remarkably similar to that of the scenes in which Tlaxcalteca lords meet the Spanish conquistador.[70] All these scenes are organized according to set pictorial formats using an agreed-upon combination of elements.

FUNCTION AND USE OF THE CONQUEST PICTORIALS

Large-sized pictorials like the Tlaxcalteca and Quauhquecholteca conquest pictorials were normally created to serve a public function. Unlike folded codices, lienzos are viewed flat and are painted on one side only. They were either put up on a wall (as is still done in some indigenous communities in Mexico) or laid out on the floor.[71]

The public reading of a lienzo was normally accompanied by orally recited texts that often included dialogues, songs, and prose.[72] These oral recitals were presented by a historian or sage who elaborated on the contents of the painting and its message. They informed the contemplators of the motivations of the persons depicted and the nature of the events and probably also revealed some of the historical awareness of the composers and the internal mechanisms within the community that had determined the presentation of the story. These oral components of the pictorials are now lost. One should therefore always keep in mind that the surviving lienzos are incomplete bodies of information of which an essential explanatory part is no longer extant.

Some of the early colonial pictorials were created primarily for internal indigenous use, while others were specifically made for the colonial administration. Given the contents, rhetoric, layout, and complexity of the iconography of the Lienzo de Tlaxcala, the Lienzo de Analco, and the Lienzo de Quauhquechollan, I believe that these documents were originally made for internal indigenous use, and only later did they serve in a Spanish context, if at all. Lienzos or other historical narratives created for a use within the indigenous sphere were normally made to remind the community of its history, to help the community members structure and acknowledge their collective memory, and to offer a framework for the understanding of certain events.[73] They also served strong purposes of identification with regard to authority and social structures. Since the Spanish conquest of Mesoamerica brought about radical changes for and uncertainties among the indigenous peoples, the need for an explanation and a redefinition of identity was strongly felt. The Lienzo de Tlaxcala and the Lienzo de Quauhquechollan provided such an explanation and identification for the people of Tlaxcala and Quauhquechollan. The lienzos explained and represented the position of the Tlaxcalteca and Quauhquecholteca in the new system and contributed to their self-image as conquerors and victors rather than victims in conquest.

The Lienzo de Tlaxcala, the Lienzo de Analco, and the Lienzo de Quauh-quechollan point to a tradition of recording conquest stories under the Spanish banner. This tradition, I believe, can largely be dated to the 1530s and 1540s and was part of the indigenous process of adapting to colonial life, redefining identity, and securing status for themselves. The lost Mapa de Totonicapan fits this image perfectly, since it must have been created at least before 1544.[74] Also, it was in the possession of the central Mexican caciques together with their Nahuatl annals and thus served in the indige-nous sphere.

The Lienzo de Quauhquechollan has alphabetic glosses on top of cer-tain images, for which originally no space was reserved. This indicates they were added later, and they might indicate a later use in a Spanish context. The early conquest pictorials from Tlaxcala seem to instead have been copied and adapted for this purpose. The Tlaxcalteca cabildo minutes of June 17, 1552, comment on a Tlaxcalteca conquest pictorial specifically made for the Spaniards, which was to be sent with a delegation to the emperor in Spain. The minutes state, "A painting of Cortés' arrival in Tlaxcala and the war and conquest is to be prepared for presentation to the emperor; two *regidores* [councilmen] are to oversee the project and to arrange for artists' supplies through the city *mayordomo* [custodian] and to choose the artists. At this point it is not decided whether the painting should be on cloth [*tilmatli*] or paper [*amatl*]."[75] Earlier versions of the Tlaxcalteca conquest narrative (the Texas manuscript and the wall paint-ings mentioned by Muñoz Camargo) were possibly used as sources for this newly created pictorial and also for later copies.

A use of the conquest pictorials in the Spanish sphere may have had to do with land claims but also, more likely, with the fact that the privileges granted to the indigenous conquistadors were often ignored and under-mined by the Spaniards. There exist quite a few alphabetic claims in which indigenous communities present before the Crown their role in the con-quest to stand up for their rights, the bulk of which were written between the 1560s and 1570s (see other chapters in this volume). Some colonial conquest pictorials may have had a "second life" in the Spanish sphere supporting such claims. Indigenous communities are known to have indeed presented to the Spanish authorities lienzos originally made for internal use in order to support certain claims.[76] The tradition of creating large paintings with conquest narratives was not strange to the Spaniards. In the very same decades that lienzos on the conquest of Mexico and

Guatemala were created in Mesoamerica, in Spain large tapestries were woven, depicting the conquest of Tunis by Charles V. These tapestries served a public function as well.[77] It can thus be presumed that the Spaniards understood the tradition of creating conquest paintings and that they recognized, and acknowledged, the value of these documents.

CONCLUSION

In this chapter I have sought to come to a better understanding of indigenous pictorials referring to the Spanish conquest by regarding them as a corpus and by comparing their contents, layouts, and the rhetorical tools used by the composers. This analysis has led to the conclusion that they not only share the theme of alliance and conquest with the Spaniards but that they also, yet more interestingly, share a similar format and rhetoric in the way in which they present these conquest stories.

One of the most important conclusions is that the rhetoric of the conquest pictorials is in line with that of later alphabetic claims. In the alphabetic claims, the indigenous conquistadors referred to themselves as "indios conquistadores"; in the pictorial sources, the Tlaxcalteca and Quauhquecholteca present themselves as conquistadors by means of their actions, their position at the Spaniards' side, their dress and attributes, and, in the case of the Lienzo de Quauhquechollan, even by skin color. The tlacuiloque skillfully played with the rhetoric of the medium to communicate and emphasize to the viewer their identity as conquistadors through their alliance with the Spaniards.

Another conclusion is that the colonial conquest pictorials follow a long and more widely practiced indigenous tradition of communicating conquest and migration stories. The similarities between the layout and contents of the initial scenes of the Codex Mendoza and the Lienzo de Tlaxcala, for example, indicate that these scenes were organized according to a set format with set components. The same applies to the remarkable similarities between the overall layout of the Lienzo de Quauhquechollan and that of the Mapa de Cuauhtinchan No. 2. Also, the format used for the initial scene of the Lienzo de Quauhquechollan is used in the Lienzo de Tlaxcala as well. Those familiar with pictorial conventions and formats would no doubt have immediately recognized the meaning of these formats and understood their function. That these colonial conquest pictorials follow precolonial formats implies that the alliances with the Spaniards were seen in the same light as prehispanic alliances and that the conquests under the Spanish banner were regarded as a continuation of precolonial conquest stories. The Lienzo de Analco, the lost Mapa de Totonicapan, and the Lienzo de Quauhquechollan indicate that this tradition was not only kept in use by the Nahua in central Mexico but also by Nahua who ended up elsewhere in Mexico and Central America.

Conquest pictorials such as that of the Tlaxcalteca and Quauhquecholteca must have played a significant role in the process of adaptation to the new colonial system and the redefinition of identities. The Lienzo de Analco, the Lienzo de Quauhquechollan, and the earliest conquest pictorials from Tlaxcala were made not long after the conquest, probably in the 1530s and 1540s. Their primary role seems to have been one of reshaping and presenting the past by creating a shared sense of understanding of what had happened and of being conquistadors. The lost Lienzo de Tlaxcala and some of its copies seem to have been specifically made for a Spanish public. The Lienzo de Quauhquechollan and the Lienzo de Analco may have had a second life in the Spanish sphere as well, when, in the second half of the sixteenth century, both Spanish and indigenous conquistadors brought their miserable situation to the attention of the king.

Each of the conquest pictorials discussed in this chapter seems to have once been accompanied by an alphabetical text. The Glasgow version of the Lienzo de Tlaxcala, for example, is accompanied by a written text by Muñoz Camargo, and there may have been others writings with the other copies. The Lienzo de Analco was found with a bundle of now lost Nahuatl documents. And from the Título de Caciques we know that the lost Mapa de Totonicapan was also accompanied by Nahuatl títulos. The only document that lacks a concrete reference to an accompanying alphabetical text is the Lienzo de Quauhquechollan, but one can presume there once existed an accompanying document to this pictorial as well.

In sum, the Lienzo de Tlaxcala, the Lienzo de Quauhquechollan, and the Lienzo de Analco were no isolated creations, and the amount of detail and the perceptions revealed in these pictorials is exceptional. With regards to the conquest of Central America, the Lienzo de Tlaxcala and the Lienzo de Quauhquechollan are the only two pictorial sources that are presently known. They are therefore indispensable historical evidence for a better understanding of both the Spanish conquest of Mesoamerica and the conquering journeys and migrations of indigenous peoples that resulted. Together with the alphabetic testimonies in the archives, the colonial conquest pictorials are essential to reveal the story of the indigenous conquistadors of the Americas.

NOTES

I would like to thank the following people for their inspiration and contributions to this paper: Maarten Jansen, Christopher Lutz, Laura Matthew, Yanna Yannakakis, Robinson Herrera, Susan Schroeder, Ruud van Akkeren, Bas van Doesburg, Michael Swanton, and Hans Roskamp. Special thanks should be extended to Michel Oudijk and Maria Castañeda de la Paz, with whom I elaborately analyzed and discussed the conquest pictorials and who generously shared their ideas, and their library, with me while writing this chapter in Sevilla. I thank WOTRO (Netherlands Foundation for the Advancement of Tropical Research) and CNWS (School of Asian, African, and Amerindian Studies) for their financial support.

1. Pictographs are stylized representations of objects found in nature (roads, water, plants, animals, persons, etc.); logographic signs are hieroglyphs with phonetic elements, normally used for personal names, place names, and dates; and ideograms are signs understood by convention: they were agreed upon standards of graphic representation, such as, e.g., footsteps for descendance or travel or a toppled temple for conquest. Presently, we know of the existence of about twenty prehispanic and seven hundred colonial pictorials, the bulk of which were made in Mexico in the sixteenth and seventeenth centuries. There are a few pictorials from Guatemala attached to K'iche' títulos and *relaciones geográficas*; however, they can be counted on one hand. There is little doubt that other peoples in Mesoamerica once held similar pictorial or hieroglyphic writing systems. Unfortunately, however, no readable examples have survived.

2. The indigenous peoples were familiar with the pictorial script, so they knew how to use it to convey messages, including hidden messages, and to provoke certain emotions with the reader. As they were less familiar with the alphabetic script, this was a much more limited medium of communication for them.

3. See Carmack and Mondloch, *El título de Yax*, 212–19: "títulos suyos juntamente con la mapa y un lienso de San Juan Bautista" (212); "esta es la berdad de que ellos son casiques y prinsipales que están en la mapa y lozas reales" (213); "ellos binieron con sus flechas y broqueles para defender la ley de Dios" (213).

4. See Mazihcatzin, "Descripción"; Alfredo Chavero, *Antigüedades mexicanas*; Gibson, *Tlaxcala*, 247–53.

5. See Chavero, *Antigüedades mexicanas*; Gibson, *Tlaxcala*, 247–53; Glass and Robertson, "Census," 215; Beltrami, *Le Mexique*, 308.

6. Glass and Robertson, "Census," 214–17. After this 1975 census was made, at least one other copy of the Lienzo de Tlaxcala was identified. This copy is presently in the Casa de Colón in Valladolid. See Ballesteros-Gaibrois, "El Lienzo de Tlaxcalla."

7. This eighty-one-folio document is in the Hunter Collection at the University of Glasgow. It was first described by Diego Muñoz Camargo in his *Descripción de*

la ciudad y provincia de Tlaxcala (written in 1585 and published as a facsimile edition with a preliminary study by René Acuña). Later, it was republished by René Acuña as an attachment to his *Relaciones geográficas*. This document presents a total of 156 scenes. The first 15 scenes present colonial Tlaxcala and mention various Europeans among whom are included Columbus, Pizarro, Cortés, Charles V, and Philip II. The document was reportedly sent to the latter. Scenes 26 through 75 present the events and conquest up to the conquest of Tenochtitlan, and the remainder of the document (scenes 76 through 156) narrates the conquests of numerous places throughout Mesoamerica, leading as far afield as Florida and California to the north and Nicaragua to the south. This manuscript seems to be an updated and adapted version of earlier conquest pictorials from Tlaxcala.

8. This document is presently kept in the Nettie Lee Benson Latin American Collection at the University of Texas in Austin, hence the name Texas manuscript or Texas fragment. See Kranz, "Tlaxcalan Conquest Pictorials," 59.

9. "La venida de Cortés y sus españoles, y del buen acogim[ien]to que se les hizo y la conquista de México." Acuña, *Relaciones geográficas del siglo XVI*, 62.

10. "Y del recibimiento y regalo que en Taxcala se le hizo, y de la paz que se le dio en toda esta provincia . . . y de las hazañas que ellos y los españoles hicieron en la pacificación de toda esta tierra." Acuña, *Relaciones geográficas del siglo XVI*, 49. See also Gibson, *Tlaxcala*, 247.

11. The accuracy of the geographic landscape was noted by König, *Die Schlacht*, 136, and also researched and confirmed by Michel Oudijk (personal communication, Sevilla, July 2003).

12. In the course of the sixteenth century, several Mixe rebellions took place in the Sierra Zapoteca. The town Villa Alta itself was attacked by Mixe among others in 1550. See König, *Die Schlacht*, 137.

13. See König, *Die Schlacht*, 136; Chance, *Conquest of the Sierra*, 18.

14. See Yannakakis, chapter 7, this volume.

15. König, *Die Schlacht*, 136, 138.

16. Blom, "El Lienzo de Analco." Shortly after Frans Blom reported the document it disappeared from the town. According to local oral traditions, the document was taken away by a private collector who was later caught at the border while trying to take it abroad. Michel Oudijk, personal communication, Sevilla, July 2003. When it was next mentioned in the literature by Howard Cline, in 1966, it was in the collection of the Biblioteca Nacional in Mexico City. See König, *Die Schlacht*, 123–24; Cline, "Native Pictorial Documents," 114.

17. So far, only one study of the Lienzo de Analco has appeared. See König, *Die Schlacht*, 122–38. In this work, Viola König comments briefly on the various scenes and presents a variety of black-and-white photographs. A more detailed study of the history, contents, and meaning of the document is yet to be made.

18. There is a reference to the existence of a possible copy in the museum in Oaxaca. See Sleen, *Mexico*.

19. For recent studies of this document I refer to Aguirre Beltran, "El códice," and Asselbergs, *Conquered Conquistadors*.

20. See Paso y Troncoso, *Catálogo*, 71–74.

21. See Asselbergs, *Conquered Conquistadors*, 195–96, 199.

22. Archivo General de Indias, Seville (hereafter, AGI), Patronato 66a-1-7, Probanza de meritos y servicios de Gaspar Martin, 1571. Ò f. 110v, transcription by Wendy Kramer. In this text, Juan Fernández Nájera declared that he had seen "un paño pintado q. truxeron a esta ciudad [Santiago de Guatemala] unos indios en q. señalaban los conquistadores y los viajes q. abian hecho a los que en las dhas conquistas mas se abian señalado y servido."

23. See Cortés, *Cartas de relación*, 89–93.

24. Gibson, *Tlaxcala*, 15–21; see also Oudijk and Restall, chapter 1, this volume.

25. See Alvarado, *Account of the Conquest*, 113.

26. See ibid., 59; Recinos and Chonay, *Memorial de Sololá*, 100.

27. The role and position of the Tlaxcalteca allies in central Mexico is well researched by Gibson and described in Gibson, *Tlaxcala*. For their role in the conquest of the Spanish borderlands in the north up to Texas and New Mexico, refer to Simmons, *Tlascalans*, and Powell, *La guerra chichimeca*. For the experiences of the Tlaxcalteca allies in Oaxaca, refer to Yannakakis, chapter 7, this volume. For a study on their services in Central America, refer to Sherman, "Tlaxcalans," and Matthew, chapter 3, this volume.

28. One of the witnesses who speaks in the AGI Justicia 291, 1, document testified that people from many places in central Mexico had come to Guatemala with Pedro de Alvarado: "eçepto los de la provinçia de guacachula [Quauhquechollan] que vinyeron con jorge de alvarado." See "El Fiscal" (1578), AGI Justicia 291, 1, f. 55v. See also ff. 67r–67v, transcription by Michel Oudijk. Likewise, in Pedro Gonzales de Nájera's probanza (1564), a witness from Quauhquechollan testified that he, together with other captains from Tlaxcala and Quauhquechollan, had assisted in the Spanish conquest of New Spain: "quando la pacifico el capitan general jorge de alvarado por ausencia del adelantado su senyor que avia ido a espanya la primera vez." See AGI Patronato 66-1-3 (1564). Díaz del Castillo, wrote, "[Pedro de Alvarado] enbió a Jorxe de Alvarado por su capitán a la paçificación de Guatimala, y quando el Jorxe de Alvarado vino truxo de camino consigo sobre dozientos indios de Tlascala, y de Cholula, y de mexicanos, y de Guacachula, y de otras provinçias, y le ayudaron en las guerras." *Historia verdadera*, ed. Sáenz de Santa María, 796. It is not surprising that Jorge de Alvarado brought Quauhquecholteca with him, as in the 1530s, and quite possibly earlier as well, the community of Quauhquechollan was granted in *encomienda* to him, and it was common practice for conquistadors to use tributaries from their own encomiendas as auxiliaries in further conquests. See Gerhard, *Geografía histórica*, 57; Paredes Martínez, *La región de Atlixco*, 52.

29. The use of the Habsburg emblem was not only granted to the Quauhquecholteca and Tlaxcalteca but also to the central Mexican conquistadors who settled in Totonicapan, e.g. Other Mexican pictorials that represent the Habsburg eagle (each with its own adaptations) are the Genealogía de Azcapotzalco / Códice García Granados, the Escudo de armas de Tzintzuntzan, the Escudo de armas de Texcoco,

the Lienzo de Pátzcuaro, and the Lienzo de Carapan. Furthermore, this privilege was granted to certain K'iche' communities in Guatemala. Variants of this image are drawn in the Título de caciques de Totonicapan, the Título de Momostenango, the Buenabaj pictorials, the Título de C'oyoi, and the Título de Totonicapan. See Carmack, *Quichean Civilization*, 1, 266; Carmack and Mondloch, *El título de Totonicapán*, folio ii; and Carmack and Mondloch, *El título de Yax*, 215, 219.

30. See Roskamp, "La heráldica novohispana," 229.

31. See Kranz, "Tlaxcalan Conquest Pictorials," 72; Buenaventura Zapata y Mendoza, *Historia cronológica*.

32. See Gruzinski, *Conquest of Mexico*, 23.

33. A similar white pyramid can be found in the place glyph of Quauhquechollan as it appears in the Mapa circular de Quauhquechollan and in the Lienzo of the Heye Foundation.

34. The word "Quauhquechollan" consists of the Nahuatl words *quauh-* (eagle), *quechol-* (quecholli bird), and *-(t)lan* (place name suffix, "place of . . .") and can be translated as "place of eagles and quecholli birds." In other Mexican pictorials, Quauhquechollan is represented by means of a mountain and an eagle as well, sometimes in combination with a quecholli bird or other elements. Depictions of the place glyph of Quauhquechollan can be found in the Historia tolteca-chichimeca, the Codex Mendoza, the Lienzo de Tlaxcala, the Lienzo of the Heye Foundation, the Genealogía de Quauhquechollan-Macuilxochitepec, the Códice de Huaquechula, and the Mapa circular de Quauhquechollan.

35. It is known that the Spaniards granted several privileges to the Quauhquecholteca in return for their services to the Spaniards. See Archivo General de la Nación (AGN), *Tierras*, vol. 2683, exp. 4, f. 164 (ff. 3r–3v). The nature of these privileges, however, is not recorded.

36. For more on Nahua warrior costumes, refer to Anawalt, *Indian Clothing*; Berdan and Anawalt, *Essential Codex Mendoza*; and Anawalt, "Comparative Analysis."

37. See Sahagún, *Florentine Codex*; Berdan and Anawalt, *Essential Codex Mendoza*; and Hassig, *Aztec Warfare*.

38. In most Mesoamerican pictorials, people are supplied with personal or calendrical name glyphs. Remarkably, most of the people depicted in the Lienzo de Tlaxcala, the Lienzo de Analco, and the Lienzo de Quauhquechollan do not have such name glyphs. Possibly, the writers of these colonial stories considered the barrios or units indicated by the insignia more relevant than the individuals, or perhaps the names of individuals were given in the alphabetic manuscripts that accompanied the pictorials.

39. See las Casas, *Brevissima relación*; MacNutt, *Bartholomew de las Casas*. For a discussion on Mexica warfare, arms and armor, refer to Hassig, *Aztec warfare*, 75–94, and Berdan and Anawalt, *Essential Codex Mendoza*.

40. See Powell, *La guerra chichimeca*, 172.

41. See Simmons, "Tlascalans," 101.

42. See Alvarado, *Account of the Conquest*, 133.

43. For a discussion on the use of dogs in the conquest, refer to Varner and Varner, *Dogs of the Conquest*. This cruel way of punishment is also depicted in other Mexican pictorials. An example is the Manuscrito del Aperreamiento (Bibliotheque Nacionale de France, Paris, Mex. 374). A color reproduction of this document can be found in the *Journal de la Société des Américanistes*, tome 84-2, fig. 17.

44. See König, *Die Schlacht*, 136; and Chance, *Conquest*, 18.

45. See Alvarado, *Account of the Conquest*, 129, and Kramer, *Encomienda Politics*, 122.

46. See Hassig, *Aztec Warfare*, 8.

47. See Kranz, "Tlaxcalan Conquest Pictorials," 142.

48. See Acuña, *Relaciones geográficas*, cuadro 13.

49. Only one place in the Lienzo de Analco is indicated pictographically by name: Tiltepec. This site is represented by means of a black mountain. Michel Oudijk, personal communication, March 2004.

50. With regards to this early campaign, the Glasgow manuscript shows a conquest route that corresponds largely to the conquest route described by Pedro de Alvarado in his letters to Cortés. See Alvarado, *Account of the Conquest*.

51. See "Probanza de meritos y servicios."

52. Laura Matthew, personal communication, Philadelphia, November 2002. In 1997 Matthew spoke to a man from Ciudad Vieja who mentioned that the Mexicans who had come to Guatemala had come with Jorge de Alvarado.

53. Díaz del Castillo, *Historia verdadera*, ed. Sáenz de Santa María, 207.

54. See Recinos, *Pedro de Alvarado*, 27, 78, 221–27; Herrera, "Concubines and Wives."

55. "Toda la mayor parte de Tlascala la acataba y le daban presentes y la tenían por su señora." Díaz del Castillo, *Historia verdadera*, ed. Sáenz de Santa María, 210.

56. See "Provanca del Adelantado D. Pedro de Alvarado."

57. It is very possible that the Spaniards referred to the Tlaxcalteca when they actually meant all central Mexican conquistadors, simply because they were the people they had most contact with. If so, much of the information given in Spanish documents on the Tlaxcalteca in Guatemala could also be applicable to the other central Mexican groups who ended up living there.

58. For an overview of the royal privileges granted to Tlaxcala, refer to Gibson, *Tlaxcala*, 229–34. Also, Tlaxcala was never placed under an *encomendero*. Instead, it became a single municipality and parish. See Kranz, "Tlaxcalan Conquest Pictorials," 133.

59. In spite of the fact that his military achievements far exceeded that of any other Spanish conquistador (including that of his brother Pedro), Jorge de Alvarado's contribution to the conquest of Guatemala has often not been fully recognized by historians. This seems to be due to (1) the fact that most well-known chronicles provide elaborate accounts about both Pedro and Gonzalo de Alvarado's military achievements but (for unclear reasons) often ignore Jorge's role; (2) conquests carried out by Jorge de Alvarado and other Spanish conquistadors were often unrightfully ascribed to Pedro de Alvarado, who, after all, was the one who

commanded the first Spanish army that ever entered Guatemala; (3) the documents that most elaborate on Jorge's achievements remain as of yet unpublished and thus are rarely used by historians and unknown to the general public; and (4) there are little specific data available on Jorge's conquests since most references are vague.

60. See Alvarado, *Account of the Conquest*, 59; Recinos, Goetz, and Chonay, *Annals of the Cakchiquels*, 119–20; and Carmack, *Quichean Civilization*, 342.

61. See Gall, *Diccionario geográfico*, 2:343.

62. Michael Swanton, personal communication, Leiden, 2004.

63. This Mexica migration is depicted in the Pintura de la Peregrinación de los culhuas-mexitin (Mapa de Sigüenza), the Tira de la Peregrinación or Codex Boturini, the Codex Aubin, and the Codex Azcatitlan. See Castañeda de la Paz, "De Aztlan a Tenochtitlan," and Castañeda de la Paz, "El largo periplo."

64. This Chichimeca migration is depicted in the Mapa de Cuauhtinchan No. 2 and narrated both alphabetically and pictorially in the Historia tolteca-chichimeca (1547–60). See Yoneda, "Los mapas de Cuauhtinchan" (1999); Leibsohn, "Primers for Memory"; and Kirchhoff, Odena Güemes, and Reyes García, *Historia tolteca-chichimeca*.

65. This Acolhua migration is depicted in the Codex Xolotl (1542). See Dibble, *Códice Xolotl*.

66. The narrative presented in the Mapa de Cuauhtinchan No. 2 includes the place glyphs for Tenochtitlan, Tlaxcala, Cholula, Tepeacac, the volcanos Popocatepetl and Iztaccihuatl, and Coixtlahuaca (Mixteca Alta). For an overview of the place glyphs represented in this pictorial, see Yoneda, "Los mapas de Cuauhtinchan" (1978), 246–47. See also Carrasco and Sessions, *Cave, City, and Eagle's Nest*.

67. See López Austin, "Aztec"; Castañeda de la Paz, "El largo periplo"; and Dibble, *Códice Xolotl*.

68. Yoneda, "Los mapas de Cuauhtinchan" (1978), 135.

69. For a comparison of these two scenes, refer to J. Gillespie, "Saints and Warriors," 5–7.

70. The elements in the initial scene in the Lienzo de Quauhquechollan are ordered according to the same layout as that of cuadro 29, 31, and 32 in the Glasgow manuscript. See Asselbergs, *Conquered Conquistadors*; and Acuña, *Relaciones geográficas*, cuadro 29, 31, and 32.

71. See Mundy, "Lienzos."

72. The Historia tolteca-chichimeca illustrates this way of presenting a narrative very vividly. The role previously assigned to spoken or chanted words is here fulfilled by the alphabetic text. There are extensive dialogues and songs related to the pictography, revealing the structure, style, and rhetoric of such previously orally recited texts. See Kirchhoff, Odena Güemes, and Reyes García, *Historia tolteca-chichimeca*.

73. See Leibsohn, "Primers for Memory," 161.

74. The Titulo de Caciques, which mentions the mapa, was written in 1544. The mapa must thus have been created before that time.

75. Lockhart, Berdan, and Anderson, *Tlaxcalteca Actas*, 51. The Nahuatl text is published in Celestino Solis, Valencia R., and Medina Lima, *Actas del cabildo*, 127–28. See Kranz, "Tlaxcalan Conquest Pictorials," 67.

76. See Mundy, *Mapping of New Spain*, 111.

77. These tapestries were painted by Jean de Vermayen and woven by Guillermo Pannemaker (1535–54). Presently, they decorate the walls of the Salón de Tapices of the Real Alcázar of Sevilla, Spain. See Fidalgo, *El real alcázar de Sevilla*, 53.

CHAPTER THREE

Whose Conquest?

Nahua, Zapoteca, and Mixteca Allies in the Conquest of Central America

LAURA E. MATTHEW

*Que este testigo hera pequeño quando el adelantado don pedro de
alvarado salio de mexico para guatimala . . . e vido que venyan en su
companya los d[ic]hos capitanes yndios y trayan consigo muchos pari-
entes y maçeguales y les vido hazer alarde a los d[ic]hos capitanes al
tiempo de la partida de mexico y esto sabe e vydo.*
[*And this witness was a child when the adelantado Don Pedro de
Alvarado left from Mexico for Guatemala . . . and he saw that there
were in his company the said Indian captains and they brought with
them many family members and commoners, and he saw them in military procession at the time of their departure from Mexico, and this
he knows and saw.*]

JOAN MONTEJO TLAXCALTECA, 1564

The most frequently cited narrative of the conquest of Central
America derives from the colonial chronicles of Bernal Díaz del
Castillo and Francisco Antonio Fuentes y Guzmán and goes something like this: The conquest of Guatemala was initiated in 1524 by an
almost equal number of Spaniards and natives from central Mexico led by
the Spaniard Pedro de Alvarado. Arriving in K'iche' territory, the several

hundred Spaniards and three hundred Tlaxcalteca, Cholulteca, and "Mexicano" allies met fierce resistance.[1] Only with the aid of thousands of Kaqchikel warriors from central Guatemala were the Spaniards able to defeat the K'iche'. The Kaqchikel subsequently rebelled against the Spaniards, chafing under Alvarado's harsh demands. Nevertheless, over the course of many years and against great odds the Spaniards managed to subjugate the region and established their capital in the Valley of Guatemala. From there, the Spanish and their native allies organized campaigns to conquer the rest of Central America.

Although oft-repeated, this narrative is incomplete in many ways. It begs the question why so many Kaqchikel would have willingly sided with the Spaniards (often assuming that they were simply Guatemala's version of the Tlaxcalteca in Mexico) and remains silent on the participation of K'iche', Achi, and other Maya in later campaigns to the south. It ignores the contributions of Jorge de Alvarado and other Spaniards who arrived in Guatemala after 1524 with reinforcements that literally saved the necks of the stranded original conquistadors. And it dramatically oversimplifies the involvement of thousands of Nahua, Zapoteca, and Mixteca from central and southern Mexico in the conquest of Central America. Many of these were captains, warriors, and porters who traveled to the region in separate military campaigns led by Spaniards. Others were colonists: women sent to join their husbands, fathers, uncles, or entire families sent to help establish colonies in the conquered areas. While precise numbers are hard to come by, the total clearly exceeded Díaz del Castillo's estimate ten-fold, at least. Indeed, the extent of Nahua, Zapoteca, and Mixteca participation in the conquest of Central America—and the ways they later remembered these events—calls into question whether they viewed it, contemporaneously or in retrospect, as a Spanish conquest at all.

In this chapter, I have two goals. The first is to retell the story of the conquest of Central America following the traditional chronology but placing Nahua and other native non-Maya allies at the forefront of events rather than treating them as a background chorus. In so doing, I follow the lead of other scholars who have noted the high levels of Nahua participation in the conquest of Central America described in petitions to the Crown in the mid-sixteenth century called *probanzas de méritos*.[2] Such probanzas detailing services to and seeking reward from the Crown were sent by Spanish and indigenous conquistadors alike on behalf of their families or their communities. In 1564, however, the Nahuatl-speaking conquistadors living in

Ciudad Vieja, Guatemala, went one step further, presenting a petition not just on their own behalf but including all the Nahua and Zapoteca warriors and settlers who remained in Chiapas, Xoconosco, Guatemala, Honduras, El Salvador, and Nicaragua.[3] In a legal battle resolved only in the 1620s, the leaders of Ciudad Vieja insisted that they, their compatriots throughout Central America, and all their descendants be granted exemption from tribute and forced labor in perpetuity. The surviving documentation from this petition, archived as Justicia 291 in the Archivo General de Indias in Seville, Spain, provides some of the most precise information we have about these native warriors' role in the conquest.

My second goal is to consider how the information and perspectives contained in documents like Justicia 291 challenge our view of the conquest period. Most fundamentally, the high number of indigenous participants attested to offers an important correction to the historical record whose implications have not been fully developed. What did these thousands of men, women, and children think they were doing when they marched south into Maya territory? Why did some choose to return home afterward, while others chose to stay and settle as colonists? Who did they think they were they fighting for, and what did they expect in return? My reading of Justicia 291 emphasizes the indigenous conquistadors' own agency in the conquest, rather than their manipulation by reputedly charismatic Spaniards like Pedro de Alvarado. The rhetoric, legal strategies employed and production of Justicia 291 suggest that these indigenous conquistadors had rather different goals, methods, and experiences of conquest than those attributed to them by later Spanish chroniclers. In Justicia 291, they offer a conquest narrative that competes, complements, and complicates Spanish-authored accounts. They also reveal their increasing frustration that by the mid-sixteenth century things were not turning out as they had expected.

NAHUA, ZAPOTECA, AND MIXTECA IN
THE CONQUEST OF CENTRAL AMERICA

Guatemala was not conquered as an afterthought. The southwestern highlands of Guatemala lie just beyond the cacao-rich region of Xoconosco, where the Mexica had established military garrisons during the reigns of Ahuitzotl and Moctezuma II.[4] Besides providing a regional market for the port of trade at Xoconosco, the Guatemalan highlands traded in obsidian, salt, and other local products with the Pipil regions of what is now El Salvador and Nicaragua to the south, Chiapas to the north, and the southern Pacific Coast. The *Popol Wuj* and the *Memorial de Sololá* both hint that the Mexica Tenochca–led empire of the Triple Alliance was extending toward Guatemala under Moctezuma II. A chronicler of the Kaqchikel Xahil lineage remarks in the *Memorial de Sololá* that Moctezuma sent messengers to the K'iche' in 1510, while the *Título de la casa Ixquin-Nehaib* reports that the K'iche' began paying tribute to Mexico at this time.[5] Carlos Navarette has suggested that in the early sixteenth century, the Mexica Tenochca were poised to conquer Guatemala in a "violent intervention interrupted by the Spanish Conquest."[6] Seen from another angle, however, the Spaniards did not interrupt this "violent intervention" but in fact enabled it to be carried out sooner and more effectively under a newly configured native-Spanish alliance.

The initial conquest of Guatemala by Pedro de Alvarado, so often memorialized by subsequent historians, was one of the first long-distance campaigns to be attempted by Mesoamerican and Spanish allies after the fall of Tenochtitlan. The original troops from central Mexico were gathered from across the region. According to Alonso López, a native of Tlalmanalco near Chalco who later settled in Gracias a Dios, Honduras, the leaders of his town gathered and announced that the "great captain who had captured Mexico was sending Don Pedro de Alvarado to conquer the province of Guatemala" and that they would receive the captains, warriors, and auxiliaries who had to go with him from each of the towns of Mexico and Tlaxcala. Asked for more information, López repeated that Cortés "brought together in Mexico all the chiefs and lords of the entire province of Tlaxcala and Mexico and ordered that Indians from each town be brought, and so a large number of Indians came."[7] Spanish participants in this first campaign also recalled how the civic and military leaders of each central Mexican province recruited soldiers who were then organized into squadrons by *altepetl* and were led by their own captains who worked together to coordinate the troops' movements.[8]

The captains traveled through their provinces, assembling warriors who marched through the streets in military procession. The warriors brought their own weapons—bows and arrows, clubs, and broadswords—and were adorned in traditional warrior garb of cotton and feathered armor, with insignias marking their altepetl affiliation.[9] It was an impressive event, capable of inspiring volunteers not only in the moment but many years later as well. Juan Montejo was a boy in Tlaxcala when the original army was recruited; he migrated to join the forces of Francisco de Montejo in Honduras a decade later. Even as an old man, he remembered vividly the native captains gathered with all their family and servants, preparing for the journey south and parading through the streets.[10] Pedro de la Lona of Texcoco was around twenty years old when Pedro de Alvarado's army of Spaniards rode through his altepetl. There, as in Tlaxcala, a native captain recruited "a great number" of soldiers and led them in procession. Lona described this captain, Don Juan, as his "lord" and continued to recognize Don Juan's authority over him at the time of his testimony some thirty years later, as did other auxiliaries who indicated their continued devotion to their captains many years after their military service had ended.[11]

Alvarado left Mexico-Tenochtitlan on December 6, 1523, during the traditional November to May season for Mesoamerican military campaigns (thus avoiding the rainy agricultural season). Accompanying him, according to Díaz del Castillo, were some four hundred Spaniards, two hundred Tlaxcalteca and Cholulteca, and one hundred "Mexicanos."[12] Cortés agrees with this account, reporting in his letter to king Phillip II of Spain on October 15, 1524, that several hundred Spaniards departed with Alvarado and an undefined number of "some chieftains from this city and from other cities in the vicinity, although not many, because the journey will be so long."[13] These oft-quoted estimates of the native auxiliaries seem low. Perhaps Cortés and Díaz del Castillo were suppressing the numbers to favor the Spaniards, although Cortés's additional explanation would seem unnecessary. Or perhaps it is true that only several hundred allies left with Alvarado on that particular date in December, and he was planning to pick up reinforcements on the way. In any case, the invasion force numbered a few thousand by the time it left Tehuantepec in Oaxaca a month or so later.

Francisco Oçelote, a young Tlaxcalteca probably in his twenties at the time, was one of those who joined Alvarado's campaign in Oaxaca. (Later, Oçelote would accompany Alvarado to Nicaragua, help found the city Gracias a Dios, and settle in the allied Barrio de Mexicanos on the city's outskirts.) In 1564 Oçelote recalled that eight hundred Tlaxcalteca, four hundred Huexotzinga, and sixteen hundred Nahua "from Tepeaca" gathered in Oaxaca with Alvarado and two hundred Spaniards, along with many more soldiers from other formerly Mexica provinces and many of their families and servants.[14] Oçelote's recollection matches that of the "mexicanos y tlaxcaltecas" of Ciudad Vieja, who said in 1547 that more than one thousand of them had served with Alvarado in the opening campaign, as well as that of the Spanish conquistador Pedro Gonzáles Nájara (whom we will revisit later).[15] As the army continued along the Pacific coastal plains to the K'iche' town of Xetulul (Zapotitlan) in the first week of February 1524, it picked up more Zapoteca and Mixteca auxiliaries as well as Nahua from the Mexica outpost at Xoconosco.[16] By the time the army reached the highland towns of Xelajuj (Quezaltenango) and Utatlan in March 1524, it probably numbered in the thousands and comprised mostly native allies from central and southern Mexico.[17]

It is a testament to the difficulty of the Guatemalan conquest and the resistance of the highland Maya that this substantial invading force was unable to defeat the K'iche' Maya without the assistance of as many Kaqchikel Maya allies in 1524. By May of that year the invading army had swelled to some six thousand from the addition of thousands of highland Maya allies and slaves.[18] A violent campaign into the Pipil territory of modern Guatemala and El Salvador caused significant casualties and only partially subdued the area; this campaign loomed large in later recollections of the Nahua and other non-Maya allies' services.[19] Pedro de Alvarado returned to Guatemala from Cuzcatlan in July 1524, founded the first Spanish capital of Santiago at the Kaqchikel site of Iximche' on July 25, and distributed the first *encomiendas*. According to the Texcoca chronicler Fernando de Alva Ixtlilxochitl, an unknown number of Nahua allies were sent home at this time, carrying letters to Cortés that detailed the campaign up to that point.[20] Within months, however, the Kaqchikel had rebelled, chafing under Pedro de Alvarado's demands for gold and his mistreatment of them despite their alliance. The moment represented a dramatic turn of events for the Spanish, Nahua, and other allies. Suddenly surrounded by hostile forces and diminished in numbers, they moved to a protective garrison at Olintepeque near Quezaltenango in the fall of 1524.[21] From there, various campaigns were launched against the Kaqchikel, Pipil, Pokomam, Mam, and other highland Maya and southern groups.

In all these campaigns, allies from the north figured prominently and casualties were high. Don Marcos Çiguacoatl, a Mexica governor of Xoconosco who joined the Spanish forces during the original invasion of 1524, remembered that some 300 allies from Xoconosco accompanied Pedro's brother Diego de Alvarado to the newly established Villa de San Salvador at the end of 1524. Around 140 returned to Guatemala alive. The rest, he said, died in the campaign.[22] Some allies were wounded or killed not in battle but in more targeted acts of violence intended as messages of defiance. Such was the case of two Nahua allies wounded in retaliation for Alvarado's kidnapping of the K'iche' lords of Utatlan in 1524. Less famously, and not uniquely, two Nahua were sent as emissaries by Cristóbal de la Cueva to demand the surrender of a small unconquered Honduran town called Colquin. The town's reply was clear: its residents killed the two allies immediately.[23]

In August 1526, Pedro de Alvarado left for Spain, leaving Pedro Portocarrero and Hernán Carillo in charge in Guatemala and sending another Alvarado brother, Jorge, to join them as his replacement. Jorge de Alvarado's assumption of power in Guatemala in March 1527, marked much more than an administrative change, for he brought with him some five to six thousand indigenous soldiers and *tameme* from central Mexico.[24] This large influx of mostly central Mexican Nahua into Guatemala—almost certainly the largest during the conquest years—helped solidify Spanish control of the region. Jorge de Alvarado and his allies defeated the Kaqchikel, founded the Spanish capital of Santiago en Almolonga, and reestablished the abandoned Villa of San Salvador.[25] Hundreds of Nahua, Zapoteca, and Mixteca allies settled in their own barrios outside both Spanish and Maya towns. The new allies came from many of the regions represented in the original campaign of 1524, including Tlaxcala, Cholula, Coyoacan, and parts of Oaxaca.[26] But the army also included a significant number of newcomers from places like Quauhquechollan, Jorge de Alvarado's encomienda (discussed at length in Asselbergs, chapter 2, this volume). In the barrio of Almolonga at the edge of Santiago en Almolonga, the Quauhquecholteca settled in their own *parcialidad* (ward), alongside Tlaxcalteca, Texcoca, Mexica Tenochca from Tenochtitlan, Otomí, and Zapoteca, among others.[27]

Warriors and colonists from central Mexico and Oaxaca would continue to enter and move through Central America by the hundreds—to fight, die, or settle there—for another decade at least. Alvarado's nephew Luis de Moscoso; yet another brother, Gómez de Alvarado; and other Spanish captains spent much of 1528 fighting in Honduras and El Salvador, with Tlaxcalteca allies reportedly at the forefront of the fighting.[28] San Miguel de la Frontera, Honduras, was founded in 1530, and most of El Salvador was pacified by 1533. In 1536 Pedro de Alvarado amassed a large army of warriors living in and around Santiago en Almolonga—perhaps as many as fifteen hundred Nahua, Oaxacans, and Maya—to carry out an expedition into Honduras and found the city of Gracias a Dios. Other Spanish captains like Alonso de Cáceres, Cristóbal de Cueva, Diego de Alvarado, and Joan de Mendoza followed with subsequent campaigns, also assisted by central Mexican and possibly Oaxacan auxiliaries.[29] Francisco de Montejo reportedly depended heavily on many hundreds of Nahua soldiers at the vanguard of his campaign in the 1530s in Honduras (see also Chuchiak, chapter 6, this volume).[30] As well, Nahua and possibly Oaxacan soldiers served in defense of newly founded Spanish ports such as Puerto de Caballos against the French and in the jungles of Chiapas against the Lacandon.[31] Several hundred of them accompanied Pedro de Alvarado on his final campaign to Nueva Galicia and Guadalajara, Mexico, in 1540, where he was fatally wounded.[32] In all these campaigns, some indigenous conquistadors were seasoned soldiers now living as colonists in Guatemala. This was the case of Francisco Oçelote, the native of Tlaxcala who joined Alvarado's original campaign in 1524 from Oaxaca and who eventually settled in Gracias a Dios after fighting in Alvarado's Honduras campaign in 1536. Others, like Joan Montejo of Tlaxcala and Pedro de la Lona of Texcoco, came as fresh recruits to the campaigns of the 1530s, stopping off first in Santiago en Almolonga where they made contacts with the indigenous conquistador community there. These new recruits were often ten to fifteen years younger than the men who had come to the region in the 1520s.[33] Thus, by the second decade of Spanish presence in Central America, a significant generational breadth had also developed among the Nahua and other non-Maya allies living in the region.

Just how many indigenous conquistadors from Mexico fought and settled in Central America during the sixteenth century? Contemporary accounts varied wildly. The most frequently cited estimates come from Díaz de Castillo. As already suggested, these numbers are clearly too low, failing to take into account either those who joined Alvarado's troops along the road to Guatemala in 1524 or any of the other waves of allies who entered the region later or with other Spaniards. At the other extreme, the Texcoca *mestizo* chronicler Fernando de Alva Ixtlilxochitl claimed in the 1570s that twenty thousand Texcoca and "Mexicano" warriors came to Alvarado's aid in the original campaign. By the battle of Acajutla, El Salvador, in 1524, Ixtlilxochitl said, only around seven thousand of these "Mexicanos and Texcoca" were left in the Spanish forces, the rest having either been killed or injured and left behind in Guatemala.[34] While high, these numbers are not impossible given the population density that existed in central Mexico at the time of the conquest, and they reflect the standard practice of fifteenth- and early-sixteenth-century military campaigns in Mesoamerica (see Oudijk and Restall, chapter 1, this volume).[35] Nonetheless, Ixtlitlxochitl had as much reason to inflate the number of native warriors as Díaz del Castillo had to underestimate them.

Reports from the actors themselves speak of thousands of warriors, porters, and colonists arriving in Central America not in a single burst but in waves and even trickles between 1524 and 1542. In 1547 the "tlaxcaltecas y mexicanos" living in Ciudad Vieja wrote to the king, somewhat poetically and thus not very usefully for an accurate count, that "a thousand and more men and combatants" had joined Alvarado in the conquest of Guatemala.[36] The leaders of Xochimilco—whose city was one of Pedro de Alvarado's encomiendas and to whose labor he therefore claimed rights—said in 1563 that twenty-five hundred of their men had gone to Guatemala and Honduras with Alvarado.[37] One of the most precise recollections of the early conquest years comes again from the Tlaxcalteca soldier Francisco de Oçelote, who said that in the original campaign alone, more than twenty-eight hundred Nahua divided by altepetl into various troops gathered in Oaxaca with Alvarado in 1524. Similarly, the Spanish captain Pedro Gonzáles Nájara—who spoke Nahuatl, acted as an interpreter during the original campaign, and later in his life maintained close relations with the Mexicano community in Guatemala—reported in 1564 that approximately seven thousand soldiers from central and southern Mexico had participated in the conquest in three separate campaigns.[38] The campaigns to which Gonzáles Nájara refers, but which he does not himself specify, are most likely those of Pedro de Alvarado in 1524 and Jorge de Alvarado in 1526 and possibly that of Pedro de Alvarado into Honduras in the 1530s.

Smaller campaigns led by less well known Spaniards and their native allies departed regularly from central Mexico toward Central America during the period 1524–42, including that of the Spaniard Diego de Rojas in 1524, dispatched from Mexico-Tenochtitlan by Cortés with some fifty indigenous conquistadors to join Alvarado in Central America, and of Hernando de Illescas, sent from Guatemala to Mexico by Pedro de Alvarado in the 1530s to bring back a contingent of Spaniards for the conquest of Honduras and who returned not only with Spaniards but with some six hundred Tlaxcalteca as well.[39] Significant numbers of native allies must have also accompanied other, less famous expeditions into Central America from Mexico, such as those, separately, of Cristóbal de Olid and Hernando Cortés into Honduras and of Pedro de Briones from Honduras to Guatemala. It is probable that some of these indigenous conquistadors also stayed in the region. Finally, family members of the indigenous conquistadors and other colonists also migrated to Central America. Some women and children traveled with the conquering armies, providing essential services preparing food, carrying supplies, and helping maintain the Spaniards' bases at Iximche' and Olintepeque (see also Herrera, chapter 4, this volume). More women and children, as well as brothers, uncles, and other relatives, followed after the initial campaigns, traveling along the main road (which was also the conquest route) apparently on their own without Spanish accompaniment.[40]

Years later, in the mid-sixteenth century, more than one Spaniard reflected that the conquest of Central America would have been impossible without the participation of these non-Maya allies. Most obviously, the indigenous conquistadors provided an enormous boost in manpower and weaponry to the Spaniards—indeed, without them the Spanish forces could scarcely be called an army. They served in the forefront and the rearguard of the troops, protecting the Spaniards against precipitous losses and thereby suffering the brunt of the casualties inflicted on their side. They continued to fight against the French on the eastern coast and rebellious native groups throughout the region and to defend newly established Spanish cities. Just as important as their military service, however, was the everyday labor the native allies provided in the journey from Mexico to Central America. The noncombatants who accompanied the soldiers— often women and children—acted as porters, carrying the army's supplies and weaponry, its wounded, and even "carriages" of able-bodied Spaniards, "for better defense." When the army came to impassable rivers or swamps, Nahua, Zapoteca, and Mixteca foot soldiers constructed bridges and created trails to allow safe passage. Often, when faced with difficult or mountainous terrain, they were burdened with the packhorses' loads as well as their own. They foraged and hunted for food to feed themselves and the Spaniards, as well as prepared it. Without this very basic assistance, said Don Marcos Çiguacoatl of Soconusco in 1564, the Spaniards would surely have perished from hunger.[41] The conquest of Central America was, from the beginning, a joint Spanish-Mesoamerican venture: planned, coordinated, guided, and fought by thousands of Nahua, Zapoteca and Mixteca and a few hundred Spaniards, in the name of their home altepetl, the Mesoamerican gods who aided them, Christianity, and the Spanish Crown.

THE SIXTEENTH-CENTURY CAMPAIGN FOR PRIVILEGES

In return for their military and colonizing services, privileges were bestowed upon the indigenous conquistadors of Central America that mirrored those granted to other indigenous allies in New Spain in the early years of colonialism. One of the Tlaxcalteca captains in Central America, Juan de Tascala, received half of the town of Citala, or Zinquinala (possibly in the Escuintla region), in encomienda from Pedro de Alvarado.[42] Several small towns were granted to the Nahua and other allies collectively in the earliest years, as well as parcels of land for cultivation outside Santiago in the barrio of Almolonga.[43] In 1532 Queen Isabella exempted the "Indians from Mexico and Taxcala and their districts" living in Almolonga from the encomienda, thus freeing them from the obligation to pay tribute and provide food and labor to local Spaniards. The edict's rhetoric emphasized the allies' singular status among the indigenous population as loyal vassals of the Spanish monarchy and *vecinos*, or residents, a term associated with proper, civilized behavior from the Spanish point of view (*policía*) and normally reserved for Spaniards in the sixteenth century.[44]

Nevertheless, very early the indigenous conquistadors' precarious position in the colony was apparent. Some had arrived in Guatemala as slaves, not soldiers. Around one hundred Mixteca, for example, were brought from Mexico by Francisco de Zurrilla, the royal accountant of the Audiencia, to work alongside local natives panning gold in the mines near Huehuetenango after Zurrilla took possession of the encomienda of Juan de Espinar from 1530 to 1531.[45] Juan de Tascala's encomienda was taken away and reassigned by Pedro de Alvarado sometime before 1537, as were the towns granted to the so-called Mexicanos and Tlascaltecas of Almolonga collectively. The queen's edict of 1532 itself reflected the tenuousness of the indigenous conquistadors' emerging position in the colony, for it was issued in response to an early request by Spanish officials to authorize using the allies as an urban labor force in Santiago. While exempting the allies from the encomienda, the edict required them to provide labor of their own "goodwill" for Santiago's maintenance.[46] The indigenous conquistadors' special status as vassals and vecinos in no way made them equal to the Spanish conquistadors, who were never instructed to perform manual labor and who expected all such tasks to be done by native or African slaves. As the Dominican Fray Bartolomé de las Casas reported, the "Mexicanos" of Almolonga were subsequently required to "construct fences for bull-fights, sweep the plazas, go on long journeys with cargo and correspon-dence, and other works, as if they were conscripts, servants and peons." It was, he noted, only another kind of forced labor.[47]

The Nahua and other allies complained vociferously about what they perceived as abuses of their position as conquistadors. In a 1547 letter to the Crown, they claimed that despite their sacrifices and the "bad treat-ment" they suffered at the hands of the Spaniards from "work and sick-ness and war," over four hundred of their party had been taken as slaves and were not heard from again. The rest of the community, they wrote, had been parceled out to provide labor to individual Spaniards. They asked the king for an order releasing them from all such subjection and reserv-ing them from all tribute and forced labor. This communal letter, written on behalf of "those of Tlaxcala and all its provinces and the Mexicans with all their subjects, new vassals of your Majesty" living in the province of Guatemala, was followed by a letter from one "Francisco, vassal of your Majesty and native of Tlaxcala," son of Tlaxcalteca *cacique* Aexotecatl.[48] Francisco, who led a regiment of Tlaxcalteca to Guatemala in Jorge de Alvarado's 1527 campaign, claimed to have expected to return to Tlaxcala as his father's primary heir. Instead, as the conquest of Central America dragged on, Francisco received word that his siblings had assumed con-trol of his share of the inheritance while he continued to be required for service in foreign lands. Reiterating the pleas of the first, collective letter, Francisco asked the king to provide restitution for all he had lost and pledged his continued service to the Crown.[49] During this same period, in 1546, Nahua allies who had settled in Chiapas also traveled to the seat of the Audiencia de los Confines in Gracias a Dios to deliver a petition ask-ing that the privileges due them as conquistadors be upheld.[50]

As these letters indicate, signs were emerging as early as the 1540s that any wealth and power conferred on the Nahua, Zapoteca, and Mixteca allies would fall short of their expectations. The allies' claims to privilege were now beginning to rankle some Spanish colonists and bureaucrats, who viewed their pretensions to difference from the highland Maya and other Central Americans as unwarranted and even offensive. The "Mexicanos and Tlascaltecas" complained the Spaniard Gregorio López in 1543 acted lordly over the native population of Guatemala with the cooperation of

Maya caciques.[51] Royal and local officials charged that Nahua neighbor-hoods had been infiltrated by Maya and others who wanted to escape labor drafts and tribute payment. Residents of Almolonga and other allied colonies, it was claimed, roamed the streets as vagabonds engaging in crim-inal activity alongside Africans and *naborías*. For these Spaniards, the blood of the native allies had by the mid-sixteenth century been irrevocably pol-luted according to the Spanish standards of *limpieza de sangre* (purity of blood). The vagabondage and criminality they claimed to witness was not, in their view, coincidental but indicated the indigenous conquistadors' degeneration into a population of *castas*.[52]

Nor were the Nahua and other non-Maya conquistadors exempt from the abuse and violence that threatened all native Mesoamericans in colonial Guatemala, although these may have been somewhat mitigated in their case. Instances of their mistreatment appear scattered throughout sixteenth-century official reviews, called *residencias* or *informaciones*, of Spanish con-quistadors and officials. In Honduras in 1544, a "Mexican Indian" approached the conquistador Francisco de Montejo, bleeding, after having been beaten; the offending Spaniard was only given a verbal warning.[53] Jufre de Loaysa, *oidor* (judge) of the Audiencia in the 1550s, was accused of using "Mexicanos" from Almolonga—now known as Ciudad Vieja after the first Santiago was destroyed in an earthquake and moved—as house servants and field laborers, without remuneration and violently enforced. The pres-ident of the Audiencia with whom Loaysa served, Juan Núñez de Landecho, was accused of similar abuses of the "Mexicanos and Tlascaltecas" of Ciudad Vieja, including forcing them to carry his wife and, on a separate occasion, his African concubine on their shoulders in a litter for over six leagues.[54] While not out of the ordinary by colonial Guatemalan standards, these inci-dents demonstrate the extent to which the native allies' status as conquis-tadors was disregarded in mid-sixteenth-century Central America.

The tenuousness of the indigenous conquistadors' situation could only have been exacerbated by the upheaval surrounding Alonso López de Cerrato's implementation of the New Laws outlawing native slavery in Guatemala in 1549. In that year, Cerrato freed some three to five thousand indigenous slaves in the Santiago area, many of them forced immigrants from other areas of the Audiencia who spoke a variety of native languages. Cerrato's actions outraged many Spanish *encomenderos* and increased already existing tensions over claims to land and native labor. A flurry of local and royal decrees followed, which attempted to redirect and regulate the ex-slaves' labor and tributary potential. These included, for example, a 1552 law outlawing vagabondage and another in 1559 insisting that fair wages be paid to native laborers with no tax taken out. Also in 1559, in recognition of the hardships caused the ex-slaves by their former condition, the Crown issued an order exempting them from personal service and tribute for a period of three years, after which time tribute could recommence. This ruling became of central importance to the Nahua and other non-Maya conquistadors, colonists, and their children in 1562, when the royal *fiscal* serving under President Landecho attempted to collect tribute from them on the basis of the 1559 *cédula*.[55]

As the indigenous conquistadors clearly realized, the official denial by the fiscal of any distinction between ex-slaves and ex-conquistadors threatened the very basis of their status in the colony. In response, they launched a campaign that superseded any of their previous efforts to secure a privileged place in Guatemalan colonial society. This fight for privileges, initiated in 1564, produced one of the most remarkable documents to have survived detailing the conquest of Central America. In January of that year, the leaders of Ciudad Vieja presented a petition to royal officials on behalf of the "yndios mexicanos, tascaltecas, çapotecas y otros" who resided in Central America, requesting that tribute exemption be reinstated and guaranteed not only to the original conquistadors but in perpetuity to their descendants as well, on the basis of their alliance with the Spanish Crown during the conquest. The surviving documentation from this petition spans fourteen years (1564–78) and includes over eight hundred pages of bureaucratic formulas, interrogations of witnesses, and royal pronouncements.[56] Copies of a number of royal edicts pertaining to the indigenous conquistadors are provided. Witnesses include native captains and warriors who joined the conquest at various points in time, Spanish conquistadors who fought alongside and were assisted by them, and Spanish vecinos who could attest to the native allies' reputation in Central America. The document is valuable most obviously for the information it provides about the conquest and settlement of Central America from both Spanish and indigenous viewpoints, much of which is reflected earlier in this chapter. But just as important for understanding the indigenous conquistadors' early colonial era experience and how they viewed it is the history of the document itself: its travels, participants, patterns, and trappings.

The document is divided into three sections. The first section, 422 pages long, is the original 1564 petition presented to Audiencia officials by the

Tlaxcalteca Don Francisco Oñate (the same Francisco, son of Aexotecatl, who wrote the Crown in 1547) and the "Mexicano" Don Juan de Tapia of Ciudad Vieja. This section includes copies of the queen's 1532 edict exempting the non-Maya allies from encomienda service and the testimony of twenty-nine witnesses from Xoconosco, Santiago de Guatemala, Gracias a Dios, San Salvador, Comayagua, and Ciudad Vieja collected over six months. The Audiencia's judge, Francisco de Briceño, received closing statements from the royal fiscal, Joan de Arguyo, and the native allies' lawyer, Diego de Ramírez, in November 1564. In January 1565, Briceño ruled that the case be forwarded to the Council of the Indies within a year's time. Meanwhile, the indigenous conquistadors continued to pay tribute until a definitive ruling was made. The conquistadors' petition was then assigned to another lawyer serving the Council of the Indies, Juan de la Peña, and delivered to him in Spain sometime in 1565.[57] De la Peña presented the case for consideration before the Council of the Indies in Madrid within days of the one-year deadline for submission, on January 21, 1566.

The second and third sections of the document resulted from the council's ruling, five years later in February 1571, that the Nahua and other non-Maya conquistadors had not proven their case and would be required to continue paying tribute to royal officials in Guatemala. Subsequently, representatives of the native allies in Spain apparently petitioned the council several more times to have the case reconsidered. In March 1572, the council agreed, and one year later, in March 1573, King Philip II issued a cédula granting "certain Indians of this province [Guatemala] who came from New Spain to help in the conquest" two more years for the preparation of a new set of documents supporting their case and ordered that the privilege of tribute exemption be honored.[58] The second part of the document thus consists of the new petition, 388 pages long, compiled by the leaders of Ciudad Vieja in 1573. It is followed by a third section, with its own numeration, that summarizes the testimony of every witness to each of the second interrogation's questions.

Perhaps the most immediately striking aspect of Justicia 291 is its sheer bulk, reflecting an enormous amount of money spent and an impressive system of sustained communications between Guatemala, Honduras, El Salvador, Chiapas, Mexico, and Madrid. In each place, local and royal officials coordinated the effort with those handling the case from Santiago and Ciudad Vieja. Scribes, lawyers, and carriers had to be paid, and some of their charges are scattered throughout the text. One series of supporting documents cost the residents of Ciudad Vieja 560 *maravedís*, at approximately 48 maravedís a page; a common laborer's wage in 1552 was around 12 maravedís a day.[59] Despite some expenses being borne by royal officials and their offices as dictated by Spanish law, then, the cost of the case to the indigenous conquistadors involved must have been significant, particularly in those years when they were also paying tribute according to Briceño's ruling. It is clear too that the colonists living in Ciudad Vieja viewed their petition as a region-wide effort. Oñate and Tapia presented the case "in the name of the rest" of the indigenous conquistadors settled throughout Central America and drew their witnesses from the most important Spanish and allied settlements existing in Central America at the time. They provided supporting documents from Chiapas as well as Guatemala, and there is some suggestion that the petition traveled to the conquistadors' home provinces in Mexico for additional material, although nothing from Mexico is provided in the text.[60]

Also impressive is the list of witnesses who testified on the Nahua, Zapoteca, and Mixteca conquistadors' behalf, which includes some extremely well known and powerful Spaniards in early colonial society. Gonzalo Ortíz, for instance, was an original Spanish conquistador, encomendero, and vecino of Santiago who, beginning in 1530, had served the city in a number of capacities. He spent time in Spain in the 1540s serving as Santiago's representative to the Council of the Indies. At the time of his testimony he was a councilman in the municipal council. Alvaro de Paz did not fight in the conquest but arrived in Guatemala from Castile in the early 1530s and became a close ally of Pedro de Alvarado, acting as his lawyer and majordomo until Alvarado's death. He was briefly granted half of Alvarado's encomienda of Totonicapan, held other encomiendas in Guatemala and Honduras, and was an active figure in Santiago's government in the 1560s. Other witnesses for the "Mexicanos and Tlascaltecas"— such as Francisco Castellón, Juan Gómez, Juan de Aragón, Pedro de Ovid, Pedro Gonzáles Nájara, Alonso de Loarca, and Diego López de Villanueva—were all conquistadors who came to Guatemala with either Pedro or Jorge de Alvarado, and were well-known members of the Spanish community in Central America. All of these Spaniards testified in support of the native allies' petition in 1564. In 1573 the witness list of Spaniards was pared down to a core group of four—Gonzáles Nájara, Paz, Loarca, and Villanueva—plus one impressive addition: Don Francisco de la Cueva, cousin of Alvarado's wife, Doña Beatríz de la Cueva, lieutenant governor of Guatemala from 1540 to 1541, husband of Alvarado's daughter and heir, Doña Leonor, and one of the richest and most influential Spaniards in Guatemala.

Significantly, not a single native Central American witness appears throughout the document. All indigenous testimony comes from natives of Mexico and their children: the conquistadors, not the conquered. In 1564 the imbalance between many more Spanish than Nahua or other indigenous witnesses suggests a further sensitivity to specifically colonial hierarchies: to whom would the Spanish Crown pay more attention? (However, this assessment seems to have varied from place to place; while no Nahua were presented as witnesses in Santiago, San Salvador, or Valladolid, Honduras, in Gracias a Dios, Honduras, they both outnumbered and preceded the Spaniards.) An important and perhaps surprising shift occurs, however, with the 1573 interrogation. Only nine witnesses were questioned as opposed to twenty-nine in 1564, and these same nine were questioned again with the same interrogation for each Nahua settlement represented in the petition so that their testimony was reaffirmed several times over. As well, the imbalance between Spanish and indigenous witnesses was practically erased, in both rank and number. Alongside the aforementioned Spaniards appear four caciques from Ciudad Vieja, all original conquistadors now approaching or in their seventies: Don Antonio Caynos from Tlaxcala, Diego Elías from Coyoacan, Diego de Galicia from Cholula, and Juan Pérez Tlapaltecatl from the Chinampa town of Huitzilopochco.[61] These were not foot soldiers or latecomers, as were many of the Nahua witnesses in 1564. Instead, they were leading members of the most important allied colony in Central America, captains, and original conquistadors.

The tone of the interrogation in 1573 changed along with the witnesses. Consistently throughout the years, the indigenous conquistadors and their representatives had emphasized their difference from the rest of the native population in Central America, especially from those who had been slaves of the Spaniards. While in their letter of 1547 the "Mexicanos and Tlascaltecas" of Ciudad Vieja had complained that the Spaniards treated them "not as sons but made us their slaves and tributaries," in 1564 no such admission was made. Instead, the allies said that before Landecho they had never paid any kind of tribute, had always lived as free persons in the manner of Spaniards, and had received nothing for their service to the Crown, for which reason they and their descendants remained penniless and stranded in Central America. The 1564 interrogation in support of these

claims consisted of twenty questions that focused on the indigenous conquistadors' specific contribution to the conquest, rhetorically tracing their
route from Mexico to Guatemala, El Salvador, and Honduras. Witnesses
were asked to describe the auxiliaries' actions: their recruitment of armies,
abandonment of families, and specific types of service as soldiers and allies.
The questions assumed a parity between the indigenous conquistadors
and their Spanish allies, using formulas similar to those of the probanzas
of the Spanish conquistadors seeking recompense in the sixteenth century
for their services in the conquest.

Eight years later, the interrogation's focus shifted from the Nahua's and
others' actions in war to their individual and communal qualities: as nobility, as conquistadors and allies, and as nonslaves. Twenty questions were
pared down to seven, which more forcefully asserted the native allies'
equality with Spaniards that had been assumed in the previous interrogation. Question 2, for instance, sought to establish that the indigenous
conquistadors had never paid tribute or been obligated "like other Indians"
to personal service but had always been treated like "Spanish vassals."
Questions 3 and 4 linked the native warriors with their Spanish counterparts by noting the similarity between Spanish and native laws that
exempted nobility and conquistadors from tribute and labor obligations.
Other questions emphasized the unity and purity of the native allies and
their descendants as cohesive communities. While in 1564 only the names
of the most prominent Nahua captains were specified in the interrogation, in 1573 over 150 individual Tlaxcalteca, "Mexicano," Cholulteca, and
Zapoteca conquistadors and their sons from Ciudad Vieja and other communities were listed by name. Each of them, the interrogation claimed, was
a conquistador or "legitimate son" of a conquistador by the terms of pre-
columbian law and the law of the Catholic Church.

This shift in tone between the two sets of interrogations can be attributed in part to the response against the allies' petition presented by the
royal fiscal, Joan de Arguyo, to Briceño in November 1564. In it, Arguyo
had sidestepped the issue of the indigenous conquistadors' worthiness by
denying that the petitioners were conquistadors at all. Labeling them "los
yndios çapotecas guatilmaltecas," he pointedly avoided associating the
petitioners with the more prestigious labels "Tlascalteca" or "Mexicano."
He charged that, in fact, the conquistadors living in Ciudad Vieja were very
few in number, having been infiltrated by a great many "yndios forasteros"
(nonlocal Indian workers) from the conquered provinces. The original

Indian conquistadors, according to Arguyo, had already been rewarded with land that had since been appropriated by these imposters, who he charged were often earning more money off their lands than some Spanish conquistadors and encomenderos. When given another chance to present their case, then, the indigenous conquistadors in 1573 devised a new set of questions that directly challenged Arguyo's claims.

But the actions and arguments recorded in the second petition of 1573 also suggest a new level of urgency on the part of the indigenous conquistadors from Mexico that is underlaid with incredulity and even desperation. In 1564 the petition was presented by Oñate and Tapia alone; in 1573 nine *principales* of Ciudad Vieja accompanied them to Santiago's municipal building to submit the second set of interrogations. They had added Francisco de la Cueva as a witness, who along with the other Spanish witnesses emphasized how different the Nahua and other non-Maya conquistadors had always been and continued to be from the rest of the Indian population in Guatemala. The four Nahua witnesses from Ciudad Vieja in the 1573 interrogation, whose testimony is long and detailed and goes well beyond the scope of the particular questions asked, hearkened back not only to their service in the conquest but to the status that brought them to Guatemala in the first place. They were all "warriors," "nobles," and "lords" who had been carefully selected to participate in the conquest on the basis of their identities as warriors and nobility.[62] As conquistadors by their own, indigenous definitions, the Nahua and other non-Maya allies were, according to Diego de Galicia of Cholula, more intelligent and capable ("más curiosa y abil") than the conquered Central Americans and were recognized and respected as such by them. As had been the case in pre-columbian times, said these witnesses from Ciudad Vieja, they and all their brethren expected that they and their children would continue to enjoy the benefits of their high social rank in their adopted homeland.

In the end, the indigenous conquistadors' expectations in Central America were only partially met. The legal case presented in Justicia 291 was finally resolved in September 1639, apparently with a decree that the allies and their direct descendants pay only a fixed and reduced amount of monetary tribute and be exempt from all personal service.[63] Despite its limitations, this was an important victory, for the indigenous conquistadors' position in colonial society continued to be challenged by those in the Spanish colonial administration who saw them only as Indians. Repeatedly, the native allies living in Ciudad Vieja and throughout Central America referred to this sixteenth-century campaign for privileges when defending their town lands from encroachment, arguing with collectors over tribute payments, or refusing to build roads or clean hospitals. Those who could demonstrate their descent from the original indigenous conquistadors from central and southern Mexico benefited for nearly two centuries from not having to provide the chickens, maize, beans, and other goods to the Spaniards that were regularly extracted from their Maya neighbors.[64] And the formal privileges granted them by the Spanish Crown also bolstered the Nahua and other allies' reputation as different from, and superior to, the Maya among a significant sector of Guatemalan creole elites.

In Ciudad Vieja, the case was remembered and revered, not only as a legal argument, but as a precious object whose physical attributes bespoke its importance. In 1799 the officials of Ciudad Vieja described the copy of the sixteenth-century proceedings in their possession, "authorized by Juan Martínez de Ferrán, Secretario de Cámara and registered by Juan de Alceda Teniente del Gran Chanciller, whose testimony is authorized in good form on parchment, in fine lettering, framed as if by a printing press, covered in crimson velvet with silver cornerpieces, with the image of María Santíssima on front, and of the royal arms." In the mid-nineteenth century it seems that this same book was still being preserved and valued long after its legal usefulness had passed. Although tribute had been abolished after independence, the leaders of Ciudad Vieja proudly showed a book to the Guatemalan archbishop, economist, and historian Francisco de Paula García Peláez, who described it as dating from November 1564. The book, which according to García Peláez contained a royal provision from November 6, 1564, exempting the descendants of the Mexican conquistadors from tribute, consisted of "parchment papers finely bound in book form, and covered in crimson velvet with silver guards on the outside, the coat of arms in the middle, and corresponding latches . . . with loose overleafs of doubled mother-of-pearl taffeta, which are still carefully preserved." In his own afterthought, García Peláez added, "A dignified monument to their antiquity!"[65]

Less jubilantly, the Nahua, Zapoteca, and Mixteca conquistadors' sixteenth-century campaign for privileges served as a bitter education in what they could expect from their Spanish allies in the new colonial order and the ways they would be required to act in order to preserve their distinction. The themes that dominated their petition for tribute exemption— whom they married, whether outsiders were diluting their community's purity, how Spanish they appeared and acted—would return again and again, for three hundred years, as measuring sticks of their difference from the conquered Central American populations. Without this difference, their privileges could be revoked. The thousands of indigenous allies from Mexico who invaded and settled in Central America in the sixteenth century became simultaneously Indians and conquistadors, their deeds largely forgotten by European chroniclers and undermined by their own colonial subjection.

NOTES

I thank Michel Oudijk, Florine Asselbergs, Robinson Herrera, Christopher Lutz, Nancy Farriss, Yanna Yannakakis, and the anonymous reviewers for the University of Oklahoma Press, as well as Leon Fink, James Grossman, Sara Austin, Massimo Scalabrini, Lisa Voight, Anthony Pollock, Mark Elliott, James Epstein, Matt Cohen, Ethan Shagan, Bruce Calder, and the Fellows Seminar participants at the Newberry Library, Chicago, for comments on earlier versions of this chapter. Research and writing was funded by the U.S. Department of Education, the Research Center for the Study of Man, New York, and the Newberry Library, Chicago.

1. For Spaniards in sixteenth-century Guatemala, "Mexicano" most often indicated anyone who spoke Nahuatl as their native tongue. The Spanish did, however, occasionally recognize the ethnic distinctions that native Mesoamericans made between altepetl, most notably and consistently in the case of the Tlaxcalteca but also, here, for the Cholulteca. The term "Mexicano" was thus very similar to the modern scholarly term adopted throughout this volume, "Nahua," which refers generally to native speakers of Nahuatl from central Mexico but does not necessarily imply a shared Nahua ethnic identification across altepetl lines. The real and perceived divisions between Tlaxcalteca and all other Nahua, or Mexicanos, in Guatemala persisted throughout the colonial period.

2. See Sherman, "Tlaxcalans"; Fowler, *Cultural Evolution*; Escalante Arce, *Los tlaxcaltecas*; Martínez Baracs, "Colonizaciones tlaxcaltecas"; Martínez Baracs and Sempat Assadourian, *Tlaxcala*, 512–26.

3. Interestingly, the Mixteca are not represented in the indigenous testimonies of Justicia 291 nor is their presence noted in the Oaxacan barrio named Teguantepeque in Ciudad Vieja, although their participation in the invasion of Maya territory is noted in Justicia 291's interrogation and confirmed by at least one Nahua witness. At least some Mixteca settled separately from other indios conquistadores from Mexico in the Valley of Guatemala. See Archivo General de Indias, Seville (hereafter, AGI), Justicia 291, 1, f 251v., testimony of Juan Perez Tlapaltecatl; Lutz, *Santiago de Guatemala*, 28, 274n67, 275n79.

4. See Voorhies, *Ancient Trade and Tribute*; Gasco, "Polities of Xoconochco."

5. Otzoy C., *Memorial de Solalá*, 183; Recinos, *Cronicas indígenas*, 84.

6. Navarrete, "Elementos arqueológicos, 347–48.

7. AGI Justicia 291, 1, ff. 174–174v, testimony of Alonso López.

8. AGI Justicia 291, 1, ff. 68r, testimony of Nicolao Lopez de Ybarraga; ff. 144v–48, testimony of Francisco de Oçelote; f. 156, testimony of Cristóbal de Campos; ff. 3v–5v (section 2), esp. testimonies of Juan de Aragón, Nicolao López, and Juan Gómez.

9. AGI Justicia 291, 1, f. 144, testimony of Manuel Hernández; f. 7r (section 2), testimony of Antonio de España.

10. AGI Justicia 291, 1, f. 178r, testimony of Joan Montejo.

11. AGI Justicia 291, 1, f. 181r, testimony of Pedro de la Lona; see also f. 170, testimony of Francisco Oçelote.

12. Díaz del Castillo, *Historia verdadera*, ed. Sáenz de Santa María, 456–57.

13. Cortés, *Letters from Mexico*, 317.

14. AGI Justicia 291, 1, f. 171.

15. AGI Guatemala 52, "Carta de los yndios Tlaxcalteca y mexicanos al Rey sobre ser maltratados" (1547).

16. "Probanzas de méritos," 147.

17. AGI Justicia 291, 1, ff. 43–46, testimony of Gonzalo Ortiz.

18. Alvarado, *Account of the Conquest*; Recinos, *Pedro de Alvarado*, 85, 89. There is some debate surrounding the Kaqchikel's early alliance with Alvarado. Adrián Recinos and Dionisio José Chonay translate the *Memorial de Sololá* to say that two thousand Kaqchikel warriors participated in the defeat of the K'iche', with no mention of dissent. A more recent translation by Simón Otzoy, however, gives this number as two hundred, followed by "But only those men of the city went, as most warriors refused to obey their lords." See Otzoy, *Memorial de Sololá*, 186. Alvarado, in his second letter to Cortés (April 11, 1524), said that four thousand Kaqchikel warriors joined him. See Escalante Arce, *Cartas de relación*, 23. Ixtlilxochitl, in his *Compendio histórico del reino de Texcoco* (1608), agrees, claiming that the Mexican and Texcocan captains were the ones who went to the "Guatemalans" (the colonial name for the Kaqchikeles, derived from the Nahuatl name for the city-state of Iximche', Quauhtemallan) to request their aid, and received four thousand more fighters. See Ixtlilxochitl, *Obras históricas*, 1:488.

19. AGI Justicia 291, 1, ff. 64–67, testimony of Juan de Aragón; ff. 67–71, testimony of Nicolao López de Ybarraga; ff. 249–51, testimony of Don Antonio de Caynos.

20. Ixtlilxochitl, *Obras históricas*, 1:490–91.

21. AGI Patronato 60-6, "Probanzas de Don Francisco de la Cueva y Doña Leonor de Alvarado sobre los servicios de sus antepasados hechos a su magestad" (1556); Kramer, *Encomienda Politics*, 39–40.

22. AGI Justicia 291, 1, f. 88v. Cihuacoatl is the lineage name of the Mexica warrior and second-in-command Tlacaelel Cihuacoatl, whose lineage it appears had strong connections with the Triple Alliance's military garrison in Xoconosco. See Gasco, "Polities of Xoconochco."

23. AGI Justicia 291, 1, ff. 11–11v (section 2). See also, e.g., García Peláez, *Memorias*, 1:66–67 ("En esta sazón había sido lanzado Diego de Alvarado de

Sacatepequez, con algunos castellanos y tlascaltecas que componían la guarnición, quedando prisionero uno de los primeros y dos de los segundos, que fueron sacrificados a los ídolos.")

24. "Probanza de méritos," 146; Kramer, *Encomienda Politics*, 67.

25. AGI Justicia 291, 1, ff. 153v; 154v; 155r; 187r; 255v.

26. AGI Justicia 291, 1, f. 253v, testimony of Diego Elías, "natural que dixo ser de la ciudad de mexico y vezino de ciudad vieja"; 255r, testimony of Diego de Galicia, "yndio natural de cholula y morador y rresidente en la ciudad vieja de almolonga."

27. AGI Justicia 291, 1, f. 55v. See also Asselbergs, chapter 2 in this volume.

28. AGI Justicia 291, 1, f. 69.

29. AGI Guatemala 44-18, "Carta del cabildo secular de Gracias a Dios al rey" (1536); AGI Guatemala 39-11, "Carta de Andrés de Cereceda al rey" (1536); AGI Justicia 291, 1, ff. 110–15, testimony of Joan de Cabrera, and f. 10v (section 2), testimony of Alvaro de Paz.

30. AGI Guatemala 9-105, "Carta del adelantado Montejo al rey sobre la pacificación de la provincia de Honduras" (1539).

31. AGI Justicia 291, 1, ff. 113–15v, 244r.

32. Recinos, *Pedro de Alvarado*, 190–92.

33. AGI Justicia 291, 1, ff. 170–80, testimonies of Francisco de Oçelote and Joan Montejo.

34. Ixtlilxochitl, *Obras históricas*, 1:487. Alvarado claimed that there were five to six thousand auxiliaries with him in total in Acajutla, some of whom certainly must have been Maya rather than Nahua. See Alvarado, *Account of the Conquest*, 80.

35. Similar numbers are reported for individual expeditions in Central America, e.g., that of Juan de Chaves in Honduras, in which he allegedly commanded sixty Spaniards and two thousand native auxiliaries, in AGI Patronato 58-3, "Gonzalo de Chaves Alvarado . . . solicita en gratificación de lo que ha servido se le encomienden en Guatemala algunos indios" (1542–72), f. 21.

36. AGI Guatemala 52.

37. Pérez-Rocha and Tena, *La nobleza indígena*, 281.

38. AGI Justicia 291, 1, ff. 171, 239.

39. Kramer, *Encomienda Politics*, 41, 54; AGI Patronato 62-1 (3), "Antonio Núñez, casado con Leonor de Illescas, hija de Hernando de Illescas, primer conquistador de Nueva España y Guatemala y vecino de Santiago, solicita un repartimiento" (1559–78), f. 1 (section 1) and f. 2 (section 2).

40. AGI Justicia 291, 1, ff. 125–125r, testimony of Bartolomé de Santiponçe; 155v, testimony of Pedro Cerón; 184, testimony of Alonso Polo; 20v–21v (section 2).

41. AGI Justicia 291, 1. For military theatres, see f. 129, testimony of Diego de Mançanares; f. 146v, testimony of Manuel Hernández; and f. 11 (section 2), testimony of Antonio de España. For Mexican casualties, see f. 56, testimony of Diego López de Villanueva. For particular services, see ff. 13–14r (section 2), esp. testimonies of Pedro Gonzáles Nájara, Juan de Aragón, Antonio de España, and Don Pedro Tlacatecute; f. 49v, testimony of Alonso de Loarca; f. 61, testimony of Pedro

de Ovid; ff. 144–46, testimony of Manuel Hernández; f. 177v, testimony of Joan Montejo; ff. 12–13r (section 2), testimony of Don Marcos Çiguacoatl, Don Pedro Tlacatecute, and Antonio de España; f. 69v, testimony of Nicolao López de Ybarraga.

42. AGI Justicia 296, "Segundo legajo de la Residencia del expresado Adelantado Don Pedro de Alvarado" (1537–39), f 80v and 87, testimony of Luys de Vivar; also AGI Justicia 291, 1, ff. 152–152v, testimony of Pedro Cerón; ff. 246v–49, testimony of Diego Lopez de Villanueva.

43. AGI Guatemala 168, "Carta de Fray Francisco de la Parra al Rey Carlos V" (1549); Remesal, *Historia general*, 175:99. See also Sherman, "Tlaxcalans," 133–35.

44. Archivo General de Centro América, Guatemala City (hereafter, AGCA), A1.23, leg. 4575/f. 9, "No es aceptado el plan sobre dar en repartimiento a los indígenas Tlascaltecas y Mexicanos, asentados en las afueras de la ciudad" (1532); AGI Justicia 291, 1, f. 198.

45. Kramer, *Encomienda Politics*, 217–20.

46. AGCA A1.23, leg. 4575/f. 9, "No es aceptado el plan sobre dar en repartimiento a los indígenas Tlascaltecas y Mexicanos, asentados en las afueras de la ciudad" (1532).

47. Las Casas, *Obras escogidas*, 5:190, "Memorial de Fray Bartolome de las Casas y Fray Rodrigo de Andrada al Rey" (1543).

48. There were several leaders of Tlaxcala at the time to whom Francisco might have been related, including Aexotecatl Quetzalpopocatzin, one of the four principal leaders of Tlaxcala and brother of Lorenzo Maxixcatzin, the grandson of the last prehispanic ruler of Ocotelulco, Tlaxcala. In his testimony for Antonio Núñez, Francisco (now known as Francisco de Oñate) mentioned his father, Cristóbal Axotecatl, and noted also that he had come to Guatemala as part of the six-hundred-strong Tlaxcalteca contingent brought to Guatemala by Hernando de Yllescas and Jorge de Alvarado.

49. AGI Guatemala 52.

50. AGI Justicia 291, 1, f. 198.

51. AGI Patronato 231, R.4, "Información de Gregorio López" (1543), cited in Sherman, "Tlaxcalans," 128.

52. AGI Guatemala 41, R.4, "Carta de los consejos de las ciudades de Guatemala y Ciudad Real, y de las villas de San Salvador y San Miguel al Rey," (1539), ff. 3–3v; AGCA A1.23, leg. 4575/f. 118v, "Para que la Audiencia resuelve sobre la cancelación de tributos por parte de los yndios que auxiliaron a la conquista" (1552); AGI Guatemala 44-21, "El cabildo de Gracias a Dios dictan las siguientes ordenanzas" (1560). On limpieza de sangre and its relationship to notions of vagabondage in early colonial Spanish America, see Martínez, "Limpieza de sangre."

53. AGI Justicia 300, "Residencia de Francisco de Montejo" (1544), testimony of Hernán Sánchez de Alvarado, qtd. in Sherman, "Tlaxcalans," 135n21.

54. AGI Justicia 322, "Visita que el Licenciado Francisco Briceño visitador, juez de Residencia, y Governador de la Provincia de Guathimala, tomó al Presidente, oydores, y demas oficiales de la Audiencia de Guathimala" (1563), ff. 28v–29, f. 347, question 14, and f. 347, question 15; AGI Guatemala 111-9, "Memorial que presenta

la ciudad de Santiago de Guatemala al Consejo de Indias, sobre los excesos de los oidores de la Audiencia" (1556), f. 2.

55. See Sherman, *Forced Native Labor*, 196, 214.

56. Sixteenth-century Spanish notation counted single, two-sided pages as folios, each with a front called the recto (r) and a back, the verso (v). Thus Justicia 291, 1, which contains 423 folios in two parts, has approximately 846 pages. I thank Deanna Matthew for reproducing Justicia 291 from microfilm to paper and Christopher Lutz and Michel Oudijk for generously sharing their own transcriptions of Justicia 291 with me.

57. In 1572 Juan de la Peña was a lawyer for the Council of the Indies and resident, it appears, in Madrid; see Falla, *Extractos*, 1:159, "Juan de Rojas, vecino, otorgó poder a su hermano Graviel de Rojas."

58. AGCA A1.23, leg. 4575/fol. 361 (1573), "Que los indígenas de México goçen de algunas merçedes."

59. Sherman, *Forced Native Labor*, 195.

60. "Para que si quisiere enbiar persona que se halle presente juara y conoser de los testigos que por parte de los dhos yndios mexicanos fuere preguntados en el pleyto con el dho fiscal tratan en las probanças que pretenden hazer asi en la cibdad de mexico como en la cibdad de santiago de guatimala como en otras qualesquier [356v] partes y lugares." AGI Justicia 291, 1, ff. 356–356v.

61. Juan Pérez's last name is variously spelled in the document as "Tlapaltecatl," "Tlapalteca," and "Tlaxcaltecatl." His birthplace is always listed as "Mexico," with one mention of the town "Huitzilipulco," which most likely refers to Huitzilopochco outside Coyoacan.

62. In Spanish, "gente de guerra, nobles y principales."

63. I have not yet been able to locate the cédula from 1639, but later documentation indicates that by that date the Mexicano residents of Ciudad Vieja and elsewhere were paying a significantly reduced amount of tribute. See e.g. AGCA A3.16, leg. 825/exp.15225 (1638), "Don Pablo Guzmán de Petapa pide exoneración de tributo"; AGCA A3.16, leg. 1587/exp. 10231/fol. 156 (1730), "Se exonere a los indígenas del barrio de los Mexicanos de Sonsonate"; AGCA A3.16, leg. 235/exp. 4668 (1735), "Razón de los tributos que deben pagar los 75 pueblos barrios etc. del valle de Guatemala"; and AGCA A1.12, leg. 154/exp. 3073 (1799), "Los justicias y principales del pueblo de Almolonga sobre no trabajar en el Hospitál de San Juan."

64. See Matthew, "Neither and Both."

65. García Peláez, *Memorias*, 156–57.

CHAPTER FOUR

CONCUBINES AND WIVES

Reinterpreting Native-Spanish Intimate Unions in Sixteenth-Century Guatemala

ROBINSON A. HERRERA

In 1579 the Audiencia de Guatemala (regional high court) authorized a small *ayuda de costos* (official subvention) for one Doña Luisa, identified as a native "of the city of New Spain who was one of the princesses that came to these provinces with the Spaniards that conquered and pacified them."[1] The Audiencia further justified economic aid with an allusion to Doña Luisa having "many grandchildren among them some Spaniards and important people."[2] Doña Luisa's successful petition for a subvention raises crucial questions about the role of native women in the Spanish conquest of Guatemala and the prestigious position that they came to occupy in colonial society. The references to her participation in the conquest and the phrase "some Spaniards" argue for close links between Doña Luisa and the Spaniards who came to Guatemala in the early sixteenth century. Far from a singular case, other indigenous women besides Doña Luisa also traveled with the Spanish conquest expeditions. As intermediaries they contributed to the mixed culture that would become synonymous with colonial rule. Unions with native noblewomen served to consolidate alliances between Spaniards and indigenous groups that once conquered became allies or with groups that sought to avert violence by entering into strategic relations with the newcomers. At times unions with native noblewomen facilitated the collection of tribute from *encomiendas*. Nonnoble native women also entered into intimate relations with Spaniards and other Europeans. Thus, whether in the military phase or in the tense early society that followed, native women fulfilled important roles within the colonial order. The *mestizo* children of intimate native-Spanish unions occupied positions that ran the gamut from the elite to the humble, depending on the status of their parents.[3]

Woefully, a general paucity of sources has hampered research on sixteenth-century native-Spanish intimate unions in early colonial Guatemala. Rather than a rich corpus of archival materials from which to recreate the lives of indigenous women in early Spanish society, historians must comb through hundreds of folios of notarial and judicial documents in search of elusive clues to weave the critical episode of sixteenth-century Guatemalan history. Indeed, such unions seldom received particular attention from the chroniclers who took pains to discuss notable events. Early histories of Guatemala hardly deem native-Spanish unions so unusual or meritorious of comment to warrant special treatment in the narratives. Only the most exceptional of native-Spanish unions, those involving celebrated conquerors or prominent *cacicas* (Arawak: indigenous noblewomen), appear in the formal historical narratives, and then only briefly, without significant commentary on the existence of their relationships. Data teased from archival sources yield information on both lesser-known and famous native-Spanish intimate unions. When compared with other areas of Spanish America, trends and patterns emerge on the importance of native-Spanish unions.

This essay discusses the creation of alliances between Spaniards and natives, the impact of those confederations on conquest expeditions bound for Central America, and the consolidation of the alliances through intimate unions between native women and high-ranking Spaniards created through the gifting of women to conquerors. It traces notable native noblewomen from central Mexico and Guatemala; the former established intimate relations with Spaniards and accompanied the conquest expeditions. Additionally, I also address female native commoners who had formal marriages and intimate unions with Spaniards and Europeans. To flesh out the lives of the individuals discussed, wherever possible information on their mestizo children will receive attention. Additionally, the attempt by some children of native-Spanish unions to distance themselves from their indigenous mothers is also discussed.

NATIVE NOBLEWOMEN IN MESOAMERICA

Instead of the fabulous and readily exploitable wealth of which they dreamed, the members of the Spanish conquest expedition to Guatemala captained by Pedro de Alvarado encountered resilient natives committed to putting up fierce resistance in defense of their homelands.[4] Here the indigenous noblewomen that accompanied Spaniards proved indispensable in safeguarding alliances. After the period of initial brutal subjugation, colonial institutions based on indigenous mechanisms sprang forth, and these in turn made possible the growth of Spanish Guatemala. Institutions such as the encomienda provided the basis of riches for the colonial elites who held sway with economic and political power. In some cases native noblewomen served as essential links between Spaniards and the tribute paying indigenous peoples that served as a crucial pillar of the colonial economy. Yet the paucity of mineral wealth contributed to keeping Guatemala's Spanish population relatively low. Even late into the sixteenth century that population numbered somewhere around five hundred *vecinos*.[5] Yet despite its size the capital, Santiago de Guatemala, remained the largest Central American city throughout the colonial period.

Guatemala's relatively poor economic situation did little to attract large numbers of Spaniards, especially Spanish women. Guatemala lacked enough suitably successful marriage partners to entice a significant number of Spanish women. Their scarcity, to use an economic term, made Spanish women highly sought after marital partners. As a result only the small group of better placed individuals, such as *encomenderos* or moneyed merchants, married women of Spanish ethnicity.[6] Fewer still could hope to marry Spanish women with pretensions to the lesser nobility, such as those who bore the honorific title "doña." Consequently, long-term unions with non-Spanish women were more commonplace. The majority of non-Spanish women tended to be of indigenous descent, although some presumably were also of African descent.[7]

Native noblewomen, especially those tied to powerful indigenous polities, made the most attractive partners after Spanish women. Later, with the growth of the mestizo population, native noblewomen lost their importance as partners to Spaniards. Yet, in the first decades of the colony, even native women of lower rank proved attractive as intimate partners, especially to humble Europeans who lived on the fringes of the colonial economy. Overall, unions between native women and European men tended to the informal. Rarely, and only in the very early years of the colony, did successful Spaniards like encomenderos actually marry native women.[8] Almost exclusively the wives in these marriages hailed from the native nobility.

While it proves nearly impossible to determine exact individual motivations, some Spaniards living in Guatemala likely consciously sought out formalized relationships with cacicas in order to access the wealth possessed by them.[9] Despite changes brought on by colonialism, cacicas continued to hold positions of authority and power within their communities.[10] They used their relations with indigenous women as a wedge into the native world, an often profitable area with a high demand for imported goods. On the other hand, native women of nonnoble lineage who had almost no likelihood of forming unions with Spanish men sanctioned formally by church ceremonies also stood to benefit. Their relations with Europeans likely garnered indigenous women higher status within their own communities because of the important roles of translators and cultural mediators that they played. As Clara Sue Kidwell writes, "Indian women were the first important mediators of meaning between the cultures of the two worlds."[11]

The sources suggest that the very success of Spanish conquest expeditions to Guatemala hinged on the ability to form links with native groups so as to elicit cooperation, essentials such as food, and in the best of cases male warriors to bolster the otherwise small number of European combatants.[12] Indeed, the group captained by Alvarado supposedly consisted of about 420 cavalry and footmen.[13] That small force could not have succeeded without the help of central Mexican native auxiliaries who perhaps totaled into the thousands. While the exact numbers of central Mexican allies remain vague, they unquestionably provided an essential service as combatants in Central America.[14] They also lent invaluable service as support personnel who took on duties such as maintaining camp. Such tasks would have otherwise fallen to Spaniards and prevented them from taking more strategic and pressing positions.

Unions with high-ranking native women, often the daughters of powerful native lords from central Mexico, served as one of the best ways to consolidate the indispensable alliances that provided highly prized interpreters, combatants, and other auxiliaries for Spanish conquest expeditions to Central America.[15] Without the presence of native noblewomen to safeguard fragile alliances, the result of Spanish expeditions to Guatemala might have turned out differently. Conquest unquestionably would have been achieved but perhaps at a far higher cost in terms of money and Spanish lives. The most notable example of this practice is undoubtedly the celebrated and much maligned Malintzin, also known as Doña Marina and Malinche.[16] One of the twenty women presented to Hernando Cortés, the leader of the conquest group that eventually subdued the natives of central Mexico, Doña Marina proved invaluable as an interpreter and advisor.[17] Guatemala does not have any examples nearly as well known, but Spaniards who traveled there nonetheless relied on the mechanism of taking on local indigenous wives, or more often concubines, either to consolidate alliances with natives or to access native sources of wealth. In this regard they acted much like Spaniards elsewhere in the newly formed colonies.[18]

From the native perspective, the practice of gifting women led to closer ties with the new dominant group. While natives themselves gained from these alliances, Spaniards in turn also benefited from closer links with natives. As Steve J. Stern has noted for Peru, "ambitious Indians sought Spanish benefactors or allies for protection or advancement; Spanish individuals and power groups, in turn, enhanced their authority and economic potential by cultivating a clientele of Indian allies and functionaries."[19] Given the similarities of the situations in Peru and Guatemala, it seems logical that the same attitudes prevailed in both areas. Thus the benefits that accrued from alliances profited both natives and Spaniards.

NATIVE NOBLEWOMEN AND GUATEMALA

Alliances formed in the indigenous central Mexican ethnic state of Tlaxcala proved invaluable to Spaniards in their later subjugation of native groups in Guatemala. Quite remarkably, the Tlaxcalteca lords used at least five young noblewomen as a means to close ranks with Spaniards. The recipients of these "gifts" included several of Cortés's top lieutenants such as Pedro de Alvarado and Cristóbal de Olid, the eventual leaders of the Spanish campaigns in Guatemala and Honduras, respectively.[20] Alvarado's brother Jorge de Alvarado met and married an indigenous noblewoman before his marriage to a Spanish woman in 1527.[21] Indeed, the brothers entered into unions with the sisters Doña Luisa and Doña Lucía Xicotencatl.[22] As daughters of the Tlaxcalan *tlatoani* (ruler) Xicotencatl, known also by his Spanish name of Don Lorenzo de Vargas, they ranked among the highest nobility in their particular sociopolitical unit.[23] While it is true that Xicotencatl had at least ninety wives and a likely multitude of children, Doña Luisa still commanded a great deal of respect among Tlaxcalteca.[24] The chronicler Bernal Díaz del Castillo states that "all of the larger part of Tlaxacala obeyed her and gave her gifts and they had her for their mistress."[25] The use of the honorific prefix "doña" also denotes the importance of the Xicotencatl sisters in the new situation brought on by the Spanish intrusion.[26]

Most accounts written soon after the presentation of native women in central Mexico are brief. They describe how the leading nobles gave daughters to Cortés. Few accounts are as detailed or as comprehensive as Díaz del Castillo's chronicles.[27] He describes the exchange in the following words:

> and it seems that they had concerted among all the *caciques* to give us their daughters and nieces, the most beautiful that they had, they were maidens in waiting, and said the elder Xicotenga [Xicotencatl]: "Malinche [Cortés], so that you may more clearly know the good we want for you, and we wish to placate you in everything, we want to give you our daughters so that they may be your women and that you bear fruit, because we want to have you as brothers, because you are so good and robust. I have a very beautiful daughter, she has not been married, and I want her for you." And likewise Mas-Escasi [Maxixcatzin] and all the other caciques said they would bring their daughters so we would receive them as women, and they made many offers.[28]

Díaz del Castillo depicts the events as codified public spectacles that required ritualized actions within a solemn performance that mandated the use of women as gifts to conquerors. Intimately aware of their own rituals of possession, Spaniards were willing actors in the indigenous rituals that reified and consolidated their power as conquerors.[29] The ritual of accepting native women as concubines also bound Spaniards and indigenous groups into a reciprocal relationship that required allegiance and service; the former would receive tribute while the latter, depending on the situation, would suspend or avoid bellicose actions against the new ally.

Despite their tenuous position as courtesans, native noblewomen like the Xicotencatl siblings had greater ties with the new colonial order than they did with the precolonial world from which they originated. Yet this in no way meant that native women ceased to enjoy status within their native communities. To be sure, they maintained their noble status that separated them from the majority of natives, and used this status to negotiate positions within the new colonial situation.[30] As a result of connections with the new dominant group, their status increased within their own societies. Additionally, native women living among Spaniards, in particular those involved in intimate unions, served as crucial bridges between the indigenous and Spanish spheres.[31] Their ability to move from one context to another allowed them to function as two-way conduits of cultural elements.

In central Mexico the native noblewomen presented to Spaniards seemed to have formed a coterie that fostered at least some connections with one another. The cacica Doña Luisa Xicotencatl traveled for some time with Doña Marina.[32] Women like Doña Luisa and Doña Marina were so essential to Spanish plans that steps were taken to ensure their safety. The fact that the two escaped death at the battle of La Noche Triste, a Spanish defeat in Mexico-Tenochtitlan for all intents and purposes, while the children of other high ranking native allies perished alludes to the care taken to protect them from harm.[33] Doña Marina's prominence lay with her abilities as translator and diplomat, and Doña Luisa's as the crucial link with the Tlaxcalteca auxiliaries who eventually proved essential to the Spanish victories in central Mexico, Guatemala, and elsewhere.

Doubtless an arduous journey, traveling to Central America took a heavy toll in terms of physical comforts and health. Doña Luisa suffered the further ignominy of giving birth to a daughter, Doña Leonor de Alvarado, in an armed Spanish camp located in hostile territory. Her onerous voyages did not end with the Spanish victory over the native peoples of Guatemala; she accompanied Alvarado wherever his conquest plans took him. Doña Luisa and the couple's young children accompanied Pedro de Alvarado even on his failed voyage to Peru.[34] As an essential element binding Spaniards and Tlaxcalteca, Doña Luisa's presence was imperative. Without her presence the indigenous auxiliaries could have abandoned the battle as they had precious little incentive to continue fighting so far from home. Much more than a mere concubine, I argue that without her presence the loyalty of the native combatants and camp aides would have diminished as Doña Luisa embodied the alliance between Spaniards and the Tlaxcalteca auxiliaries along with the traditional authority of her father the tlatoani Xicotencatl.

Doña Luisa was far from alone in having to accompany the Spaniards on their conquest expeditions. Other cacicas were taken along to serve the same purpose of consolidating alliances. In fact, Doña Luisa's sister Doña Lucía also accompanied the first large-scale Spanish expedition to Guatemala. Unfortunately, little information exists on Doña Lucía; even details of her journey to Guatemala remain sketchy. Despite the relative dearth of information, it seems that Doña Lucía Xicotencatl likely died before 1527.[35]

While the children of the Alvarado-Xicotencatl unions entered into the elite of early Guatemala, details of their lives remain vague.[36] After the death of her father Pedro de Alvarado, Doña Leonor, the daughter of Luisa Xicotencatl, was left a wealthy encomendera and an extremely influential person in local society, largely because Alvarado left no other heirs besides his mestizo children.[37] She married the shrewd Don Francisco de la Cueva. Apparently Don Francisco did not let the fact that his cousin Doña Beatriz de la Cueva had been married to Pedro de Alvarado prevent his marriage to Doña Leonor.[38] The marriage made Don Francisco fabulously wealthy as he gained access to Doña Leonor's rich encomiendas.[39] Even less is known of Alvarado's two mestizo sons, Don Diego and Don Pedro. After Pedro de Alvarado's death the two lost any influence they may have had. Don Diego died either in Spain or on his way there, and Don Pedro was murdered on a roadside by natives in Peru, where he had traveled to seek his fortunes once his mixed ethnicity became an issue.[40] It was truly an inglorious end for the scion of the once formidable Alvarado-Xicotencatl union.

The use of women to consolidate alliances, while practiced among the Tlaxcalteca and diverse groups such as the Guaraní in Paraguay, did not occur in the same structured manner among the natives of early Guatemala as it did in central Mexico, at least not where the Spaniards were concerned.[41] During the initial Spanish conquest of Guatemala the Kaqchikel, one of three main indigenous groups located in the highlands of Guatemala, contributed two thousand warriors to the Spanish campaign against their rivals the K'iche'.[42] But they did so without the apparent necessity of having to consolidate the alliance with the gifting of native noblewomen. Indeed, the Kaqchikel, who had once been crucial allies, rose in a fierce revolt against Spanish domination in part as a result of anger at Alvarado's kidnapping of an important native noblewoman in 1524. The traditional interpretation has long held that Alvarado, in love with the beautiful wife of the powerful Kaqchikel cacique named Sinacam, kidnapped Sinacam to gain possession of his spouse.[43] Given Alvarado's central Mexican experience, it seems likelier that he understood the importance of possessing indigenous noblewomen with connections to important native nobles but that he saw little benefit from following Kaqchikel cultural practices. The singular documented example of Alvarado forcefully taking the wife of the Kaqchikel cacique supports the contention that by the time the Spaniards arrived in Guatemala they (the Spaniards) no longer felt it necessary to rely on noblewomen as a means to safeguard the loyalty of indigenous auxiliaries. The presence of the Tlaxcalteca auxiliaries could have offset the need to create binding military ties with native groups in Guatemala through intimate links with daughters of powerful local lords. There also exists the possibility that a hierarchal system immediately took root that placed the Tlaxcalteca above the Guatemalan native groups because of their close association with Spaniards.[44]

More commonly, instead of indigenous noblewomen, local native groups supplied Spaniards with women as laborers. This they did like their counterparts in central Mexico. The Kaqchikel contributed eight hundred men and eight hundred women to labor in Santiago and in some ephemeral gold mines. The corvée labor was given as part of tribute obligations established after the native group had been subdued.[45] Alvarado and his Spanish companions also received tribute in the form of gold.[46]

As time passed, the conquest came to serve as a foundation for elevated status and as justification for royal patronage for natives and Spaniards alike. Participation in conquest expeditions, or even a connection to a participant on the expeditions, made native women part of a small, elite group that diminished in size as the years progressed. Spaniards like Juan de Ecija went before the Audiencia to seek favors not because of services he had rendered but rather because of his marriage to the mestiza daughter of a famous conqueror.[47] Native women acted in much the same manner. They used connections to the conquest to safeguard rewards from colonial institutions. Indeed, rather than unique, Doña Luisa's successful petition to receive a subvention for her services during the conquest was typical of behavior observed elsewhere in Spanish America. Native women in Mexico also used their connection to conquest events in attempts to seek royal rewards.[48]

BEYOND THE CONQUEST

While Doña Luisa and Doña Lucía represent the two best-known examples of native noblewomen who created ties with important Spaniards in

Guatemala, after the period of violent conflict other cacicas also engaged in relations with well-placed Spanish members of the colonial order.[49] Overall it seems that the status and concomitant wealth of indigenous noblewomen increased the possibility of having marriages with Spaniards sanctioned by a church ceremony. Doña María de Molina is representative. As the daughter of the wealthy Don Juan, lord of Xoconosco, a profitable area of intense cacao cultivation, Doña María commanded quite a fortune.[50] Perhaps to create an alliance with the influential Spanish family of Doña Francisca de Molina and her husband, Martín de Guzmán, Don Juan entrusted Doña María to their care at an early age.[51] Placing noble-born daughters in the home of influential Spaniards did not prove unique. Indigenous nobles in other Spanish American areas such as Peru did much the same thing.[52] As part of an influential family, Martín de Guzmán moved among the most powerful local elites. His connections were likely not lost on Don Juan. Likewise, a link to Don Juan granted Guzmán access to the rich cacao fields of Xoconosco. Doña María's position in the Molina-Guzmán household, in her circumstance as a *doncella* (unmarried young woman), served to cement the mutually beneficial relationship. Doña María probably became fluent in the Spanish language and learned Spanish cultural norms during her formative years spent in the Molina-Guzmán household.[53] To safeguard a marriage worthy of his daughter, Don Juan set aside a dowry of three thousand pesos, a formidable sum for anyone but especially an indigenous person in sixteenth-century Guatemala. Additionally Doña María likely continued to receive tribute payments from the commoners in her sociopolitical unit as did noblewomen in early Peru and Mexico.[54] Finding a suitable marriage partner proved essential. To further consolidate their connection to her wealth, the Molina-Guzmán couple arranged a marriage between Doña María and the Spaniard Alonso de Paz in 1548.[55] It seems that at the time of the marriage Paz worked as the mayordomo of Guzmán's estates. As time went on, Alonso de Paz's economic position improved, no doubt as a result of having gained access to Doña María's wealth.[56] Paz's brother, Alvaro de Paz, enjoyed far greater financial success, eventually becoming one of the wealthiest men in Guatemala. Despite the changes in the position of indigenous women in the local Spanish society and the Paz brothers' economic prosperity, Alonso de Paz and Doña Maria remained married for over thirty-six years, separating only when Alonso died.[57] It is noteworthy that Doña María's ethnicity appears only rarely in the documentation. Due to their status, native

women like Doña María who had successfully entered into the Spanish
world escaped the constant ethnic labeling that characterizes mundane
documents, such as land sales, municipal records, and so on. At the same
time Spaniards rarely appear without an ethnic label that helped connote
their status.

Indigenous noblewomen did not always marry Spaniards of distinction, however. After the mid-sixteenth century, once the heyday of essential and strategic native-Spanish alliances had waned and Spaniards had
either brought over their wives or married locally available Spanish or mestiza women, cacicas seeking to marry nonnatives had little likelihood of
finding high-ranking Spanish spouses. Native noblewomen even wed mestizos and non-Spaniards like Portuguese who generally occupied marginal
social positions, though the evidence indicates that what the men lacked
in ethnic prestige they made up for in economic success.[58] In 1569 Doña
Catalina, the daughter of Doña Catalina and Don Juan de Fuentes, indigenous nobles of the cacao-rich region of Escuintla, located in southeast
Guatemala, married the Portuguese Antonio Almeida Botello.[59] Despite
his Portuguese ethnicity, Botello possessed respectable capital. He owned
a sizable cattle ranch in Masagua (a town close to Escuintla). He sold cattle, hides, and cacao and kept close ties to two wealthy, Spanish
encomenderos.[60] Botello was closely linked to Escuintla. The fact that he
became a vecino of the town suggests a high degree of localization on
Botello's part.

NONNOBLE NATIVE WOMEN

Native women commoners also played a crucial role in early Guatemala.
But unlike noblewomen nonnoble indigenous women rarely had formalized and church sanctioned unions with Spaniards. In marriage rare
concubinage seems to have been the normative type of union. The
encomenderos Sancho de Barajona, Sebastián de Mármol, and Diego de
Monroy all had at one time or another maintained unions with native
women.[61] Barajona and his native mistress Magdalena had a daughter
named Isabel de Barajona. And, as in other cases involving mestizo children in early Guatemala, he made sure to arrange a marriage for Isabel
with one of his dependents, the Spaniard Hernando de Castroverde.
Barajona also arranged for Magdalena to marry, although she wed one of
his indigenous dependents. Isabel's death left her husband and her mother

embroiled in a legal suit. Magdalena and her native husband, Juan, successfully won over five hundred pesos from Castroverde.[62] Thus, even after death Isabel's connection to the Spaniard Castroverde served her native relatives well. In some instances, indigenous women used the colonial legal system not only for their own gain but also to influence the raising of their mestizo children. In one case an indigenous woman filed a suit to change the legal guardianship of her mestiza daughter from one Spaniard to another.[63]

While Barajona later married a Spanish woman, Mármol and Monroy did not do so. In fact, the two never married, although it remains unclear whether they continued their relationship with their native concubines. Not even fear of losing their profitable encomiendas sufficed to convince them to wed.[64] In later years their mestizo children, coincidentally wed to each other, stressed that their fathers had been "solteros por que nunca fueron casados en yndias" (single men because they were never married in the Indies).[65] The children specifically avoided naming their mothers, possibly as a way to distance themselves from their indigenous connections. In the records their unnamed mothers receive the generic label of "una yndia soltera" (an unwed Indian woman). The mothers of these mestizos did not hail from indigenous nobility, for if they had, the children would most likely have had greater reason to identify them. The categorization of native women as "yndia soltera" further reinforces the distance that the children of Mármol and Monroy sought to establish. It was not only Spanish encomenderos who were enthusiastic to distance themselves from their native concubines. Even humbler encomenderos such as the Greek Juan Griego followed the same pattern. In his testament Griego describes his relationships with native women and identifies each one with the label of "yndia soltera."[66] Humble native women, unlike members of the indigenous nobility, stood little chance of formalizing their unions through church sanctioned matrimony when involved with encomenderos. Furthermore, their nonnoble lineage led their mestizo children to shroud their names in anonymity for fear of seeing their own prestige tinged by their humble maternal roots.

Unlike elite members of society, humble Spaniards in Santiago married native women as late as the 1570s, but these marriages occurred with lessening frequency. Native women married to humble Spaniards enjoyed the same types of benefits as their noblewomen counterparts. Connections to Spaniards could serve them well especially in times of duress or when under investigation by the local authorities. In 1576 when the natives Juana and her friend Theresa stood accused of bludgeoning a Spaniard to death, Juana's husband, Francisco de Palencia, came to their defense.[67] He argued that the women were "good Christians" and that they had treated the victim with "love and charity." At first a rather modest group of people that included a Spanish carpenter and an African slave testified in Juana and Theresa's defense. A few days later, no doubt due to Palencia's intercession, local grandees testified that the victim suffered from maladies that may well have caused his death. The prestige of the witnesses marshaled in Juana and Theresa's defense apparently spared the women prison. Palencia's actions must be viewed as an attempt to assert his patriarchal prerogative as protector of his and his wife's honor.[68] But that does not change the fact that Juana and Theresa's fate would have been very different without the benefit of Palencia's help, as few things would have been punished with greater severity than the murder of a Spaniard at the hands of two indigenous women. As Sonya Lipsett-Rivera writes, "Members of the elite . . . reacted with fury when they believed their social inferiors had crossed an invisible line."[69]

CONCLUSION

Conquest expeditions to Guatemala depended on the aid of indigenous groups. The assistance provided by central Mexican auxiliaries, although disputed in so far as the actual number of combat reinforcements, proved vital for success. Once established in Guatemala, even after the tentative peace that developed between conqueror and conquered, native auxiliaries continued to play crucial roles.[70] Consequently, establishing and maintaining alliances with native peoples were essential. Native noblewomen from central Mexico excelled in the role of bonding Spaniards to powerful indigenous groups. For no small reason did the Alvarados carefully cultivate their unions with the likes of the noble-born Xicotencatl siblings. Links with local indigenous noblewomen also permitted access to wealth and labor paid them in the form of tribute. Although the Spanish intrusions fundamentally changed many aspects of native economic and social structures, native nobles in Guatemala, at least for most of the sixteenth century, retained their preeminent positions within their communities. As such, the daughters of the local native nobility made for ideal companions, if not outright wives, for middling Spaniards seeking to use these relations as a wedge to gain access to the wealth held by native communities. As the century progressed, marriage with successful Spaniards became less and less a possibility, even for indigenous noblewomen. Some members of humbler groups, like Spanish and Portuguese yeoman farmers continued to marry native women, however. Marriages and unions to Europeans accrued benefits to native women, not the least of which was the possibility to better contest criminal charges brought against them by unsympathetic authorities.

For the most part, nonnoble indigenous women had little likelihood of marrying Spaniards or other Europeans. Unions between these humble women and Europeans tended to be either fleeting or unsanctioned through legal or religious means. In the case of fleeting relations, such as those between domestic servants and employers, elements of exploitation and coercion took place. Here the paucity of evidence requires circumspection when attempting to discern motivations. Occasionally in cases involving humble native women, Spanish fathers bequeathed substantial amounts of money to their mestizo children.[71] Unlike their noble counterparts, humble native women rarely received recognition even from their children. By aligning themselves with their Spanish fathers, mestizo children denigrated, perhaps unwittingly, the importance of their mothers. Following males seeking to distance themselves from their female companions, mestizo children of humble native women stated that their fathers never married. This stands in stark contrast to the children of native noblewomen who would boast of their parentage. Pedro de Alvarado's daughter, Doña Leonor de Alvarado, proudly boasted that she was the daughter and heir of Doña Luisa Xicotencatl.[72] In her case the boast had practical implications, as it helped her establish a legal claim to her mother's assets.

Traditional views of native women as passive victims must give way to reinterpretations that seek to reanalyze the complex positions occupied by them in colonial society. Understanding the challenges to colonial rule undertaken by native women does not take away from their terrible suffering. If anything it helps to better understand the constant negotiations between the ruler and the ruled. As Camilla Townsend warns, "our new knowledge of the ways in which these women conceived of themselves and why they made the decisions that they did will become self-referential and of limited interest if we do not also explore the social and political *impact* of their self-conception and decisions" (emphasis added).[73] An investigation of the long ignored role of indigenous women in early

Guatemala reveals that regardless of their lineage, whether noble or commoner, they helped shape the contours of the society that developed. Understanding this aspect of Guatemala's history serves to better understand the complex nature of colonial rule and the interethnic interaction that characterized Spanish America.

NOTES

I am grateful to Ed Gray, Rebecca Horn, Susan Kellogg, Michel Oudijk, Laura Matthew, Susan Schroeder, Lisa Sousa, Michael Uzendoski, and the anonymous readers for their insightful comments and suggestions.

1. The original reads, "natural dela ciudad dela nueva españa y fue delas princezas que pasaron en estas provincias con los españoles que las conquistaron y pacificaron." Archivo General de Centro América, Guatemala City (hereafter, AGCA), A1.39, 11.737, 1751, f. 7 (10-20-1579).

2. The author's translation from "tiene muchos nietos y entre ellos algunos españoles personas principales."

3. Due to its complexity and moderately tangential relation to the topic at hand, the phenomenon of *mestizaje* will only receive discussion when it directly bears on the native-Spanish unions discussed. For a discussion of mestizos and mestizaje, see Altman, "Spanish Society"; Burns, "Gender and Politics"; Cahill, "Colour by Numbers"; Chance, "On The Mexican Mestizo"; Lutz, *Santiago de Guatemala*; Martínez Peláez, *La patria del Criollo*; and Seed, "Social Dimensions of Race."

4. Lutz, *Santiago de Guatemala*, 4. On wealth, see Cortés, *Cartas de relación*, 184, and Díaz del Castillo, *Historia verdadera*, Alianza edition, 616. See also Leonard, "Conquerors and Amazons."

5. See Pineda, "Descripción," 465, and Markman, *Architecture and Urbanization*, 110–11.

6. A similar situation developed in other areas of Spanish America. See Davies, *Landowners in Colonial Peru*, 67–68.

7. For an excellent treatment of the growth of the population of African descent in Guatemala see Lokken, "From Black to Ladino," esp. chaps. 4 and 5.

8. Israel, *Race, Class, and Politics*, 61.

9. See Carrasco, "Indian-Spanish Marriages," 92, and Socolow, *Women of Colonial Latin America*, 36.

10. Terraciano, "Colonial Mixtec Community," 15.

11. Kidwell, "Indian Women as Cultural Mediators," 97.

12. Rodríguez Becerra, *Encomienda y conquista*, 16; Stern, "Rise and Fall."

13. Recinos, *Pedro de Alvarado*, Ibarra edition (1986), 50.

14. See Ixtlilxochitl, *Obras históricas*, ed. Chavero, 391; Sherman, *Forced Native Labor*, 22.

15. For the importance of women in conquest ventures, see Navarro and Sánchez Korrol, *Women in Latin America*, 29.

16. The literature on Malintzin is vast. See, e.g., Núñez Becerra, *La Malinche*, and Herren, *Doña Marina*. For an excellent account of Malintzin's time among the Spaniards, see Karttunen, *Between Worlds*, 1–3.

17. Sahagún, *War of Conquest*, 20n1.

18. Lockhart identifies several Andean noblewomen who entered into unions with Spaniards, some as mistresses and others as wives. See Lockhart, *Men of Cajamarca*, 153–57 note, 199 note, 222, 272, 302, 304 note, and 358–59. Perhaps most prominent among these women was Quispe Sisa, known also as Inés Huaylas Yupanqui, the mistress of Francisco Pizarro. See María Rostworowski de Diez Canseco, *Doña Francisca Pizarro*, 16–30.

19. Stern, *Peru's Indian Peoples*, 170.

20. Clavijero, *Historia antigua*, 3:70–71.

21. According to José Milla, Pedro de Alvarado married Doña Lucía Xicontecatl in a church sanctioned ceremony. See Milla, *Historia*, 299n1.

22. Aparicio y Aparicio, *Conquistadores de Guatemala*, 3. How Doña Lucía came to marry Jorge de Alvarado remains unclear. While Doña Luisa appears numerous times in the chronicles, Doña Lucía does not. Indeed of the two, Doña Luisa stands as the most easily recognized by contemporary Guatemalans due to her importance in national histories. See, e.g., Gorriz, *Luisa Xiconténcatl*. Recently Doña Luisa has been revived as a symbol of pride in her homeland under the name of Doña Luisa Teohquilhuastzin. See Meade de Angulo, *Doña Luisa Teohquilhuastzin*.

23. The difference in the orthography of Xicontecatl and Xicotencatl results from local practice. In Guatemala the former occasionally appears, while in Mexico the latter surfaces as most common. For the importance of the Xicotencatl see Gibson, *Tlaxcala*, 5, 25, 98.

24. For Xicotencatl's numerous marriages see Gibson, *Tlaxcala*, 98.

25. Here the word mistress should be taken in the seigniorial sense. Díaz del Castillo, *Historia verdadera*, Alianza edition, 200.

26. Lockhart, *Nahuas after the Conquest*, 125–26.

27. For a criticism of Díaz del Castillo's accounts see Adorno, "Discursive Encounter."

28. This writer's translation. The original wording of "las recibiésemos por mujeres" leaves no doubt as to the sexual intent of both the presenters and recipients of the noblewomen. In the passage above "Malinche" refers to Hernando Cortés. Díaz del Castillo, *Historia verdadera*, Alianza edition, 197. See also Karttunen, "Rethinking Malinche," 293–94.

29. Seed, *Ceremonies of Possession*, 69–71.

30. Compare with Silverblatt, *Moon, Sun, and Witches*, 117–19.

31. Restall, *Maya World*, 136.

32. Recinos, *Pedro de Alvarado*, Ibarra edition (1986), 41.

33. "Provanca del Adelantado," 480.

34. See "Provanca del Adelantado," 481, 483, 484, 487. Indeed Doña Luisa accompanied Alvarado on nearly all his campaigns. See Recinos, *Pedro de Alvarado*, Ibarra edition (1986), 27.

35. See Milla, *Historia*, 299n1.

36. See Aparicio y Aparicio, *Conquistadores de Guatemala*, 3.

37. Kramer, *Encomienda Politics*, 157.

38. Marta Casaus Arzú, *Guatemala*, 34.

39. Don Francisco proved rather unpopular because of his avaricious ways. See Sanchíz Ochoa, *Los hidalgos de Guatemala*, 97–100.

40. Kramer, *Encomienda Politics*, 171, 191–92; Recinos, *Pedro de Alvarado*, Ibarra edition (1986), 78, 221–27.

41. Mörner, *Race Mixture*, 23–24.

42. *Memorial de Solola*, trans. Recinos and Chonay (1980), 125. Alvarado claimed the Kaqchikel contributed four thousand auxiliaries, yet Díaz del Castillo supports the number given by the Kaqchikel. See Alvarado, *Account of the Conquest*, 45; Díaz del Castillo, *Historia verdadera*, Alianza edition, 621–22. See also Kramer, *Encomienda Politics*, 32n29.

43. Kramer, *Encomienda Politics*, 38–40.

44. Matthew, "Neither and Both," 7.

45. *Memorial de Solola*, trans. Recinos and Chonay (1980), 133.

46. Ibid., 128–29.

47. Alvarez-Lobos Villatoro and Palomo, *Libro de los parecers*, 15.

48. See Icaza, *Conquistadores y pobladores*, 124–25, 129, 131–32, 160, 177.

49. Sherman, *Forced Native Labor*, 305.

50. For a discussion of this region's wealth see Janine Gasco, "Una visión conjunta."

51. AGCA A1.20, 732, 9225, f. 146 (1-14-1538).

52. Lockhart, *Spanish Peru*, 237.

53. In cases such as this, of an isolated individual living in a Spanish household and raised in the Spanish manner, a high level acculturation likely took place. Kuznesof's point that an automatic assumption of Spanish cultural hegemony is much too simplistic is important to keep present when analyzing these situations. See Kuznesof, "Ethnic and Gender Influences." Yet, in cases of individuals such as Doña María, as a member of the quickly acculturating native nobility who lived in an elite Spanish home with all the cultural accoutrements that wealth could purchase, retention of native ways likely gave away to full adoption of Spanish practices.

54. See Martín, *Daughters of the Conquistadors*, 50–51; Himmerich y Valencia, *Encomenderos of New Spain*, 195–96.

55. AGCA A1.20, 1129, 9622, f. 79 (1-28-1548).

56. See Carrasco, "Indian-Spanish Marriages," 97.

57. AGCA A1.20, 424, 8827, f. 204 (12-12-1586).

58. Compare to Lockhart, *Spanish Peru*, 27.

59. AGCA A1.20, 438, 8841, f. 12293 (4-21-1569) and f. 12324 (2-5-1569).

60. AGCA A1.20, 443, 8846, f. 13371 (11-19-1579), AGCA A1.20, 444, 8847, f. 13714 (6–26-1581), and AGCA A1.20, 1507, 9994, f. 23 (10-11-1585).

61. AGCA A1.20, 1362, 9853, f. 26 (3-6-1555).

62. Ibid.

63. AGCA A1.20, 443, 8846, f. 13524 (9-11-1579).

64. See Marshall, "Birth of the Mestizo."

65. Informaciones: Sebastián de Mármol y María de Monroy: Archivo General de Indias: Sig.: Guatemala, 113, n. 4 (fechas extremas 1572).

66. AGCA A1.20, 440, 8843, f. 11884 (9-29-1572), Last Will and Testament of Juan Griego.

67. AGCA A1.15, 4074, 32340 "A" (5-8-1576).

68. See Stern, *Secret History of Gender*, 6–8.

69. Lipsett-Rivera, " Slap in the Face," 188.

70. Remesal, *Historia general*, tomo 175, 1:82.

71. AGCA A1.20, 446, 8849 f. 14153 (7-8-1581).

72. AGCA A1.20, 442, 8845, f. 13288 (12-9-1569); "Provanca del Adelantado," 475–87.

73. Townsend, "Story without Words," 52.

CHAPTER FIVE

CONQUEST, COERCION, AND COLLABORATION

Indian Allies and the Campaigns in Nueva Galicia

IDA ALTMAN

When he went to the War of the Chichimecas, Don Francisco Acacitli carried for his insignia and arms a feathered face covering with green plumes, a shield of the same with a center of worked gold, his sword, and his cloak, and [he was] dressed in a red doublet, breeches, shoes and half-boots, a great white hat and large kerchief tied around his head, and a necklace of stones with two chains.

FRANCISCO DE SANDOVAL ACACITLI,
CONQUISTA Y PACIFICACIÓN DE LOS INDIOS CHICHIMECAS

Thus colorfully attired Don Francisco de Sandoval Acacitli, the "cacique y señor" of Tlalmanalco in the central Mexican province of Chalco led a group of men, including two of his sons, to fight alongside the viceroy of New Spain, Don Antonio de Mendoza, in the pacification of Nueva Galicia in what has come to be known as the Mixton War (1540–42).[1] During the western campaign the ruler of Tlalmanalco at one point was nearly captured, became seriously ill, and found himself reduced to eating kernels of roasted corn. Don Francisco nonetheless survived to receive the warm thanks of the viceroy and, some six months after his departure, a triumphal welcome home, apparently still in the company of his sons.

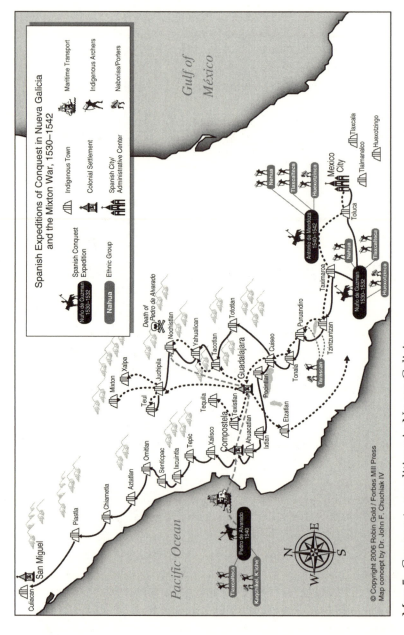

Map 5. Conquest expeditions in Nueva Galicia

In the course of little more than a decade the Spaniards waged two wars of conquest in the west-central and northwestern region of New Spain they called Nueva Galicia. Although characterized by differences in leadership and objective, these campaigns shared a heavy reliance on large armies of so-called indios amigos recruited in central Mexico and Michoacan. The latter served as the gateway especially for the campaign of 1530–31, which was led by the president of the first Audiencia, Nuño de Guzmán.[2] Force and intimidation marked Guzmán's recruitment efforts for this expedition. The heavy-handed tactics he used to muster an army were directed not only at Indians from central Mexico and Michoacan but in some cases toward Spaniards as well.[3] The devastation that Guzmán's campaign left in its wake and subsequent attempts to impose the *encomienda* on indigenous groups in Nueva Galicia that differed considerably from those of central Mexico in their sociopolitical organization fomented almost constant disorder and conflict in the region during the 1530s. As a result, just ten years after Guzmán's *entrada* the viceroy, Don Antonio de Mendoza, had to muster an army in central New Spain to relieve the overwhelmed settlers and officials in Nueva Galicia, who by then were struggling to suppress a massive indigenous uprising. In contrast to Guzmán, however, Mendoza exercised much greater diplomacy in dealing with his Indian allies. Thus the experience of the Indian allies recruited for the two campaigns differed in some significant regards, although in both cases they suffered privations and losses and were assigned the most onerous tasks. Notwithstanding Spanish coercion and control, however, in both campaigns it is possible to discern certain objectives and actions of the indios amigos that were at least partly distinct from those of Spaniards and seem to have influenced Spanish tactics.

Given the miserable experience of the indigenous troops that accompanied Guzmán in his violent entrada into Nueva Galicia, it is something of a wonder that only a decade later Mendoza was able to attract a substantial degree of support among both Indians and Spaniards for his campaign. Don Francisco de Sandoval Acacitli stated that "I went to the said city [Mexico] and begged the lord Viceroy that he grant me the favor that I and others from my province of Chalco should serve in this war."[4] Guzmán's recruitment techniques, in contrast, were characterized by extortion and intimidation, and there is little indication of voluntary indigenous participation.

Because of the disparities in emphasis and reporting in the accounts of Guzmán's entrada, a brief synopsis of the events of that campaign may be helpful. At the time he departed from Mexico City for Nueva Galicia, Guzmán was president of the first Audiencia as well as governor of the northeastern area of New Spain known as Panuco, where he had been responsible for taking thousands of slaves, most of whom were shipped to the islands of the Spanish Caribbean. When Guzmán left Mexico City for Michoacan at the very end of 1529 he took with him the indigenous ruler of the former Tarascan (Purepecha) state, the Cazonci, whom he had been holding prisoner in the capital. On reaching Michoacan he increased the pressure on the Cazonci to provide manpower and supplies and, apparently, to reveal the location of his treasure. That effort, coupled with indications that the Cazonci's submission to Spanish rule might not have been as thorough as had been thought, led to Guzmán's decision to torture several leading nobles of Michoacan, including the Cazonci himself, in order to obtain information on the deaths of Spaniards and, possibly, the whereabouts of the ruler's treasure. Obtaining only limited results from these interrogations, Guzmán tried and executed the Cazonci as he left Michoacan for Nueva Galicia.[5]

Guzmán's party headed northwest on a zigzagging route, skirting north of Lake Chapala and eventually reaching the Pacific coast. In the second year of the entrada the remnants of the expedition, which had suffered catastrophic losses in a great flood while encamped for the winter at Aztatlan near the coast, reached Culiacan (in modern Sinaloa). From there a smaller party entered the Sierra Madre Occidental but accomplished little beyond exposing the group to starvation and the hostility of the local inhabitants. After the expedition was reunited in Culiacan, Guzmán founded a town he named San Miguel, which for many years remained a precarious Spanish outpost far removed from other centers of Spanish settlement in Nueva Galicia. Returning to the south Guzmán established towns at Tepic (Compostela, the first capital of Nueva Galicia) and Guadalajara (the second and permanent capital). While Guzmán was on this campaign the second Audiencia arrived in New Spain, and he was replaced as president. In addition his rival Hernando Cortés had returned to Mexico from Spain. After completing the entrada Guzmán continued to hold office as governor of Nueva Galicia, but his political ascendancy was at an end. Within a few years he lost the governorships of both Panuco and Nueva Galicia and found himself exiled to Spain.[6]

There are at least ten full or partial accounts of Guzmán's 1530–31 campaign, including Guzmán's own letter, which differ from one another in length, detail, and emphasis.[7] The complex politics and rivalries of early New Spain, together with Guzmán's increasingly controversial tactics in dealing with New Spain's indigenous peoples—perhaps most notoriously his execution of the Cazonci of Michoacan—and the gradual fraying of his political power, a process that began even as he conducted his campaign in Nueva Galicia, all guaranteed there would be considerable scrutiny of his actions during the two-year entrada. Thus, even before the initiation of a formal *residencia* of Guzmán's term in office, the second Audiencia had begun to elicit testimony regarding aspects of the entrada into Nueva Galicia, accounting in part for the numerous *relaciones* that were generated.

Cristóbal Flores, who was a participant although not one of Guzmán's officers, wrote a chronicle that was highly critical of Guzmán's actions and those of some of his officers.[8] The interpreter García del Pilar also depicted Guzmán's behavior in harsh terms, as to a slightly lesser extent did Pedro de Carranza.[9] In contrast, Gonzalo López, one of Guzmán's closest associates who served as his field marshal in the second half of the campaign, was a consistent supporter of the captain general. López himself was personally responsible for one of the most controversial episodes of the entrada, the taking of large numbers slaves in Jalisco and other towns and apparently forcible recruitment of additional Indian troops or auxiliaries when he returned to Michoacan halfway through the campaign to obtain reinforcements for the decimated expedition. As one might expect, Guzmán's letter, covering only the first six months of the campaign, emphasized his efforts to bring Christianity to the territory he tried to subjugate and discipline and religious enlightenment to both his indigenous troops and the people they encountered as they marched through Nueva Galicia.

The tone of the other accounts for the most part is fairly neutral, which is to say they could be considered largely pro-Guzmán. Juan de Sámano's is one of the most detailed, and the "Primera relación anónima'" includes quite a lot of ethnographic and topographical information, although mainly for the area of Culiacan. Perhaps the least accurate of the accounts is one that the historian Gonzalo Fernández de Oviedo wrote, based mainly on an interview with Francisco de Arceo, the ensign of Captain Francisco Verdugo (one of Guzmán's close associates), although it is not without interest. Taken together these relaciones offer quite a full picture of the campaign, albeit with significant discrepancies.

One of these discrepancies has to do with numbers. Just how large were the indigenous forces that accompanied the Spaniards into Nueva Galicia?

In central Mexico Guzmán recruited troops mainly from Tlaxcala, Huexotzingo, and the capital itself. These provinces were logical targets for recruitment. Mexico City was solidly under the authority of the first Audiencia, which approved and supported the president's planned entrada into Nueva Galicia, and thus could be readily tapped for manpower. Tlaxcala had forged an alliance with the Spaniards during Cortés's conquest of central Mexico, as had Huexotzingo; during Cortés's absence from Mexico, Huexotzingo had come directly under Guzmán's sway.

According to Oviedo, Arceo reported that fifteen thousand "indios de guerra" left Mexico City with the captain general. In his testimony to the second Audiencia in 1531 Cristóbal de Barrios, who had participated in the first half of the Nueva Galicia entrada, claimed that ten or twelve thousand "naturales de la tierra" had accompanied Guzmán, while Fray Juan de Zumárraga (first bishop of Mexico) thought that Guzmán had taken with him as many as twenty thousand Indians.[10] Guzmán himself, however, stated that he had left Mexico City with 150 horsemen and about an equal number of foot soldiers and seven or eight thousand indios amigos.[11] In addition to these forces Guzmán demanded that the Cazonci supply him with manpower when they reached Michoacan. García del Pilar reported that Guzmán ordered the Cazonci to provide eight thousand men in Michoacan, although he admitted that he did not know how many men he actually had produced.[12]

A lawsuit brought in 1531 by Cortés against Guzmán and the other members of the first Audiencia included testimony from natives of Huexotzingo regarding the men that the province sent to the war, but the numbers offered by witnesses vary. One man, "who was formerly known as Tamavaltetle, *vecino* and *principal*," mentioned the "thousand Indian men whom the said Nuño de Guzmán took from the said town to the war." Another witness, however, stated that "Nuño de Guzman said to the lord of Huexotzingo that he should give him men to go to the war with him—six hundred men outfitted for war ... and among the said men whom he took to the war there were eleven leading men of eleven houses of Huexotzingo." The painted codex that accompanied the lawsuit indicated only 320 warriors.[13] These numbers suggest that the higher Spanish estimates might have been exaggerated. Perhaps, then, Guzmán initially conscripted a total of ten to fifteen thousand natives in central Mexico and Michoacan for the campaign.

Also complicating the issue of numbers of native warriors is the question of what proportion of total indigenous manpower they represented.

The accounts refer to the Spaniards' *naborías*, or servants as distinct from the indios amigos, and some of the Tarascans might have been used more in this capacity than as fighting men, although their roles probably varied over time. References to Spaniards being assigned Indians, however, further confuse the issue. J. Benedict Warren notes that "the Relacion [de Michoacan] indicates that 8,000 men did assemble but that when the Spaniards began distributing them among themselves, without any account or order, many of them fled. The Spaniards then used chains to make sure that no more of them ran way."[14] Pedro de Carranza probably was referring to this incident when he noted that the Cazonci gave to the Spaniards "muchos tamemes," who were divided up among the Spaniards of the army.[15] The chronicle that is credited to Cristóbal Flores gives perhaps the most detailed account of the recruitment and treatment of the Tarascans: "Each ruler of a town came with the portion of his subjects that had been assigned by the *repartimiento* [labor draft], all of whom were divided up by the Spaniards who went to war so that they would carry their goods; and for security that these Indians would not flee and leave their belongings, the lords and nobles marched with chains around their necks, and many of them died prisoners." Flores alleged that Guzmán treated the Tarascans as if they were rebels and noted that there was no lack of individuals "who told him how badly this was done." He also mentioned that Guzmán became angered at a cousin of the *maestre* of Roa, an *encomendero* of Michoacan, and made him march with a chain around his neck for two days.[16] Thus Guzmán employed his harsh methods against Spaniards as well as Indians who failed to bend to his will.

In the second year of the campaign López returned from a detour back to Michoacan with as many as one thousand Indians "and many of the principales from there whom he had in chains," according to García del Pilar. Although the evidence is ambiguous, there is a strong implication that these new recruits, along with the slaves that López had taken in Jalisco and elsewhere, again were divided up among the Spaniards when López's party rejoined Guzmán and the main force in Chiametla.[17]

The expedition's personnel probably included women as well as servants, slaves, and captives, although women are barely mentioned in the accounts, making it impossible even to guess at their numbers. Francisco de Arceo claimed that the Cazonci, in addition to supplies, had provided for each Spaniard "an Indian woman to cook food" as well as a total of ten thousand men "to carry the packs of the Christians."[18] Of the other accounts only Carranza's alludes to the presence of women in the entrada, mentioning that when they left Chiametla many "indios e indias" remained there ill.[19] In the preconquest period women did not accompany Mexica armies, but large numbers of porters and young men did. The practice might have been different in Michoacan, however, as Warren notes that Tarascan women carried burdens for the Spaniards during Gonzalo de Sandoval's campaign in Colima.[20]

It is possible, then, that the ambiguous status of the indios amigos stems in part from longstanding indigenous military practice: when called upon by Guzmán to send men to war, native rulers in central Mexico might have followed preconquest tradition by sending both fighting men and porters and young men to accompany them. Whether or not the Spaniards called their indios amigos "tameme," they certainly used them in that capacity. Although Francisco de Arceo claimed that when the warriors recruited in Mexico City departed the capital "they did not carry any burdens for the Christians, only those things they needed for themselves," there is plenty of evidence that later, if not at the very outset, they would do exactly that.[21] The author of the third anonymous chronicle wrote that when they were in the Sierra Madre Occidental near Culiacan many of the indios amigos "left their loads, their own as well as those of the Spaniards."[22] Cristóbal Flores noted that as they left for Tonala there were always "many of the amigos in chains, with Nuño de Guzmán's consent, so they wouldn't flee and leave the packs."[23]

The Spaniards used their Indian allies for any and all forms of physical labor. As they left Michoacan the indios amigos erected a church two leagues beyond Purandiro at Guzmán's behest. López described the construction of bridges made of earth and branches to allow the expedition to cross over swollen rivers, commenting that "on these bridges the indios amigos of this city [Mexico] worked a great deal and with much good will."[24] Flores painted a darker picture. According to him Guzmán ordered his field marshal, Antonio de Villarroel, to have rafts made to cross a river after they left Cuinao. Villarroel "ordered the cacique Tapia, lord of Mexico, to bring wood and equipment for them, which his macehuales made. And because the said cacique, because he was ill, did not enter the water to help them, the field marshal treated him in such a way, putting his hands on him, that he never again was well until he died."[25] Much later, when the captain general himself became ill, he ordered that a litter be made on which "the lords, Indians of this city [Mexico], would carry him up into the sierra."[26] Guzmán and his officers did not hesitate to demonstrate their authority by humiliating and abusing the high-ranking Indians who accompanied them.

Above all the Spaniards relied on the indios amigos to forage for food and other supplies and to loot and plunder the local communities they terrorized into submission. Guzmán had attempted to provision the expedition when he departed Mexico and later Michoacan, bringing with him stores of wine, vinegar, flour, and oil as well as thousands of pigs and sheep.[27] The testimony from Huexotzingo in 1531 referred to a number of items the town had supplied, most famously the golden, feathered banner with the image of the Virgin Mary and child that is reproduced in the Codex Huexotzingo. The town's contribution to Guzman's campaign was substantial. Tamavaltetle testified that

> a Christian Spaniard who was at the time overseer in the said town of Huexotzingo asked the lord and leading men of the said town to give him gold to buy a horse so that Don Tomé, the lord of the said town, could go to the war on horseback. . . . They said Nuño de Guzmán asked them for ten painted banners to take to the war, and they gave them to them. And he also asked them for a thousand and six hundred pairs of the shoes which they wear, which are called *cutaras*, and also four hundred small awnings [*toldillos*] . . . and four thousand arrows, and another four thousand breeches and blankets . . . and also six leather-covered chests and also another two thousand eight hundred blankets.[28]

The livestock that Guzmán brought did not fare well in the face of bad weather, floods, and a local populace that was generally hostile to the intrusion of the Spanish-Mexican host and their voracious herds but ready to enjoy the bonanza of fresh meat the latter offered. Problems of supply for the huge war party began early on; while leaving Michoacan, Guzmán noted the "abundant food, of which they had begun to have considerable need" that they found at Cuinao.[29] The need to supply the expedition was a constant concern and one for which the indios amigos appear to have been primarily responsible, when local groups were unable or unwilling to provision their conquerors.[30]

Guzmán disciplined his huge and motley force with an iron hand, in Nochistlan burning three Indians from Toluca who had been accused of making sacrifices and in Tepic hanging two Indians from Huexotzingo who wanted to return home.[31] The pivotal event of the entrada, the great storm and flood that engulfed the winter camp at Aztatlan, however, severely tested Guzmán's leadership. Quite unprepared for a disaster on this scale, the actions he took in the flood's aftermath exacerbated its impact. Notwithstanding the great mortality that resulted from the flood, he proceeded to take disciplinary measures that compounded the disastrous losses of men and provisions and further demoralized his already sorely tested forces.

Guzmán had chosen Aztatlan, near the Pacific coast, for his first winter camp because of its ample supply base, described by López: "Here there was great abundance of provisions and fowl . . . of which a great amount was collected, in such quantity that it should have sufficed for two years if what later occurred had not happened. . . . The countryside was full of cultivated plots. . . . Houses and huts having been made for the Christians as well as the Indians, they settled in."[32] Exactly how long they enjoyed their camp before disaster struck is unclear—at least a month or two—but around mid-September 1530 a huge storm swept through, knocking down most of the temporary quarters that had been erected (with the exception of Guzmán's house).[33] The real catastrophe, however, occurred overnight, when the river along which they were encamped overflowed its banks; "when it dawned, all the land was sea."[34] In a day or two the waters receded, but by then the expeditionary force was devastated. Supplies had been lost or ruined, the bewildered horses could not penetrate the watery and treacherous swamps, and hundreds, even thousands, of Indians drowned or subsequently died of illness and starvation. Not surprisingly, all the accounts that cover that period of time mention the episode, although details vary. García del Pilar referred to the drowning of more than a thousand Indians "who were lying in their beds sick" and wrote that after the flood "more than eight thousand Indians and naborías fell ill, in such manner that there weren't two hundred of them who could walk on their own two feet."[35]

The extent of the immediate damage is difficult to assess. López estimated that three thousand died in the flood itself, and Flores commented that "so high was the mortality, that of the great multitude of allies that we had I don't believe that five hundred were left healthy."[36] For the unfortunate survivors, however, the suffering had only begun. Some of them "fearing death . . . fled in order to return to their homes, although they knew they would be killed on the way." In the midst of the chaos and wreck-age of his camp, Guzmán ordered some of the would-be deserters hung; Pilar claimed there were fifty such executions.[37]

A number of the Indian lords pleaded with Guzmán to allow them to return south to recuperate. Flores described the scene as follows:

> Seeing the lord of this city of Mexico, who was named Tapia, and the lord of Tlatelolco, and the lord of Tlaxcala, and the lord of Huexotzingo and many other lords and principales from this province of Culhua how bad their health was, and that hardly a subject remained who wasn't dying, and other necessities they experienced, they went to beg and ask mercy from Nuño de Guzmán for the love of God, since all their people had died, would he please take their jewels and ornaments of war and let them return to Jalisco which was healthier country to spend the win-ter. . . . I know that not one of those lords who went to plead escaped, that they all died.[38]

Guzmán refused to let anyone return south and instead insisted that the main part of the expedition, "the healthy as well as the ill," continue north to Chiametla. They were forced to wade through swamps as bodies accumulated along the banks of the river and the road. On Guzmán's orders Pedro de Carranza took three horses and two black slaves to try to trans-port some of the Indians, but he found that it was impossible to carry more than one on his horse. He alleged that Guzmán then ordered that the ill and suffering Indians be rounded up and distributed to "those who wanted to carry them so they could brand them, and those they didn't take away remained there, and he ordered them brought to a house where later I saw them all dead." López, in contrast, insisted that the sick, Spaniards and Indians alike, "were treated and helped by the captain general with such solicitude and care, as if they were his children."[39] Guzmán directed that the dead be buried, but the sheer numbers of bodies and the stench over-whelmed the efforts of the survivors. Some men began throwing the bod-ies into the river, but as the water level had fallen, instead of being carried off by the current the corpses remained along the banks.[40]

By this time the Indian lords were hardly the only ones desperate to abandon the expedition. Flores reported that before leaving Aztatlan Guzmán hanged a Spaniard "who had been brought by force from the province of Michoacan" and wanted to return home and started to hang another; he also allegedly imprisoned and tortured "certain hidalgos" who wanted to leave.[41] Pedro de Carranza recounted a pitiful episode that took place after they had reached Chiametla in which Guzman again ordered the hanging of a Spaniard who tried to desert. The unfortunate man prayed to the Virgin Mary as they placed the noose around his neck. The rope broke when it was thrown over a tree. The onlookers begged Guzmán on their knees not to carry out the execution, to no avail. The condemned man also fell to his knees and, with a cross in his hands, promised to become a friar, but Guzmán's constables threw another rope around his neck and dragged him off to be hanged.[42]

The march to Chiametla took nearly three weeks and proved to be a nightmarish prolongation of the disaster that began at Aztatlan, with Indians dying along the road and, according to García del Pilar, many hanging themselves in despair. Possibly some of the afflicted stragglers were taken in by local people along the way.[43] After reaching Chiametla and with the reinforcements that López brought from Michoacan, Guzmán continued his entrada into the province of Culiacan. By this time there was considerable disarray, as both Indians and Spaniards attempted to escape, even if it meant certain death. In Piastla "many of the allies wanted to return." Guzmán ordered one burned alive and another hanged, but notwithstanding the double threat of Guzmán's brutal justice and hostile locals a certain number escaped anyway, the majority apparently perishing as they attempted to reach home.[44]

What was left of the expedition spent the second winter in Culiacan, where Guzmán founded the town of San Miguel, "where he left many amigos."[45] Flores described what for him was a heartrending scene as they departed from San Miguel:

> Leaving in that town . . . a large number of the Indians from this country [i.e., central Mexico] that he had taken with him to help make war, in payment for their good service and work at the end of two years in which they traveled the roads and mountains loaded down, every day making huts and looking for food for us, he [Guzmán] left them in that town among the vecinos, free men made slaves, chained by the neck or in stocks so that they would not follow us, shouting and weeping when they saw us leave because of the great wrong that was done to them in repayment for their work.[46]

For the survivors who accompanied Guzmán's party when it finally returned south, their trials by no means were at an end. They went back to Chiametla, where they discovered the remains of most of the Indians who had stayed there because they were too ill to go on to Culiacan. Before leaving Chiametla Don Tomé of Huexotzingo attempted once again to bribe Guzmán into releasing him. He probably was ill, as he had to be carried on the back of another man, who led Don Tomé's horse when he went to see Guzmán. Guzmán later told some of the Spaniards that Don Tomé had offered him "todas las joyas y que no eran buenas" and given him his horse—presumably the same one that the town of Huexotzingo had purchased for him when he went off to war. Two or three days after this meeting Don Tomé was dead.[47]

Organizing an expedition into a region that for the most part was little (if at all) known to the Spaniards on the scale that Guzmán did was an enormous undertaking. The logistical and supply challenges of leading several hundred Spaniards with their African slaves and Indian servants, together with thousands of Indian allies, into unfamiliar territory were staggering. The evidence suggests that Guzmán and his officers often did not meet those challenges very well. What advantages, then, did having such large numbers of indios amigos confer?

One advantage was tactical. Having large numbers of Indian fighting men organized under their own native leaders allowed the entrada to split up at certain points, making it possible to cover and conquer more territory without losing the advantage of superior numbers. The latter surely was the main benefit of having thousands of indios amigos; they helped to constitute an intimidating host. Indications are that many of the local groups they confronted might have had the military edge over the invaders had they not been overwhelmed by their sheer numbers. Referring to the Indians who tried to defend Tonala Guzmán commented that "I saw that they fought very stoutly with our allies."[48] In some instances it seems clear that when Spaniards and indios amigos did not have a numerical advantage, they did not necessarily prevail.

The Indian allies themselves seemingly were well aware of the military prowess of the people they confronted. After leaving Tepic and sighting a large war party, Guzmán wrote that he had ridden ahead to reconnoiter and saw that the enemy warriors were "withdrawing into the sierra, and our allies, who always go ahead, more to test than to fight, were following them with the support of the horsemen, because without them they wouldn't dare to do it." Furthermore, when engaged in pitched battle the indios amigos apparently could be in as much danger from Spaniards as from their enemies. Guzmán mentioned that in one battle that took place before they reached Omitlan ten or twelve indios amigos died, "some of them lanced by Christians, who didn't recognize them."[49]

All the accounts mention the systematic burning of pueblos through which the entrada passed (with the rather rare exception of those villages that offered no resistance and submitted immediately), a practice consistently attributed to the indios amigos and probably often initiated by them. Even Flores, who wrote one of the accounts most hostile to Guzmán, admitted that despite Guzmán's efforts to prevent it, the Indians could not be dissuaded: "This burning went on always wherever we went, and . . . Nuño de Guzmán had made every effort so they would not burn the pueblos. . . . The amigos that we took with us are such that even though you burned them alive, they would not cease to set fires wherever we went."[50] Yet it appears that in time the Spaniards incorporated the practice of putting enemy pueblos to the torch into their overall strategy. Francisco Verdugo early on adopted a scorched-earth policy on his campaigns, and López commented when they arrived in Jalisco that "the allies, seeing that there were very few people, began to burn, and the captain-general ordered it."[51] According to the third anonymous chronicler Guzmán also had ordered the burning of temples at Cuiseo.[52]

Notwithstanding the brutality that Guzmán himself employed to maintain discipline or to extract information or aid from Nueva Galicia's inhabitants, he had a particular horror of human sacrifice. The incident at Nochistlan that resulted in the execution of two or three Indians under Guzmán's command was reported in several of the accounts, although the details are murky. Guzmán seemed to assume that, given the opportunity, his Indian allies would sacrifice enemy captives. Once when he had sent some of his men to gather up the indios amigos, they came across "some women and children that the amigos had killed and even sacrificed," a practice from which he thought they would not desist no matter what punishment he imposed "although some of them affirm that they are very good Christians." He was convinced that the Indians secretly continued to sacrifice "as formerly they did."[53]

Despite the travails of the two-year campaign, mortality among Spaniards was fairly low compared to the catastrophic losses suffered by the indios amigos, as was typical in such situations. It seems likely that only a small fraction of the indigenous participants survived to return home or were permitted to do so. Referring to the departure from San Miguel (Culiacan) García del Pilar reported that "of one thousand two hundred who went from Tlaxcala, no more than twenty escaped, and these remained chained, save perhaps two that Gonzalo López brings [with him]."[54] On the campaign the indigenous recruits found themselves subject to the authority of a callous leader and stranded in hostile territory, although they occasionally encountered local people who were friendly. Juan de Sámano, for example, reported that in Tonala a "barrio de naguatatos" offered the amigos some fruit and water.[55] It is possible that some deserters or refugees from the disaster at Aztatlan found asylum among the locals in the sierra.[56] Safe havens and sympathy were in short supply, however, as the local inhabitants of Nueva Galicia had little reason to empathize with the Spaniards' Indian allies. Probably most of the amigos perished miserably— from illness, starvation, drowning, or at the hands of their enemies or the Spaniards themselves—or lived out the remainder of their lives far from their homes and families.

The experiences of the Indians from central Mexico and Michoacan who accompanied Viceroy Mendoza to Nueva Galicia in 1541 differed significantly. Possibly nearly as numerous as the recruits whom Guzmán initially led—Mendoza reported that he brought five thousand Indian allies from central Mexico, and they were joined in Nueva Galicia by another five or six thousand from Michoacan—the indios amigos who participated in the Mixton war were better supplied and organized.[57] Geographically this second campaign for the pacification of Nueva Galicia was far more circumscribed than Guzmán's entrada, meaning that neither Spaniards nor their allies were venturing into unfamiliar territory with unexpected dangers. Furthermore, this second campaign was much shorter in duration. Although the war itself raged for nearly two years, the involvement of recruits from central Mexico and Michoacan for the most part lasted little more than six months, an important factor in limiting their exposure to disease, starvation, and other hazards.

In contrast to Guzmán's campaign, which generated multiple and sometimes conflicting accounts, information on the prosecution of the Mixton war is largely confined to testimony in the lengthy residencia into Mendoza's conduct in office. Thus the account set down at the behest of Don Francisco de Sandoval Acacitli, mentioned at the outset, is exceptional in two regards: it is possibly the only full-length chronicle of events generated by

a participant independently of any official inquiry, and it was authored by
an indigenous leader.[58] This latter point is important for understanding the
role of the indios amigos, as not surprisingly Don Francisco was especially
concerned with recording their activities and contributions to the campaign.

What has come to be known as the Mixton war began in late 1540, but
initially the Spanish settlers and officials living in Nueva Galicia—many
of them veterans of Guzmán's campaign ten years earlier—thought they
could put down the rebellion without outside aid. Mendoza himself actually had been touring the region at the time the rebellion broke out, but he
allowed himself to be persuaded that local officials could handle the situation. If in retrospect that decision seems shortsighted, it should be borne
in mind that Nueva Galicia had never really been pacified, and unrest and
violent conflict were endemic all through the 1530s. Local Spaniards probably viewed the early stages of the revolt as a continuation of the disorder
they had faced since Guzmán's entrada.

Furthermore at the time of the outbreak the interests of the viceroy and
others lay elsewhere. Not long before Nueva Galicia's governor, Francisco
Vásquez de Coronado, had departed from Culiacan in the north on an expedition sponsored by the viceroy to find the fabled Seven Cities of Cíbola
(a mythical locale that apparently had interested Guzmán as well). The
lure of new conquests to the north perhaps overrode concerns about maintaining control over Nueva Galicia. The individual who took over as acting governor—Cristóbal de Oñate—did have long experience in Nueva
Galicia, whereas Vásquez de Coronado was a newcomer to the region. Both
before and after the war, Oñate was considered by all—the residents of
Nueva Galicia as well as officials in Mexico City—to be highly competent.

The viceroy did continue to monitor the situation in the west closely.
He finally made the decision to intervene personally against the advice of
some of his close associates who feared that the rapidly swelling tide of
rebellion might engulf central Mexico as well and that the viceroy's departure from the capital with so many troops would leave the city vulnerable
to attack.[59] As events turned out, Mendoza's arrival with a large Spanish
and Indian host turned the tide of the conflict against the rebels. Although
local Spanish residents had managed—just barely—to save the town of
Guadalajara from utter destruction, the first decisive Spanish victory of the
war came only when Mendoza brought his forces, and the royal authority he represented, to bear on the local defenders of the high strongholds,
or *peñoles*, that had been fortified in defiance of Spanish rule.[60]

Before reinforcements arrived from central Mexico and Michoacan, the Spanish residents of Nueva Galicia tried to mobilize local groups they thought they could count on for support. They called these recruits their indios amigos—although as it turned out, they sometimes were neither friends nor allies. Early on one of the key Spanish officers (and local encomendero), Miguel de Ibarra, had tried to reason with or confront the defenders of one of the peñoles. Seeing that he and his companions were seriously outnumbered, however, he had sent back to Guadalajara for reinforcements. These were dispatched in the form of sixteen Spanish horsemen and "one thousand five hundred *amigos de Tonala* and more than three thousand Cazcanes." While en route from Jalpa to the peñol of Tepetitaque, another Spaniard, Toribio de Bolaños, who led the vanguard of the forces while Ibarra brought up the rear, encountered and detained two "indios Tecuexes de la lengua de Tonala."[61] To Ibarra's dismay and initial disbelief, when questioned separately the two insisted that Ibarra's "amigos de Tonalá" had been in constant contact with the people fortified at Tepetitaque. They revealed the existence of a detailed plan involving both the Tecuexes of Tonala and the Cazcanes who accompanied the Spaniards to turn on the latter and make common cause with the enemy fortified in the peñol.[62] This episode strongly suggests that the Spaniards had few "amigos" in Nueva Galicia on whom they could rely. Given that less than a decade had passed since Guzmán's bloody entrada into the region, it is not surprising that during the intervening years these people had not been transformed into trustworthy allies.

Nonetheless it appears that in the early stages of the conflict the Spaniards were able to mobilize some local people for their defense. Referring to an early defeat in the first battle for Mixton, Jerónimo López noted that the Spaniards "lost some of the people, including many of the indios amigos they had with them," although he later mentioned the treachery of "other indios amigos such as Tenamaztle and Don Francisco, lords of Nochistlan."[63] Although the rebellion was extensive and multiethnic, there seem to have been communities (or parts of communities) that attempted to remain neutral, notwithstanding the pressure exerted on them by both sides to join the deadly fray. In any case the Spaniards gained a substantial base of indigenous support only with the arrival of Mendoza and his recruits.

In contrast to the near total isolation of the Indian troops that accompanied Guzmán to Nueva Galicia, the indios amigos who went to fight in the *guerra de Jalisco* were able to make at least limited friendly contacts with local people. Possibly the conquests of Michoacan, Colima, and Nueva Galicia had fostered increased contact with people from central Mexico and Michoacan. Many local groups, including the Cazcanes and Tecuexes, spoke languages related to Nahuatl, and Nahuatl itself apparently had made some headway as a lingua franca in the west, facilitating communication with people from central Mexico.[64] Don Francisco de Sandoval Acacitli's account includes the following description of the celebration of Christmas near Jalpa at the end of the fourth month of the campaign:

> On the Sunday that was the day of the nativity . . . all the people went to a field. . . . And the day of the festival of our lord Jesus Christ, those from Amaquemecan had their dance. And the third day of Christmas . . . Don Francisco danced, and they sang the *chichimeca* song. There were flowers and incense, food and cacao which they gave to the lords, and all the nations from different provinces danced, with their arms and shields and wooden swords; everyone danced, without exception.[65]

Just before these celebrations Don Francisco befriended, or was befriended by, a local ruler of Tonala named Don Pedro, who claimed he had been in the mountains and had come forth to declare his loyalty to the viceroy. Don Pedro and Don Francisco exchanged gifts "and became great friends," following which Mendoza arrived at the camp and Don Pedro met him with gifts of food.[66] Despite the apparent perfidy of some of the "amigos" from Tonala, the Spanish nevertheless made the town one of their bases; Don Francisco mentioned taking the sick and wounded to recover there after the battle at Tototlan (Coyna).[67]

Such peaceful interludes as the Christmas celebrations were rare. Don Francisco's account on the whole paints a picture of grueling marches, short supplies, illness, and other hazards. In the fourth week some drowned as they attempted to cross a river, and in the fifth week Don Francisco and the people from Chalco engaged in their first battle, at Tototlan. The following week a few people fell from a precipice. The region's topography posed considerable risks, especially as the indios amigos had to care for the livestock and were responsible for hauling heavy artillery and other equipment over difficult terrain. For the battle of Nochistlan the people of Chalco carried the artillery, "pulling or dragging it, with which their work was doubled, and they also were responsible for carrying the shot and other ammunition and equipment for it, and for guarding the sheep."[68]

Such physically taxing and onerous duties did not prevent the allies from participating in combat, which for them surely was the real point of the campaign. Don Francisco described the allies' role in the battle of Nochistlan, which started early in the morning:

> The order that they had for the battle . . . was that they set up the artillery in the middle, and on one side of the road went the Tlax-caltecas, Huexotzincas, Quauquecholtecas, followed by the Mexi-canos and Xilotepecas, and then the Aculhuas; and on the other side [were] those from Michoacan, Mestitlan, and the Chalcos, and they were setting up the artillery [aimed] at the wall of wood and then of stone, which left the Chichimecas without protection, and against them Señor Don Francisco with his green feathered insignia of wide quetzal plumes, with which they gained the wall and broke it, and burned their huts, and began to fight with them. . . . It was there that all those from the provinces took many captives, and no more than four Spaniards died in this battle.[69]

In addition to the groups listed above he elsewhere referred to "Tzapotecas" and "uno de nación Otomi." Usually neither Don Francisco nor the Spanish participants offered precise numbers for the casualties that the amigos suffered during the battles, although they greatly exceeded those of the Spaniards. When Cristóbal de Oñate led the first Spanish attack on the peñol of Mixton, "after having fought for four hours they defeated them [the Spaniards] and set their camp on fire and robbed it. They killed thirteen Spaniards and six blacks and more than three hundred Indians."[70]

While giving other groups their due, Don Francisco naturally high-lighted his own contributions. In the battle for Juchipila,

> The enemy that sought to confront us went out at night, and the Chichimecas descended to the foot of the mountain where we were, and those in the lead were those of Chalco, and of Quahuitlan and Coyoacan and Xilotepec. . . . The Chalcos . . . defended their position very well, and the Señor Don Francisco was almost captured, because he engaged with two of them armed only with an old shield and without a sword, and then he armed himself with his quilted armor, with his shield and sword and other insignia, and then strongly engaged with the Chichimecas, with which they did not dare return again, and seven of them died there and they took two alive.[71]

Don Francisco's account makes it clear that the indigenous nations or provinces retained their integrity as distinct units for work and combat. He and his people functioned primarily under the authority of licenciado Francisco Maldonado, the *oidor* (judge) of the Audiencia who served as one of Mendoza's principal captains. The viceroy himself generally led the Mexicanos; Don Francisco mentioned Don Martín of Tlatelolco and Hernando de Tapia as their *caudillos*.[72] Tapia served as an interpreter for the Audiencia and in the 1530s had visited the royal court in Castile. Like Don Francisco of Chalco, Tapia survived the campaign in Nueva Galicia and returned to Mexico, although the rewards he received from the viceroy for his participation were meager.[73]

Relations between Don Francisco and Maldonado might not always have been cordial. When the time finally came to return to central Mexico, Don Francisco was reluctant to accompany Maldonado. Ultimately he did, but he might have had good reasons to distrust the Spaniard. At one point Maldonado had taken Don Francisco with him to Jalpa, seemingly without having made adequate preparations. "And there the lord suffered greatly, because he had nothing to eat except toasted maize, and without clothing, because he only carried his arms and a thin blanket called Yczotilmantli, and he slept armed with his quilted armor on, and all the rest of the people suffered greatly because they were all without clothes or food."[74]

Conditions had begun to deteriorate by the end of the fourth month of the campaign. Soon after the Christmas festivities nearly everyone, Indians and Spaniards alike, including the viceroy himself, Don Francisco, "and all the principales," was reduced to eating hearts of palm for several days.[75] The situation did not improve. A few weeks later as they left the pueblo of Temicie Don Francisco had nothing more to eat than some "fruit kneaded between the hands, and *pinole* which the people of Tlalotlacan gave him, and his horse no longer ate maize, and there in Tequila he had for breakfast what the people of San Juan gave him, and in the days that it took to arrive in Temicie he didn't eat anything." As they fanned out from Temicie looking for maize, the "Chichimecos" attacked, and a man from Chalco named Bartolomé was shot. Soon afterward Don Francisco fell ill. Mendoza heard and wanted to send him to be treated elsewhere, but Don Francisco insisted he wished to stay with the viceroy. He remained ill off and on for the next two weeks.[76]

As supplies ran short, the native troops began to abandon the campaign en masse. Many fled from Texistlan, especially the Tlaxcalteca, whom the viceroy chastised, saying that "from here on out you shouldn't brag of being good soldiers." The viceroy's restraint in dealing with deserters very likely hinged on his realization that he and his officials simply could not continue to supply adequately such large numbers of troops. Don Francisco's account noted that "the hunger began in Texistlan." From there they went on to Tequila, "and there we experienced much thirst. It was necessary to finish the water since the maize that the señor ate was gone, and there the people of San Juan helped them with a large basket of maize, and a bowl... of beans, which he ate in two days, and the third [day] there was only enough for breakfast." From Temicie also "many of the natives left, and from there fled Felipe Quahuihuitl, he of Texcoco, and the captains from Tlailotlacan, Amistlato, and others."[77]

Looking back to Guzmán's campaign ten years before, perhaps the greatest reward for Mendoza's indios amigos was that many—perhaps even most—survived to return home. The viceroy insisted that mortality among the allies was "miraculously" low and that supplies were ample.[78] Although Don Francisco's account makes it clear that already by the end of the fourth month of the campaign shortages began to plague the Spanish and Indian forces, the viceroy and his mayordomo Agustín Guerrero seem to have devised a reasonably effective system for supply. In his testimony for the residencia Alonso de Santa Cruz explained the system as follows: "There was great abundance of many supplies, for Spaniards as well as Indians, and in many pueblos of the said province a Spaniard had been placed at the orders of the viceroy ... who gave [supplies] to Spaniards as well as Indians without their having to pay anything, rather it was all at the expense of the said viceroy."[79] Although obviously he exaggerated the system's effectiveness, after the war's conclusion records reflect the viceroy's efforts to repay debts for supplies and the presence of his officials in places like Toluca, a key location on the route from Mexico City to Nueva Galicia.[80]

Mendoza did allow his Indian allies to take captives in compensation for their efforts, especially after the first victory at the peñol of Coyna (Tototlan). In his response to charges brought against him in the residencia regarding the distribution of slaves captured in the war, he explained why he had turned captives over to his Indian allies, dispensing with the legal process of branding and registering them. He declared that he had done so "to encourage them for the war and because it was the first thing that they had taken by force of arms" and also to prevent the allies from killing all the potential captives, as they would have done had they thought that they would all be handed over to the Spaniards. In the official distribution of slaves after the battle for Coyna Don Martín, lord of Tlatelolco, received one slave, and "Tapia naguatato" (surely Hernando de Tapia) received eleven.[81] There is no record of how many captives unofficially were handed over to the indios amigos.

Although Mendoza and his officers succeeded in maintaining much greater discipline among their troops, as in Nuño de Guzmán's campaign indigenous practices associated with conquest did figure. In contrast to the earlier entrada Don Francisco's account makes only infrequent references to burning, and these few incidents appear to have been limited in extent and to have taken place under the supervision of Spanish officers. The account does refer, however, to the practice of uprooting *magueyes* and other plants. In Apozolco "all day they pulled up the magueyes and cut the mesquites." From there they went on to Juchipila, where they spent two days; "as soon as we arrived they began to uproot the magueyes, the Tlaxcaltecas and Mexicanos."[82] The destruction of useful plants and shrubs, like the burning of pueblos, was more than symbolic; it threatened the rebels' very livelihood. At Nochistlan the defenders of the peñol offered to come to terms in an apparent effort to save their *tunales* (prickly pear plants) from destruction.[83]

Despite shortages of food, casualties, and the occasional mistreatment of Indian allies at the hands of Spaniards, the relations between Spanish and Indian participants in this second war for Nueva Galicia seem to have been substantially more restrained and balanced than had been the case ten years earlier. The largely voluntary nature of recruitment for the campaign surely made a difference from the very outset. Alonso de Santa Cruz explained that the viceroy's personal commitment to the campaign persuaded Spaniards and Indians alike to participate: "When the lord viceroy decided to go in person to the said pacification, he prepared his departure and left the city of Mexico with many of the leading people of the land on horseback, conquerors and settlers, married and single, all of whom went with the said lord viceroy to the pacification. . . . And I saw that many caciques and principales of the country came voluntarily to the said lord viceroy to go with him."[84] Significantly, Don Francisco de Sandoval Acacitli and many of the other indios amigos kept faith with Mendoza to the end of the campaign, despite the privations they had suffered. The viceroy sent them home from Etzatlan: "[There] the lord viceroy said farewell to all the people of the various provinces, and the lord viceroy said to them:

Sons, natives that you are of many provinces, go in good fortune, because now the war is finished and has come to an end. . . . Those of you who have followed in my company, whom I regard as sons, and I will favor you in everything that should present itself. . . . And those of Tlalmanalco the viceroy sent first of all."[85] Don Francisco's journey home, although not without points of interest, such as the steaming hot geyser they encountered whose waters could cook meat, took place without mishap.[86] He received a gratifying welcome in Michoacan, where he was met by the trumpeter Tequimotzil, who brought a meal with plenty of tortillas, ground cacao, and pinole. Don Francisco and "all the principales" also were given blankets, shirts, breeches, and footwear. In another town the local ruler, also named Don Francisco, provided two turkeys, a side of bacon, and wine. The next day, Ash Wednesday, they arrived in a town where they lodged in the house of a Spaniard and were entertained by the ruler of Michoacan himself, Don Pedro. In Toluca the local lords, Don Luis and Don Felipe, fed them. The next day Don Francisco's brother Don Pedro Tlacatecuitzin met the party, and they spent two days in Mexico City. There they made their final farewell to the viceroy, exchanging speeches of congratulation with the aid of interpreter Antonio Ortiz. Don Francisco addressed Mendoza as follows: "Your illustrious lordship, I come to kiss your hand and extend a welcome for having returned well from the journey that your lordship has made in the land of the Chichimecos, with so many prosperous events and without any disaster or illness, and that God has brought you well to your house and court in this city of Mexico. . . . I have come to ask permission to go to your pueblo of San Luis Tlalmanalco." The viceroy replied as graciously: "I am deeply grateful to Don Francisco, and very satisfied with the good that the Chalcas have done with the Marqués when he came for the conquest and pacification of this kingdom, and that they helped in all the wars that the Marqués fought. Go with congratulations to your house and pueblo of Tlalmanalco to rest, and in each and any thing that arises I will do what you ask me and favor you." Notwithstanding the viceroy's solicitousness, surely the most gratifying moment of all was the festive welcome home in which all the *principales* and their ladies and the commoners as well came out to greet the veterans. Arches covered with rushes had been set up along the route and boards covered with the same placed at intervals leading up to the church. The way from the church to Don Francisco's house was similarly decorated with rushes and a profusion of flowers.[87]

Beyond the failures and successes of the two campaigns for Nueva Galicia and the individual and collective experiences of the participants, detailed examination of the role of the indios amigos provides insight into the formation and functioning of early Spanish-indigenous relations and the progressive establishment of effective Spanish rule, both in central Mexico and the west. Nuño de Guzmán's entrada into Nueva Galicia was predicated on extending his control over Michoacan, which became the immediate base for his campaign in the west. His drive to consolidate his authority there transformed the earlier somewhat collaborative relationship between Spaniards and their subjects in Michoacan into one characterized by intimidation, use of force, and coercion, elements that would shape Guzmán's western campaign as well. Few of Guzmán's indios amigos survived, and the entrada left a legacy of resentment, defiance, and disorder in the region that contributed quite directly to the massive rebellion of 1540–42, thus paving the way for the second campaign for the west.

In contrast to Guzmán, Don Antonio de Mendoza attracted the genuine and even enthusiastic support of Indian rulers. Mendoza was popular among many Spaniards and higher-ranking Indians of central Mexico, who probably welcomed his generally balanced and moderate approach to governance after more than a decade of squabbles generated by rivalries among Cortés, treasury officials, and the first Audiencia headed by Nuño de Guzmán. Perhaps equally important, by this time some Spanish officials, encomenderos, and others had begun to form effective working relationships with Indian leaders. Alonso de Santa Cruz, who claimed that he understood "la lengua mexicana," and other witnesses testified to the qualities of character and distinguished service in the war of such native leaders as Don Francisco of Chalco, Don Francisco of Culhuacan, Hernando de Tapia, and others.[88] These statements stand in considerable contrast to Guzmán's contemptuous and even cruel treatment of Indian lords and principales during his campaign.

Guzmán's efforts to position himself favorably in the politics of New Spain and the royal court affected his actions and choices in Michoacan and Nueva Galicia and led to his political downfall. Shrewd, ambitious, and possessed of tremendous physical stamina, Guzmán certainly had his loyal supporters, but he lacked both Cortés's gift for diplomacy and the legitimacy that Mendoza—member of a powerful, high-ranking noble Spanish family and, as viceroy, the highest-ranking representative of royal authority in New Spain—brought to bear. If Mendoza, like Guzmán, also hoped to be associated with new conquests—hence his sponsorship of Vásquez de Coronado's expedition—he had none of Guzmán's anxieties about retaining his position. Indeed he was supremely, and justifiably, confident of his ability to orchestrate and ultimately to control local politics and power struggles and retain the support of the Crown. An episode that took place after Mendoza left Mexico City with his Spanish and Indian troops to pacify Nueva Galicia reflects this confidence. The viceroy was warned of an ostensible plot in which Indians from Michoacan had met with the governor of Tlaxcala to make common cause and take advantage of his absence from Mexico City to assert themselves. The source of this warning, Jerónimo López, was indignant that when Mendoza was informed of the alleged conspiracy, he made light of it and initiated no inquiries.[89] The viceroy had few doubts about his ability to maintain his, and the emperor's, authority in New Spain.

It probably would be an exaggeration to claim that the two leaders' treatment of their Indian allies during the Nueva Galicia campaigns played a decisive role in determining the direction of their political careers. Nonetheless Guzmán's flagrant abuse of indigenous allies and enemies alike certainly undermined his position and fostered serious doubts regarding his ability to govern. In contrast, Mendoza's moderation, reflected both in his balanced treatment of his indios amigos and the restraint he showed in dealing with many of the defeated rebels of Nueva Galicia, helped to solidify not only his own position but Spanish rule in New Spain itself. The experience and fate of the indios amigos in the campaigns for Nueva Galicia, then, far from being merely an interesting sideline to the early history of New Spain, were instead an important element in influencing the form that Spanish rule and Spanish-indigenous relations would take.

NOTES

The author gratefully acknowledges research support from the National Endowment for the Humanities and the University of New Orleans as well as comments from Richmond F. Brown and James Lockhart; the latter in particular provided very helpful insights regarding Don Francisco de Acacitli's account.

1. I have translated the word *calavera* (lit., "skull") as "face covering"; it might have been something like a visor. Don Francisco is mentioned in Chimalpahin's history of Chalco; see Schroeder, *Chimalpahin*, 98. For a discussion of the equipment, arms, and attire of central Mexican warriors, see Hassig, *Aztec Warfare*, chapter 6. On 86 and 90 he discusses the use of feathers on helmets and shields. Miguel

León-Portilla discusses the youthfulness of many recruits for the campaign in *La flecha en el blanco*; see esp. p. 47. Don Francisco's personal account of his participation in the pacification of Nueva Galicia was set down in Nahuatl by Gabriel de Castañeda, who accompanied him on the campaign. In 1641 Pedro Vásquez, an interpreter for the Audiencia, translated the account into Spanish, the only form in which it now exists, as the Nahuatl original was lost. José María Muriá edited and transcribed the account for the edition used here. It also appears in García Icazbalceta, *Colección de documentos*, 2:307–11.

2. See Warren, *Conquest of Michoacan*.

3. The bishop-elect of Mexico, Fray fray Juan de Zumárraga, testified to the Audiencia in 1531 that Guzmán should not lead the campaign in Nueva Galicia because of "having taken many forcibly, in chains." See "Información sobre los acaecimientos de la guerra que hace el Gobernador Nuño de Guzmán a los indios . . . tomada por el muy noble Señor Licenciado Salmeron para el efecto," in *Colección de documentos inéditos*, 16:371. See also Warren, *Conquest of Michoacan*, 213. Pedro de Carranza began his account by stating that he was taken prisoner from Mexico to Michoacan, where he was released. See Zaragoza, *Crónicas de la conquista*, 155. See also the 1544 account of Bartolomé de Zárate in Paso y Troncoso, *Epistolario de Nueva España*, 6:133.

4. Acacitli, *Conquista y pacificación*, 14.

5. These events, and their relationship to the politics of early New Spain, are well covered in Warren, *Conquest of Michoacan*.

6. See Gerhard, *North Frontier*, 42–46, on Guzmán's campaign and the political struggles of early New Spain in which he played a part and Chipman, *Nuño de Guzmán*. See also Manuel Carrera Stampa's brief *Nuño de Guzmán*.

7. The accounts used here have been published in two edited volumes: García Icazbalceta, *Colección de documentos*, vol. 2, and Zaragoza, *Crónicas de la conquista*. There is some redundancy in the two collections.

8. Joaquín García Icazbalceta believes that Flores probably was the author of what appears in his collection as the fourth anonymous chronicle; the same account appears under Flores's name in Zaragoza, *Crónicas de la conquista*.

9. García Icazbalceta suggests that because Pilar's abilities as an interpreter were not of great use to Guzmán during his entrada, he was able to distance himself from Guzmán's excesses. Like some other early interpreters in New Spain, García del Pilar had a shady reputation. He died soon after the end of Guzmán's campaign, in January 1532, at the age of thirty-eight. García Icazbalceta, *Colección de documentos*, 2:xlii–xliv. See also Warren, *Conquest of Michoacan*, 143–44.

10. See "Informacion sobre los acaecimientos de la guerra" in *Colección de documentos inéditos*, 363, 370.

11. See Guzmán's letter, "Carta a S.M. del presidente de la audiencia de Méjico Nuño de Guzmán en que refiere la jornada que hizo a Mechoacan, a conquistar la provincia de los tebles chichimecas que confina, con Nueva España. MDXXX," in Zaragoza, *Crónicas de la conquista*, 21–59, esp. 25 (hereafter, Guzmán, "Carta").

12. J. Benedict Warren suggests that according to the *Relación de Michoacan* around eight thousand men were recruited but many deserted before leaving Michoacan. *Conquest of Michoacan*, 228.

13. See *Harkness Collection*, 104, 109, 114, 117, 119. This volume includes portions of the lawsuit (transcribed and translated by J. Benedict Warren) as well as reproductions of the Codex Huexotzingo; see p. 64 for painting 6 and the reference to the number of warriors. See also Warren, *Conquest of Michoacan*, 213–14.

14. Warren, *Conquest of Michoacan*, 228. It is highly unlikely that the Spaniards would have been able to come up with the quantity of metal (and the necessary blacksmiths) to fashion the chains that would have been needed for so many men; more likely, as Flores stated, they kept the lords and nobles in chains as hostages for the rest.

15. Pedro de Carranza, "Relación sobre la jornada que hizo Nuño de Guzmán de la entrada . . . hecha por Pedro de Carranza," in Zaragoza, *Crónicas de la conquista*, 153–80, quote on 156 (hereafter, Carranza, "Relación").

16. Cuarta anónima in García Icazbalceta, *Colección de documentos*, 2:462, 464.

17. García del Pilar in García Icazbalceta, *Colección de documentos*, 2:256, 258. According to Flores, "fueron repartidos entre los españoles los indios que traia de paz de los pueblos del Marqués y de los de Alonso de Avalos . . . y de otros pueblos . . . como quien alquila bestias, ansi se alquilaban los pobres indios amigos entre algunos de los españoles por preseas." Cuarta relacion anónima, in García Icazbalceta, *Colección de documentos*, 2:474.

18. Francisco de Arceo, "Relación, hecha de viva voz por el alférez Francisco de Arceo, al capitán e historiador Gonzalo Fernández de Oviedo y Valdés," in Zaragoza, *Crónicas de la conquista*, 239–68, quote on 243 (hereafter, Arceo, "Relación").

19. Carranza, "Relación," 171.

20. Hassig, *Aztec Warfare*, 63–64; Warren, *Conquest of Michoacan*, 67.

21. Arceo, "Relación," 242.

22. Tercera anónima, García Icazbalceta, *Colección de documentos*, 2:458.

23. Cuarta anónima, García Icazbalceta, *Colección de documentos*, 2:467.

24. Gonzalo López, "Relación del descubirmiento y conquista que se hizo por el gobernador Nuño de Guzmán y su ejército en las provincias de la Nueva Galicia, escrita por Gonzalo López y autorizada por Alonso de Mata, escribano de S.M., año MDXXX," in Zaragoza, *Crónicas de la conquista*, 61–112, quote on 84–85 (hereafter, López, "Relación").

25. Cuarta anónima, García Icazbalceta, *Colección de documentos*, 2:467. The Tapia in question probably was Don Andrés de Tapia Motelchiuhtzin, who had been interim ruler of Tenochtitlan and accompanied Guzmán. See also *Epistolario de Nueva España*, 2:188.

26. Carranza, "Relación," 175.

27. See Warren, *Conquest of Michoacan*, 213.

28. See *Harkness Collection*, 107, 109; see also 117 for a description of how the gold and feathered banner was made.

29. Guzmán, "Carta," 27.

30. E.g., according to Gonzalo López after leaving Omitlan the expedition came to a pueblo where there was no maize but plenty of fish and dogs "de lo cual los amigos cargaron cuanto pudieron." López, "Relación," 84.

31. Both García del Pilar and Flores mention the punishment of the Indians of Toluca; possibly the latter was familiar with the testimony of Pilar.

32. López, "Relación," 87.

33. García del Pilar states that they reached Aztatlan in July and had been there approximately two months before the river flooded. García Icazalceta, *Colección de documentos*, 2:254.

34. López, "Relación," 88.

35. García del Pilar, García Icazbalceta, *Colección de documentos*, 2:254, 255. He is the only one who suggested that a number of Indians already were ill before the flood.

36. López, "Relación," 89; Cuarta anónima, García Icazbalceta, *Colección de documentos*, 2:471. Arceo thought that two-thirds of the twenty thousand indios amigos had died and noted that all the cattle and pigs died. "Relación," 261–62.

37. Cuarta anónima, García Icazbalceta, *Colección de documentos*, 2:471; García del Pilar, García Icazbalceta, *Colección de documentos*, 2:255.

38. Cuarta anónima, García Icazbalceta, *Colección de documentos*, 2:471, and Carranza, "Relación," 167. The author of the Tercera relación anonima, García Icazbalceta, *Colección de documentos*, 2:447, stated that "in the pueblo of Aztatlan Tapiezuela and other principales, lords of Mexico and Tlatelolco, died."

39. López, "Relación," 89–90.

40. Carranza, "Relación," 169.

41. Cuarta anónima, García Icazbalceta, *Colección de documentos*, 2:472.

42. Carranza, "Relación," 173.

43. Gonzalo López mentions finding in a pueblo in the sierra near Culiacan during Semana Santa: "four Indians of our allies, of which two were mine, who had been brought there by the Indians of the country who had taken them from the rear guard that remained sick." López, "Relación," 101.

44. Gonzalo López stated that Guzmán had been informed that many of the indios amigos had made an agreement to mutiny. Ibid., 92. Flores said that of those who left, "the enemies" killed all except one who escaped. Cuarta anónima, in García Icazbalceta, *Colección de documentos*, 2:475.

45. Carranza, "Relación," 176.

46. Cuarta relación anónima, García Icazbalceta, *Colección de documentos*, 2:480–81.

47. Carranza, "Relación," 177. Carranza wrote that he had subsequently seen Don Tomé's horse in Guzmán's stable and that Guzmán had kept Don Tomé "a donde tenia a sus puercos" for two or three days.

48. Guzmán, "Carta," 38.

49. Ibid., 43, 57.

50. Cuarta anónima, García Icazbalceta, *Colección de documentos*, 2:467. See also López, "Relación," 65, 72, 73, 75, 78.

51. López, "Relación," 78.

52. Tercera relación anónima, García Icazbalceta, *Colección de documentos*, 2:441.

53. Guzmán, "Carta," 45. Flores alone mentioned that when Gonzalo López returned from Michoacan with reinforcements to Zacualpa, where he was received peacefully, López took five hundred or one thousand captives. Flores reported (he had not been present) that the "amigos say that they killed and sacrificed more than two thousand souls, because they were their enemies, with the sanction of the Christians." Cuarta anónima, in García Icazbalceta, *Colección de documentos*, 2:473–74.

54. García del Pilar, García Icazbalceta, *Colección de documentos*, 2:261. A letter to the Crown from the Audiencia of Mexico in late April 1532 mentioned having sent to Guzmán a provision stating that "he should allow to come to their houses and estates certain Indians of this city and its district who remain of those whom he took on his conquest, that there were few who returned." *Epistolario de Nueva España*, 2:124.

55. Juan de Sámano, García Icazbalceta *Colección de documentos*, 2:269. The phrase "barrio de naguatatos" must refer to an enclave of Nahuatl speakers who perhaps originated in central Mexico rather than to a group of interpreters, the primary meaning of the term.

56. The Primera anónima states that after the flood "algunos de los indios que aqui quedaron vivos se fueron veinte, treinta leguas a la sierra a vivir y juntar con otros que en ella estaban." The statement is ambiguous as here "indios" might refer to amigos or to local people. García Icazbalceta, *Colección de documentos*, 2:289.

57. Hernando Cortés and Jerónimo López both wrote that Mendoza took forty or fifty thousand recruits to Nueva Galicia. See their letters in García Icazbalceta, *Colección de documentos*, vol. 2.

58. Apart from the depositions that appear in the residencia, another source for firsthand observations of the war are *informaciones* later compiled by some participants. These usually discuss only episodes in which the petitioner played a role. There exists a partial account of the war in the form of a letter from Jerónimo López, who was not a participant, in the Archivo Histórico Nacional, Madrid (hereafter, AHN), Diversos, Colecciones, leg. 22, no. 33 (also published in Zaragoza, *Crónicas de la Conquista*, 329–43).

59. Cortés made this criticism explicitly in his "Peticion que dio Don Hernando Cortes contra Don Antonio de Mendoza," probably written in 1543; see García Icazbalceta, *Colección de documentos*, 2:63.

60. The speed with which Mendoza's presence changed the direction of the war suggests that his success perhaps did not hinge solely on the military superiority of his forces.

61. This probably is the *estancia* of Cuistlan, not far from Guadalajara, that Peter Gerhard lists as Tepoquitequi, which he thinks may be the same as Tepacatengo. *North Frontier*, 137.

62. For a lengthy and detailed description of this episode, see Hernando Martel's response to question 133 of the *interrogatorio* in Archivo General de Indias, Sevilla (hereafter, AGI), Justicia 261, pieza 3.

63. AHN Diversos, Colecciones, leg. 22, no. 33.

64. Gerhard lists Cazcan, Coca, Cora, Guachichil, Huichol, Tecuexe, and Zacateco all as belonging to the "Aztecoidan Family." *North Frontier*, 42. Some of these languages are now extinct. On the ethnohistory of this region see Donald D. Brand, "Ethnohistoric Synthesis," and articles in Foster and Weigand, *Archaeology*.

65. Acacitli, *Conquista y pacificación*, 26.

66. Ibid., 25–26.

67. Ibid., 18.

68. Ibid., 19.

69. Ibid., 18. According to Lockhart, Quahquechollan is the same as Huaquechula, located near Tlaxcala and Huexotzingo, and so they were likely grouped together. The Acohuas are from the area of Texcoco; Mestitlan is Metztitlan.

70. See AGI Justicia 262, question 150 of the interrogatorio.

71. Acacitli, *Conquista y pacificación*, 20.

72. Ibid., 20.

73. See testimony of Alonso de Santa Cruz in AGI Justicia 262, pieza 1, and Archivo General de la Nación (hereafter, AGN) Mercedes vol. 2, expedientes 237 and 381 (1543).

74. Acacitli, *Conquista y pacificación*, 24. According to Lockhart, *yczotilmantli* (*iczotilmatli*) means a blanket or cloak of palm fiber, pretty poor stuff for an Indian lord.

75. Acacitli, *Conquista y pacificación*, 28.

76. Ibid., 33, 36.

77. Ibid., 31, 33. Texistlan (spelling used in Gerhard, *North Frontier*, 121, 123) was near Copala, northwest of Guadalajara.

78. AGI Justicia 262, question 196.

79. AGI Justicia 262, response of Alonso de Santa Cruz to question 128.

80. See, e.g., AGN Mercedes vol. 2, expedientes 19 and 31.

81. See AGI Justicia 259 pieza 3, response to charge 39 and the charge in AGI Justicia 262, question 174.

82. Acacitli, *Conquista y pacificación*, 27.

83. See AGI Justicia 262, question 179.

84. AGI Justicia 262, testimony of Alonso de Santa Cruz, question 167.

85. Acacitli, *Conquista y pacificación*, 36–37.

86. See ibid., 38–39 for a detailed description of the hot springs, which clearly impressed him.

87. Acacitli, *Conquista y pacificación*, 39–41.

88. See AGI Justicia 262, responses to questions 72–76.

89. See Carta de Jerónimo López al Emperador, Mexico, October 20, 1541, in García Icazbalceta, *Colección de documentos*, 2:143–44.

CHAPTER SIX

FORGOTTEN ALLIES

The Origins and Roles of Native Mesoamerican Auxiliaries and Indios Conquistadores in the Conquest of Yucatan, 1526–1550

JOHN F. CHUCHIAK IV

I have fought beside these Indians and I have seen their loyalty and the great service that they have done for Your Majesty. . . . They have fought and suffered along beside us, and many a Spanish soldier owes them his life. . . . I can say in all honesty that without them we would never have conquered this land.

FRANCISCO DE BRACAMONTE, 1576

On March 16, 1576, Pedro Xochimilco and Miguel Damián, both Nahuatl speaking natives of central Mexico serving as the *alcaldes* of the village of Santiago, which lay just outside of the walls of the Spanish city of Mérida, appeared before the governor of the province of Yucatan, Francisco Velázquez de Guijon. Xochimilco and Damián, both veteran Indian conquistadors in the Spanish conquest of Yucatan, presented a complaint in the company of the *defensor de los indios* (Indian defender) Francisco de Palomino. Along with the rest of the non-Maya village council from Santiago, they petitioned the governor for his aid in relieving them of a fiscal burden that they saw as unjustly placed upon them by a previous governor. According to their petition, they and other citizens of the villages of Santiago and San Cristóbal had originally come from outside of the

province as allies and auxiliaries during the wars of conquest conducted by
the *adelantado* Francisco de Montejo and his son and nephew. They argued:

> We left behind our own lands and our families in order to come to
> this province and to serve our lords the Spaniards and to aid and
> help them in their conquest . . . and in this dangerous duty we
> always served and fought beside them as their friends and we have
> always served His Majesty with our own persons, our arms and our
> servants in the conquest and defense of this land . . . and even after
> the conquest we have served in times of need for defense and
> against rebels by land and corsairs who have come by sea. . . . [I]n
> all of this we have served voluntarily . . . and now we are seeking
> justice for so many injustices that have been committed against us.[1]

The non-Maya Indian petitioners also noted that they had once been
among a great number of Indians from many places outside of the province
of Yucatan, but after the wars, decades of exploitation, disease, impover-
ishment, and death, their numbers were reduced to a pathetic few. Now,
aged and impoverished from many financial exactions that were unjustly
placed upon them after the conquest, they sought justice at the hands of
the king of Spain. The Indian petitioners claimed that their service was
essential in conquering and pacifying the land but that their contribution
to the conquest and colonization of Yucatan had been long since forgotten. They were, in their own words, the "forgotten allies" of the conquest,
and only by their own struggle, sacrifice, and aid to the Europeans could
the Spaniards subdue the Maya of the province.

Their impoverished economic situation and the struggle for recognition
of the merits and services of these non-Maya Indians in Yucatan reveal the
extent to which they had been forgotten as useful allies in the conquest.
Along with their petition, these forgotten allies attached lists of non-Maya
inhabitants of the region. These two separate lists serve as a clue to the origins of what had once been a vast number of Indian auxiliaries, servants,
and slaves, all of them brought by force from central Mexican and other
neighboring provinces, in order to aid the Spaniards in their long and brutal conquest of the Yucatan peninsula. Just reading down the list of those
few allies and auxiliaries who survived the conquest gives us a hint of the
makeup of the army that won Francisco de Montejo final victory in the

Maya region: a mix of peoples from the central Mexican towns of Xochimilco, Azcapotzalco, Huexotzingo, and Texcoco, who fought beside Chontal, Popoluca, and Zoque Indian auxiliaries from Tabasco, as well as Lenca and Jicaque Indians from Honduras. Along with these auxiliaries, a large host of other Mesoamerican Indians served as slaves and burden carriers (*tameme*) including Tabascan, Chiapanec, Zapoteca, Mixteca, Mixe, and other Mesoamerican Indians who carried the expeditions' equipment and supplies.[2] (See table 6.1.)

Unlike the well-documented deeds of the Tlaxcalteca and other Nahua allies of Hernando Cortés in Tenochtitlan and Pedro de Alvarado in Guatemala, history has chosen to forget the indigenous allies who served both during and after the conquest in Yucatan.[3] Even colonial era historians of Yucatan such as Fray Bernardo de Lizana (1633), Fray Diego López de Cogolludo (1686), and Fray Francisco de Ayeta (1693) all remain silent concerning the nature, origins, and significance of these Indian allies.[4] Barely mentioning the native allies, these historians left behind few clues for modern scholars to unravel the mystery of the role of indigenous auxiliaries and allies in the conquest of Yucatan. More recent historians have also chosen to ignore the role played by the host of auxiliaries who participated in Montejo's conquest of the Yucatec Maya. Thus, Nancy Farriss, Grant Jones, Robert Patch, Manuela Cristina García Bernal, and others have failed to devote more than a few sentences in passing concerning these auxiliaries.[5] Nevertheless, as this chapter will show, these native auxiliaries played a pivotal role in the final successful conquest of Yucatan, and abuses committed against them directly led to changing Crown policies concerning the *encomienda* system, indigenous labor, and personal services.[6] Without the aid of these Mesoamerican allies, Montejo and his men could not have succeeded in their venture.

The story of Pedro Xochimilco and the other indios conquistadores shows that in truth, as they argued, their Spanish allies had forgotten them. Although they had once numbered in the thousands, by 1576 the Indian allies of the conquest were a demoralized and oppressed group of native Mesoamericans who had come to Yucatan during the conquest from many places and provinces, only to end up impoverished and forgotten a generation later. The story of how and why they had come to join the conquest of Yucatan is a story that has never been told. This chapter is an attempt to unravel the details of this allied army long since lost to history.

TABLE 6.1

Place of origin of surviving indios conquistadores, ca. 1576

	NUMBER OF SURVIVORS
Azcapotzalco	17
Xochimilco	6
Huejotzingo	1
Texcoco	1
Province of Tabasco	8
Province of Honduras	3
Province of Guatemala	2
Unknown Origin	18
Total	56

Source: AGI, Audiencia de Mexico, 100.

THE INITIAL ENTRADAS OF YUCATAN, 1526–39

Although the Yucatan peninsula was the first part of the Mexican mainland discovered, it would be the last region conquered. The more wealthy lands of the Mexica of central Mexico occupied the Spaniards for several years. It was not until 1526 that Francisco de Montejo, a veteran of two earlier expeditions to Yucatan and of Cortés's conquest in Mexico, received a royal patent and charter to explore and conquer the region of Yucatan.[7] Anxious to begin his undertaking, while still in Spain Montejo used his title and commission as adelantado to organize a Spanish expedition of conquest. This first expedition, made up exclusively of Spaniards who were enlisted in Seville and the surrounding regions, arrived in the eastern part of the Yucatan peninsula in 1527.[8] At first, the Maya of the region met the Spaniards in peace and agreed to their demand to swear loyalty to the king of Spain. The Maya also began to supply the expedition with food and other necessary supplies. Apparently, this expedition included no Indian allies because the soldiers were required to carry their own supplies. Several soldiers even had the duty of carrying other supplies, like the barrels of powder and shot for the small artillery pieces brought by the expedition. The Spaniards had not come knowingly with the understanding that they would serve as burden carriers. After much grumbling and the death of several dozen Spaniards by disease and overwork, Montejo set out to explore the region to the north of their camp at Dzama.[9] The Maya grew angered at their continued presence and demands and attacked the Spaniards. Despite the loss of more than one thousand Maya at the Battle of Chauaca, the Maya refused to surrender, forcing Montejo to return to the coast under constant harassment. The Spaniards set up a small fort on the coast in 1528, but they had no further success in conquering the country. With the deaths of most of his expedition's soldiers, Montejo found himself forced to return to Mexico City in 1529 in order to gather a larger army.

Once again, Adelantado Montejo neglected to bring along any serious number of Indian auxiliaries or servants, and his second attempt at the conquest of Yucatan met a similar fate. Nevertheless, in Mexico City Montejo was quickly joined by his son Francisco de Montejo (*el mozo*, the younger) who helped him plan his second expedition. The younger Montejo had accompanied Cortés on his 1524–25 journey through the region to Honduras. During that expedition, the younger Montejo traveled in the Chontal Maya speaking region of Acalan in the province of Tabasco.[10] He urged his father to launch his conquest of the peninsula from that western region.

Following his son's advice, the elder Montejo returned in 1531 with a larger force but one still short on Indian burden carriers and allies. The Spaniards quickly conquered the Maya port city of Campeche, where they established a fortress. From this western base of operations, Montejo sent his son inland with an army. The younger Montejo went deep into the peninsula and established a base at the sacred Maya city of Chichen Itza, which he renamed the royal capital, Ciudad Real de Chichen Itza. After the expedition had lingered there for several months, the local Maya rose up against him, and the Spaniards were constantly under attack. Desperate and losing men, the younger Montejo fled back to his father's base at Campeche.

The elder Montejo had already sent out an expedition east across the peninsula to the Maya province of Chetumal under the command of his lieutenant, Alonso de Avila. Although Avila met with initial success, the Maya of the Chetumal region eventually defeated his army, forcing them to escape to Honduras for safety.[11] Seeing the defeat of both his son and Avila's forces as a sign, in 1535 the adelantado withdrew his forces to Veracruz, leaving the Yucatan peninsula once again completely in control of the Maya. In one of the last letters from his base of operations in Campeche, the adelantado examined the reasons for his failure. He wrote that he decided to leave the land and abandon the conquest because "we did not even have an Indian left to serve us a cup of water."[12] Montejo unconsciously answered his own question when he wondered why he had been defeated. He revealed the central weakness of his two previous expeditions: the lack of any significant number of Indian allies and servants. No major conquest in the Americas, either before or after 1540, took place successfully without the aid and service of indigenous allies. In truth, it was Cortés's alliance with the Tlaxcalteca and other Mesoamerican Indian groups that produced the final fall of the Mexica of Tenochtitlan. In Peru, the Pizarros might never have conquered any part of Peru without the aid of various Inca factions, themselves engaged in a civil war at the time of the capture of Atahualpa. Even as late as the 1690s, when Don Diego de Vargas undertook the reconquest of the province of New Mexico, his victory would not have occurred without the aid of other Pueblo Indian communities. What Montejo's first attempts at the conquest of Yucatan illustrate is the inability of the Spaniards to conquer any indigenous people by themselves, unaided by military and logistical support from other native groups.[13]

As the younger Montejo earlier counseled his father, the key to success in the conquest of Yucatan relied on using the surrounding regions (like that of Tabasco to the west) as bases of support for operations and logistics. Almost prophetically, the younger Montejo had given his father the key to formulating the final plan for the ultimate conquest of the peninsula. However, with his father away in Honduras conquering that region for the Crown, that seed had to germinate a while longer. By the time that the elder Montejo successfully conquered the region of Honduras-Higueras and had the ability to finally embark upon his own conquest of Yucatan, a political conflict with the conqueror of Guatemala, Don Pedro de Alvarado, had surfaced and forced him to set aside his own plans for conquest. In 1536 the conqueror of Guatemala, Pedro de Alvarado, entered the Honduras and Higueras regions with eighty well-armed Spaniards, on horse and foot, together with over three thousand Nahua and Guatemalan Indian auxiliaries.[14] A year later, with royal permission and the title of governor, Francisco de Montejo, only recently defeated in his second *entrada* to Yucatan, led an army of eighty to one hundred Spanish soldiers and several hundred Nahuatl-speaking native auxiliaries from his encomienda of Azcapotzalco to Honduras, arriving early in 1537.[15]

Alvarado reluctantly left the region, returning to Guatemala and leaving behind a large number of his Indian auxiliaries, who joined Montejo's army.

An Indian rebel leader named Lempira, using the confusion between the Spaniards to his advantage, began an Indian rebellion in central Honduras. At first, Lempira appealed to Montejo's Guatemalan and Mexican auxiliaries, as racial brothers, to desert the Spaniards and join him in a common war on the European invaders.[16] These warriors, however, remained loyal to Montejo, who later reaffirmed his preference for central Mexican auxiliaries, especially the Nahuatl-speaking Azcapotzalca, whom he came to regard as his most trusted indigenous allies.[17] Toward the end of 1537, Francisco de Montejo commissioned one of his Spanish captains, Alonso de Cáceres, to attack the rebels under Lempira with a force of eighty Spaniards and several hundred Guatemalan and Mexican auxiliaries.[18] Here in Honduras Montejo realized the value of Indian auxiliaries in warfare. From this point onward, he included large bodies of Indian auxiliaries, posting them with each Spanish squad.[19]

In Honduras, Montejo also came to appreciate the value of Indian burden carriers, servants, and slaves and their necessary role in supplying and transporting goods and supplies. Due to a lack of Indian burden bearers, his army became bogged down and lost mobility. Montejo sent repeated appeals to adjacent provinces for men and materials of war, supplies of all kinds, and especially native auxiliaries.[20] The Spanish authorities in San Salvador offered Montejo their cooperation, making available to Montejo's emissaries munitions of all kinds, powder, harquebusiers, and iron bars from which to make crossbow bolts. They also provided livestock and, most importantly, one hundred native auxiliaries (probably Pipil) and placed one thousand Indian burden bearers at their disposal. The burden bearers were not only to carry the munitions from San Salvador to Higueras but were also to remain to serve the Spaniards. However, even these native burden bearers did not remedy the situation. The Spaniards remained shorthanded, and, according to witnesses, they "lacked burden carriers to bring in distant supplies and could spare neither warriors nor auxiliaries from the siege of Lempira's forces to make up foraging parties."[21]

During the final conquest of the Valley of Comayagua, Montejo utilized a large number of Indian auxiliaries. In late 1538, on his march into the valley, Montejo raised more than fifteen hundred native auxiliaries of high fighting quality from among those Lenca and Jicaque natives he had recently conquered.[22] Now allied with Montejo, many of these Jicaque

and Lenca Indians would serve beyond their own province as allies and
auxiliaries for Montejo's later conquests. Both he and other conquerors
who later left the province of Honduras for the conquest of Yucatan took
with them numbers of Lenca and Jicaque Indian allies. Montejo often
rewarded his favorite soldiers, relatives, and supporters who served with
him in Yucatan with titles to encomiendas from which they extracted a
great number of slaves and porters for their own expeditions and later
participation in the conquest of Yucatan.[23] Montejo revoked many of the
encomiendas created by Alvarado and distributed them among the soldiers who served in his campaigns. (See table 6.2.)

As the changing tributary population of these encomiendas may suggest, the new *encomenderos* removed and forced into service large numbers of their tributaries. Montejo and his supporters often used brutal
methods to procure allies and porters from among their Lenca and Jicaque
encomiendas in Honduras. The conquistador Francisco Trejo, for instance,
on several occasions used violence to force the Lenca Indians of his
encomiendas and from the surrounding regions to serve him as porters
and servants. Apparently, on one occasion Trejo and one of his fellow
Spaniards, Alonso Hernández, went to the home of a local Lenca Indian
noble named Capaxuaca and demanded that he and several others serve
them as porters. When the native resisted and protested that he did not
want to serve him, Trejo and his men began to beat him in the head with
clubs until they drew blood, and then they burned down his house, steal-
ing all of his turkeys, mantas, and other belongings as a lesson for others.[24] Other natives similarly accused Trejo of beating them and forcing
them to serve as porters and slaves.[25] Another Montejo supporter and ally,
Simon de Bravante, reportedly killed an Indian in the Jicaque town of
Laguaracha with a sword and wounded several others in an attempt to
force them to accompany him as porters and servants.[26]

Montejo concluded the successful campaigns in the Valley of Comayagua and beyond in the first months of 1539, bringing the bloody war to
an end. At that time, the Spaniards and colonists of Honduras all believed
that Indians from outside who served as auxiliaries in war could later be
settled among the natives as allies of the Spaniards. The practice of settling Indian allies among recently conquered peoples had become common. Alvarado and Montejo both subscribed to this belief in the view that
a policy of colonization was desirable. However, Montejo would not remain
long in the province. Pedro de Alvarado, angry at Montejo's usurpation

TABLE 6.2

Net tributary losses in encomiendas in Honduras held by Spanish conquistadors of Yucatan, 1539–1550

SPANISH CONQUISTADORS OF YUCATAN (FROM HONDURAS CAMPAIGN)	ENCOMIENDA(S) HELD	NUMBER OF TRIBUTARIES OF ENCOMIENDA, 1539	NUMBER OF TRIBUTARIES OF ENCOMIENDA, 1550
Pedro de Casos	Lacampay	250	50
	Oxuera	—	—
	Guacarequin (*Lenca*)	—	—
Juan de Esquivel	Lexamanij	350	120
(step-son of adelantado Francisco de Montejo)	Caruza	—	—
	Tencosquin (*Lenca*)	150	—
Alonso Reinoso	Yamala	300	180
	Tencoa	—	—
	(*Lenca*)	—	—
Juan Ruiz de la Vega	Cocuyagua (*Lenca*)	200	70
Francisco de Trejo	Lacayan	—	—
	Camaxca (*Lenca*)	500	20

Sources: AGI, Patronato, 56, 67, 68, 72, 80; AGI, Indiferente General, 1004, 1018; AGI, Justicia 299; AGI, Justicia 298; AGI, Audiencia de Mexico, 100, 126, 127, 359, 364.

of his claims to Honduras, filed suit in both Mexico and Spain against Montejo, eventually winning the dispute and having Montejo removed from his governorship in Honduras. In return for peacefully relinquishing the province to Alvarado, Montejo received the control and governorship of the province of Chiapas, along with the cession of Alvarado's claims to his central Mexican encomienda of Xochimilco, which he handed over to Montejo in late 1539 in compensation for his loss of Honduras.

Not wanting to leave Alvarado with the services of his own Indian auxiliaries, Montejo left the province of Honduras for his post as governor of Chiapas in late 1539, taking along with him not only the auxiliaries that he had brought with him, some of whom were Nahua from his central Mexican encomienda of Azcapotzalco, but also several hundred Lenca and Jicaque natives who had served him in Honduras.[27] During his march to Chiapas, Montejo's armies included not only these native auxiliaries but also a large number of Indian slaves and porters, many of them from Guatemala and still others from Honduras (see map 6). Now realizing the significance of these Indian porters in his conquests, he sent a large number of them forward from Chiapas to his son, who then served as his lieutenant governor in the province of Tabasco. These Indian porters and slaves would aid in the logistics of the final conquest of Yucatan.

After Montejo left, several other Spanish conquistadores, all Montejo supporters, also departed to participate in the conquest of Yucatan. Juan Ruiz de la Vega, Alonso Reinoso, and Francisco Trejo all served in Yucatan, taking with them Lenca Indian allies and a number of Lenca and Jicaque porters from their own encomiendas in Honduras.[28] Embarking from the port of San Pedro, these conquistadors and their small contingent of Indian allies went with Montejo's blessing by ship to Tabasco to take part in the final conquest of Yucatan.

By 1539, at least in theory, the Montejo clan controlled a large swath of territory including Yucatan and, more importantly, including the major provinces and territories that bordered the peninsula. In reality, this control was limited to the territories in which the Montejos actually had a military presence (i.e., Tabasco and Honduras-Higueras) by late 1538. Nevertheless, in the struggle for ultimate legal control over Honduras, the Montejo-Alvarado dispute would work itself out in the favor of the Montejos. In 1539, in exchange for control over Honduras, the Crown required Pedro de Alvarado to yield control of the province of Chiapas to Adelantado Montejo and to compensate him for his financial loss by trans-

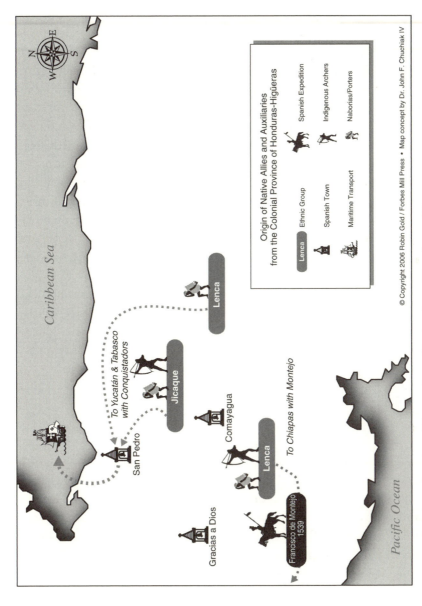

Map 6. Origins of native allies and auxiliaries from Honduras-Higueras

ferring control over the wealthy and populous central Mexican encomienda of Xochimilco to the adelantado. With the control and governorship of Chiapas, Montejo the elder could resupply and support his son's efforts at the final conquest of Yucatan more effectively. Due to the harsh conditions of the Honduran coast and the lack of any major port city, the province of Honduras did not serve as an effective place to supply and maintain an expedition of conquest. The Montejos' final control over the province of Chiapas, with its close connection to the more populated provinces of New Spain and Guatemala, made it an excellent base for mustering men and supplies to be sent to the younger Montejo's province of Tabasco, which soon came to serve as a staging point for all supplies, men, and equipment arriving from Mexico, Guatemala, Chiapas, Honduras, and Spain (see map 7).

With the exchange of Honduras for Chiapas—and with the younger Montejo already in firm control of Tabasco, with its close connection to the Spaniards in the bordering provinces of Guazacoalcos, Zapotecas, and Chiapas—the Montejos prepared for their final conquest of Yucatan. The Mesoamerican Indians of the provinces either claimed or controlled by the Montejos all played a major role in the supply, transportation, and military conquest of the province of Yucatan. Although colonial historians have ignored their role in the final conquest, it was only the military and logistical assistance of these Indians that enabled the Spaniards under Montejo to complete the conquest of a province that had eluded their domination for more than twenty years.[29]

NATIVE ALLIES AND FORCED LABOR IN MONTEJO'S FORCES

Francisco de Montejo and his commanders gathered their growing allied Indian army from the neighboring provinces either directly under their control or from which their soldiers and captains originated. In this manner, the native allies that aided in the final conquest of the Yucatec Maya came from all over central Mesoamerica. Ranging from Chontal and Nahuatl natives from the province of Tabasco to Zapoteca and Mixe warriors from the region of the Zapotecas to Lenca and Jicaque allies from Honduras, Montejo continuingly added native Mesoamerican allies to his army throughout the final months of 1539.

A large number of the allied warriors and porters came from the nearby provinces of Guazacualco and Tabasco. These provinces had both been at

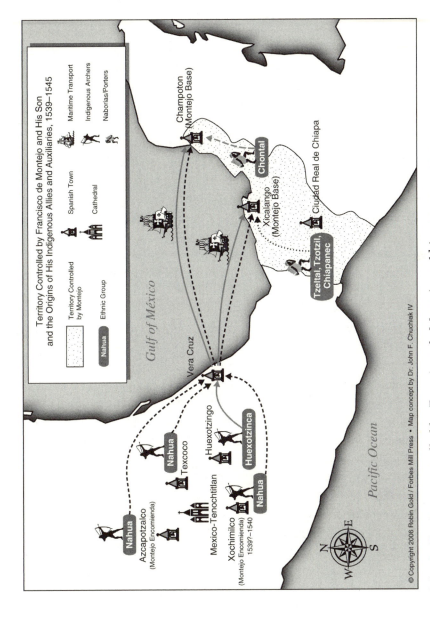

Map 7. Territory controlled by Francisco de Montejo and his son, 1539–1545

Within the map:

Territory Controlled by Francisco de Montejo and His Son
and the Origins of His Indigenous Allies and Auxiliaries, 1539–1545

- Territory Controlled by Montejo
- Ethnic Group
- Nahua
- Spanish Town
- Cathedral
- Maritime Transport
- Indigenous Archers
- Naborías/Porters

Gulf of México

Pacific Ocean

Champoton (Montejo Base)

Chontal

Xicalango (Montejo Base)

Ciudad Real de Chiapa

Tzeltal, Tzotzil, Chiapanec

Vera Cruz

Texcoco

Huexotzingo

Huexotzinca

Mexico-Tenochtitlan

Xochimilco (Montejo Encomienda) 1539?–1540

Nahua

Azcapotzalco (Montejo Encomienda)

N E S W

least nominally conquered by the Spaniards as early as 1526. Later, a Spanish captain, Baltazar de Gallegos, arrived from Mexico with a force and conquered the provinces, becoming an encomendero and later a participant in Montejo's final expedition of conquest. The province of Tabasco proved of paramount importance for Montejo's plans for the ultimate conquest of Yucatan. Unfortunately for the many Nahuatl-, Chontal-, and Popoluca-speaking peoples of the region, Montejo's plans included a massive mobilization of Indian burden bearers, servants, and military auxiliaries, a majority of whom would be extracted from the province (see map 8). After Francisco de Montejo received official royal commission as governor of Tabasco in 1533, he named his younger son as his lieutenant and his effective governor in Tabasco. With the arrival of the younger Montejo, the exploitation of the human resources of the region began in earnest.

Crown policy concerning Indian slavery was in transition at the very time that Montejo and his supporters enslaved and impressed Indian allies from Tabasco and beyond to participate in the conquest.[30] To some degree, it may have been Montejo's abuse of Indian porters and slaves from nearby provinces that urged Fray Bartolomé de las Casas to campaign for the celebrated New Laws of 1542. Regardless of Las Casas's attempts to protect them, the lives of thousands of native Mesoamericans from the region of Tabasco changed with the arrival of the Montejos. After a series of initial rebellions, Montejo consolidated his power over the province of Tabasco. These Indian uprisings gave the Montejo clan the justification that they needed to begin to enslave massive numbers of natives from the region. According to one contemporary source, during his period of control over the region, Montejo branded, enslaved, and utilized the forced services of more than thirty thousand Indians from Tabasco alone.[31] These Tabascan slaves, mostly Chontal- and Nahuatl-speaking peoples, served as integral parts of the logistical and transportation aspect of conquest implemented by the Montejos and their men. As late as 1547, tameme from Tabasco served as the main means of transporting goods and supplies to and from the province of Yucatan via the port town of Xicalango, from where large trains of indigenous porters left by way of canoe and on foot to reach the Yucatecan ports of Champoton and Campeche. One of the Spanish conquistadors later commented, "These Indians of Tabasco are our main means of transportation by canoe and by land to this province of Yucatan."[32] Later in 1552, the *cacique* of the demographically devastated town of Xicalango testified to the importance of his town's assistance to the Spaniards in the

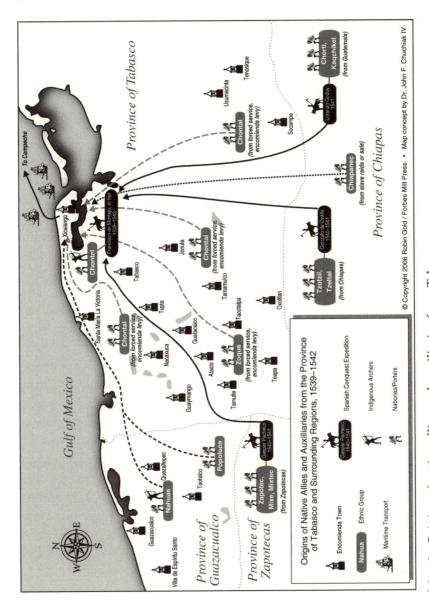

Map 8. Origins of native allies and auxiliaries from Tabasco

conquest of Yucatan. However, he noted that they not only contributed slaves and porters but also allied Indian warriors. The cacique Don Francisco testified that "all of the caciques, principales, and common Indians of this town have participated in the activities of this conquest, not only in giving all aid in the form of food, supplies, and many canoes in order to transport soldiers, horses, food and supplies through the many rivers, swamps and lagoons . . . but this town as friends and loyal vassals has also given the Spaniards many guides and a great number of people who served as soldiers in war."[33]

Even the Spaniards who testified on behalf of the town of Xicalango, which had served as the base of transportation and supply for their army of conquest, testified to the fact that it was "only thanks to these natives and their support and supplies that it was possible to conquer the provinces of Yucatan."[34] Much earlier with the services of several Chontal guides and interpreters, the Spaniards first established a peaceful connection with the Yucatec Maya town of Champoton with whom the Chontal had trading relations.[35] The service of these Chontal interpreters became instrumental in establishing an advance base of support for their later conquests.

Regardless of the small numbers of Tabascans who served as allied auxiliaries, the majority of Tabascan Indians served as slaves and porters. Although most slaves used as tameme had been taken semilegally by means of conquest or suppression of native rebellions, it appears that, especially in Tabasco, the Montejos used and authorized other means of making slaves. Also, although his actions remained patently illegal, Francisco de Montejo apparently gave permission to his men to enslave many of their encomienda Indians and use them as burden carriers without payment for their services.[36] This abuse of encomienda service not only enabled the Spanish conquistadors of Yucatan to equip themselves and transport their goods during the final conquest of the Maya; it also played a large part in the rapid depopulation of the provinces of Tabasco and Guazacoalcos.

In his long battle against Spanish injustice in the conquest, Fray Bartolomé de las Casas complained about the many abuses of the encomienda system.[37] There is no better example of the extent to which the early conquerors abused their encomiendas than that of Montejo and his supporters in the provinces of Guazacoalcos and Tabasco (see map 9). Originally a densely populated region, with more than 160,000 tributaries in 1524, the region of Tabasco suffered from abuse by Montejo and his men to such a degree that by 1549 there were no more than 13,454 natives

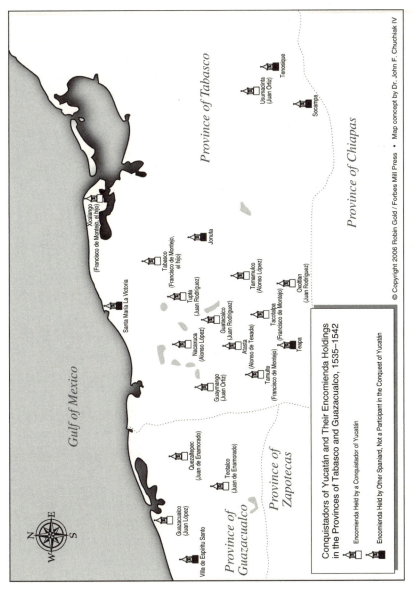

Map 9. Conquistadors of Yucatan and their encomienda holdings in Tabasco and Guazacualco, 1535–1542

on the tribute rolls. Regardless of the onset of major epidemic diseases that afflicted the population of Tabasco beginning in 1524, as late as 1530 the province still contained over 105,000 Indian tributaries.

By 1533, when Francisco de Montejo came to control the province with the assistance of his son as lieutenant governor, the population began to suffer a rapid decline not attributed to epidemic diseases or any other identifiable cause. By the 1540s an absolute pillaging of the human resources of the province occurred in order to secure the logistics of conquest. Moreover, upon examining several figures and historical records, it appears that the highest levels of depopulation occurred only in those encomiendas held by Montejo and those conquistadors who accompanied him on his conquests. In fact, neighboring towns held in encomienda by other Spaniards who did not participate in the conquest of Yucatan experienced little or no population loss, and several actually witnessed population increases.

No single encomienda town in Tabasco held by a conquistador of Yucatan witnessed an increase in population. Instead, as table 6.3 illustrates, a net loss of more than 828 indigenous tributaries and their families occurred from 1541 to 1549. This figure suggests that more than 828 tributaries disappeared or were forcibly impressed into Spanish service during the era of the final conquest of Yucatan between 1541 and 1546.[38] In contrast to the staggering population loss in encomiendas held by Spanish conquistadors of Yucatan, those few encomiendas held by other Spaniards, including those held by the Crown, actually witnessed population increases, even though these same towns were located less than a few kilometers away from those that became depopulated.

Just as in their earlier campaigns in Honduras, Montejo and his conquistadors used brutal tactics to force native Chontal, Nahuatl, and Popoluca speakers into the service of their army. No doubt many of the 2,810 Indians missing from these encomiendas served as tameme and other auxiliaries with Montejo's army, either perishing in the conquest or remaining behind in Yucatan as slaves after the hostilities ceased. According to the Mexican scholar Mario Humberto Ruz, it was from the region of Tabasco in particular, especially from its coastal towns, where the Spaniards obtained a large part of the manpower necessary to transport their soldiers, weapons, horses, and other supplies to the province of Yucatan.[39] He also attributes this factor as significant in the demographic decline that occurred during the period from 1530 to 1549.

Instances of Spanish conquistadors violently forcing their encomienda tributaries into service as tameme or forced Indian auxiliaries became widespread. For example, Alonso López, the brother-in-law of the adelantado, used violence on many occasions to force native caciques to provide him with large numbers of Indian tamemes and auxiliaries. In 1541, while recruiting native auxiliaries and tameme for the final expedition of conquest to Yucatan, López attacked Don Francisco, the indigenous cacique of the town of Copilco-Zacualco, apparently for protesting against his forced impressments of natives from the town as burden carriers for the Spanish army. The Indians of the town later told their encomendero that "Alonso López had passed through there and he beat the cacique with a club and a whip until blood ran from his mouth, ears and nose and two days later he died ... all because he had not given over the tameme that López had asked to have."[40] Many other Tabascan natives received inhumane treatment when they resisted their own encomenderos' demands for service and auxiliaries.[41]

In the encomienda towns held directly by Francisco de Montejo and his son, population decline and the forced labor of Tabascan natives reached epic proportions, with an average of more than 80 percent of the population forced into service in their army. From 1541 to 1546 more than 413 Tabascan Indian tributaries from their encomiendas may have been forced to serve them in the conquest (almost 50 percent of the total number of tributaries lost). The Montejos also contrived unique ways of hiding the illegal forced service given to them by Tabascan Indians. Desperate to conceal their illegal use of encomienda Indians from Tabasco as slaves, auxiliaries, and servants, the Montejos engaged in the now age-old use of the *prestanombre* system by which they laid claim to more encomiendas and Indians by means of granting them to dead or absent Spaniards whose encomiendas they controlled themselves.[42]

A similarly large number of Indian allies and porters came from the neighboring province of Chiapas, which the Montejo's began to control in 1539 (see map 10). After ceding his claims to Honduras, Montejo received the governorship of Chiapas in 1539. Late in that same year, the adelantado made his way overland with a large column of Spaniards and Indian auxiliaries from Azcapotzalco and Guatemala, along with a large number of Lenca and Jicaque porters from Honduras. Having previously realized the value of indigenous allies and auxiliaries in his campaign in Honduras from 1537 to 1539, the adelantado began actively to recruit both Spaniards and native auxiliaries from his base in Chiapas for the conquest of Yucatan.

TABLE 6.3

Comparison of net population loss/gain on encomiendas held by Spanish conquistadors of Yucatan compared to those controlled by other colonists and the Crown

Spanish conquistadors of Yucatan	Encomienda(s) held (Tabasco)	Number of tributaries of encomienda town, 1541	Number of tributaries of encomienda, 1549	Net population loss/gain No. (%)
Rodrigo Alvarez	Taxaguan	53	0	−53 (−100)
Alonso Lopez (brother-in-law of Francisco de Montejo)	Soyataco	53	32	−21 (−40)
	Tamamulco	14	0	−14 (−100)
	Oxiaco	18	10	−8 (−44)
	Anaxuxuca	149	60	−89 (−60)
Adelantado Montejo	Tlacotalpa	200	60	−140 (−70)
	Tamulte	160	60	−100 (−63)
Francisco de Montejo (son)	Xicalango	150	30	−120 (−80)
	Tabasco	53	0	−53 (−100)
Juan Ortiz	Gueymango	170	100	−70 (−41)
	Usumacintla	60	40	−20 (−33)
Juan Rodriguez	Olcuatitan	53	29	−24 (−45)
	Guatacalco	35	20	−15 (−43)
	Tupta	46	22	−24 (−52)
Alonso de Texeda	Atasta	53	5	−48 (91)
	Masateupa	60	31	−29 (−48)
	Texomaxiaca	?	0	? (100)
TOTAL NET LOSS:				828 tributaries lost

SPANISH COLONISTS/CROWN	ENCOMIENDA(S) HELD (TABASCO)	NUMBER OF TRIBUTARIES OF ENCOMIENDA TOWN, 1541	NUMBER OF TRIBUTARIES OF ENCOMIENDA, 1549	NET POPULATION LOSS/GAIN No. (%)
Alonso Grado	Teapa	53	70	+17 (+32)
Garcia de Ledesma	Tecomaxiaca	100	160	+60 (+60)
Crown-held encomiendas	Tapijualpa	70	110	+40 (+57)
	Oxolotlan	170	240	+70 (+41)
TOTAL NET GAINS:			187 tributaries lost	

Sources: AGI, Audiencia de Guatemala, 111; AGI, Indiferente General, 1004; AGI, Justicia, 195; AGI, Justicia, 135, 195, 299, 300; AGI, Audiencia de Mexico, 100, 359, 364; AGI, Audiencia de Mexico, 900–1005 (*Confirmaciones de encomiendas de indios*).

In 1540 the adelantado, as governor of Chiapas, declared a new conquest of Yucatan. He immediately named his son Francisco de Montejo el mozo as his lieutenant and captain general and began to gather men and supplies.[43] Montejo had the conquest announced in Chiapas and the adjacent province of Zapotecas, as well as in Mexico and Guatemala. He promised independent captains that "with their own expenses they could raise companies that would serve in the conquest of Yucatan and that they would enlist them under their own banners, promising them recompense in the form of high offices and special privileges."[44]

In spite of the incentives offered, the need for reinforcements for his son's advance camp in the Maya town of Champoton soon became desperate. Shortly after announcing the conquest, Juan de Contreras arrived from Champoton in order to request more reinforcements for the Champoton garrison. With Montejo's aid he raised a small army and secured many Indian allies and slaves as porters and then returned to Champoton after sending Alonso Rosado in advance to give the garrison word of reinforcements. Along with this column, Montejo sent five hundred of the central Mexican Indian auxiliaries from Azcapotzalco that he had brought with him from Honduras. He also dispatched the remaining Guatemalan Indians with Contreras so that when he departed for Tabasco and Yucatan, he had an army of thirty Spaniards and more than one thousand Indian auxiliaries. From Chiapas, Montejo named competent lieutenants such as Juan de Urrutia, Gonzalo de Ovalle, and Hernán Centeno, each of whom brought with him a small army of Spanish servants and dependents, as well as Indian slaves and other native auxiliaries. Montejo also recruited several outstanding captains such as Lorenzo de Godoy from Guatemala, and Francisco Gil from Chiapas, both of whom raised large companies of men, including both Spaniards and several hundred Indian slaves and auxiliaries, all at their own expense.[45] Also a number of vecinos and encomenderos from Guatemala and El Salvador enlisted under the command of Lorenzo de Godoy in the conquest of Yucatan. Together over twenty Spaniards from Guatemala formed a company under Godoy, whose contingent included more than 140 Pipil, Chorti, and Xinka native porters and naborías.

Continuing to use the province of Chiapas as his base, the adelantado named Francisco Gil, a resident of Chiapas, as captain of a second expeditionary force to follow Contreras's army first to Tabasco and from there on to Yucatan. Gil organized a large group of 60 Spanish soldiers on horse

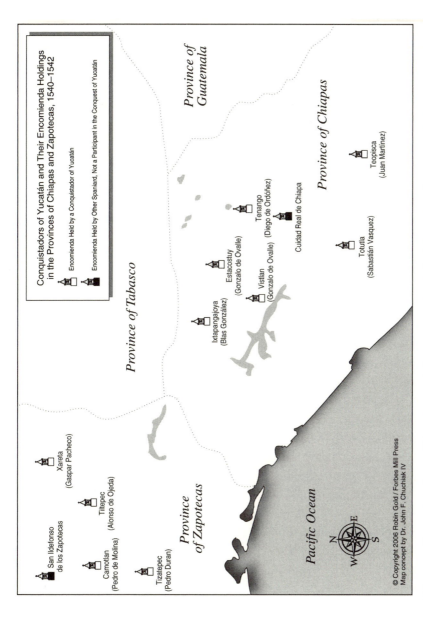

Map 10. Conquistadors of Yucatan and their encomienda holdings in Chiapas and Zapotecas, 1540–1542

and foot from Chiapas and Guatemala, all of whom brought with them Tzeltal or Zoque Indian allies and porters. To this column Adelantado Montejo added his remaining Lenca and Jicaque naborías, slaves, and auxiliaries that he had brought from Honduras, a party of several hundred in all. His Honduran porters carried the heavy artillery (three cannons), shot, powder, and other iron bars and ingots to be used as replacement bolts for the crossbows and shoes for the horses that Montejo had purchased with his own funds.[46] These were meant as reinforcements and supplies for his son in Tabasco. The other Spaniards in this column who held encomiendas brought along with them more than 230 Tzeltal and Zoque naborías, porters, and slaves to carry their own personal goods and supplies (see table 6.4).[47] Juan de Urrutia was commissioned to command the 10 Spanish horsemen as *alferez de la caballería,* and Hernán Centeno received a commission as *maestre de campo* in command of the infantry and allied Indians of the column.[48] The commanders themselves brought 30 Tzeltal Maya slaves to carry their provisions, spare weapons and other materials such as nails, tools, and iron ingots for crossbow bolts.

As Francisco Gil and his column prepared to leave, the adelantado decided to go to New Spain to obtain permission from the viceroy, Don Antonio de Mendoza, to take a large number of central Mexican Indians in order to conquer Yucatan. During his sojourn in Mexico City, Montejo enlisted many captains and soldiers from New Spain, Puebla, and Jalisco. On the way back to Chiapas, the adelantado stopped in Oaxaca in the town of San Ildefonso de los Zapotecos, where he recruited Gaspar Pacheco. Pacheco, a wealthy landowner and encomendero, raised a small army that included his brother, Melchor, together with his son, also named Melchor, and a nephew, Alonso Pacheco.[49] Together with Jorge de Villagomez, they recruited 15 other Spaniards from the province and over 345 Zapoteca, Mixteca, and Mixe retainers, porters, and slaves (see table 6.5).

Although Montejo's army drew its support troops from natives from a large number of ethnic groups from a wide geographical region controlled by Montejo, it was central Mexican Indian allies who made up the bulk of the Indian auxiliaries destined to serve as actual combatants. Although Adelantado Montejo amassed a large force of allied Mesoamericans from throughout the region, he continued to only trust Indian auxiliaries from central Mexico to bear arms and fight alongside of the Spaniards as true indios conquistadores. The majority of the auxiliaries who served Montejo as active combatants came from the central Mexican towns of Azcapotzalco and Xochimilco. Several other Spanish conquistadors who enlisted with Montejo in 1540 in Mexico City brought along with them a smaller number of Nahua speakers from other towns in central Mexico, such as Texcoco and Huexotzingo. In proven Spanish style, Montejo and his men discriminated against other ethnic groups, believing them to be inferior to the fighting quality of the central Mexicans.[50] As early as 1530 the adelantado expressed his opinion that most of the natives of Tabasco were only fit for service as porters, guides, and slaves.[51] Only with much reluctance did the adelantado allow his son, Francisco, to convince him that the Chontal Maya from the coastal towns like Xicalango fought as loyal allied auxiliaries. Apparently, the majority of Tabascan Indians were relegated to the position of servants, porters, and guides, while only a handful of Chontal Maya from Xicalango actively participated as indios conquistadores.[52] Along with these Tabascans few other Mesoamerican Indians actively served as combatants. The only exceptions were the few Guatemalan and Honduran Indians who had fought loyally with the adelantado in his Honduran campaign. Numbering no more than three hundred Indian warriors, these two groups who had earned Montejo's trust with loyal services in the past were the exception.[53]

Francisco de Montejo's choice of taking along "Mexicano" allies from central Mexico and not Tlaxcalteca auxiliaries may have been motivated more by historical and temporal factors than his preference for Mexica warriors. During the initial battles with the Tlaxcalteca in Tenochtitlan, Montejo had been absent (having left earlier with the first installment of treasure of the royal fifth back to Spain in 1520), and he did not return until 1522. Montejo would not have had the time or experience to forge close alliances or connections with important Tlaxcalteca nobles like Pedro de Alvarado and Hernando Cortés had done, both taking Tlaxcalteca mistresses and making close friendships with Tlaxcalteca nobles. In the case of Alvarado, he joined with one of the Tlaxcalteca daughters of the *tlatoani* (hereditary ruler) of Tlaxcala, Xicontecatl, ensuring future Tlaxcalteca support for his conquests in Guatemala, El Salvador, and his later exploits in Peru.[54]

Montejo, who had no such connections to local Indian elites, was forced to rely upon the Indians of the encomienda that Cortés granted him in reward for his valuable services as envoy to the Crown (which helped to secure for Cortés his own privileges), given to him in an encomienda grant in 1523.[55] Montejo first chose to take approximately five hundred Indians from his encomienda of Azcapotzalco in 1537 when he went to conquer

TABLE 6.4

Spanish conquistadors of Yucatan from the provinces of Guatemala and Chiapas, their encomienda holdings, and the ethnicities of their accompanying Indian slaves, servants, and auxiliaries.

SPANISH CONQUISTADORS OF YUCATAN FROM GUATEMALA	ENCOMIENDA(S) HELD (GUATEMALA)	ETHNIC GROUP OF TRIBUTARIES OF ENCOMIENDA	NATIVE NABORÍAS/CRIADOS AND SLAVES TAKEN
Juan de Guzman	Izalco	Pipil	10 naborías
	Sonsonate		20 slaves
Blas Cota	—	Chorti	10 slaves
Lorenzo de Godoy	Chiquimula	Chorti	20 naborías
			50 slaves
Cristóbal Velazquez	Jumaytepeque	Xinka	10–20 naborías

Totals: 30 Pipil naborías and slaves
30 Xinka naborías and slaves
80 Chorti naborías and slaves

Sources: F. De Icaza, *Conquistadores v. Pobladores de la Nueva España*; AGI, Guatemala, 111n23; AGI, Guatemala, 112n10; AGI, Guatemala, 113n36; AGI, Indiferente General, 2070n78; AGI, Patonato, 87, N.1,R.4; AGI, Justicia, 300; AGI, Audiencia de Mexico, 100, 359, 364.

SPANISH CONQUISTADORS OF YUCATAN FROM CHIAPAS	ENCOMIENDA(S) HELD (CHIAPAS)	ETHNIC GROUP OF TRIBUTARIES OF ENCOMIENDA	NATIVE NABORÍAS/CRIADOS AND SLAVES TAKEN
Hernan Centeno	—	—	5 naborías 10 slaves
Francisco Gil	—	Tzeltal	10 naborías 50 slaves
Blas Gonzalez	Ixtapangajoya	Zoque	10 naborías
Juan Martinez	Teopisca	Tzeltal	20 naborías
Diego de Ordóñez	Tenango	Tzeltal	—
Gonzalo de Ovalle	Estacostuy Vistlan	Zoque	20 naborías 50 slaves
Juan del Rey	—	—	10 naborías
Alonso Rosado	—	Tzeltal	10 naborías
Sebastián Vasquez	Totutla	Tzeltal	20 naborías 20 slaves
Juan de Urrutia	—	—	
	Totals: 75 Tzeltal naborías 80 Tzeltal slaves 30 Zoque naborías 50 Zoque slaves		

Sources: F. De Icaza, *Conquistadores y Pobladores de la Nueva España*; AGI, Guatemala, 110, n 34; AGI, Guatemala, 112, n. 10; AGI, Guatemala, 113, n. 29; AGI, Indiferente Genmeral, 2070, n. 78; AGI, Audiencia de Mexico, 203, n. 22; AGI, Patonato, 56, n. 1, r.2; AGI, Justicia, 300; AGI, Audiencia de Mexico, 100, 359, 364.

TABLE 6.5

Spanish conquistadors of Yucatan from the province of Zapotecas, their encomienda holdings, and the ethnicities of their accompanying Indian slaves, servants, and auxiliaries.

SPANISH CONQUISTADORS OF YUCATAN FROM ZAPOTECAS	ENCOMIENDA(S) HELD (ZAPOTECAS)	ETHNIC GROUP OF TRIBUTARIES OF ENCOMIENDA	NATIVE NABORÍAS/CRIADOS AND SLAVES TAKEN
Garcia de Aguilar	Igualtepec	Mixtec	10 naborías
			20 slaves
Hernando de Aguilar	—	—	10 naborías
Hernando de Bracamonte	—	—	10 naborías
Francisco de Bracamonte			10 naborías
Pedro Duran	Tizatepec (Quelabichi)	Zapotec	20 naborías
			5 slaves
Pedro Franco	—	Zapotec	5–10 naborías
Pedro de Molina	Camotlan	Zapotec	10 naborías
Alonso de Ojeda	Tiltepec	Zapotec	10 naborías
			20 slaves

	Xareta	Mixe	
Gaspar Pacheco		Mixe	10–20 naborías
Melchor Pacheco	—		100 slaves
Melchor Pacheco (son)		Zapotec	30 naborías
Alonso Pacheco (nephew)			
Alonso Reinoso	—	Zapotec	10 naborías
Jorge de Villagomez	—	Zapotec	10 naborías
			20 slaves

Totals: 160 Zapotec, Mixtec, and Mixe naborías
185 Zapotec, Mixtec, and mixe slaves

Sources: F. De Icaza, *Conquistadores y Pobladores de la Nueva España;* AGI, Indiferente General, 2070; AGI, Audiencia de Mexico, 100, 103, 105, 106, 110, 112, 113; AGI, Patonato, 58, 62, 65, 68; AGI, Justicia, 300; AGI, Audiencia de Mexico, 100, 359, 364.

and pacify the province of Honduras. During that campaign, these Nahua warriors proved their loyalty. During the famed Lempira rebellion in central Honduras, when the Indian rebel leader appealed to the Azcapotzalca as racial brothers to betray Montejo, his allies refused and fought bravely beside Montejo and his lieutenant, Alonso de Cáceres.

The surviving Azcapotzalca who went with Montejo to Chiapas in 1540 eventually made their way to Tabasco to aid the adelantado's son in his plans for conquest. At the same time, Montejo came to control the encomienda of Xochimilco only briefly but long enough to take advantage of its manpower. Having lost his claim to the valuable province of Honduras, Montejo renewed his plans for the final conquest of Yucatan. He immediately took advantage of Alvarado's cession of his large encomienda of Xochimilco, sending for several hundred armed warriors from the town to serve him as auxiliaries. Apparently, more than five hundred Xochimilca, along with several hundred Nahua from Texcoco and Huexotzingo, joined a second expeditionary force of Nahua from Azcapotzalco which Montejo raised late in the year 1540.

Realizing the value of the town, Pedro de Alvarado almost immediately backed out of the exchange, launching a series of complaints in order to regain control over Xochimilco.[56] Viceroy Mendoza, interceded in the dispute, giving the encomienda of Xochimilco back to Alvarado but not before several hundred Nahua from the town left as Montejo's auxiliaries, traveling first to Chiapas and then overland to Tabasco and Yucatan.

The adelantado's visit to Mexico City from late 1540 to early 1541 had as its primary goal the gathering of supplies and Nahua auxiliaries for the final conquest of Yucatan. Having come to trust his Azcapotzalca allies, Montejo chose to take more than fifteen hundred Azcapotzalca with him, sending them in contracted ships by sea to Xicalango, where his son, Francisco, was assembling the forces for the final conquest of the Yucatec Maya.[57] The loss of so many young men caused great alarm among the leaders of the town of Azcapotzalco, yet they were given promises that once the conquest ended, they would return. These promises, however, were lies, as the adelantado had no intention of returning these auxiliaries and instead had already begun to formulate his plans to use them as colonists along with Spaniards so that they might serve as buffers against future Maya rebellions or resistance. However, the adelantado did not convey his plans to resettle these Nahua to his son and lieutenant until much later. This lapse in communication led to hardship for the Nahua allies after the conquest, for no free lands were set aside for them to inhabit near the Spanish cities. Instead of rewarding them with grants of land, the adelantado's son forced them to purchase land that had already been given to Spaniards, adding to their postconquest burdens. As far as the historical record is concerned, no more than a handful of Azcapotzalca returned to their homeland after the conquest.[58] The situation was so bad that the Crown later reprimanded the adelantado for his abusive use of the Azcapotzalca in a *cédula* dated January 28, 1550, which stated, "The said adelantado forcibly removed from the said town [Azcapotzalco] a large quantity of people which he took to the province of Yucatan, and a major part of this large number of Indians died during the conflict and only a few, almost none, returned due to the great sufferings and labors that they experienced in the journey . . . and of more than 10 or 12,000 that once inhabited this town, now there are no more than 800 residents and these few are forced to pay the same tribute."[59] Regardless of the Crown's attempt to curb the abuse, the officials of the town of Azcapotzalco a decade later still blamed Montejo and his impressments of Nahua auxiliaries for their poverty, the gradual loss of their town's landholdings, and the demographic collapse that occurred after 1540.[60]

MONTEJO'S ARMY IN THE THIRD ENTRADA, 1540–42

As this chapter has shown, the allied Indian auxiliaries who gradually came together in the final months of 1540 to accompany Montejo's third and final entrada were a polyglot and multiethnic group. Although the Nahuatl-speaking allies from central Mexico made up the bulk of the allied Indian soldiers permitted to fight, a whole host of other natives served in a support capacity (see table 6.6). The army also counted on the support of thousands of porters, servants, and slaves, including Nahua, Chontal, and Popoluca speakers from Tabasco; Zoque and Tzeltal Maya speakers from Chiapas; Mixe and Zapotec speakers from Oaxaca; Lenca and Jicaque speakers from Honduras; and Chorti Maya, Xinka, and Pipil speakers from Guatemala and El Salvador.[61]

Late in 1537 the adelantado's son sent an expeditionary force from Tabasco under the command of Captain Lorenzo de Godoy, who organized a group of thirty Spanish horsemen and foot soldiers. Along with them went a large number of Tabascan Indian porters and approximately one hundred Chontal allied warriors from Xicalango. Godoy's forces established

TABLE 6.6

Active combatants and auxiliary and support forces available to Francisco de Montejo
during the final entrada of conquest, 1540–1542

COMBATANTS / ACTIVE SOLDIERS	AUXILIARIES / SUPPORT SERVICES / SLAVES
150 Spanish cavalry 250 Spanish infantry	20–30 African slaves
2,500–3,000 central Mexican warriors (Nahuatl speakers from the cities of Azcapotzalco, Xochimilco, Huejotzingo, and Texcoco)	5,000–8,000 Chontal, Populaca, Nahua porters, naborías, and slaves (from Tabasco)
200–300 Chontal allied warriors (from Xicalango and Tabasco)	300 Lenca and Jicaque porters, naborías, and slaves (from Honduras)

100–200 Guatemalan allied warriors (from Honduras campaign: Kaqchikel, K'iche')	345 Zapoteca, Mixteca, and Mixe porters, naborías, and slaves (from Oaxaca)
100 Lenca and Jicaque warriors (from Honduras campaign)	150 Chorti, Xinka, and Pipil porters, naborías, and slaves (from Guatemala and El Salvador)
500–1,000 allied Maya warriors (from Champoton, Campeche, and Mani)	200–500 Yucatec Maya slaves (taken from conquered provinces)

Sources: For specific information on numbers of combatants and their origins see AGI Indiferente General, 2070; AGI Guatemala 110, n. 34: AGI Guatemala 111, n. 23; AGI Guatemala 112, n. 10; AGI Guatemala 113, n. 29; AGI Guatemala 113, n. 36; AGI Justicia 300; AGI Mexico 100, 103, 105, 106, 110, 112, 113; 203, n. 22; 359, 364; AGI Patronato 56, 58, 62, 65, 68; AGI Justicia 300. For estimates and figures on the numbers of auxiliaries and support servants, see AGI, Justicia, 195, 299, 300, 1004.

a base of operations and a fortified post at the town of Champoton, which served Montejo as an advanced camp. From 1537 until 1539, Lieutenant Commander Montejo resupplied the post at Champoton with small bands of Spaniards, large numbers of Indian slaves, and a small number of allied Indian warriors. Together father and son had begun gathering supplies and soldiers for the final conquest.[62] By late 1539 the younger Montejo was ready to send larger forces.

Once in charge of the government of Chiapas, the elder Montejo organized and sent Captain Francisco Gil to Tabasco with his organized group of soldiers from Chiapas and Guatemala. Along with the sixty Spaniards, Montejo sent along a large number of his central Mexican and Guatemalan allied warriors and a few warriors whom he trusted from Honduras. With their Indian allies and several hundred porters, the group left for Tabasco and Campeche in the spring of 1540.[63] By the end of 1540, this army went with the younger Montejo to Champoton, leaving a small group at Xicalango and Tacotalpa to secure those sites as bases of operations and reinforcements.[64]

Captain Juan de Contreras left the base at Champoton early in 1540 and went to Ciudad Real de Chiapa to receive more reinforcements for the Champoton garrison. In Chiapas, he raised a small army of Spaniards and many more Indian allied warriors from central Mexico and several hundred more Indian slaves to serve as burden carriers. Sending Captain Alonso Rosado ahead of him with a squad of central Mexican warriors to give the garrison at Champoton the good news of reinforcements, Contreras himself left for Champoton before the end of 1540. At the same time the adelantado went to New Spain and got permission from viceroy Mendoza to send central Mexican Indians to the conquest of Yucatan. In Mexico, the elder Montejo enlisted many captains and soldiers from Jalisco and New Spain, and on the way back to Chiapas, they stopped in Oaxaca at the town of San Ildefonso de los Zapotecas.[65] Here the brothers Gaspar and Melchor Pacheco armed a small army of mounted Spanish soldiers with their sons and joined Montejo, adding several hundred more Zapoteca, Mixteca, and Mixe auxiliaries and slaves to the expedition.[66] At the end of 1540, the younger Montejo left Tabasco with all his forces to make Champoton and then Campeche his advanced base of operations for the final conquest.[67]

Central Mexican auxiliaries saw active combat in the very first pitched battle fought during the final conquest. After having proclaimed their arrival and demanding submission from the Maya around Campeche, the younger Montejo ordered his forces to advance. The first battle occurred not too far from Campeche along the Maya road north at the small town of Sihochac. Montejo feared an imminent attack. Cautiously dividing his forces into three major groups, Montejo sent out a small party of Spanish and Indian scouts under the command of Alonso Rosado. Rosado, four other Spaniards, and a group of about twenty-five armed Mexican auxiliaries went ahead to investigate and scout out the area.[68]

They quickly returned with the news that the Maya had made a large barricade of wood and stone along the road before the entrance to the town of Sihochac. On either side of the blocked road, the dense jungle brush prevented the army from advancing. They had to take the barricade and the town in order to proceed. Worse news followed: the denseness of the jungle precluded outflanking the Maya with the cavalry. Montejo then ingeniously came up with a plan that the Spaniards would use time and again in confronting these Maya fortresses and barricades. He divided the army into several groups. Three columns would attack the barricade. The Spanish cavalry and a large force of Indian allied archers would attack the barricade from the front, and two other columns of mixed Spanish and allied Indian warriors on foot would attack the rear of the barricade after circling around them through the jungle and outflank the Maya defenders. The two columns of foot soldiers on the flanks were named the Squadron of Santiago and the Squadron of San Francisco. The central column of cavalry then received orders to attack the barricade head-on once the two allied squadrons hit the Maya from the sides. This tactic proved successful time and again.

On July 7, 1540, with Alonso Rosado in command of the column in the front, the two other columns attacked the Maya barricade from the flanks. Rosado's group quickly dismounted and threw themselves at the wooden barricade before the signal for attack. A hail of Maya arrows met the advanced column, and the first Spaniard to scale the wall was rapidly killed by arrows.[69] Rosado quickly jumped over the wall, and with the aid of a dozen Spaniards and several dozen Azcapotzalca and Xochimilca warriors he broke through the main wall. Receiving an arrow wound in his arm, Rosado and his force managed to drive the Maya back.[70] The two Spanish columns on the flanks finally attacked, driving the Maya into retreat, winning the battle of Sihochac with only one Spaniard and several dozen allied Indians dead and about a dozen Spaniards wounded.[71] With the abundance of provisions, both food and water, that they found in the town of Sihochac, the army supplied itself for its continued advance. Montejo decided to set up camp in Sihochac and tend to his wounded. A Spanish soldier who also served as a doctor and a surgeon, Juan del Rey, nursed the wounded Spaniards and Indians alike.[72]

Montejo and his forces eventually arrived in Campeche on August 10, 1540. They called for all of the Maya caciques of the region to come and renew their oaths of loyalty. All but two Maya cities obeyed the call. Through his two Maya slaves who served as interpreters, Montejo quickly understood that the Maya caciques Na Poot Canche Canul and Na Chan Canche Canul, rulers of the towns of Teabo and Calkini, chose to resist and fight the Spaniards. Montejo mustered his forces and prepared for the long war he knew would come. The Spaniards founded a Spanish town in Campeche on October 24, 1540, and new reinforcements arrived shortly after on November 2, 1540.[73] The reinforcements included more than fifteen hundred central Mexican allied warriors from Azcapotzalco, Xochimilco, Texcoco, and Huexotzingo, who arrived with new Spanish forces, including the heavily armed cavalry troop under the command of Captain Gaspar Pacheco and his relatives. From this point on, the younger Montejo controlled an army of more than four hundred Spaniards and approximately three thousand allied Indian warriors, with a large supply train of several thousand porters and other Indian slaves and servants. He was ready to advance upon the final conquest.

Montejo decided to divide his large army into several groups and to send advance parties out to occupy posts and towns along the way.[74] Once news arrived of a secure base ahead, Montejo would leave Campeche and begin hopping from secured base to base, ensuring the security of their supply lines and connection to Champoton and the coast from where all future reinforcements came. On November 8, 1540, two large columns separated and headed for the town of Tenabo. One column commanded by Captain Gonzalo Méndez, made up of twenty Spaniards and more than five hundred Nahua allied warriors from central Mexico, served as the spearhead of the advance.[75] In front of their advance, this column drove a herd of several hundred pigs as supplies. Behind this column, Captain Francisco de Tamayo followed a few hours behind with a force of fifty Spaniards on horse and foot and another five hundred allied warriors. A third column, under the command of the adelantado's nephew, also named Francisco de Montejo, followed closely behind them in command of the three groups with an army of sixty Spanish horse and foot soldiers and another contingent of several hundred allied Nahua warriors.[76]

Along with Captain Gonzalo Méndez went several important Mexican Indian leaders from the town of Azcapotzalco. The Mexican warrior squads were led by Nahua Indian captains and lieutenants. One of the Azcapotzalca Indian captains, a Nahua named Gaspar de Castro, would loyally command allied auxiliaries throughout the war.[77] Other groups of Nahua warriors from Xochimilco were commanded by captains such as Pedro Xochimilco and Miguel Damián. Gonzalo de Méndez and the Nahua captain Gaspar de Castro and their group would be the first to make contact with the Maya of Tenabo, Xechelchakan, and Calkiní.

Once a town had been taken, in order to secure the supply line and maintain open communications with reserves in Champoton and Campeche, Montejo would leave behind a small force of one or two Spaniards and several dozen central Mexican auxiliaries to hold down each town as a defensive force. By the end of 1540, towns throughout the countryside had small forces of Indian allies and a few Spaniards serving as guard posts to protect the supply line of the army. Nevertheless, supplies of food and water ran low. The Maya who fled before the advance of the Spanish army quickly took with them all of their foodstuffs and covered and hid their wells, the only source of fresh water in the area. Montejo and his captains therefore employed long supply trains of several hundred Chontal, Popoluca, Maya, and other Indian slaves as porters, bringing fresh water from secured wells behind their lines and transporting it in large ceramic jugs and other heavy wooden containers.[78] Montejo also commissioned Esteban de Oliva to conduct scouting and exploratory missions into enemy territory to discover the enemy's food and water supplies. In the company of a squad of thirty Mexican warriors, Esteban de Oliva went out deep into enemy territory in order to discover supplies of food and water to provision the army.[79] Hunting around in the jungles and hills, Esteban de Oliva and Diego Quiyauit, the Nahua commander of his accompanying Mexican warriors, located several stores of corn and other food. Returning to the army they reported their discoveries and were given permission to take a large number of Indian naborías and slaves to bring the supplies back to the army. Esteban de Oliva later reported that he conducted these dangerous expeditions many different times, wandering around enemy territory for several days with no other protection than that of a company of Quiyauit and several other Mexican warriors. He also stated that he risked the safety and lives of many of his own slaves and Indian naborías, leading them into the jungles and back to the army laden with supplies.

After the path to Calkini had been secured, Francisco de Montejo advanced with the rest of his army. The defeat of the Maya at Sihochac had made the Maya of Calkini abandon their plans of resistance. Montejo allowed Captain Gonzalo Méndez and his allied Nahua warriors to be the first ones to enter the recently surrendered town of Calkini. The Maya at Calkini described the arrival of these Spanish and central Mexican conquerors stating, "Na Pot Canche held the governorship here in Calkini; it was on his patio that the tribute was delivered to the captain Montejo, when he and his soldiers arrived here in Calkini, when they arrived near the well at Sacnicte. . . . Their swine and their Culhua allies arrived first; the Captain of the Culhuas was named Gonzalo."[80] The Maya of Calkini also later complained that the central Mexican allies, whom they called Culhuas, rushed forward and grabbed at their tribute and gifts, greedily taking handfuls of whatever they had offered to the Spaniards. They recorded that after Montejo demanded the tribute, he let his allied warriors rush in and take it: "Then the Culhuas and their companions grabbed it all, some seizing much and some seizing a little . . .'Hey you, one at a time!' [Montejo yelled at them.] Thus they quickly made their take before their Captain Montejo, who oversaw the tribute distribution."[81] According to their report, a disorganized mob of central Mexicans plundered the gifts.

After securing the towns to the north of Campeche the road was open for the conquest of the province of Chakan, where the younger Montejo intended to found his Spanish capital. Francisco de Montejo, the nephew, stopped his advance and fortified his position in the town of Tuchicaan in March of 1541. From their base, scouts and spies reported that the Maya of Chakan had amassed a large force to resist them. Alonso Rosado and small groups of Spaniards and allied Mexican warriors served as advanced scouts and spies on numerous occasions.[82] On May 28, 1541, the allied Maya cacique of the town of Mani arrived in Tuchicaan and renewed his offers of support, bringing with him gifts and supplies.[83] Several months later, on July 15, 1541, Montejo's nephew led an army divided into three columns with Alonso Rosado and Blas González as captains of the other two columns.[84] All three columns contained several hundred Mexican allies as well as between twenty and thirty Spaniards each. The three columns marched unopposed into the Maya town of Maxcanú, where they fortified their positions and waited for the younger Montejo and the rest of the army to arrive. Once the army reunited on August 15, 1451, they left Captain Juan Vela, ten Spaniards, and a number of Mexican Indian allies behind to establish their control over Maxcanú.[85]

Montejo and the rest of his army marched into the territory of the town of Chochola, where they discovered that a local Maya cacique and priest, Ah Kin Chuy, had organized fierce resistance against the Spaniards. They arrived in Chochola to discover the town abandoned and food supplies either gone or destroyed. Leaving Captain Juan Sandoval in charge of the town with a garrison of several Spaniards and several dozen Mexican Indian allies, Montejo commissioned a special mixed unit of Spaniards and allied warriors to go and seek out and apprehend the Maya priest Ah Kin Chuy. The unit of ten Spaniards under the command of Captain Hernando Muñoz Zapata and a dozen or more Mexican Indian warriors found the Maya priest Ah Kin Chuy and quickly arrested him without a fight.[86] The capture of their leader stopped the planned Maya offensive and allowed Montejo's nephew's army to be reinforced with the younger Montejo's army that arrived in early November 1541. Throughout the months of November and December the army faced sporadic Maya resistance; however, by December 25, 1541, they managed to occupy the large and important Maya town of Ichcaanziho, where on Janurary 6, 1542, they established the capital of their new colony, naming it Mérida.[87] The establishment of their capital marks the end of the final active phase of conquest in the western part of the peninsula.

CONCLUSION

The Nahua—and especially Tlaxcalteca—allies and auxiliaries of Hernando Cortés and Pedro de Alvarado are well known. As this study has shown, although there is no evidence that a single Tlaxcalteca ever served as an ally in the conquest of Yucatan, there were thousands of other central Mexican and various other Mesoamerican peoples who played an active part in the conquest of Yucatan. Matthew Restall, in a book titled *Maya Conquistador*, argues that there were four main reasons why Montejo's third entrada was successful: (1) the Maya had been weakened by disease in early 1530s; (2) by successfully using one Maya group against another, Montejo successfully stimulated rivalries among Maya regions; (3) a severe drought and plague of locusts had exacerbated a food crisis causing starvation; and (4) the Spaniards enjoyed advantages of more men and better experience of the land.[88] Although I agree with Restall on these four points, I think that the most important, fifth reason for Montejo's final success was his use of Indian allies.

The valuable role of the Indian allies remained forgotten until 1576, when the paltry few survivors petitioned for their rights to freedom from tribute. According to the survivors, twelve years before (1564) the previous governor, Diego de Quijada, had written a "sinister letter and relation to His Majesty and to the Real Audiencia of New Spain . . . and based on his lies the Crown issued a royal provision so that we should be visited by members of the Royal Fiscal office and that we should be counted and assessed as tributaries . . . and once this census was made the governor Doctor Diego de Quijada placed upon us a certain excessive tribute quota without taking into account our own merits and the services that we have given His Majesty."

Pedro Xochimilco, Miguel Damián, and the other indigenous petitioners had initially complained against the imposition in 1564 and filed a legal appeal that was still pending, but they had no reliable agent in the viceregal capital and were too poor to afford the legal expenses involved.[89] They begged to be forgiven these new taxes because their "land was not fertile and they are now very poor and suffer from much necessity for they do not have any wealth and the only thing that they can do to pay these taxes is to rent themselves out for daily labor and live from their work."[90] However, since their appeal they had received no justice; instead, they suffered even more. Not only had the previous governor, Quijada, imposed upon them an excessive tribute quota, but successive governors received new orders from the Real Audiencia to impose additional contributions on the Indians. That very year, the petitioners lamented, the royal officials of the province were demanding that the native Indian auxiliaries pay back taxes and tribute in arrears dating from the conquest itself.

The very generation of Spanish conquistadors that owed these indigenous conquistadors their lives and the success of the conquest itself went to their graves without recognizing their efforts or rewarding their struggles. While a long line of indios conquistadores and indios hidalgos continued basing their later claims to freedom of service and tributes on the actions of their ancestors, only a handful of Spaniards remembered the forgotten allies.[91] Few had such courage and conviction as Captain Francisco de Bracamonte, himself a commander of a combined column of Spaniards and several hundred Nahua auxiliaries, when he remembered those forgotten allies and testified to the Crown, "I can say in all honesty that without them we would never have conquered this land."[92]

NOTES

1. "Carta y Petición de los indios mexicanos y de otros lugares que viven en los pueblos de Santiago y San Cristóbal ante el gobernador de Yucatán Francisco Velázquez de Gijón," March 16, 1576, Archivo General de Indias, Sevilla (hereafter, AGI), Audiencia de México, 100, 3 folios.

2. Surviving Indian allies on these two lists apparently came from a variety of regions throughout New Spain. The surviving historical documentation similarly reveals that indeed the army was multiethnic, made up of indigenous people from more than twenty separate ethnic and linguistic groups.

3. A large literature exists concerning the role played by auxiliaries and allies from Tlaxcala in the conquest and colonization of the New World. For just a few examples, see Gibson, *Tlaxcala*; Gibson, "Conquest"; Gibson, "Significación"; as well as the colonial history of Diego Muñoz Camargo, *Historia de* Tlaxcala, ed. Vásquez. Also see Toulet Abasolo, *Tlaxcala*; Escalante Arce, *Los tlaxcaltecas*. For the Tlaxcalteca role in settlement and colonization, see Sheridan Prieto, "Indios madrineros"; Sego, *Aliados y adversarios*; Martínez Baracs, "Colonizaciones tlaxcaltecas"; and Sherman, "Tlaxcalans."

4. See Lizana, *Historia de Yucatán*; López de Cogollado, *Los tres siglos*; Ayeta, *Ultimo recurso*.

5. Many modern scholars have confused the origins of these native auxiliaries, believing that they were made up of a majority of Tlaxcalteca and other central Mexicans. In her book on the Maya, Nancy Farriss postulates that these allies were "referred to simply as Mexicans in later documents [and] these troops may have been predominately Tlaxcalans and were certainly all Nahuatl speakers from the central highlands." *Maya Society*, 230. Grant Jones barely mentions them at all in his own study on Maya resistance to colonial rule. It is only Manuela Cristina García Bernal who gives us our best information in a secondary source about the allies. See Farriss, *Maya Society*; G. Jones, *Maya Resistance*; and García Bernal, *Yucatán*.

6. Besides the study of the Tlaxcalteca, the important role of native allied auxiliaries in Spanish conquest and expansion has been well studied for other regions, especially for the American Southwest, where Pueblo Indian auxiliaries were used in Spain's wars against the Apaches, Comanches, and other hostile groups, and in South America. See Stern, "Rise and Fall"; O. Jones, *Pueblo Warriors*; O. Jones, "Pueblo Indian Auxiliaries"; Riley, "Mesoamerican Indians"; Brugge, "Pueblo Factionalism."

7. See "Petición de una licencia para conquistar a Yucatán presentado por Francisco de Montejo al Rey," November 19, 1526, AGI Indiferente General 2048. Also see the Crown's patent and instructions to Montejo, "Capitulación entre el Rey Carlos V y Don Francisco de Montejo para la conquista de Yucatán," December 8, 1526, AGI Indiferente General 415.

8. There is evidence that perhaps at least a few African slaves went with this expedition. According to Matthew Restall, Montejo brought several Africans on all of his expeditions, see Restall, "Black Conquistadors," 181. Also see Chamberlain, *Conquest of Yucatan*, 30–34. However, besides these slaves, Montejo's first army had no other Indian servants or porters. For information on his army and its supply see Rújula y de Ochotorneo and Solar y Tabaoda, *Francisco de Montejo*. Also see the extensive testimony of two of Montejo's initial ships' owners, Juan Ote Duran and Martin de Ibiacabal, who testified to the men and supplies and their costs. See "Proceso de Juan Ote Duran contra el adelantado Montejo por ciertos pesos de oro," 1537, AGI Justicia 126, ramo 4; Relación de los méritos y servicios de Martín de Ibiacabal en la conquista de Yucatán, 1534, AGI Indiferente General 1204.

9. Chamberlain, *Conquest of Yucatan*, 41–43.

10. "Relación de los méritos y servicios de Francisco de Montejo, hijo del adelantado de Yucatán," 1563, AGI Patronato 65, ramo 2, n.1.

11. Chamberlain, *Conquest of Yucatan*, 99–127. For more information on the Avila entrada, see "Relación de la Entrada que hizo Capitan Alonso de Avila," 1535, AGI Patronato 63.

12. Chamberlain, *Conquest of Yucatan*, 174n30.

13. For other examples of Spain's successful use of Indian allies, see Sego, *Aliados y adversarios*; Flagler, "Defensive Policy"; and O. Jones, "Pueblo Indian Auxiliaries." Other European powers in the New World would also be forced to rely on Indian allies and auxiliaries in their own wars of conquest and wars of colonial expansion. The literature on this topic is similarly vast; for a few examples see P. MacLeod, "Microbes and Muskets"; Johnson, "Search for a Usable Indian"; Desbarats, "Canada's Native Alliances"; and Davis, "Employment of Indian Auxiliaries."

14. Chamberlain, *Conquest of Honduras*, 55.

15. Ibid., 74; also see the description of the conquest period in Newson, *Cost of Conquest*, 93–127.

16. In his letter to the Crown written on May 18, 1539, the Licenciado Pedraza, protector de los indios de Honduras, wrote that the Indians who had rebelled and fled to the stronghold of the peñol of Cerquin attempted to convince many of Montejo's allied Indians to join them. According to Pedraza, "ellos gritaban a los indios amigos, diciendoles que eran como sus hermanos y con ellos juntos podrian matar a todos los cristianos." See "Carta del Licendiado Pedraza, protector de los indios de Honduras, al Rey," May 18, 1539, AGI Audiencia de Guatemala 9, ramo 8, 23 folios. The adelantado Francisco de Montejo also mentions that the Indian rebels led by Lempira called to have his Indian allies join them. See "Carta del Adelantado Francisco de Montejo al Rey," June 1, 1539, AGI Audiencia de Guatemala 9, 8 folios.

17. Chamberlain, *Conquest of Honduras*, 81.

18. Ibid., 81–82.

19. Ibid., 83.

20. Ibid., 87.

21. Ibid., 88.

22. Ibid., 93.

23. Newson, *Cost of Conquest*, 100.

24. For the entire trial and testimony from the native Lenca principal Capaxuaca, see "Querella de un indio principal del pueblo de Olotempe llamado Capaxuaca contra Francisco Trejo, vecino de Gracias a Dios y de Alonso Hernández, por abusos," May 28, 1544, AGI Justicia 300, "Residencia contra Francisco de Montejo y su gobierno en Honduras" (1544), 6 folios.

25. See "Querella de los indios del pueblo de Lacayan contra Francisco Trejo por haber golpeado a un cacique llamado Xuy, y a dos indios macehuales llamados Lepaxan y Lepaloaca," 1544, AGI Justicia 300, "Residencia contra Francisco de Montejo y su gobierno en Honduras" (1544), 4 folios.

26. See "Querellas de los Indios del pueblo de Laguaracha contra Simon de Bravante, por haberlos maltratado y herido a muerte a un indio y su esposa," April, 1, 1544, AGI Justicia 300, in "Residencia contra Francisco de Montejo y su Gobierno en Honduras" (1544), 5 folios.

27. Chamberlain, *Conquest of Honduras*, 122.

28. See "Relación de los meritos y servicios de Alonso Reinoso en la conquista de Honduras y Yucatán," 1542, AGI Patronato 56, ramo 3, n. 3; "Probanza de los méritos y servicios de Juan Ruiz de la Vega, conquistador de Tabasco y Yucatán," 1548, Archivo General de Centroamérica, Sección Colonial; "Información sobre las acciones de Francisco Trejo en la provincia de Honduras," 1544, AGI Justicia 300 in the "Residencia en contra del adelantado Francisco de Montejo."

29. The only modern historian to examine the conquest of Yucatan was Robert Chamberlain, and he too is guilty of ignoring or slighting the efforts of the Mesoamerican Indian allies of Montejo in his own book *History of the Conquest and Colonization of Yucatan*. Unlike the rest of Mexico, where colonial era chroniclers and historians recounted endless details about the conquest, what little is known of the conquest focuses on the final siege and battles for Merida and the surrounding region. Only vague details concerning Montejo's previous attempts to conquer the peninsula are extant in their works. Instead, the real history of the conquest lays hidden in the thousands of manuscript pages still available in the archives of Spain, Mexico, and Guatemala.

30. For the best discussion and sources on the evolution of Indian slavery and its legislation, see Závala, *Los esclavos indios*, and Závala and Castelo, *Fuentes para la historia*. For an examination of the specific case of Yucatan, see García Bernal, *Los servicios personales*.

31. See "Quejas y capitulas puestos en contra del adelantado de Yucatán, Don Francisco de Montejo," 1546, AGI Audiencia de México 359, r. 1, n. 1, folio 20.

32. See "Testimonio de Juan Mendez de Sotomayor," May 1533, in "Pleito entre el adelantado de Yucatán Don Francisco de Montejo en contra del Adelantado Pedro de Alvarado, sobre el gobierno de la provincia de Tabasco y la region del Rio de Grijalva," 1533, AGI Justicia 1005, r. 1, n. 3.

33. See "Probanza de los servicios de los indios de Xicalango elaborada en la Villa de la Victoria a pedimento de Don Francisco, cacique del pueblo de Xicalango,"

July 13, 1552, AGI Audiencia de Guatemala 111, n. 2. For a complete description of the services and abuses of the Indians of Tabasco during the conquest of Yucatan, see the excellent works of Mario Humberto Ruz, esp. *Señor Alonso López* and *Un rostro encubierto*.

34. See "Testimonio de Jorge Hernández, vecino de Campeche, sobre los servicios de los indios de Tabasco," 1552, AGI Audiencia de Guatemala, 111, n. 2, 3 folios; "Testimonio de Juan Colon, vecino de la villa de Santa Maria de la Victoria de Tabasco," 1552, AGI Audiencia de Guatemala, 111. Also see "Testimonio de Diego de Córdoba, vecino de la villa de Santa Maria de la Victoria de Tabasco," 1552, AGI Audiencia de Guatemala, 111; and the statements of one of the major suppliers and backers of Montejo's expeditions in Tabasco, Juan de Ledesma, in "Testimonio de Juan de Ledesma, vecino de la villa de Santa Maria de la Victoria de Tabasco," 1552, AGI Audiencia de Guatemala, 111.

35. It was also Chontal and Nahuatl speakers from Tabasco who accompanied and made safe passage for the first Franciscan missionaries led by Fray Jacobo de Testera in 1535. See Chamberlain, *Conquest of Yucatan*, 311–13.

36. "Quejas y capitulas puestos en contra del adelantado de Yucatán, Don Francisco de Montejo," 1546, AGI Audiencia de México, 359, r. 1, n. 1, folio 23.

37. For the best study of the various aspects, tributes, and labor services of the encomienda system in general, see Simpson, *Encomienda in New Spain*. For perhaps the best studies of the encomienda, Indian labor, and the economic history of Central America see M. MacLeod, *Spanish Central America*, and Sherman, *Forced Native Labor*. For specific information on the encomienda and its abuses by conquistadors in all regions, including Yucatan, see Závala, *La encomienda indiana*. For specific information on the abuses of labor and tribute in the encomienda system in Yucatan, see Chuchiak, "Ca numiae."

38. If we use the figure of 3.2 people per tributary as suggested by Sherburne F. Cook and Woodrow Borah for the region of greater Yucatan before 1583, these 878 tributaries would have amounted to a population of 2,810 Indians removed from these towns. For discussions of Cook and Borah's methods and reasoning behind this figure and others, see Cook and Borah, *Essays in Population History*, 2:1–179.

39. See Ruz, *Un rostro encubierto*, 64.

40. Ibid., 70.

41. See various testimonies of Indigenous caciques, Spanish clerics and others in the "Residencia hecha contra el gobernador Don Francisco de Montejo," AGI Justicia 300.

42. See Fernandez Tejeda, *La comunidad indígena*, 47. Also see the discussion of these and other abuses of the encomienda in Yucatan in Rodríguez Losa, "La encomienda"; García Bernal, "Indios y encomenderos"; and Quezada, "Encomienda."

43. See "Instrucciones y ordenanzas para Francisco de Montejo el mozo para la conquista de Yucatán, hecha por el adelantado en la Ciudad Real de Chiapas," 1540, AGI Audiencia de México, 299.

44. Chamberlain, *Conquest of Yucatan*, 185. Also see Chamberlain, *Governorship*, 184–85.

45. Ibid., 184.

46. See "Relación de los méritos y servicios del adelantado Don Francisco de Montejo en la conqusita de Honduras, Tabasco y Yucatán," 1549, AGI Patronato, 81, n.1.

47. Each Spanish soldier was required to bring along with him his own food and supplies or else purchase them from Montejo and his captains, who all made fortunes selling them materials when they were in need. Most captains and even foot soldiers brought as many Indian slaves and porters as they could. Encomenderos, of course, had the ability to muster larger numbers of Indian porters and bearers, whereas simple soldiers had to rely on slaves either taken previously in war or bought from other Spaniards. For more information on the abuse of encomienda Indians in Chiapas, see Wasserstrom, "Spaniards and Indians." See also Chamberlain, *Governorship*, 178–80.

48. "Titulo de Alferez de la Caballeria hecho por el adelantado Don Francisco de Montejo a Juan de Urrutia en la Ciudad Real de Chiapa," May 29, 1540, AGI Patronato, 56, r. 2, n. 1, 3 folios.

49. See "Información de los méritos y servicios de Gaspar Pacheco, capitán general de la provincia de los Zapotecas en Nueva España, y conquistador de ella. Constan los méritos de Melchor Pacheco, hijo de Gaspar, quien sirvió en la provincia de Zapotecas como teniente de capitán general y maestre de campo," 1581, AGI Patronato, 76, r. 12, n. 2. Also see "Información de los méritos y servicios de Juan Gómez de la Camasa, uno de los primeros conquistadores y pobladores de la provincia de Yucatán, y de Gumiel, Chitemal, y Zueveniques con el capitán Gaspar Pacheco," 1562, AGI Patronato, 65, r. 17, n. 1.

50. In many instances, Montejo and his men expressed their feelings that the Nahua allies were valiant and good soldiers. For a few instances, see "Información de los servicios hechos en las Indias por Alonso Rosado, vecino de la ciudad de Mérida, provincias de Yucatán," 1573, AGI Patronato, 66A, r. 4, n. 1; "Probanza de los méritos y servicios de Cristóbal Delgado, vecino de Salamanca de Yucatán, y de su padre Juan Delgado, un de los primeros conquistadores de Yucatán," 1571, AGI Patronato, 73, r. 7, n. 2; and "Relación de los méritos y servicios de Juan cano el mozo y de su padre Juan Cano el viejo en la conquista y pacificación de las provincias de Yucatán," 1576, AGI Patronato, 73, r. 3, n. 2.

51. See "Testimonio de Don Francisco de Montejo en el pleito con Don Pedro de Alvarado sobre los limites de la provincia de Tabasco," 1534, AGI Justicia, 1004.

52. In 1550, Don Francisco, the cacique of Xicalango, mentioned, as if it were exceptional, that his town also provided many "hombres de guerra." See "Probanza de los servicios de los indios de Xicalango elaborada en la Villa de la Victoria a pedimento de Don Francisco, cacique del pueblo de Xicalango," July 13, 1552, AGI Audiencia de Guatemala, 111, n. 2.

53. This exception must explain the extremely small numbers of surviving Honduran, Tabascan, and Guatemalan Indians who petitioned for recognition as

indios conquistadores in 1576. Of a total of fifty-six surviving petitioners from the towns of San Cristóbal and Santiago, only eight were from Tabasco (no doubt Xicalango), three from Honduras (probably Lencas or Jicaques), and two from Guatemala (ethnicity not specified). The remaining indios conquistadores were originally from Azcapotzalco, Xochimilco, Texcoco, and Huexotzingo. The small number of surviving indios conquistadores is evidence of their brutal treatment and the huge losses they sustained in the conquest and later rebellions. Between 1540 and 1543 more than one thousand perished; in the rebellion of 1546 another six hundred were reportedly killed; and several hundred more perished from diseases and overwork in Valladolid before the town was moved to a healthier place (1544–50). Counting the several other towns populated by these indios conquistadores, their total population according to the census and tribute records of 1580 was only 323. This would mean that the Mexican and other Indian allies that had numbered around 4,600 (including Nahua, Hondurans, Tabascans, and allied Yucatec Maya) in 1540 suffered casualties and losses of 35 percent by 1550, and by 1580 93 percent of their numbers had perished either by war, disease, or old age, leaving only 323 survivors. A large number of these survivors may have been servants, naborías, or slaves rather than active indios conquistadores. Of the 323 survivors, according to the petitioners of 1576, only 56 were surviving soldiers of the conquest. See "Carta y Petición de los indios mexicanos y de otros lugares que viven en los pueblo de Santiago y San Cristóbal ante el gobernador de Yucatán Francisco Velázquez de Gijón," March 16, 1576, AGI Mexico, 100.

54. It was especially Alvarado's first union with Doña Luisa, Xicotencatl's daughter, that solidified his ties to Tlaxcala. See Meade de Angulo, *Doña Luisa Teohquilhuastzin*, and Herrera, chapter 4, this volume.

55. For specific information on Montejo's encomienda holdings in New Spain, see Himmerich y Valencia, *Encomenderos of New Spain*, 198. Montejo's grant of encomienda also included the Nahua towns of Matlactlan and Chila, with their surrounding villages.

56. In the end, the dispute between the two over the encomienda was settled amicably with Montejo offering Alvarado the option of turning over the encomienda or returning to him the governorship of Honduras. Alvarado replied, and his lawyer stated to the offer, "Since Montejo was so good as to give him free choice, he would prefer to retain Xochimilco and would restore to Montejo the governorship of Honduras-Higueras whenever Montejo might desire." See Chamberlain, *Conquest of Honduras*, 193. The entire case has several interesting letters and exchanges between the two conquerors. See "Pleito del adelantado Francisco de Montejo contra el Adelantando Pedro de Alvarado," AGI Justicia, 134, r.3. The most ironic thing, however, appears to be that Montejo had already removed several hundred tributaries from Xochimilco before he made his "kind offer."

57. Several men lost valuable ships and merchandise in several mishaps, including the unfortunate shipwreck of one vessel in Tabasco that lost Indian servants, horses, and cattle. See "Información de oficio y parte de Lorenzo de Godoy, encomendero de Chiquimula," 1562, AGI Audiencia de Guatemala, 111, n. 23;

"Proceso de Juan Ote Duran contra el adelantado Montejo por ciertos pesos de oro," 1537, AGI Justicia, 126, r. 4; "Relación de los méritos y servicios de Martín de Ibiacabal en la conquista de Yucatán," 1534, AGI Indiferente General, 1204. As late as 1542 Montejo lost another ship with supplies and goods. See "Relación de lo que sucedió al galeón San Miguel, que salió de San Juan de Ulúa para España, y uno de las flotas del adelantado Don Francisco de Montejo," 1542, AGI Patronato, 257, r. 1, n. 1.

58. The officials of the town of Azcapotzalco would petition the king to remedy the many abuses and exactions of labor and services that the Montejos had conducted in their town. See "Cartas del pueblo de Azcapotzalco a su Magestad con otros documentos," 1561, AGI Audiencia de México, 1842, ff. 44–50. The dramatic loss of so many male Azapotzalca and Montejo's abuse of tributes and labor from this town would later lead to the Crown's confiscation of the town from his successor, his daughter Catalina. See "Proceso con el adelantado Montejo sobre la suplicación que interpone de una cedula sobre el pueblo de Azcapotzalco," 1555, AGI Justicia, 204, r. 1, n. 2. Apparently, during his long years of fighting in Yucatan and Central America, Montejo had removed several thousand Azcapotzalca, forcing them to serve him as auxiliaries in his campaigns.

59. See "Cedula Real de la emperadora sobre los abusos que cometio el Adelantado Francisco de Montejo en su pueblo de encomienda de Azcapotzalco," AGI Audiencia de México, 1089, r. 4, 146v–47r.

60. "Carta de Don Hernando de Molina, de Don Baltazar Hernández y de los alcaldes, regidores y otros oficiales del cabildo de Azcapotzalco al rey Felipe II," February 10, 1561, AGI Audiencia de México, 1842.

61. Based upon rough calculations from material gathered from reading hundreds of primary documents, the final allied army that invaded and conquered Yucatan was approximately made up of the figures listed in table 5.6.

62. See Chamberlain, *Conquest of Yucatan*, 188–90. For a description of later surviving conquistadors of the province of Yucatan, see "Relación de los conquistadores y pobladores que habia en la provincia de Yucatán," 1551, AGI Patronato, 20, r. 4, n. 2.

63. More detailed information on these reinforcements and their composition is given in the testimony and description of the ship's owner and captain of the expedition of reinforcements. See "Probanza de los méritos y servicios de Juan de Contreras y Diego de Contreras en la conquista y pacificación de Yucatán," April 27, 1565, AGI Patronato, 56, r. 2, n. 4. Also see "Relación de méritos y servicios de Esteban de Oliva, Ginoves, uno de los primeros conquistadores de la provincia de Yucatán a instancias de Giuseppe López de Ricarde," 1618, AGI Patronato, 87, r. 4, n. 1. For more general information on the expedition, see Chamberlain, *Conquest of Yucatan*, 200.

64. See ibid., 200–201.

65. For several testimonies on the success of Montejo's recruitment campaign among other conquerors of central and northern Mexico, see "Información de los méritos y servicios de Juan de Rivas, que se hallo en la pacificación de Jalisco, y en

la conquista y pacificación de Yucatán," 1576, AGI Patronato, 74, r. 4, n. 2; "Información de los méritos y servicios de Juan de Magaña, uno de los conquistadores de Nueva España, y en la provincia de Yucatán," 1564, AGI Patronato, 66A, r. 6, n. 1.

66. See "Información de los méritos y servicios de Gaspar Pacheco, capitan general de la provincial de los Zapotecas en Nueva España, y sus hijos en la conquista de Yucatán," 1579, AGI Patronato, 76, r. 12, n. 2.

67. See "Información de los méritos y servicios de Juan de Parajas, uno de los primeros conquistadores de la provincial de Yucatán, donde pasó con Don Francisco de Montejo en cuya compañía llegó al puerto de Champoton y salieron de aquí y siguieron el descubrimiento, poblaron el pueblo de San Francisco de Campeche, siendo el primero que se pobló," 1586, AGI Patronato, 79, r. 1, n. 2.

68. For more detailed information on the use of Indian allies at the battle of Sihochac, see "Información de servicios hechos por Alonso Rosado, vecino de la ciudad de Mérida de Yucatán, y conquistador de estas provincias," 1573, AGI Patronato, 66A, r. 4, n. 1. Also see "Probanza de Luis Rosado, hijo de Alonso Rosado," 1596, AGI Audiencia de México, 115, r. 5. Based on his actions with the allied Indian auxiliaries at Sihochac, the Crown later rewarded Rosado by giving him the town as an encomienda. See "Confirmación de encomienda de Sihochac a Alonso Rosado," AGI Audiencia de Audiencia de México, 242. Also see "Información de los méritos y servicios de Juan de Urrutia que sirvio en la conquista y pacificación de la provincia de Yucatán, en compañía del capitan general Don Francisco de Montejo," April 13, 1540, AGI, Patronato, 56, r. 2, n. 1. For further eyewitness accounts of this battle, see Información de Pedro Díaz Monjibar, conquistador de Yucatán, 1573, AGI Audiencia de México, 99, r. 3; "Relación de los méritos y servicios de Blas Gonzalez, conquistador de Yucatán," AGI Patronato, 68, r. 2, n. 1. For a good study of this soldier and his contribution to the final entrada of conquest, see Chamberlain, "Probanza de meritos."

69. See testimony and eyewitness accounts of this battle in "Información de servicios hechos por Alonso Rosado, vecino de la ciudad de Mérida de Yucatán, y conquistador de estas provincias," 1573, AGI Patronato, 66A, r. 4, n. 1, esp. the detailed accounts and testimony of Francisco de Montejo el mozo, Francisco Tamayo, Hernando de Bracamonte, and Gomez de Castrillo. For a description of the battle by another Spanish soldier and surgeon of the expedition, Juan del Rey, see "Probanza de los méritos y servicios de Juan del Rey, uno de los primeros conquistadores de la provincial de Yucatán presentado por García de Medina, su yerno," 1582, AGI Patronato, 76, r. 6, n. 1.

70. "Información de servicios de Alonso Rosado," AGI Patronato, 66A, r. 4, n. 1. Also see "Probanza de los méritos y servicios de Juan de Contreras y Diego de Contreras en la conquista y pacificación de Yucatán," April 27, 1565, AGI Patronato, 56, r. 2, n. 4. Another similar relation of the battle and its outcome is found in "Probanza de los méritos y servicios de Diego Muñoz, conquistador de Yucatán," 1579, AGI Mexico 947.

71. See "Relación de los méritos y servicios de Blas Gonzalez, conquistador de Yucatán," AGI Patronato, 68, núm. 1, ramo 2; also see "Información de servicios de Alonso Rosado," AGI Patronato, 66A, núm. 1, ramo 4; as well as "Información de los méritos y servicios de Juan de Urrutia que sirvió en la conquista y pacificación de la provincia de Yucatán, en compañía del capitan general Don Francisco de Montejo," 13 de Abril 1540, AGI Patronato, 56, núm. 1, ramo 2. More detail is also found in "Información de los méritos y servicios de Diego de Contreras y de su hijo Juan, que se hallaron en el socorro y ayuda que dieron en la provincia de Tabasco al adelantado Francisco de Montejo, y estuvieron en la pacificación de las villas de San Francisco de Campeche, y de la provincia de Yucatán," 1583, AGI Patronato, 79, núm. 1, ramo 7. The conquistador Gómez de Castrillo also describes the details of the events. See "Información de los méritos y servicios de Gómez del Castrillo, uno de los primeros conquistadores de las provincias de Yucatán," 1583, AGI Patronato, 77, núm. 2, ramo 19.

72. See "Probanza de los méritos y servicios de Juan del Rey, uno de los primeros conquistadores de la provincial de Yucatán presentado por García de Medina, su yerno," 1582, AGI Patronato, 76, núm. 1, ramo 6.

73. See "Información de los méritos y servicios de Juan de Parajas, uno de los primeros conquistadores de la provincial de Yucatán, donde pasó con Don Francisco de Montejo en cuya compañía llegó al puerto de Champoton y salieron de aquí y siguieron el descubrimiento, poblaron el pueblo de San Francisco de Campeche, siendo el primero que se pobló," 1586, AGI Patronato, 79, núm. 2, ramo 1.

74. For specific information on these orders and other details of the campaign see "Información de los méritos y servicios de Don Francisco de Montejo, hijo del adelantado Don Francisco, que se halló en la conquista de la Nueva España, Higueras, y Honduras, y después por mandado de su padre fue conquistador de las provincias de Yucatán," 1563, AGI Patronato, 65, núm. 2, ramo 1; also see similar details of the campaign found in the documents relating to his cousin and the nephew of the adelantado, "Información de los méritos y servicios de Francisco de Montejo, uno de los primeros descubridores y conquistadores de las provincias de Yúcatan, con su tio, el adelantado Don Francisco de Montejo, a petición de su hijo Juan de Montejo," 1596, AGI Patronato, 81, núm. 1, ramo 1.

75. See "Relación de los méritos y servicios de Gonzalo Mendez," AGI Audiencia de México, 123; as well as "Información de los méritos y servicios de Pedro de Ledesma, conquistador, pacificador y poblador de la provincia de Yucatán," 1556, AGI Patronato, 60, núm. 5, ramo. 1. Also see "Información de los méritos y servicios de Francisco Ronquillo, uno de los conquistadores de la provincia de Yucatán," 1554, AGI Patronato, 60, núm. 3, ramo. 2.

76. For details on this part of the campaign see the documents produced by the adelantado's nephew "Información de los méritos y servicios de Francisco de Montejo, uno de los primeros descubridores y conquistadores de las provincias de Yucatán, con su tio, el adelantado Don Francisco de Montejo, a petición de su hijo Juan de Montejo," 1596, AGI Patronato, 81, núm. 1, ramo 1. Also see "Información de los méritos y servicios del capitan Francisco Tamayo Pacheco, uno de los

primeros conquistadores y pobladores de la provincia de Yucatán," 1597, AGI Patronato, 82, núm. 2, ramo 1.

77. See "Libro de Probanzas de hidalguia de la familia Castro de Tekanto, Yucatán (1611–1815)," Archivo de la Parroquia de Tekanto. For information on the role of the Central Mexican indigenous captain Gaspar de Castro see "Probanza y testimonios sobre los indios mexicanos y los méritos como indio conquistador en la conquista de esta provincia, de Gaspar de Castro, natural del pueblo de Azcapotzalco en la Nueva España," 18 de junio, 1583, Archivo de la Parroquia de Tekanto.

78. See "Información de los méritos y servicios de Esteban de Oliva, uno de los primeros conquistadores de la provincia de Yucatán," 1618, AGI Patronato, 87, núm. 1, ramo 4. Also see "Información de los méritos y servicios de Francisco de Montejo, uno de los primeros descubridores y conquistadores de las provincias de Yucatán, con su tio, el adelantado Don Francisco de Montejo, a petición de su hijo Juan de Montejo," 1596, AGI Patronato, 81, núm. 1, ramo 1.

79. See "Información Esteban de Oliva," 1618, AGI Patronato, 87, núm. 1, ramo 4.

80. Restall, *Maya Conquistador*, 89.

81. Ibid., 88

82. See "Información de servicios de Alonso Rosado," AGI Patronato, 66A, núm. 1, ramo 4.

83. See "Información de los méritos y servicios de Pedro Gómez, que se halló en la pacificación de la provincia de Guatemala y en la de Yucatán con el adelantado Montejo," 1562, AGI Patronato, 65, núm. 1, ramo 11. Also see "Información de servicios de Alonso Rosado," AGI Patronato, 66A, núm. 1, ramo 4; as well as "Relación de los méritos y servicios de Blas Gonzalez, conquistador de Yucatán," AGI Patronato, 68, núm. 1, ramo 2; and finally "Información de los méritos y servicios de Alonso Ruiz de Arévalo, uno de los primeros conquistadores y pobladores de la provincia de Yucatán," 1566, AGI Patronato, 69, ramo 9.

84. See "Relación de los méritos y servicios de Blas González, conquistador de Yucatán," AGI Patronato, 68, núm. 1, ramo 2.

85. See "Relación de los méritos y servicios de Juan Vela, uno de los primeros conquistadores de la provincia de Yucatán," 1576, AGI Patronato, 74, núm. 2, ramo 3.

86. See "Relación de los méritos y servicios de Hernando Muñoz Zapata," 1568, AGI Patronato, 68, núm. 1, ramo 9.

87. See "Información de los méritos y servicios de Don Francisco de Montejo, hijo del adelantado Don Francisco, que se halló en la conquista de la Nueva España, Higueras, y Honduras, y después por mandado de su padre fue conquistador de las provincias de Yucatán," 1563, AGI Patronato, 65, núm. 2, ramo 1; also see "Relación de los méritos y servicios de Blas Gonzalez, conquistador de Yucatán," AGI Patronato, 68, núm. 1, ramo 2.

88. Restall, *Maya Conquistador*, 11–12.

89. According to the petitioners, "since that time and until now we have attempted to file a case of appeal and due to our lack of someone in the said royal Audiencia who knows and can competently seek justice and redress." See "Memoria de los indios Mexicanos y de otras provincias que residen en los barrios de Santiago y San Cristóbal," 1576, AGI Audiencia de México, 100.

90. AGI, Audiencia de México, 100.

91. See Thompson, *Tekanto*.

92. See "Relación de los Méritos y servicios de Francisco de Bracamonte, uno de los conquistadores de Yucatán," 1572, AGI Patronato, 72, ramo 1.

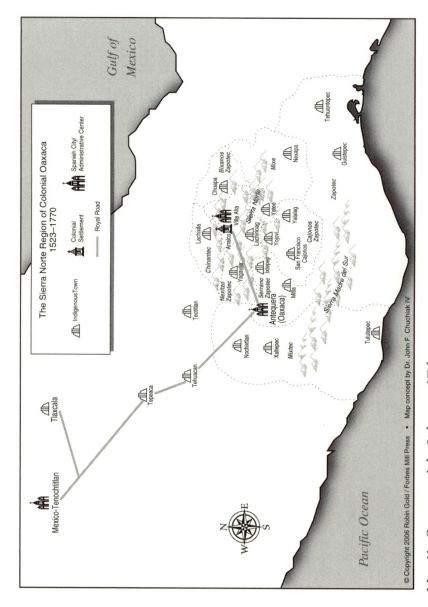

Map 11. Oaxaca and the Isthmus of Tehuantepec

CHAPTER SEVEN

THE INDIOS CONQUISTADORES OF OAXACA'S SIERRA NORTE

From Indian Conquerors to Local Indians

YANNA YANNAKAKIS

Indigenous military auxiliaries from the Valley of Mexico facilitated the conquest of the remote and rugged Sierra Norte of Oaxaca. Through their specialized role in the region's security, which continued well into the eighteenth century, the Indian conquerors made possible the maintenance of Spanish colonial rule in the Sierra. This chapter focuses on the establishment, maintenance, and decline over time of the political, cultural, and military roles of the Sierra Norte's indigenous conquerors in an effort to illuminate one of the persistent puzzles in the history of colonial Mexico: how did Mexico's imperial overlords maintain colonial rule in the empire's hinterlands despite a notoriously underdeveloped provincial bureaucracy and the lack of a standing army? In response to this question, the historical literature has emphasized hegemonic processes such as the evangelization of the native population or "spiritual conquest," the incorporation of indigenous elites into the colonial bureaucracy through the system of native *cabildos* and the channeling of indigenous grievances through the legal system.[1] This trend in the literature has both contributed significantly to our understanding of Spanish colonialism and yielded its own set of problems. For instance, the persistence of systematic coercion in the Spanish colonial system, particularly in the more remote regions of New Spain, has tended to be ignored or deemphasized. The example of the indigenous conquerors of the Sierra Norte reveals how the cultural and political incorporation of the Spanish empire's indigenous allies not only coexisted with but also insured colonial military security through the threat and exercise of violence.

In order to examine the history of the role of the indigenous conquerors of the Sierra, I have organized this chapter into three sections that correspond with historical changes in the indigenous conquerors' role in the Sierra's colonial system. The conquest, which enveloped the better part of the sixteenth century, marks the first phase of the indigenous conquerors' role, which was primarily military. The indigenous conquerors capitalized upon their invaluable contribution to the conquest of the Sierra by petitioning for special rights and privileges, which were granted to them by the Real Audiencia. Following the pacification of the region, they made use of the Spanish colonial legal system to maintain those rights and privileges.

The history of the early seventeenth century in the Sierra Norte remains somewhat murky due to the relative lack of administrative and legal documentation, which may have been the result of the devastating epidemics that wracked the region and all of New Spain during the late sixteenth and early seventeenth centuries. This gap in the historical record leaves us unsure as to the workings of the indigenous conquerors during this time. Analysis of the second phase of the indigenous conquerors' role in the Sierra Norte therefore begins with the region-wide rebellion of 1660, a significant flash point in the political history of the region, which started in the Isthmus of Tehuantepec and spread through the regions of Nexapa and the Sierra Norte. The second phase also included a second uprising in the Spanish administrative center of Choapa in 1684 and lasted until the first decades of the seventeenth century, during which time the Spaniards worked to reconsolidate colonial rule following the Cajonos uprising of 1700. During this period, the indigenous conquerors maintained their privileged status on two fronts: in the context of three major violent uprisings and in the labyrinthine colonial court system. On the first front, the indigenous conquerors enacted and performed their role as guarantors of Spanish security through violent suppression of local resistance to colonial rule. On the second front, the cabildo of Analco turned to the courts to fend off threats posed by the region's Spaniards to their collective privileges and to maintain their special status vis-à-vis the local indigenous population.

Finally, the third phase, which spanned the late eighteenth century, was marked by a sharp decline in the special status of the indigenous conquerors.

The relative political stability of this period diminished the coercive role of the natives of Analco. Furthermore, colonial racial ideology eventually grouped all natives together under the racial and legal category of "Indian," which overshadowed the privileged category of "conquistadores." Two legal disputes from the 1760s and 1770s between the cabildo of Analco and the Spanish authorities of Villa Alta bear witness to these changes and reflect larger political changes in the Sierra's colonial system.

Sources concerning indigenous participation in the conquest of the Sierra include official accounts and reports written by the conquerors themselves and by Luis de Berrio, the first *alcalde mayor* of Villa Alta. These sources can be found in the Archivo de las Indias in Seville. The Reales Provisiónes that established and reaffirmed the indigenous conquerors' privileges and obligations and formed the foundation for their relationship with the Spaniards of Villa Alta and the local indigenous population can be found in the Archivo General de la Nación, Mexico City. In his narrative of the colonial period in the Sierra Norte, John Chance has mined and interpreted many of these sources, as well as sources from the Archivo del Juzgado de Villa Alta (currently located in the Archivo del Poder Judicial de Oaxaca) and the Papeles de Analco in the Archivo Parochial de Villa Alta.[2]

In addition to these written documentary sources concerning the early colonial period, scholars of the Sierra Norte are fortunate to have access to a painted *lienzo* whose provenance was the barrio of Analco. The lienzo was first identified and written about by Franz Blom, who encountered it in the barrio of Analco itself.[3] Some time thereafter it was taken from the barrio by a private collector, and finally the lienzo ended up in the National Library of Anthropology in Mexico City. Viola König dates the lienzo to the sixteenth century, and both König and Florine Asselbergs identify its style with the Tlaxcalteca tradition.[4] We do not know how the lienzo was used, whether, for example, it was ever presented as evidence in a legal case, although we can guess that this might have been its purpose since lienzos were often used by indigenous litigants in court during the early colonial period. Despite its availability to scholars, the Lienzo de Analco has been little studied.

For the first phase of the indigenous conquerors' role in the Sierra, I rely primarily on the work of John Chance. For the second and third phases, I utilize court documents from the Archivo del Juzgado de Villa Alta and the Archivo General de la Nación to trace and analyze the legal negotiations between the ruling elite of the barrio of Analco and their former

Spanish allies. These petitions, legal disputes, and royal decrees concerned the rights and privileges that the indigenous conquerors were to enjoy and are replete with the rhetorical strategies that the municipal authorities and the natives of Analco deployed to distinguish their collective identity from that of the local population and justify their rights as conquistadores.

CONQUEST AND SERVICES IN EXCHANGE FOR PRIVILEGES

In the wide sweep of the Spanish conquest of Mexico, the military campaign against the Zapoteca of Oaxaca's remote and rugged northern Sierra proved especially bloody and brutal. Local resistance and the difficult terrain made it necessary for the Spanish conquistadors to make at least three attempts to subdue and pacify the region. The first two forays, led by Rodrigo de Rangel in 1523–24, met with some initial success until native rebellion forced the Spaniards to retreat. A third campaign in 1526, led by Gaspar Pacheco and Diego de Figueroa, owed its partial success to the excessive force used by the Spaniards, most notably the deployment of fearsome mastiffs to hunt and devour Indian rebels. A war between the Zapoteca and their neighbors and rivals, the Mixe, also contributed to the eventual military success of the Spaniards and their indigenous allies. Finally, and most importantly for the establishment and maintenance of colonial rule in the region, the participation of a few hundred indigenous military auxiliaries proved indispensable to Spanish expansion into the Sierra.[5]

In 1527 Pacheco and Figueroa established the Spanish seat of power at San Ildefonso de Villa Alta. A few hundred of the indigenous auxiliaries, all of whom were recognized as *naborías*, set up camp adjacent to the small Spanish settlement. There, they built a garrison and served as an occupying force. In this naboría settlement, which came to be known as the barrio of Analco, the indigenous conquerors and their descendants converted to Christianity, learned both the Spanish and Zapotec languages, and married local women.[6] Their identification with Spanish culture and language and their social relationships with the local population positioned them as cultural intermediaries and power brokers in the region.

The tiny settlement of Spaniards in Villa Alta (which never exceeded more than thirty families) and their indigenous allies spent much of the sixteenth century attempting merely to achieve stability and establish the most basic foundations of colonial rule. In this regard, we should think of the conquest of the Sierra Norte as a protracted process rather than as a single event. The Spaniards carved the region into *encomiendas* and initiated a regime of forced labor that resulted in a rebellion centered in the Nexitzo Zapoteca community of Tiltepec in 1531. The Spaniards and the indigenous conquerors responded swiftly and cruelly, torturing and executing a number of village leaders. The indigenous conquerors continued to prove themselves as key players in the prolonged conquest of the Sierra, as they helped the Spaniards to put down a general rebellion that shook the region in 1550, a second uprising that erupted in Choapa in 1552, and a fierce Mixe rebellion in 1570. The overwhelmingly destructive effects of epidemic disease on the indigenous population and the accompanying disarray of indigenous society and its political leadership eventually broke the back of native resistance in the Sierra Norte, and facilitated the consolidation of Spanish power.[7]

This narrative of the conquest of the Sierra Norte relies on interpretation of documents written by the Spanish conquerors, which provide little access to the perspective of the indigenous allies who participated in the conquest. The Lienzo de Analco, produced by an indigenous artist and most likely commissioned by the ruling elite of Analco in order to commemorate or possibly provide evidence in court of the role of the natives of Analco in the conquest, allows us a glimpse of the indigenous conquerors' perspective. Of course, the Lienzo de Analco is burdened as much by the political agenda of its author(s), as are the documents produced by the Spanish conquerors. But coming to terms with that agenda helps us to understand how the indigenous conquerors attempted to position themselves in an emerging colonial society.

König identifies the lienzo as both a map and pictorial narrative of the conquest of the Sierra Norte, and as discussed earlier, she describes the lienzo's style as Tlaxcalteca. She posits that Tlaxcalteca military auxiliaries must have brought their own codices or lienzos with them to the Sierra, which provided models for colonial era lienzos made by artists in the barrio of Analco and in surrounding Zapoteca, Chinanteca, and Mixe villages. König notes the distinctive influence of Tlaxcalteca and Aztec styles in the colonial era lienzos painted by native artists of the Sierra Norte, such that we can discount the possibility of a tradition of codices and lienzos autochthonous to the Sierra.[8]

The artist who painted the Lienzo de Analco rendered the territory of the Sierra Norte through representations of mountains, rivers, roads, and

FIGURE 7.1.
*Lienzo de Analco. Reproduced courtesy of the Biblioteca Nacional de Antropología
e Historía, México, DF.*

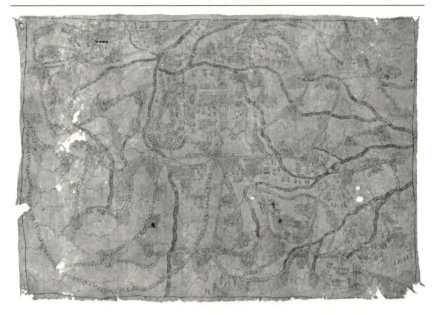

indigenous settlements, with the Spanish settlement of Villa Alta occupying the center of the lienzo.[9] The artist also indicated the route of the conquerors' military incursion through a maze of footprints that crisscross
the territory (see fig. 7.1). As a pictorial narrative of the events of the conquest of the Sierra, the lienzo portrays different facets of the military support provided to the Spaniards by the indigenous conquerors. The
indigenous auxiliaries appear as guides and porters, leading Spaniards
up and down the endless layers of mountains, gullies, and drainages and
carrying their persons, possessions, and equipment (fig. 7.2).[10] The artist's
rendering of the Spaniards perched on the backs of indigenous porters
and on horseback, leading their indigenous allies into battle against
Zapoteca resistance, position the Spaniards as the commanders of the military operation (fig. 7.3). But despite clear signaling of Spanish leadership
in the conquest, the lienzo's artist put the integral role of the indigenous
conquerors into relief through sheer numbers, juxtaposing dozens of fierce-
looking indigenous foot soldiers with pointed spears at the rear of the handful of Spanish commanders (fig. 7.4). This juxtaposition of a few Spaniards
supported by a hefty rear flank of indigenous auxiliaries appears partic-

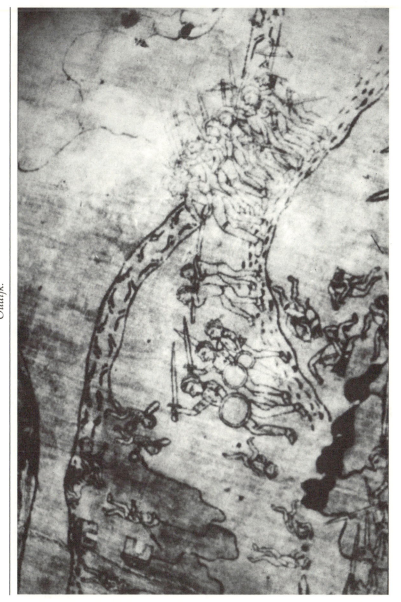

FIGURE 7.2.
Scene from the Lienzo de Analco. Photography by Burkhard Brinker. Reproduced courtesy of Viola Koenig and Michel Oudijk.

FIGURE 7.3.

Scene from the Lienzo de Analco. Photography by Burkhard Brinker. Reproduced courtesy of Viola Koenig and Michel Oudijk.

FIGURE 7.4.

Scene from the Lienzo de Analco. Photography by Burkhard Brinker. Reproduced courtesy of Viola Koenig and Michel Oudijk.

ularly poignant in the artist's rendering of the Battle of Tiltepec, portrayed in the upper left quadrant of the lienzo. The grisly depiction of battle scenes, which include dogs devouring the local population, the hanging of local leaders, and the dismemberment of local fighters, gives the impression that the conquest of the region was hard fought. The artist's communicative strategy is quite effective. As one ponders the lienzo, one is left to wonder how the conquest of the Sierra would have been at all possible had it not been for the Spaniards' native allies.

As we contemplate the perspective of the indigenous conquerors concerning their role in the conquest of the Sierra and their construction and projection of that role through the lienzo's narrative strategy, we are left to wonder who these people were and where they came from. The only means we have of answering these questions is to examine how they identified themselves and how others identified them. Three aspects defined both their ascriptive identity and the categories imposed upon them by the Spaniards and local population of the Sierra: their residence in the barrio of Analco, their role in the conquest, and their preconquest ethnic heritage.

The central question—a political one—about the identity of the indigenous conquerors of the Sierra is to what degree they can be collectively categorized as Tlaxcalteca. As discussed in other chapters in this volume, "Mexicano" as a term encompassed a variety of groups from Mexico's central valleys, the valley of Oaxaca, and the Isthmus of Tehuantepec. But the term "Tlaxcalteca" held special import because of the touted role of the Tlaxcalteca as the most significant allies in Hernando Cortés's conquest of Tenochtitlan.

As has been well documented in the historiography of colonial Mexico, the Tlaxcalteca, fierce enemies of the Mexica, played a crucial role in the military conquest of Mexica territory and in the "civilizing" and evangelizing projects of the Spanish colonizers. Through the skill of Cortés's interpreter Doña Marina, the Spaniards formed a longstanding alliance with the city-state of Tlaxcala. Tlaxcalteca rulers agreed to send tens of thousands of their best-trained men to serve as guides, interpreters, and foot soldiers for the small band of Spanish conquerors. First, Tlaxcalteca auxiliaries and other longstanding enemies of the Mexica made possible the conquest of the heart of the Mexica empire. Afterward, they and military auxiliaries from other indigenous groups led the Spaniards through southern Mexico and Guatemala, subduing resistance and brokering alliances along the way.

Once the furthest reaches of the Mexica empire had been conquered, the Spanish Crown made a formal agreement with the rulers of Tlaxcala that guaranteed them special privileges as "Indian conquerors." In exchange for these privileges, the Tlaxcalteca leadership sent hundreds of families to the frontiers of the new Spanish empire. The Spaniards envisioned that the Tlaxcalteca—sedentary agriculturists who were hispanized and evangelized—should provide a "civilizing" influence on indigenous groups in the north. These Tlaxcalteca families formed model Christian communities and served as examples of "civilized Indians" in places as far-flung as the Chichimeca frontier in the north of Mexico and the Philippine Islands. Other Tlaxcalteca settled alongside their Spanish comrades in arms in the newly conquered regions.[11]

The Tlaxcalteca style of the Lienzo de Analco hints at a connection between Tlaxcala and the barrio of Analco. In his work on the colonial history of the Sierra Norte of Oaxaca, Chance identifies the indigenous conquerors of the Sierra Norte as "Nahuatl-speaking indios naborías from central Mexico, especially Tlaxcala."[12] Although he makes a nod to the diverse ethnic affiliations of the indigenous conquerors through the general identification of "indios naborías from central Mexico," he emphasizes the Tlaxcalteca aspect of their group identity by referring to the "Tlaxcalteca heritage" of the barrio of Analco. He points out, however, that by the 1770s the Tlaxcalteca ethnic identity of the barrio's inhabitants had been significantly diluted by migration of locals to the town and by intermarriage.[13]

In a 1761 legal dispute over exemption from tribute and the right to patrol their own barrio, eight individuals from the barrio of Analco identified themselves as "of origin of the first Tlaxcalteca auxiliaries of the first conquerors of these provinces."[14] However, in a 1591 decree concerning the privileges and obligations of the indigenous conquerors of the Sierra, the reference to Tlaxcala is nowhere to be found as the Real Audiencia referred to the "naturales de Analco" as "Mexican Indians living in the barrio of Analco."[15] In a Royal Provision of 1683, the Audiencia referred to them as "natives, naborías of the barrio of Analco."[16] Francisco de Burgoa, the Dominican curate who chronicled the evangelization of Oaxaca, referred to them as "very loyal Mexican Indians" and "Mexicans of Analco."[17] In a 1683 case, the cabildo of Analco referred to the natives of their barrio as "conquistadors from these provinces that we acquired."[18]

What are we to make of these varying identifications? Were the natives of Analco descended primarily from Tlaxcalteca auxiliaries, or were they a more diverse group of indigenous conquerors from other regions? Given the Tlaxcalteca's special place in the Spanish colonial project and the privileges associated with Tlaxcalteca identity, it would have been tempting for the natives of Analco to emphasize or claim Tlaxcalteca heritage, even if their forefathers had more diverse ethnic roots. Perhaps, then, we should emphasize the utility of Tlaxcalteca identification rather than attempting to categorize the indigenous conquerors of the Sierra as Tlaxcalteca or not.

Since we do not know the exact origins of the indigenous conquerors of the Sierra nor the terms of their alliance with the Spaniards, we are left to wonder what they expected when they agreed to participate in the conquest of this reputedly fearsome, wild, and rebellious region. Did they expect to be awarded some of the spoils of conquest, or did they consider the military campaign against the Zapoteca as their own campaign of expansion? Whatever their objectives and expectations, the indigenous conquerors who accompanied the Spaniards as naborías must have been sorely disappointed when following the conquest of the Sierra their Spanish allies soon drew little distinction between them and the recently conquered locals. As early as 1549, the indigenous conquerors complained to the viceroy of their treatment at the hands of Villa Alta's Spaniards. Recognizing their service to the Crown, Viceroy Mendoza reinforced their status as naborías, insisting on their freedom from coerced labor and payment for their work.[19] '

The viceroy's decree provided a foundation upon which the Indian conquerors could negotiate a relationship with their former comrades in arms. This relationship, based largely on the logic of services in exchange for privileges, endured despite significant challenges through the first half of the colonial period. As Chance points out, in 1552 the cabildo of Villa Alta (the Spanish settlement in the Sierra) granted the indigenous conquerors land to the west of their town. In the 1560s the settlement came to be known as Papalotipac and soon thereafter as the barrio of Analco, the name it still bears today. In exchange for the land, the indigenous conquerors had to agree to the following conditions: its inhabitants were to remain part of the Spanish settlement of Villa Alta and subject to its political authorities; they could not take water illegally; they could not plant crops in the *ejidos* (community lands) of the Spanish settlement; they could not crowd the roads entering and leaving the Spanish settlement; they had to provide messenger service to Antequera and Mexico City and repair the roofs of the church and Dominican convent when necessary; and, finally, they had to serve as firemen.[20]

The population of the barrio of Analco, always larger than that of Villa Alta, fluctuated from about 175 to 270 from 1548 to 1703. Although the indigenous foot soldiers who inhabited Analco had outnumbered their Spanish allies from the start, migration of Zapoteca and other local indigenous groups to the barrio and intermarriage increased the barrio's population over the course of the colonial period.[21] Collectively, the barrio's inhabitants came to be known as the natives of Analco.

Within the next few decades, the natives of Analco won a series of royal decrees from the Real Audiencia in Mexico City, which recognized their status as indios conquistadores, and secured for them a series of special privileges in recognition of their service to the Spanish Crown. In 1572 the Real Audiencia granted them exemption from tribute in exchange for voluntary services to Spanish residents of Villa Alta, a relationship that the Spaniards often abused.[22] In 1591, in response to Spanish abuses, the natives of Analco petitioned the Audiencia to reinforce their rights and privileges. The Audiencia complied and issued a Real Provisión that prohibited the Spaniards of Villa Alta from forcing the natives of Analco to work against their will.[23] Other privileges recognized by the Audiencia included the right to be buried in the parochial church of Villa Alta, to be baptized in the baptismal font of the same church, and to carry the staff of office (*barra de justicia*) in Villa Alta. In exchange for these privileges, the indigenous conquerors were to provide special services to the local Spanish administration, which included the collection of tribute from the region's native population and service as governors and municipal authorities in politically unstable or rebellious communities.[24]

In addition to these services, in the centuries that followed the natives of Analco played an indispensable role in law enforcement and peace keeping in the Sierra, continuing to serve as a coercive occupation force under Spanish oversight and as midlevel legal and civil administrators. Their roles included deputy to the bailiff, transporters of prisoners from village jails to the prison in Villa Alta, messengers of orders and decrees to village governments, interpreters, schoolmasters, "prestige witnesses," and spies.[25] Their conduct in these roles inspired a combination of respect, fear, and loathing among the local indigenous population, particularly since their roles as spies and schoolmasters constituted part of a larger colonial strategy of social control and eradication of native religious practices. These roles became especially important during the late seventeenth and early eighteenth centuries, when Spanish officials called upon the natives of Analco to assist in squelching the region-wide rebellion of 1660, a local uprising in 1684, and another major uprising in 1700.[26]

THE SWORD AND THE PEN: THE MAINTENANCE OF PRIVILEGE

The political instability in the Sierra Norte from the 1660s until the 1720s helped the Indian conquerors to maintain their privileged position. The 1660 rebellion that initiated this tumultuous period terrified Spaniards all over Oaxaca and throughout New Spain for two reasons: its huge geographic expanse and the speed and apparent coordination with which it spread.[27] The rebellion began on Palm Sunday, March 21, 1660, when the elected indigenous leaders of Tehuantepec, the jurisdictional seat of the Zapoteca Isthmus of Tehuantepec, presented themselves at the administrative quarters of the alcalde mayor, Juan de Avellán, to issue a protest regarding the *repartimiento* labor draft's high production quotas for cotton thread and cloth and the low prices paid to native producers. The alcalde mayor, notoriously abusive, berated the officials and had them whipped publicly and imprisoned. The following morning, a crowd of over one thousand from Tehuantepec and its outlying settlements gathered in the town plaza and made their way to the municipal buildings. When they encountered the alcalde mayor and two of his assistants, the crowd killed all three of them. The rebels then organized a local government, garnered the support of surrounding villages, and succeeded in maintaining virtual political autonomy and control in the area for the following year. In the meantime, the rebellion spread, in the words of Spanish officials, like "wildfire" to the neighboring jurisdictions of Nexapa, Villa Alta, and Ixtepeji, following the lines of regional indigenous political and commercial networks.[28] Although the rebellion in Villa Alta did not reach the intensity of that in Tehuantepec, several smaller uprisings from 1659 to 1661, involving some four thousand natives, proved sufficient to put the alcalde mayor, parish priests, and the native officials of the region on notice.[29] The natives of Analco played a central role in pacifying the Mixe and Cajonos Zapoteca communities that participated in these uprisings.

The rebellion of 1660 reinforced deep anxieties and fears within the Spanish community and convinced them that they needed the Indian conquerors for the purposes of defense and social control. The fear, anxiety, and "bunker mentality" of the Sierra's Spanish population are attributable to a variety of sources. First, the land itself provided cause for anxiety. Spanish narratives of the region's landscape frequently emphasized its awesome and dreadful mountains and its broken, wild, and treacherous nature. Home to wild animals, poisonous snakes, and sometimes renegade natives and thieves, the environment haunted the Spanish imagination throughout the colonial period.

Second, despite its relatively small size and fluctuation over the course of the early and middle colonial period due to epidemic disease, the region's indigenous population greatly outnumbered its Spaniards and surrounded the tiny settlement of Villa Alta like a vast sea. From the vantage point of Villa Alta, indigenous communities dotted the landscape as far as the eye could see, with no other Spanish settlements even remotely close by. Over the course of the colonial period, the total population of the jurisdiction of Villa Alta averaged about 10,000 families in comparison with the 30 Spanish families who resided in the jurisdictional seat.[30] According to Spanish records, in 1570 tributaries in the jurisdiction numbered 7,850 overall, including 4,500 Zapoteca, 1,500 Mixe, and 1,850 Chinanteca.[31] The epidemic of 1576–77 hit the native population quite hard. A recovery appears to have occurred between 1588 and 1623, and the tributary population jumped from 6,000 in 1600 to 11,000 by 1743.[32]

From the Spanish perspective, this stark demographic imbalance had its advantages and disadvantages. On the one hand, the surrounding natives provided the Spaniards with what constituted in their opinion the only exploitable resource in the region: cheap labor. On the other, it created a situation of perpetual insecurity and fear of Indian rebellion. If the surrounding native communities were to join together and rise up against the Spaniards as happened in 1660, 1684, and 1700, the Spaniards alone would have been helpless to defend themselves. History contributed to Spanish fears of native rebellion. The fierce resistance of the local indigenous population to the conquest and to the first decades of colonial rule conferred a wild and rebellious reputation on the region's Zapoteca, Mixe, and Chinanteca natives. The Spaniards seemed to believe that these unruly locals had never wholly resigned themselves to Spanish domination.

Finally, for the Spaniards a preponderance of idolatry provided proof of the local population's undisciplined, savage, and dangerous nature.[33] In fact, the case of the Sierra Norte reveals the centrality of the discourse of idolatry to the Spanish colonial project. In the absence of state presence in the Sierra, the Catholic Church was in effect the Crown's representative and the embodiment of colonial authority. Driven by what they perceived to be a righteous mission of evangelization, Spanish priests went places that no other Spaniard would go, including remote communities, where, from their perspective, the Christian doctrine was misunderstood and malpracticed.

"Idolatry"—the worship of images—became a catchall term to define a spectrum of sacred practices, including the production, possession, and care of stone, wooden, or clay objects deemed "idols" the sacrifice of turkeys, dogs, or deer; communion with natural features of the landscape such as caves or mountains; or the use of ritual calendars for the purposes of divination or name giving. Priests and indigenous people alike wielded accusations of idolatry against perceived enemies of the Catholic faith and against perceived political rivals. Accusations of idolatry carried heavy weight and served as potent weapons of cultural and political power. To be an idolater meant that one lived outside the boundaries of colonial society. At best, idolatry connoted cultural incompetence. At worst, it implied willful resistance to colonial power with full knowledge of the basic tenets of the Christian faith.

It was these willful resistors that scared the Spaniards the most. In some cases of idolatry, local elites who had been assistants to the parish priest proved to be the worst offenders. Although they had been brought into the Christian fold, they continued their pagan ways. From an indigenous perspective, there was little contradiction in the simultaneity of native and Christian practice; they could exist side by side. But for Spanish officials, idolatry among the native elite was the ultimate sign of treason. Throughout the colonial period, the Zapoteca, Mixe, and Chinanteca communities of the Sierra Norte were reputed idolaters.[34]

The indigenous conquerors of the barrio of Analco were keen readers of this situation. They turned to colonial courts and utilized rhetorical strategies that played upon Spanish fears, justified their continued role as keepers of regional peace and security, and distinguished them culturally and politically from the local indigenous population.[35] A late-seventeenth-century conflict with the Zapoteca community of Lachirioag illustrates the legal and rhetorical efforts on the part of the natives of Analco to define their collective identity against that of local indigenous communities. In January 1683 what appears at first glance to have been a turf war between the neighboring communities of Analco and Lachirioag eventually turned out to be a platform for the officials of Analco to distinguish themselves along the lines of culture and power from the neighboring Zapoteca community. The case was provoked by the conduct of the Lachirioag natives during the fiesta of Villa Alta's patron saint, Ildefonso. Many of the communities of the district, including those of the Rincón region, Lachirioag, and Analco, participated in the fiesta of San Ildefonso in Villa Alta, which commemorated the conquest of the region. It was customary during the celebration for the natives of these communities to carry and play their drums and horns (*tambores y clarines*), musical instruments that were used in prehispanic warfare. And although it was technically illegal for indigenous people of the Sierra (with the exception of the natives of Analco) to carry firearms, the natives of Lachirioag appear to have broken this law in order to carry rifles in their procession to Villa Alta, and colonial officials appear to have looked the other way—at least until 1683.

The procession from Lachirioag, which required passage through Analco to get to Villa Alta, included men bearing arms and the staff of office. The officials of Analco claimed that this was an affront to the privilege of the indios conquistadores—exclusive among the region's Indians—to carry firearms. Furthermore, the officials of Analco interpreted the display of Lachirioag's staff of office within the confines of their territory as a challenge to the authority of Analco's officials to govern their own community. These complaints represented an effort on the part of the officials of Analco to police not only their territory but also the boundaries of their privileged collective identity.[36]

In the course of the same case, the Indian conquerors defined themselves culturally against the natives of Lachirioag, whom they cast as frequent instigators of rebellion and unrest in the volatile Cajonos region. In their characterization of the natives of Lachirioag as rebellious, they made specific reference to the regional rebellion of 1660, thereby identifying Lachirioag as a threat to regional peace. More importantly, however, they characterized the natives of Lachirioag as idolaters, pointing to the fact that many were currently jailed in the jurisdictional prison on idolatry charges. The discourses of idolatry and rebellion drew the boundary from the perspective of the colonizers between good and bad Indians, loyal vassals and the colonial "other." By contrast, the officials of Analco defined the residents of their barrio as "loyal vassals," "good Catholic Christians," and defenders of the Crown by virtue of their role in the military defense of Villa Alta during the 1660 uprising.[37]

The rhetorical opposition between loyalty to the Crown versus idolatry and rebellion convinced the judge to decide in favor of the Indian conquerors in the case against the natives of Lachirioag. However, this decision did not ensure the privileges of the indigenous conquerors of Analco, nor did it represent a permanent recognition of their rights on the part of the region's Spaniards. In the space of the same year, the officials of Analco complained to the Audiencia of abuses visited upon them by the Spaniards of Villa Alta. Their petition resulted in a royal provision issued in September 1683, reinforcing their privileges as Indian conquerors, and therefore a temporary victory in their power struggle with the jurisdiction's Spaniards.[38]

These late-seventeenth-century cases against the Zapoteca community of Lachirioag and the Spaniards of Villa Alta demonstrate that the Indian conquerors' privileged position resulted from constant legal and rhetorical work on two fronts, the first oriented toward halting Spanish challenges to their rights and the second toward distinguishing themselves from the region's indigenous population.

The uprising in Choapa in 1684—one year after these legal disputes—justified the Spanish administration's maintenance of the privileges of the natives of Analco. Other than the district center of Villa Alta, the town of Santiago Choapa was a hub of political and economic power in the Sierra, as it had been during the prehispanic era. As a crossroads for important trade routes, Choapa hosted the Sierra Norte's most prominent market, drawing Indian traders from as far as the Isthmus of Tehuantepec as well as Spanish merchants from the jurisdiction and beyond. It served as a center for ecclesiastical and civil administration and provided a gateway between the highlands and lowlands.[39]

Given the strategic centrality of Choapa, the Spanish colonial administration was alarmed and dismayed when in November of 1684 a crowd from surrounding communities besieged Choapa's taxation house with the alcalde mayor of Villa Alta and a delegation of Spaniards inside. Although the motives for the uprising remain unclear, the rebels were most likely protesting excessive tribute and taxation. Once again, the Spaniards of Villa Alta called upon the natives of Analco to pacify violent unrest and secure the region. The uprising was significant enough that colonial authorities in Antequera had to send militia units twice into the Sierra to break the siege, which lasted a few days.[40]

Sixteen years later the Cajonos region of the Sierra Norte erupted in the most serious uprising that the region had experienced since the conquest period. On September 14, 1700, the *fiscales* of the town of San Francisco Cajonos reported to the parish priest that the *mayordomo* of one of the town's *cofradías* (confraternities) was hosting a feast and leading his guests in idolatrous rites. Two Dominican friars and several Spaniards accompanied the fiscales to the house, burst in, and startled and dispersed the crowd gathered at the celebration. The three men investigated the remains of the feast and confiscated evidence of idolatry: beheaded turkeys, a bleeding doe, and other ritual implements. They reported their findings to the ecclesiastical authorities and local officials in Villa Alta.

The next day, violence erupted when a furious crowd from San Francisco Cajonos and some of the nearby towns surrounded the monastery with the priest, fiscales, Dominican friars, and a handful of Spaniards inside. The crowd demanded that the priest turn the fiscales over to them. The Spaniards, terrified for their lives, complied, and the crowd left with the two men, whom they whipped, tortured, and put to death for their betrayal and intervention in the community's affairs. The repression that followed was horrific. A criminal investigation of the entire municipal authority of San Francisco and other leaders of and participants in the rebellion ensued, involving torture on the rack and forced confessions. Almost two years later, in January of 1702, fifteen men from San Francisco Cajonos were garroted in the jail of Villa Alta. Their corpses were drawn and quartered and their remains displayed around the town of San Francisco and on the Camino Real as a warning to would-be idolaters and rebels.[41]

According to the narrative of events that emerged from court records published in part by the bishop of Oaxaca and church historian Eulogio Gillow in 1889, the ferocity of Spanish reaction to the uprising in San Francisco Cajonos had more to do with rebellion than idolatry.[42] In this particular instance, what disturbed the Spanish clergy and civil authorities most was not the idolatrous rites themselves but the brutal murder of the fiscales, the assault on the parish church, the violence with which the crowd had threatened the priest, and the widespread uprising—encompassing eighteen communities—that ensued. These actions breathed new life into Spanish nightmares of native sedition and violent rebellion.

The Cajonos uprising and the repression that followed proved a nightmare for the local indigenous population and a boon for the privileged status of the natives of Analco. As was the case with the regional rebellion of 1660 and the Choapa uprising of 1684, the Spaniards of Villa Alta turned to their indigenous neighbors and allies in the barrio of Analco to help them restore law and order. In this regard, the Cajonos uprising contributed to the maintenance of the privileged collective identity of the natives of

Analco, bolstering the military and legal work conducted during the previous decades. The violence and enormity of the incident convinced the
local Spanish population that they still needed the Indian conquerors for
the purposes of military defense and social control.

Following the uprising, colonial civil and religious authorities deployed
the natives of Analco to restore order in the region's communities and participate in an extirpation campaign. They stationed many as schoolmasters, following the logic that the Spanish language provided an important
means of combating idolatry.[43] Andrés González, a principal from the barrio of Analco who spoke Spanish, served as a teacher of Spanish language
and Christian doctrine in the Zapoteca community of Yatee in the years
following the uprising. In addition to his duties as schoolmaster, he was
also expected to report any suspicious or idolatrous conduct to church officials in the Dominican convent in Villa Alta. The details of the case against
him demonstrate the ways in which individual power brokers from Analco
used the language of idolatry and the legal system to exercise political
power, much the way that the officials of Analco had done in the service of
collective power in the 1683 case against Lachirioag.[44] The case also demonstrates the hostility and tension that permeated the relationship between
the Indian conquerors and the local indigenous population and the persistence of the coercive role of the indigenous conquerors into the early eighteenth century.

The case begins with an accusation of idolatry on the part of Andrés
González against two men from Yatee who had been imprisoned in Villa
Alta for idolatry following the Cajonos uprising. Because of their history
as "idolaters," these men made convenient targets. According to González,
the two men entered the church when he and the community were pray-
ing and shouted, "first, there was the common doctrine" ("primero era la
doctrina del comun"). The two men, backed by Yatee's village officials,
denied the charges and countered with a case of their own. In their petition to the court, they presented a litany of abuses on the part of González
against their community, including adultery, corruption of children, abuse
of power, extortion of money and services, interference in village politics,
desecration of municipal buildings, and theft of church property.[45]

In their complaints against him, the former "idolaters" from Yatee cast
González as a "hispanized Indian" ("indio ladino") who "knew how to
write and talk to your majesty."[46] They feared that González's linguistic
skills and cross-cultural knowledge would win the Spanish magistrate's

sympathy, thereby hurting the community's case against the schoolmaster. This characterization of González reveals the association of hispanized indigenous conquerors with colonial power and highlights the fear and contempt that they inspired in the local population. Their words also hint at the continued power that the Indian conquerors wielded in the region in the context of a perceived threat of idolatry and rebellion and the considerable room for maneuver afforded them by the fears and insecurities of the Spanish ruling elite.

DECLINE: BECOMING LOCAL INDIANS

The special status of the natives of Analco persisted through the early eighteenth century, thanks to their legal vigilance and to the Cajonos uprising of 1700, which justified their continued coercive role. However, during the middle and late eighteenth centuries, changing conditions eroded the cultural and political power of the natives of Analco. Increased political stability during this period decreased their utility in matters of defense and social control. Their exemption from tribute impeded the push toward economic efficiency imposed by the Bourbon reforms, which had been issued in the late eighteenth century in order to squeeze as much revenue as possible out of the colonies.

By the late eighteenth century, the natives of Analco appear to have lost the documents—the royal decrees—that secured their rights and privileges, a mishap that justified their mistreatment and exploitation at the hands of Villa Alta's Spaniards. In this instance "lost" is probably a euphemism. It is highly likely that Spaniards stole the decrees. Furthermore, migration of Indians from all over the jurisdiction to Analco and the intermarriage of these migrants with the Indian conquerors diluted the ethnic identity upon which their privileges were based.[47] Finally, a general hardening over time of racial attitudes toward indigenous groups and individuals, true for the colony as a whole, contributed to the demise of the Indian conquerors' special status. Their assertions of cultural superiority to the local Zapoteca no longer carried the weight that they had in the past.

Each of these factors appeared to play a role in two late attempts (in 1761 and 1774) on the part of the Indian conquerors to defend their privileges in court. In the first case, the municipal authorities of Analco complained that local Spaniards had disrespectfully ignored the privileged status of the natives of Analco by attempting to collect tribute from them. They also complained that the Spanish magistrate no longer used them in the service of the administration of justice but preferred to use Spanish residents of Villa Alta instead.[48]

The authorities of Analco defended their privileges and exemption from tribute by emphasizing a collective identity based on past deeds, particularly instances in which they had pacified the local population. In addition to the 1684 Chuapa uprising and the 1700 Cajonos uprising, they referred to a number of other uprisings in the towns of Lachixila, Yalalag, Guistepec, Yagavila, and Yojovi. With regard to this impressive record of military service, they claimed, "In all of these instances we have conquered and remained victorious thanks to our Lord God and his saintly mother Mary who have favored us in so many valuable ways that we cannot enumerate them all in this petition because it would make it too long; so much has happened to us since the conquest of New Spain until the present."[49]

In an even more forceful attempt to prove their continued loyalty and military utility and thereby defend the collective privileges of the residents of their barrio, the cabildo of Analco submitted to the court a robust list of men from their community who would volunteer themselves and their sons "spontaneously as soldiers of your majesty without any motive except their honor."[50] In sum, these legal strategies appear as desperate attempts to hang on to privileges that were clearly slipping through their fingers.

The Spanish magistrate responded to these grand claims of loyalty by demanding proof of their privileges and of the precise identities of the descendants of the Indian conquerors. He argued that since Indians from many local communities had migrated to Analco, they could therefore claim privileges to which they were not entitled. He also argued that their exemption from tribute would hurt the royal coffers. Finally, he claimed that according to his understanding, the natives of Analco performed their services not in exchange for privileges but voluntarily.[51]

Beyond the larger issue of exemption from tribute, the case also addressed the physical and racial boundaries that separated the Indian conquerors from their Spanish neighbors. The Spanish magistrate complained that the officials of Analco—in particular an alcalde named Juan Carpio—had chased the Villa Alta night patrol from their barrio. The alcalde argued that since the natives of Analco had always patrolled their own barrio, and the Villa Alta patrol had never before entered their jurisdiction, they had assumed that the Spanish patrol were either a band of thieves or vagabonds. The Spanish judge did not accept this explanation, claiming that the actions of the alcalde represented a contravention of royal justice.[52]

In yet another desperate attempt to hold on to the privileges afforded them as indigenous conquerors, eight men from the barrio of Analco singled themselves out from their community and claimed that they should be exempted from any erosion of their privileges given their direct descent from the indigenous conquerors of Tlaxcala. We never learn of the effect of their claim of particularity from their fellows and to Tlaxcalteca identity, since the case ends with a mandate for further testimony on the matter.[53] However, in this context, the claim to Tlaxcalteca identity hints at the power of the category "Tlaxcalteca."

In a 1774 follow-up case regarding the privileges of the natives of Analco and the jurisdiction of its cabildo and civil patrol, the Spanish judge upheld the right of the natives of Analco to patrol their own barrio. But he rescinded the long-standing role of the natives of Analco as night watchmen in Villa Alta. In stark contrast with the rhetoric of loyal vassalage and honor deployed by the natives of Analco, the prosecutor argued that the Spanish residents of Villa Alta could not have Indians patrolling their streets at night because of their "innate incapacities."[54]

Clearly, the principles of racial hierarchy came to override the aspects of intimacy and interdependence that had in part characterized the long-term relationship of the Spaniards of Villa Alta to the Indian conquerors who lived in the barrio of Analco.[55] Although tensions based on racial differences had marred the relationship from the start, in practice interdependence and the logic of services in exchange for privileges had mitigated the identity of the natives of Analco as Indians. At the very least, it had served to distinguish them from the local population. Toward the end of the eighteenth century, the legal system that had upheld their privileges in the past recognized this distinction less frequently. Gradually, after the Cajonos rebellion, the Spaniards of Villa Alta ceased to require the services that the natives of Analco had performed from the beginning of the colonial period, particularly in the realms of military defense and social control. The rigors of the post-Cajonos extirpation campaign and the repression that followed the rebellion may have succeeded in deterring similar uprisings. Further, Bishop of Oaxaca Angel Maldonado increased social control in the region through the formation of new parishes and the installation of secular priests (twice the number of their Dominican predecessors) who would answer to him directly. Now colonial authorities had more eyes and ears in villages throughout the district, and the new priests worked to suppress the idolatry that in the eyes of the Spaniards had plagued the region.[56] As a result of all of these factors, the indios conquistadores' privileges disappeared.

These privileges and services had defined their power, status, and collective identity, and without them the indios conquistadores were nothing more than local Indians.

CONCLUSION

Notwithstanding these late colonial dynamics, for the better part of three centuries, the natives of Analco, alongside the descendants of their Spanish comrades in arms, formed part of the Sierra Norte's ruling elite. Rebellion, resistance, political autonomy, and illicit religious practices characterized the communities of the Sierra Norte well into the eighteenth century. In this context, the exigencies of regional security helped the role of the Indian conquerors as military allies of the Spanish to evolve into one of guarantors of Spanish security. We must also acknowledge the skilled use of the colonial legal system on the part of the natives of Analco as the other central factor in the maintenance of their privileges, given the Spanish tendency to abuse the relationship of services in exchange for privileges. Spanish reliance on coercion and indigenous recourse to the legal system therefore worked in tandem to maintain the privileged status of the Sierra's indigenous conquerors and colonial control of the region. In this regard, the natives of Analco both inserted themselves and were co-opted into the Sierra's colonial system. Unfortunately for them, once they had outlived their coercive role, the legal system no longer served their purposes.

NOTES

1. Louise Burkhart and Kenneth Mills have written against Ricard's notion of the "spiritual conquest." See Ricard, *La conquista espiritual*; Burkhart, *Holy Wednesday*; Burkhart, *Slippery Earth*; Mills, *Idolatry and Its Enemies*. Susan Kellogg makes explicit arguments about the role of colonial law and its courts in the emergence of a hegemonic system in New Spain. See Kellogg, *Law and Transformation*. Steve Stern and Karen Spalding make strong arguments about the incorporation of Andean elites into the Spanish political order in colonial Peru. See Spalding, *Huarochirí*; Stern, *Peru's Indian Peoples*.

2. Chance, *Conquest of the Sierra*.

3. Blom, "El Lienzo de Analco."

4. König, *Die Schlacht*, 21–23; Florine Asselbergs, personal communication, November 2002. I would like to thank Florine Asselbergs for discussing the Lienzo of Analco with me and for sharing her expertise regarding Mesoamerican pictorial writing.

5. Chance, *Conquest of the Sierra*, 16–20; Gerhard, *Historical Geography*, 367–73.

6. Chance, *Conquest of the Sierra*, 33–34, 42–43.

7. Ibid., 16–29.

8. König, *Die Schlacht*, 21–23.

9. Although König makes many of these observations about the lienzo, the commentary in the rest of this paragraph comes from my own study of the Lienzo de Analco. I would like to thank Michel Oudijk for facilitating this study by sharing his slides of the Lienzo de Analco with me.

10. Figures 7.1–7.3 are sepia-toned photographs taken by Michel Oudijk of black-and-white photographs of individual scenes in the Lienzo de Analco taken by Burkhard Brinker 1984, (c) Viola König. König's photographs were taken in 1984 under extremely difficult technical conditions, most notably lack of light. I would like to thank Michel Oudijk and Viola König for allowing the publication of these images in this volume.

11. See Gibson, *Tlaxcala*; Cavazos Garza, "Los tlaxcaltecas"; Frye, *Indians into Mexicans*; Sego, *Aliados y adversarios*.

12. Chance, *Conquest of the Sierra*, 33. Chance relies on the Papeles de Analco from the Archivo Parochial de Villa Alta for this particular categorization.

13. Chance, *Conquest of the Sierra*, 43.

14. Archivo del Poder Judicial de Oaxaca (hereafter, APJO), Archivo del Juzgado de Villa Alta (hereafter, AJVA) Civil exp. 259 (1761), "Los naturales del barrio de Analco piden se les respete los privilegios que gozan como el de no pagar tributos."

15. Archivo General de la Nación, Mexico City (hereafter, AGN), Indios vol. 3, exp. 917, ff. 223v–24 (1591).

16. AGN Tierras vol. 2968, exp. 121, ff. 296–99v (1683).

17. Burgoa, *Geográfica descripción*, 2:147.

18. APJO, AJVA Ramo Civil exp. 18 (1683), "Los naturales del barrio de Analco contra los del pueblo de Lachirioag para que respeten el contrato celebrado entre ambos con motivo de la festividad del patron del pueblo."

19. Chance, *Conquest of the Sierra*, 33.

20. Ibid.

21. Ibid., 62. According to his figures, the total population of Analco fluctuated as follows: in 1548, there were 200; in 1622, 177; in 1703, 271; in 1742, 135; and in 1781, 355.

22. Ibid., 34.

23. AGN Indios vol. 3, exp. 917, ff. 223v–24 (1591).

24. APJO, AJVA Ramo Civil exp. 104 (1709), "Los naturales del barrio de Analco reclaman para que no se les quiten los privilegios otorgados por Real Provisión como el de no pagar tributos y otros." In this case, the cabildo of Analco petitioned the Real Audiencia to uphold the privileges granted to the indios conquistadores and their descendants after the conquest.

25. For examples of these roles, see the following cases: APJO, AJVA Civil exp. 16 (1677), "Los naturales de los pueblos de San Andres Yaa, San Francisco Yatee y

Yohueche contra los de Betaza and Lachitaa por tierras"; APJO, AJVA Criminal exp. 200 (1725), "Contra Juan Martin gobernador y Nicolas Geronimo alcalde por ebrios consetudinarios."; APJO, AJVA Ramo Criminal (uncataloged) (1753), "Idolatría en Zoogocho"; Rosenbach Museum and Library, New Spain 462/25, pt.25 #1 (December 22, 1736–November 20, 1741), ff. 24v–25; AGN Indios vol. 62, exp. 57, ff. 77v–79 (1769); APJO, AJVA Criminal exp. 227 (1736), "Contra las Autoridades y el común del pueblo de Yalalag por idolatras"; APJO, AJVA Civil exp. 52 (1677), "Los naturales de los pueblos de San Andres Yaa, San Francisco Yatee y Yohueche contra los de Betaza y Lachitaa por tierras"; AGN Civil vol. 1607, exp. 1, ff. 45–50 (1783).

26. APJO, AJVA Ramo Civil exp. 104 (1709), "Los naturales del barrio de Analco reclaman para que no se les quiten los privilegios otorgados por Real Provisión como el de no pagar tributos y otros." In this petition to the Real Audiencia for the preservation of their privileges, the cabildo of Analco cited the role of the descendants of the indios conquistadores in maintaining security during various uprisings and rebellions.

27. Judith Francis Zeitlin argues forcefully that the speed, coordination, and geographical expanse of the 1660 rebellion was exaggerated by Spanish officials for political purposes. For this new interpretation, see Zeitlin, *Cultural Politics*, 168–202.

28. See the narratives of the 1660 rebellion in Díaz-Polanco, *El fuego de la inobediencia*, and Romero Frizzi, *El sol y la cruz*, 195–206.

29. Chance, *Conquest of the Sierra*, 110.

30. Romero Frizzi, *El sol y la cruz*, 190.

31. Gerhard, *Historical Geography*, 369.

32. Gerhard, *Historical Geography*, 370. Chance puts the total population at 20,751 in 1622, 36,396 in 1703, and 49,123 in 1742. Tributaries were counted as male heads of families. Chance, *Conquest of the Sierra*, 62–63.

33. Burgoa, *Geográfica descripción*, 1:110–11, 2:137–38. Burgoa expresses this opinion about the Sierra repeatedly in his chronicle of the evangelization of Oaxaca.

34. AGI *Mexico* 357, 60–4-22. A series of documents makes clear the persistent preoccupation with idolatry on the part of the clergy and civil authorities in the Sierra Norte. In a 1679 report to the Crown, the bishop of the Puerto de Oaxaca expressed concern for continued idolatry in the Cajonos region and commended the alcalde mayor of Villa Alta, Don Christobal del Castillo, for his "zealous" persecution of idolaters. In a 1689 report to the Crown, Bishop Sariñana of Oaxaca discussed his plans (approved by the Crown) to build a "prison for perpetual idolators" in Oaxaca. See also Gillow, *Apuntes históricos*, who echoes Burgoa in his characterization of the idolatrous nature of the people of the Sierra, in particular those of the Cajonos Zapoteca region. For an historical study of idolatry and extirpation in the Sierra Norte, see Tavárez, "Invisible Wars."

35. For examples of these rhetorical strategies, see AGN Tierras vol. 2968, exp. 121, ff. 296–99v (1683); APJO, AJVA Ramo Civil exp. 104 (1709), "Los naturales del barrio de Analco reclaman para que no se les quiten los privilegios otorgados por

real provision como el de no pagar tributos y otros"; APJO, AJVA Civil exp. 259 (1761), "Los naturales del barrio de Analco piden se les respete los privilegios que gozan como el de no pagar tributos"; APJO, AJVA Civil exp. 366 (1774), "Los naturales del barrio de Analco piden se les respeten los privilegios de que gozan de imemorable año."

36. APJO, AJVA Ramo Civil exp. 18 (1683), "Los naturales del barrio de Analco contra los del pueblo de Lachirioag para que respeten el contrato celebrado entre ambos con motivo de la festividad del patron del pueblo."

37. Ibid.

38. AGN Tierras vol. 2968, exp. 121, ff. 296–99v (1683).

39. For a brief discussion of the history of the town of Chuapa, see Chance, *Conquest of the Sierra*, 98, 117.

40. AGPEO Leg. 6, exp. 9 (1684) Antequera, "Autos y diligencias hechas sobre el socorro que se envió al alcalde mayor de la Villa Alta." This document outlines the events surrounding the Chuapa uprising, the request on the part of the alcalde mayor of Villa Alta for military backup from the alcalde mayor of Antequera, and the actions taken by Antequera's civil authorities, which included the deployment of militias to the Sierra Norte.

41. APJO, AJVA Criminal (uncataloged) (1701), "Contra los naturales del pueblo de San Francisco Cajonos por sedición, sublevación e idolatría." For a narrative of the events of 1700–1702 from the perspective of the Catholic hierarchy, see Gillow, *Apuntes históricos*.

42. Ibid. Gillow reproduces many of the official documents from the case.

43. José Alcina Franch, *Calendario y religión*, 20.

44. APJO, AJVA Criminal (uncataloged) (1706), "Idolatria en Yatee."

45. Ibid.

46. Ibid., f. 27.

47. Chance, *Conquest of the Sierra*, 43.

48. APJO, AJVA Civil exp. 259 (1761), "Los naturales del barrio de Analco piden se les respete los privilegios que gozan como el de no pagar tributos."

49. Ibid.

50. Ibid.

51. Ibid.

52. Ibid.

53. Ibid.

54. APJO, AJVA Civil exp. 366 (1774), "Los naturales del barrio de Analco piden se les respeten los privilegios de que gozan de imemorable año."

55. An erosion of privileges and a closer approximation to the status of local Indians proved to be the trajectory for the Tlaxcalteca settlers of the San Luis Potosí region as well. See Frye, *Indians into Mexicans*, 50, 53.

56. Chance, *Conquest of the Sierra*, 164–68.

CHAPTER EIGHT

Nahua Christian Warriors in the Mapa de Cuauhtlantzinco, Cholula Parish

STEPHANIE WOOD

A century or more after the Spanish seizure of the Mexica capital Tenochtitlan, conquerors' descendants were still writing the Crown for recognition of their ancestors' meritorious deeds. Since participants had regularly financed their own conquest expeditions in the sixteenth century, they had been eager to gain rights to collect tributes from any new subjects they could subdue. They also felt compelled to win official approval of their activities, for advancing the interests of the Crown brought legitimacy and security to their own individual endeavors. Bernal Díaz del Castillo's account of the conquest of Mexico, written late in life, is just one of many examples of this tradition. His memoirs, though completed in 1568, were published and circulated in New Spain after 1632.[1]

Díaz del Castillo was a figure of prominence in the area around Tlaxcala. A large part of what we know about the Tlaxcalteca warriors who joined the Spanish by the thousands, taking a major role in defeating the Mexica, comes from his account. His expedition to Guatemala, where he ultimately settled, was accompanied by large numbers of Tlaxcalteca. The example set by Díaz del Castillo in writing about the conquest may have served not only to inspire other Spanish conquerors to write about their exploits; it also may have planted a seed in literate circles of the indigenous nobility or their descendants who claimed a role in the victory over the Mexica in 1521.

The Mapa de Cuauhtlantzinco or Códice Campos, a series of paintings in watercolor with short texts in Nahuatl, mentions the "Señor Don Bernal Díaz del Castillo" among other Spanish conquerors whose histories supposedly recognized the deeds of a local *cacique*, Tepoztecatl.[2] The mapa actually touts the meritorious activities of not just one but four local caciques who aided or even took the lead in local battles of conquest. The mapa comes from a small community, San Juan Cuauhtlantzinco, in the parish of Cholula, not far from Tlaxcala. It seems to date from no earlier than the 1650s, a temporal framework that would support the mapa's author(s) having been influenced by Díaz's writings.[3]

Certain caciques actually got started much earlier in their quest for rewards.[4] One such example is Don Joaquín de San Francisco Moctezuma, "cacique y gobernador" of Tepexí de la Seda, who petitioned the Crown in 1584 for exemption for himself, his family, and his entire community from taxes, in honor of his having welcomed Hernando Cortés, having given him gifts and for having performed royal service by independently conquering a number of communities in the area of Oaxaca.[5] People such as this gentleman, who claimed to be the great-great-grandson of the Moctezuma who was reigning in Mexico at the time of the Spanish invasion, were encouraged in their pursuit of royal favors by the awards that the king had given to their relatives, such as Isabel, a daughter to Moctezuma, who received a large *encomienda*.[6]

The Mapa de Cuauhtlantzinco follows the lead established by merit-seeking caciques in the sixteenth century, but it also draws from other traditions. The post-1650 period in which the mapa was probably produced was also a time of fairly intense activity across Mesoamerica in the production of ad hoc local histories written in indigenous languages. These records, called *títulos primordiales* (primordial titles), can share this desire to win recognition for caciques, but they go farther, seeking to underwrite the antiquity of the pueblo in question and its rights to landholdings. Further, títulos often have a religious component, recounting the selection of the local patron saint and the construction of a church in his or her honor, for the relative prominence of the local church came to serve as a measure of the stature of the community as a whole.

The Mapa de Cuauhtlantzinco, as a series of large paintings, diverges in form from both the petitions for merit and the primordial titles, but it has definite thematic elements in common with these traditions. It does show a concern for the benefit of the town, and it has references to land grants and the defense of lands. One of the mapa's dominant themes is the great effort made by the local caciques to advance the Christian faith among the neighboring communities. According to this account, these four native men became fervent allies of the Spanish conquistadors and Christian warriors in their own right. They forcefully evangelized neighboring communities with and without the help of the foreign invaders. In passionate Nahuatl-language speeches and colorfully explicit paintings, the mapa storyboards a clear indigenous agency. Native actors are the major players in a drama set in motion and then supported by Hernando Cortés and his men shortly after their landfall on the Gulf Coast.

This drama hails from a small community in the Nahua cultural zone of the central highlands that had been under Mexica domination, unlike its neighbor, the city of Tlaxcala. The smaller Nahua communities around Cholula, a traditional enemy of Tlaxcala, seem to have followed the lead of both of these cities, however, in choosing to ally themselves with the Spanish invaders.[7] Cholula, after suffering a devastating massacre at the hands of the Spanish and Tlaxcalteca in the fall of 1519, surrendered and joined the march on Mexico-Tenochtitlan. Cholulteca even fought alongside their traditional enemies, the Tlaxcalteca, on subsequent conquering expeditions. According to Díaz del Castillo, a group of two hundred Cholulteca and Tlaxcalteca went with Pedro de Alvarado on the expedition he led into Guatemala in 1524.[8] The Mapa de Cuauhtlantzinco upholds this tradition, mentioning not only Cortés but also Alvarado and Díaz del Castillo (in the text to scene 22) as familiar figures.[9]

The reference to these "conquistadores" (using the Spanish loanword in the Nahuatl text) is not intended to shed any particular honor on them but, rather, to elevate the importance of the native men from Cuauhtlantzinco who were smart enough to take them on as their allies.[10] Minimizing the role of the Spaniards and, in fact, largely suppressing the presence of any possible, competing Tlaxcalteca on the local scene, the mapa shines its brightest light on its local leaders. It was not out of any apparent anti-European position that the Cholulteca would make themselves into the primary conquistadors. They were even less likely to make other Nahuas, such as the Tlaxcalteca, into key figures of their local history. It was their own heroes, and by extension their own pueblos, they wished to exalt.

Still, because Tlaxcala was the more vocal and relatively more successful of the Spanish allies to win favors from the Crown, the Cholulteca found it prudent to learn from the example of the Tlaxcalteca and to borrow from their discourse about their roles in conquest and evangelization. As will be shown, the mapa embraces some of the major elements of Tlaxcalteca early colonial memory. Granted, the elements they embrace, as well as the Tlaxcalteca sources themselves, have some distinct later-colonial influences that have shaped the nature of those contact-era events in the minds of those who created the mapa, possibly first writing the script of the drama later in the sixteenth century, although existing copies appear to be from after 1650. Together, the mapa and the Tlaxcalteca sources border more on legend and lore than eyewitness historical records, and yet they have their foundation in some degree of actual, lived experience. San Juan Cuauhtlantzinco was a small, quiet settlement that, in all probability, played a relatively minor role in conquest-era events except perhaps at the local level.

DATING THE MANUSCRIPT

In 1836 the curate of Cholula, Jose Vicente Campos, visited one of the pueblos of his jurisdiction, San Juan Cuauhtlantzinco, where the local people showed him what he described as a multiscene, painted "historical document," which he calculated to be 312 years old (which would give it a date of 1524, momentous for coinciding with the founding of the Franciscan monastery in Tlaxcala, the launching of the evangelical campaign by native youth, and the departure for Guatemala of indigenous conquistadores from Tlaxcala and Cholula).[11] Campos found this series of paintings on paper, glossed with Nahuatl texts, much deteriorated. It was not until 1855–56 that he was able to revisit the pueblo to have the approximately thirty original paintings (with twenty-nine numbered texts), plus some duplicates, mounted on two long, wooden frames.[12] Also in the 1850s, Campos asked for help from the local people to translate the Nahuatl texts into Spanish. He found the native language speeches of the mapa to be "more pure and old-fashioned" than the dialect still in use in the pueblo at that time, but it is nevertheless difficult to say whether that Nahuatl could have been sixteenth-century.[13]

When I visited the pueblo in 1989, I was not given access to the original, or oldest, copies of the paintings and texts, which people in the municipal palace said had been taken to Mexico City. Turning to the copies that exist at Tulane University and the University of Oregon, I have found the orthography of the Nahuatl of these versions to be what James Lockhart would call Stage 3, or roughly post-1650.[14] We have no firm dates for either of the copies in Louisiana or Oregon, but both of these seem to have been made late in the nineteenth century. The Protestant missionary Adolph F. Bandelier visited the pueblo in 1881 and apparently obtained a copy.[15] It is possible, perhaps, that his copy ended up in the William Gates collection and, subsequently, the Tulane library.[16] Following Bandelier's lead, anthropologist Frederick Starr went with photographers to Cuauhtlantzinco twice in the 1890s, publishing some of those photos in his study of 1898. The copy of the mapa at the University of Oregon comes from the Starr estate, so it surely dates from that period too. What is not clear is whether the transcriptions of the Nahuatl texts on these nineteenth-century copies are precise, allowing us to be sure of the timing of their original composition, or whether the post-1650 Nahuatl in them reflects the influence of their copyists.

Clearly, the events depicted in the mapa occurred—or were later believed to have occurred—in the first half of the sixteenth century. But the paintings and their scripts refer to Cortés as the marqués del Valle, a title he did not win until 1529, so we know the original texts could not be from the purported date of 1524 (unless Cortés's title was added by later copyists). Furthermore, as Charles Gibson found in his study of Tlaxcala, religious conversion was somewhat delayed, taking place for the most part during and after the 1530s. Friars' accounts of a supposedly successful religious campaign date from the 1530s through 1550s. Legend produced by subsequent generations, however, projected conversion back to the moment of contact, reducing the degree of resistance and exaggerating the local people's piety. Gibson refers to this tradition as "late and contradictory."[17] Although difficult to date precisely, the mapa shares these characteristics of later colonial lore.

TLAXCALTECA DISCOURSE

Tlaxcalteca discourse on the conquest contains many of the same elements we find in the Mapa de Cuauhtlantzinco from the Cholula jurisdiction. It is as though a formulaic narrative evolved, mimicked by neighboring communities and likely carried by Tlaxcalteca and missionaries into distant frontiers. Exemplary sources include the Lienzo de Tlaxcala from the 1550s and the Historia or Descripción de Tlaxcala of Diego Muñoz Camargo from the 1580s. Later-colonial examples that also embody these perspectives are the eighteenth-century cartographic-historical Códice de Contlantzinco and Códice de Santo Tomás Xochtlan.[18] These ethnohistorical sources additionally appear to draw from Spanish-language chronicles that recorded noteworthy events in conquest-era Tlaxcala.[19]

FIGURE 8.1.
Scene 1 from the Mapa de Cuauhtlantzinco.

FIGURE 8.2.
Scene 2 from the Mapa de Cuauhtlantzinco.

FIGURE 8.3.
Scene 3 from the Mapa de Cuauhtlantzinco.

FIGURE 8.4.
Scene 4 from the Mapa de Cuauhtlantzinco.

FIGURE 8.5.
Scene 5 from the Mapa de Cuauhtlantzinco.

FIGURE 8.6.
Scene 6 from the Mapa de Cuauhtlantzinco.

FIGURE 8.7.
Scene 7 from the Mapa de Cuauhtlantzinco.

FIGURE 8.8.
Scene 8 from the Mapa de Cuauhtlantzinco.

FIGURE 8.9.
Scene 9 from the Mapa de Cuauhtlantzinco.

FIGURE 8.10.
Scene 10 from the Mapa de Cuauhtlantzinco.

FIGURE 8.11.
Scene 11 from the Mapa de Cuauhtlantzinco.

FIGURE 8.12.
Scene 12 from the Mapa de Cuauhtlantzinco.

FIGURE 8.13.
Scene 13 from the Mapa de Cuauhtlantzinco.

FIGURE 8.14.
Scene 14 from the Mapa de Cuauhtlantzinco.

FIGURE 8.15.
Scene 15 from the Mapa de Cuauhtlantzinco.

FIGURE 8.16.
Scenes 16 and 17 from the Mapa de Cuauhtlantzinco.

FIGURE 8.17.

Scene 18 from the Mapa de Cuauhtlantzinco.

FIGURE 8.18.

Scenes 19 and 20 from the Mapa de Cuauhtlantzinco.

FIGURE 8.19.
Scene 21 from the Mapa de Cuauhtlantzinco, left and right sides (below and opposite).

FIGURE 8.20.
Scene 22 from the Mapa de Cuauhtlantzinco.

FIGURE 8.21.
Scene 23 from the Mapa de Cuauhtlantzinco.

FIGURE 8.22.
Scene 24 from the Mapa de Cuauhtlantzinco.

FIGURE 8.23.
Scenes 26 and 29 from the Mapa de Cuauhtlantzinco.

FIGURE 8.24.
Scene 27 from the Mapa de Cuauhtlantzinco.

FIGURE 8.25.
Scene 28 from the Mapa de Cuauhtlantzinco.

One of the elements in the formula of Christian fervor in Tlaxcala that emerges in these various sources involves the early baptism of four native nobles, which we also see illustrated in scene 13 of the mapa. The names may change in the local histories from particular Tlaxcala-area towns, but the number four tends to remain the same. It is as though four became a requisite number used even in towns where there was no equivalent to the four-part division that characterized Tlaxcalteca political leadership. In the Mapa de Cuauhtlantzinco, the stories of caciques from different towns may have been pooled to bring the number up to four, since we learn that one was from Cuauhtlantzinco and another was from Santiago Xalitzintlan (see the texts of scenes 22 and 29).[20]

Another element in Tlaxcalteca lore is the miraculous apparition of a cross at the various sites where the indigenous nobles forged their alliances with Cortés. Typically, the special cross is decorated with plants and flowers.[21] Such a cross is featured in scenes 16 and 17 of the mapa. This one, ironically, has a sword as its crossbar. A branch forms the vertical component, providing the leaves and flowers. The native couple's prayers, in the form of speech-scrolls, drape over the sword, linking them organically to the cross as the couple also reverently steadies it with their hands.

An even more influential episode in Tlaxcalteca religious history, from the point of view of the authors of the mapa, involves the activities of the youths trained by the Franciscan missionaries in 1524, the monastery's first year. Gibson recounts, "The youths learned readily and rapidly. . . . [A] group of children from the monastery took so literally the friars' injunctions against the former religion that of their own accord they stoned to death one of the native Tlaxcalan priests . . . insisting that they had killed a devil rather than a man."[22] Juan Buenaventura Zapata y Mendoza, in his *Historia cronológica de la Noble Ciudad de Tlaxcala*, emphasizes how a subsequent (1527) investigation to stamp out idolatry (*tlatetemolo y tlatlacatecolo*) was carried out by the "students of the friars" (*itlamachtilhuan teopixque*).[23] The friars themselves also executed several Tlaxcalteca nobles in 1527 for continuing prehispanic practices, setting an example of the extremes to which the religious war could go.[24]

Related to this is the story of the Tlaxcalteca boy martyrs, fervent Christians who overstepped their bounds and were killed by their own people. Cristóbal, one of the martyrs, died at the hands of his own father, Acxotecatl, in 1527. The latter also killed his wife and was hanged for both murders. When he and the other Tlaxcalteca leaders were executed by hanging, that was when "the terror began" ("oca peuhqui ye nemauhtiloc"), according to the annalist Buenaventura Zapata y Mendoza.[25]

Ironically, Acxotecatl, who put an end to his zealous son's Christian-ization efforts, actually saw himself as a pioneer in the evangelization process. Cortés gave him an image of the Virgen de los Remedios, which became one of the key symbols of Christianity in the region, ending up in a church in Puebla.

The Virgen de los Remedios also became the patron saint of the Christian church built atop the giant *tlachihualtepetl* (artificial hill/"pyramid") in Cholula.[26] Her image appears several times in the mapa (scenes 7, 18, 19, and 20), with the proud appellation "conquistadora" taken into the Nahuatl text (scene 18).[27] Rather than a European conqueror, was she becoming an indigenous one? Parading her around on a dais, much as they would one of their most exalted dignitaries, were they transforming her into a sym-bolic partner in their own conquest endeavors?

While the enthusiasm of new Christian youth of Tlaxcala and Cholula offended some, it probably inspired others. Much of the work of the fri-ars, from the perspective of the local histories, was actually carried out by these young men, taking up the sword to advance the cross. Sometimes the clergy were shocked by what they had set in motion, but they also held up the example of the boy martyrs as praiseworthy. By encouraging religious theater, the friars also helped propagate these legends and carry them into neighboring jurisdictions to serve their missionary aspirations.

Religious festivals described by Motolinía, beginning at least as early as 1536, encouraged the enactment of theatrical elements, such as the bring-ing of gifts for presentation on Easter Sunday, including blankets, religious items, lambs, and pigs, as recalled in the left side of scene 21 in the mapa, where native people bring such things to provide a feast for Cortés.[28] In another festival, in 1539, native actors performed mock battles between Tlaxcalteca and Mexica or between Christians, Moors, and Jews, reminis-cent of the battle we can see in scenes 5 and 7 of the mapa.[29] Even if the clergy encouraged these dramas, the local people embraced such prac-tices and made them their own.

According to Gibson, these festivities declined somewhat in the sec-ond half of the sixteenth century, but the messages they carried survived through oral and written traditions in the affected communities.[30] One late-sixteenth-century play, the *Colloquy of the Last Four Kings*, performed in 1585, has four indigenous recent converts convincing other native "kings" of the Christian message.[31] These kinds of plays, generally called *colloquios*, were performed into the seventeenth and eighteenth centuries. Recollections of the foundation period not only survived but tended "to represent Tlaxcalan leaders as more sympathetic toward Spanish practices than was actually the case."[32] What these memories also achieved was the preservation of indigenous participants as key figures in a forceful native Christian evangelism, showing them wielding considerable independence practically from the start.

NAHUA CHRISTIAN WARRIORS

In the Mapa de Cuauhtlantzinco, which clearly draws from the colloquios tradition, the main protagonists are men named Tepostecatzin, Cacalotzin, Cencamatzin, and Sarmiento.[33] Although Spaniards figure in many scenes and Cortés is prominent and respected, these four indigenous nobles are the main characters, performing most of the action, whether as depicted in the visual materials or as described in the texts and glosses that accompany the paintings. In most scenes, the native leaders wear either their own battle dress of animal skins and carry stylized *macanas* (indigenous, obsidian studded clubs), or they carry staves of authority and dress in capes and decorative, knee-length pants.

Spaniards generally appear in armor, carrying banners, drums, and firearms. In comparison with the indigenous figures, the Spaniards' appearance is more obviously and probably more exaggeratedly that of the Western "soldier," even if they were not trained as such and even if this militaristic role was historically fleeting in the central areas, where the invaders quickly became settlers.[34] But the native people do show themselves ready and willing to fight to introduce the new faith, even if their evangelism only rarely leads to bloodshed.

In scene 1, the story's heroes greet Cortés and his men in Jalapa, supposedly shortly after they had started their overland journey in search of the Mexica capital.[35] Tepostecatzin bows humbly to Cortés, offering him his hand. But this native leader occupies the physical space at the center of the scene, dominating the action. He also overshadows the other native men who are present. A possible contender for power, Cacalotzin here receives the least attention and does not even have a gloss for his name next to his apparent portrait.[36]

In the text for scene 1, Tepostecatzin emphasizes two points about this historic meeting (and alliance): that he took the initiative to inquire about the new religion and that he agreed to be the Spaniards' guide along their journey.[37] He thus places himself in a leadership role and establishes his early interest in the new faith. For Tepostecatzin, to be a guide would not imply a position as a subordinate aide but, rather, would transfer to him the lead and initiative from the foreigners who did not know their way through this countryside.

Tepostecatzin's alliance with the Spanish was apparently controversial among some of his indigenous neighbors. In scene 3, Tepostecatzin tells how Nezahualcoyotl (1402–72, or was this meant to be a descendant of his, alive in the sixteenth century?), regent of Tetzcoco, ordered five neighboring lords to bring the upstart before a tribunal. There, Tepostecatzin was sentenced to enter a hot bath fully clothed, which he felt would have put his life in peril. Somehow, he escaped and led his Spanish allies against the five men who had tried to curb his activities. In this scene, the foes appear asleep, having not seen the light of Christianity. He catches them by surprise, wielding his mighty sword, and they beg forgiveness and agree to baptism, without an obvious fight.[38] Apparently in the same location and with the same protagonist, in scene 4, Tepostecatzin threatens punishment for those who resist conversion. His ferocious words nearly frighten them to death, while, again, no blood is shed.[39]

In the most violent of all the scenes, scene 5, Tepostecatzin once again leads the Spanish troops against some indigenous neighbors, this time in the community of Santa María Malacatepec, near San Juan Cuauhtlantzinco. The people of Malacatepec fight back with clubs, while Tepostecatzin, like the distant Spanish troops who are his allies, raises his newly acquired sword.[40] One Spaniard, more in the foreground, has fallen under the threat of the advancing opposition. We might presume that Tepostecatzin would arrive in time to save him, but the downtrodden Spaniard's fate is not the central concern here. What the mapa emphasizes is that the people of Malacatepec were successfully converted and chose to believe in the Christian God.

Occasionally, Tepostecatzin steps out of the spotlight. He does not appear at all in scene 6. Rather, Cencamatzin, Sarmiento, and an off-stage Cacalotzin take power over a neighboring ruler, Tlamacospili, who has both a throne and a turban made from a coiled green snake. The three local leaders only have to threaten violence, with "valor and boldness," to win his subjugation. No Spaniard assists them in this scene; they operate completely on their own, advancing the rim of Christendom against what some Western observers might see as a Moorish figure.[41]

In scene 7, the threat of battle shifts to San Jerónimo Tecuanipan, a pueblo subject to Santa Isabel Cholula. Here, indigenous warriors with bows and arrows square off against Spaniards, whose firearms discharge at no particular target. Tepostecatzin and the other three heroes do not appear at the battle scene, but Cacalotzin's name has been tagged onto the end of the text box, preceded by the Nahuatl particle *ni*, the first person "I," apparently intending to give him the command. No arrows fly, and no one lies fallen in this otherwise tense setting.

Again, in scene 8, the main protagonists are not pictured. A Spaniard leads the captured noble, Tecpaxotzin, before a person who seems to be Cortés, who holds the rope that binds the captive's hands. Although the four indigenous leaders of this story do not appear in the scene in person, the text box has a speech about how "we conquered him and drew him forth from a great gorge," as though they were either entirely responsible for capturing Tecpaxotzin or certainly participated.[42]

Tecpaxotzin may have been from Tecuanipan, for the conquest of Tecuanipan seems to continue in scene 9, where the people are said to have dressed in the skins of wild beasts (*tecuani*). Here Tepostecatzin takes central stage again, bringing indigenous nobles from yet other communities, whom he has taken prisoner, before Cortés. Tepostecatzin credits himself with having induced these captives to believe in the Christian faith and accept baptism.

The forcible conversion of neighboring communities progresses in scene 10, where Tepostecatzin brings more unbelievers before the Spaniards for baptism. The leader reports that these men accepted baptism out of respect for his example, having been baptized himself and having aided Cortés and being strong. As in several other scenes, he achieves his objective without obvious violent conflict and largely unaided by the foreigners. Also following the example of other scenes, figures who have not yet converted cover their eyes in a rather submissive gesture.

A particularly prominent leader arrives for baptism in scene 11. The Nahuatl text of the Tulane version calls him the "pili" (*pilli*, noble) "Oquatemoqui" (intending Cuauhtemoc?).[43] His arrival on a dais does suggest a figure of note. The use of such a lowly title, *pilli*, instead of *tlatoani* (ruler) or *teuhctli* (lord) would be surprising for anyone of this prominence, but pilli is, curiously enough, the preferred title for all the major indigenous figures in this manuscript, including the four heroes themselves.[44] Still, one doubts that this particular lord was the Cuauhtemoc of the royal Mexica lineage. It would have been unlikely, historically, for him to appear in this context.[45] It seems likely, however, that these Cholula-area men or their descendants, in an effort to boost their own importance and expand the geographical reach of their influence, were building a story that was larger than life many years after the supposed events occurred and when few memories would be sharp enough to contradict it.

More credible is the appearance of the Tlaxcalteca lord Citlalpopocatzin, who "was baptized" in scene 12. I presume that Citlalpopocatzin, rather than being the kneeling figure in this scene, is the one who stands holding the staff, or macana, and who wears the uniquely checked pants, suggestive of a different ethnicity or a higher status. Other accounts more credibly place his baptism in Tlaxcala itself, as one of the famous four first baptisms. To its author's credit, the mapa does not indicate the location of this momentous event, and perhaps it is simply borrowing a leaf from the history of Tlaxcala. In the text, the local heroes perhaps wisely do not try to take credit for this particular conversion. Furthermore, their own baptisms follow, suggesting perhaps that their own celebration of the sacrament came in the wake of and was inspired by that of Citlalpopocatzin and his colleagues.[46]

Cacalotzin (glossed as "Coalotzin," presumably a copyist's error) appears next to Citlalpopocatzin in scene 12 and again on his knees ready to receive the sacrament in scene 13. In line awaiting their turns are Sarmiento and Cencamatzin, and, one would presume, Tepostecatzin, unless he was already baptized by this time. Remaining scenes show celebrations, processions with the Virgin of Los Remedios, prayer, a farewell feast for the Spaniards, and the receipt of titles and coats of arms for Cacalotzin and Tepostecatzin. The religious conquest of neighboring towns has ended, and the local leaders prepare to bask in the glory.

Although they are sad to have Cortés and his men depart for Spain (scenes 22, 23, 24), they are anxious to have the rewards that will come when Carlos V hears about their own accomplishments.[47] It is also convenient that the Spanish conquerors have disappeared, leaving these local men with full authority to represent their own kingdoms (symbolized by the arrow, macana, nopal cactus, and, throwing in a European element, the brass horn in scene 28) as well as Castile (shown as the royal crest in

FIGURE 8.26.

The Four Heroes of Cuauhtlantzinco. Reproduced from Frederick Starr, The Mapa de Cuauhtlantzinco, or Códice Campos *(Chicago: University of Chicago Press, 1898).*

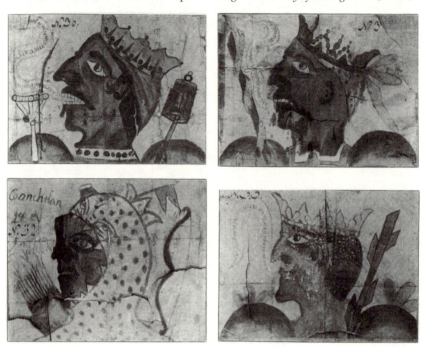

scenes 27 and 28). The story concludes with close-up facial portraits of, presumably, the four local heroes (fig. 8.26).[48]

INDIVIDUAL POSTURING AND ORATORY

Among the notable features of this Christian crusade led by Nahua against Nahua (with some Spanish support) is the relative lack of violent conflict. While we see weapons, hear threats of confrontation, and witness one battle scene, perhaps the details of conflagration have faded from memory. In actual fact or as they are remembered, the heroes have their greatest successes as a result of posturing and oratory. It is as though their stature and initiative were sufficient to overcome most of their neighbors, who only rarely stand up prepared to fight. While the four heroes' speeches were apparently effective, they rarely appear to be more than brief statements, often occupying only a speech scroll in the pictures. But these were possibly mnemonic devices that triggered longer speeches whenever this drama was performed to bolster community memory.

Upon occasion, the speeches in the text boxes provide somewhat more substance. In scene 15 we are shown a site of religious instruction in Christian doctrine, where men and women contemplate the word of God, salvation, and Mary's grace.[49] This strengthens the mapa's position in favor of local people accepting the new faith, elucidating its benefits. The caciques also intermittently stress the errors of Mesoamerican religion. These had to be simplified in the mapa, probably to appease the clergy, who would not want to encourage any extensive preservation of elaborate pre-Columbian rituals even within an otherwise Christian drama. We see references in scenes 2, 6, and 7 to the worship of the snake (interestingly, not a plumed serpent, the patron deity of the Cholulteca temple and the object of ancient pilgrimages).[50] Once, in scene 9, we read about the impropriety of making of animal spirits (*nanahualtin*) into gods (*oquimoteotialla*). Less ominous is scene 14, where people perform song and dance for a prehispanic deity. The use of the *teponaztli* and *huehuetl*, indigenous drums, would be allowed to continue in Christian religious festivals.

In the Mapa de Cuauhtlantzinco, the posturing, heroics, and valor of individual indigenous warriors outweigh troop size or military strategy. As one might expect from a history told with hindsight, the eyes are on the prizes—territory and legitimacy for the local community, status and perquisites for its leaders. Of the four nobles, not all share equally in the rewards. The one who plays the most prominent role in the history of the crusade, Tepostecatzin, earns the greatest prestige. In scene 27 he holds a royal grant from emperor Carlos V. His name is also most closely linked to San Juan Cuauhtlantzinco (also scene 27). His son of the same name makes a brief appearance in the mapa (scene 21) and possibly became an heir to power and property in that town.

Another who benefited greatly was Cacalotzin, possibly from Santiago Xalitzintlan, not too far away. He claims Cortés was present at his baptism and took that surname, becoming Don Jacinto Cortés.[51] He apparently won the coat of arms featured in scene 28 (next to the royal arms), although it is not completely clear that Tepostecatzin was not the beneficiary. The two men may have been rivals, or perhaps they enjoyed an equal status in separate communities, both of which looked to this manuscript as proof of their glorious, shared heritage. Both men claim to have been given the title of "cacique" (an Arawak term that took the place of "tlatoani").

The use of terminology such as "cacique" and "cacicazgo" adds years to this story about events that supposedly occurred in 1524. Nahuatl texts are rare prior to the 1540s. But even in native-language manuscripts from the second half of the sixteenth century, one would expect to see Nahuatl titles for local leaders or a borrowing of Spanish terms such as *señor* (lord), *gobernador* (municipal governor), *juez* (judge), or some combination thereof.[52] Furthermore, it was more likely in the seventeenth century that the indigenous elite, anxious about its precarious status, began producing documentary evidence of its illustrious heritage. The mapa's account of extreme religious devotion and services rendered in the 1520s or 1530s, influenced by sixteenth-century events and campaigns for privileges, lent itself to later colonial struggles in Cholula-area towns to strengthen their grip on the land and their leaders' need to counteract the undermining of their authority in the face of colonial changes.[53] The ironies of the native-European alliance and resulting dependence on favors from the Crown are more apparent today as we reflect on the growing desperation that resulted in the proliferation of records like the mapa, which, when they were composed and possibly reenacted in local festivals, thrived as a source of local ethnic pride.

COMPARISONS WITH OTHER GENRES

The Mapa de Cuauhtlantzinco exhibits well the Mesoamerican consciousness that linked community pride with the historical deeds of its native governors that can be found in many genres, from stelae to codices. While we have not yet found in the mapa's text boxes the use of the term *tlalmaceuqui*, "land-deserver" or "land-achiever" (Nahuatl for conqueror in some primordial titles, such as Techialoyan Codices), we do see a concern to make the leaders both great and deserving of their dominion. The mapa's position is also reminiscent of Fernando de Alva Ixtlilxochitl's effort to "pull Christian warrior culture over to his side," as Rolena Adorno sees it, placing his own meritorious behavior center stage.[54] One could further imagine how the *relaciones geográficas*, or sixteenth-century royal questionnaires about local history, when eliciting the names of the conquerors of Cuauhtlantzinco and Xaliztintlan, would be given the names of Tepostecatzin and Cacalotzin over those of Cortés and Alvarado.[55]

The "Señor Don Fernando Cortés" is remembered with great respect in the mapa, but he is just a name and a figure, usually standing benignly as a witness to the deeds of the native heroes and interceding with the emperor somewhere offstage to see that the town received its rewards. This representation of Cortés is reminiscent of the títulos primordiales, which rarely fail to name the key Spanish figures who strengthened the status of the local community, recognizing its territory and leadership, but often without obvious direct action. Pueblo histories focus on the enterprise, movements, and undertakings—in effect, the agency—of the indigenous men (and sometimes women) whose descendants were either still in power or struggling to increase their own influence in such towns. While *alcaldes mayores* and other colonial officials occupied provincial capitals and intermittently supervised local political affairs, those daily affairs were managed by native authority figures making many of the critical decisions.[56]

Annals and town council minutes, such as Juan Buenaventura Zapata y Mendoza's *Historia cronológica* or the *Tlaxcalan Actas*, are full of these men's names and their business of governance.[57] Once in a while some Spanish official or priest makes his presence felt in such records, but a Western preoccupation with the foreigners' power is out of line with the indigenous way of contemplating that time and place. It is the same with the Spanish seizure of power and foreigners' missionary work. Native histories concentrate on their ancestors' crucial roles in these activities and their outcome—not subjugation but increased strength.

The Mapa de Cuauhtlantzinco contributes a unique, locally centered view of some of the larger events of 1519–21 that became so pivotal in Mexican history. What we learn from this manuscript is the way one group of native nobles in a small, rural community looked back upon their heritage as both people with deep roots in this landscape *and* proud Christians. Having little memory of the actual battles, yet casting their ancestors as warriors, they painted storyboards for what were probably annual reenactments of eloquent oratory, passionate struggle, and ultimate religious victory. Whether consciously conceived this way or not, the mapa's perspective replaces what might be imagined as a story of downtrodden, colonized natives with a story of indigenous initiative and success. These native authors and artists relished giving their forebears not simply multiple options but actually according them the upper hand, choosing to welcome and lead the foreign invaders forward on the predestined path.

In doing so, they leveraged for their families and their town a prominent place in history, worthy of being recounted to all who might hear.

While the format of multiple paintings, the considerable emphasis on religious activities, and the particular details of local events sets this historical record somewhat apart from other native accounts of conquest-era events, the mapa does share with other genres of indigenous history writing, such as primordial titles, annals, or chronicles, what we may increasingly come to expect as standard features. Local, native, and largely male nobles are the central figures, the dominant players. They think and act for themselves, not as directed by any outside colonizers. They recognize some authority in Spanish officials but mainly as figures who can grant *them* some authority. These leading native men make pragmatic adjustments to foreign invasion. The wisdom of their decisions and the merit they earn strengthens the community as a whole. While the memory of their actions may ensure a favorable outcome and intentionally or inadvertently inflate the importance of such actions, at the core of these narratives is a truth that was apparently embraced by significant numbers of indigenous people over long stretches of time, sometimes up to the present day.[58]

NOTES

1. Carmack, *Quichean Civilization*, 93–94.

2. Starr, *Mapa de Cuauhtlantzinco*. I have also consulted copies of the mapa in the Latin American Library at Tulane University and in the Museum of Natural History, University of Oregon. Photographs from the Tulane copy are reproduced here with permission. A few images from Starr's 1898 publication also appear here, having fallen outside the temporal reach of copyright.

3. Wood, *Transcending Conquest*, 79–80; for more evidence of Díaz del Castillo's interest in the region around Tlaxcala and the apparent impact of his writings on indigenous manuscripts, see 81n6.

4. In fact, natives in the Canary Islands had embraced the Spanish pursuit of the *fuero*, a privilege that rewarded service and loyalty, in their own conquest during the fifteenth century. The same was seen in the Caribbean islands after 1492. Gibson, *Tlaxcala*, 162–63.

5. Archivo General de Indias, Seville (hereafter, AGI), Patronato 245, R. 10. Thanks go to Michel Oudijk for bringing this example to my attention.

6. As recently as 2003, a fourteenth-generation descendant of Isabel was suing to have his income from the historic pensions reinstated (they were curtailed in 1934). BBC News, August 22, 2003, http://news.bbc.co.uk/1/hi/business/3172569.stm. For a biography of the princess, see Chipman, "Isabel Moctezuma."

7. Cholula and Tlaxcala were both declared *ciudades* (cities) by the Spanish government. Gerhard, *Historical Geography*, 116, 326.

8. Gibson, *Tlaxcala*, 23, notes how Cholulteca fought with Tlaxcalteca in Guatemala, citing Díaz del Castillo. This is corroborated by the contributions in this volume of Laura Matthew and Florine Asselbergs, both based on the document Justicia 291 in the Archivo General de Indias.

9. Photographs of individual scenes from the Mapa de Cuauhtlantzinco have been digitized and put online as part of the Mapas Project at the University of Oregon. A full transcription and translation is under construction within a "distance research environment," with features for visiting scholars to collaborate by making suggestions or comments. The Nahuatl of the University of Oregon copy, scene 22, reads: "yn llehuatzin yn Sr Bardiaz del Castillo Carcuantzin (?) ynpil Sr. Don pedro de albarado Conquistadores famosos in Sr. Dn. fernando Cortes y marques del Balle."

10. While men are the main protagonists in so many of these stories of indigenous conquerors, women do appear in some records. Scene 2 of the Mapa de Cuauhtlantzinco features a noblewoman (*cihuapilli*) as a kind of founding mother with a special association with Matlalcueye volcano, a focal point of prehispanic religious devotion in this region. Women are also prominent in the scene showing prehispanic religious music and dance (scene 14). A woman stands by Citlalpopoca in scene 12; three study the Christian doctrine and make speeches in scene 15; a woman and a man pray together next to the cross in scenes 16–17; and a woman kneels closest to the virgin in scenes 19–20.

11. Starr, *Mapa de Cuauhtlantzinco*, 9.

12. The count will vary. Some paintings represent two scenes (such as 2 and 25, 16 and 17, 19 and 20, and 26 and 29). The four portraits of the main figures, apparently at the end of the series of paintings but not always counted, were not incorporated into either the copy in Louisiana or in Oregon, but they are found in the Princeton copy (see *http://libweb5.princeton.edu/mssimages/GarrettGates%20Mesoamerican/garrettgatesmeso258a.jpg* and *http://libweb5.princeton.edu/mssimages/meso-garrett gates24.html#258*).

13. Starr, *Mapa de Cuauhtlantzinco*, 10.

14. See Wood, *Transcending Conquest*, 80, and Lockhart, *Nahuas after the Conquest*, 336. The copies may or may not be faithful transcriptions of the original texts, but they do take surprising pains to reproduce the graphic images accurately, judging from the photographs Starr published in his 1898 book.

15. Starr, *Mapa de Cuauhtlantzinco*, 3. Bandelier was in the pueblo more than once, but presumably both visits took place in 1881. Bandelier, *Report*. Given the disparaging attitudes of Bandelier and Starr toward the local people, it is remarkable that these visitors were allowed to see the paintings, let alone leave with copies.

16. See Glass and Robertson, "Census," 120–22. There are other, various copies of the mapa described in the *Handbook of Middle American Indians*. It is not clear which of these might have been the one acquired by Bandelier.

17. Gibson, *Tlaxcala*, 29.

18. Gibson, *Tlaxcala*, 265, 266.

19. The use of Spanish-language sources by the authors of primordial titles is a topic under investigation. Having the Franciscan convent in Tlaxcala from an early time (1524) meant the presence of men who would research and write about local events almost as they happened. Fray Toribio de Benavente ("Motolinía") (d. 1568) is one. He wrote an influential history of the Indians of New Spain later cited by the prolific Jerónimo de Mendieta (1525–1604), another friar who was a resident of Tlaxcala. Subsequent residents, such as Juan de Torquemada, would quote and summarize their forebears, providing more material that may have circulated among the more educated native authors. Gibson, *Tlaxcala*, 29, 31n8. Perhaps the tomes of elite *mestizo* authors of Nahua heritage were even better known to indigenous writers. The primordial titles, or *tlalamatl*, of Huaquilpan mention Don Fernando Alvarado Tezozomoc (1519–98), whose chronicle was published in 1609. See Dyckerhoff, "Dos títulos." The *Historia chichimeca*, written by the Texcoca chronicler Don Fernando de Alva Ixtlilxochitl (1570–1649), contains many themes that parallel Tlaxcalteca discourse on religious history, as Gibson found. *Tlaxcala*, 29–32.

20. The University of Oregon copy reads, e.g., "in altepetzin Xalitzintlan."

21. Gibson, *Tlaxcala*, 30–31.

22. Ibid., 33.

23. Buenaventura Zapata y Mendoza, *Historia cronológica*, 102–103, paragraph 63.

24. Gibson, *Tlaxcala*, 35.

25. Buenaventura Zapata y Mendoza, *Historia cronológica*, 104–105, paragraphs 67–68.

26. Gibson, *Tlaxcala*, 35–36. "Toltecatepetl tlahchihualtepetl" appears on the reverse of the Códice de Cholula (120, gloss 1). See González-Hermosillo A. and Reyes García, *El códice de Cholula*.

27. In the copy from the University of Oregon, scene 18: "tzihuapili los Remedios conquistadora."

28. Gibson, *Tlaxcala*, 37.

29. Ibid., 38.

30. Ibid., 40–41.

31. Baumann, "Tlaxcalan Expression of Autonomy."

32. Gibson, *Tlaxcala*, 30.

33. It is not clear if this first cacique is the Tepuztecatl who appears in Bernardino de Sahagún's account of the conquest of Mexico as one of five lords who were sent by Moctezuma to meet Cortés after his landfall. See *Florentine Codex*, book 12, chapter 3, p. 725. Juan de Torquemada also mentions him, citing Gómara and Antonio de Herrera: see *Los veynte*, book 4, chapter 13, p. 418. (Thanks to Michel Oudijk for facilitating these citations.) While we might think of the name meaning "one from Tepoztlan" (in what is now Morelos), the name does have local authenticity. A shortened version, "Tepos," was used by distinguished citizens of Cuauhtlantzinco in the mid-nineteenth century. Starr, *Mapa de Cuauhtlantzinco*, 10.

34. In *Early Latin America*, James Lockhart and Stuart B. Schwartz write about Spanish conquerors: "The men had no connection with a royal army, received no pay, had no uniforms, no rank, and in nine cases out of ten no professional military training or experience. Only distant or posterior commentators have called them 'soldiers,' a term they never applied to themselves in the conquest years" (80).

35. We should bear in mind that the order of these scenes may have been jumbled at some point as a result of fires and having multiple copies that may have become mixed up. But there is also a logic to the storyline that unfolds following the order as the scenes are numbered, with a few minor exceptions.

36. Cacalotzin, perhaps not to be overshadowed, does not appear in the next scene, but the all-important mountain, Malintzin, is shown with the land that he reigns over. His consort, Lady Matlalcueye, sits weaving at the base of the mountain. Nearby is a sweat bath that Cacalotzin built for her. Cacalotzin reemerges later in the story with a stature nearly equal to Tepostecatzin and takes the name Don Jacinto Cortés after baptism.

37. In the University of Oregon copy, scene 1, the Nahuatl text reads, "Ca niCan namehnextilia quename onicmonamiquilito in icuac omohualquin yteh im alteptli yn xalapan canpa onicmotlatlanilito yn tlaneltoquilistli Ca lle onpa onehmotlatlatitli ca nicmollecaniliti nemic quiname Onicmotlatlacamachititzino."

38. In Starr's translation the text for scene 3 reads, "Hail Sons! The many labors which I have endured have two or three times imperiled my life (the five kings who are represented asleep in this mountain, envious because I was the first to go to meet the Spaniards and to inform myself regarding their religion, gathered to deliberate upon a mode of punishing me, in accordance with the order which the King Nezahualcollotzin had given; they dragged me before the tribunal, where I was sentenced to enter clad into a very hot bath, where I should infallibly have perished if, by a miracle of God, I had not been delivered). When I saw myself free from danger I took to flight from my enemies. I found them sleeping and, awakening them suddenly with the sword which I held in my hand, so great was the surprise with which they were overcome that they begged my pardon and resolved to be baptized, for which reason I spared their lives. Learn to be valiant, oh sons of Cacalotl! Believe today in God, oh ye who decreed my death." Starr, *Mapa de Cuauhtlantzinco*, 12. I am still working on the transcription and translation of the Nahuatl in the copies I have.

39. In Starr's translation the text for scene 4 reads, "Know that these young men, owners and governors of these mountains as soon as they are ready will embrace the religion of Jesus Christ, and I shall threaten to punish them if they will not be converted; on hearing my words they will be left almost dead with grief. They are and are called the owners of the mountain." Ibid., 13.

40. In what seems to be an older version, published by Starr as series "a," scene 5 does not show a cacique leading the Spaniards. Could this discrepancy be the result of a late-colonial revision, intended to increase indigenous agency? In the older version too the native resisters do not hold clubs but stones, which they rain

down upon the Spaniards from behind the hill. The Spaniards use their firearms, shooting directly at the resisters. In general, the older scene 5 makes the Spaniards more active than in the newer one. See ibid., 54.

41. Could this represent influence from the Spanish priest(s) who may have helped shape this drama?

42. Starr read this name as "Teopaxotzin," but in the Tulane copy, at least, it clearly reads "Tecpaxotzin."

43. While "Oquatemoqui" has the appearance of a preterite verb, it is not unusual for the Nahuatl in these nineteenth-century copies to have such errors. The use of "q" for the name Quauhtemoc is shared by Buenaventura Zapata y Mendoza, *Historia cronológica*, 134 (paragraph 132, left margin note).

44. While *pilli* might seem somewhat lowly in other Nahua zones, perhaps its usage in the Tlaxcala-Puebla-Cholula region was not so unusual, particularly as time passed and governance could be achieved by lower nobles. In *El Códice de Cholula* (118, gloss 163) we see the designation "pilli" for a man who was also a gobernador and a don supposedly in 1586. Similarly, the use of "pilli" for a man who was governor and who bore the title "don" as of the late seventeenth century occurs in Buenaventura Zapata y Mendoza, *Historia cronológica*, 638 (paragraph 594). Still, Buenaventura Zapata y Mendoza was far more likely to refer to an indigenous gobernador as "tlatoani" or "teuctli." We even see "tlatoani" in an entry as late as 1688 (640, paragraph 596).

45. Cuauhtemoc was captured in a canoe on Lake Tetzcoco in 1521 and taken on an expedition to Honduras, where he was hanged. See Díaz del Castillo, *Conquest of New Spain*, 403, and Buenaventura Zapata y Mendoza, *Historia cronológica*, 134 (paragraph 132, left margin note). Buenaventura Zapata y Mendoza refers to him as a "tlatoani."

46. Buenaventura Zapata y Mendoza has Citlalpopocatzin being baptized with Xicotencatl, Maxixcatzin, and Tlehuexolotzin. Ibid., 96–97, paragraph 44. He humorously reports that "ayamo huel momatia" (they still did not know it well), meaning that they still did not fully understand baptism or had not yet learned much about Christianity. Notice that this appearance of Citlalpopocatzin in the mapa breaks with the general tendency to leave Tlaxcalteca out of the story, even when borrowing liberally from their discourse of conquest and evangelization.

47. Some Tlaxcalteca lords actually traveled to Spain to put their requests for rewards straight to the king, and some won exceptional favors, spurring others to try for the same through petitions if not through actual visits. Gibson, *Tlaxcala*, 163–65.

48. Neither the Tulane nor the University of Oregon copies retain these final four paintings, and the speech scrolls they contain are not legible in Starr's publication.

49. In Starr's translation scene 15a reads, "Know, my sons, that this place is where we acquired our religious instruction, where we gathered together our parents and relatives with the purpose of repeating the Christian doctrine; this little piece of fruitful land, known as Capultiopan, is ours; it is situated outside of our house, close to my little brook, and we have chosen it to solace ourselves and to strengthen ourselves with the Word of God, and to meditate in it upon the eternal truths of

salvation, fulfilling there the charge given me by the conquerors from whom we received the faith of Christ. God bless thee, Mary, full thou art of grace; the Lord is with thee. Blessed thou art among all women; blessed is the fruit of thy womb, Jesus; Santa Maria." Starr, *Mapa de Cuauhtlantzinco*, 25.

50. The snakes in scenes 6 and 7 do not have the rattler's tail of classic iconography. The snake I have identified in scene 2 may actually be simply a spring-fed river, such as those in scene 15, but it has the appearance of a snake.

51. It is fascinating that the four caciques in the mapa, while supposedly valiant Christians from the start and crusaders against their neighbors, do not have Christian names until the end of the story. Only Sarmiento has no indigenous name, simply this foreign surname. But none of them has a Christian given name until the end. We never learn the first names of all of them. This conflicts with the eighteenth-century Códice de Contlantzinco and Códice de San Santo Tomás Xochtlan, from Tlaxcala, which often give first baptismal names to their caciques—Pedro, Pablo, Juan, and Leonardo.

52. A "juez gobernador" with the noble title "don" appears, e.g., in the Códice de Cholula, (98, gloss p). In the same manuscript (96, gloss h, and 101, gloss 12), we also find "juez" and "gobernador" singly. Naturally, the term "cacique" was not unheard of in the sixteenth century, for it was brought to New Spain by the Spaniards coming from the Caribbean experience. Diego Muñoz Carmargo uses the term in his *Historia de Tlaxcala* (from the second half of the century). See, e.g., his reference to the baptisms of "muchos señores y caciques de esta república" in the wake of the famous four. Muñoz Carmargo, *Historia de Tlaxcala*, ed. Reyes García and Lira Toledo, 205.

53. Community territory receives a few references, and particular zones that may have been crucial to cacicazgo holdings, such as Capulteopan and Acatopitlan (scenes 15 and 18), receive attention in the texts. Gibson supports the assessment that "the disruptive consequences of Spanish intrusion occurred late in the [sixteenth] century," taking time to alter indigenous social and economic life. *Tlaxcala*, 156.

54. Adorno, "Arms, Letters," 210–11.

55. See Wood, *Transcending Conquest*, 117.

56. Robert Haskett's *Indigenous Rulers* draws from election records, petitions, and political disputes to illustrate this point very well.

57. See Lockhart, Berdan, and Anderson, *Tlaxcalan Actas*.

58. On May 22, 1994, I visited the community of Santo Tomas Ajusco for its momentous transfer of power from one guardian of local land documents to the next. In the ensuing ceremony, the town's dramatic narrative of conquest, originally written in Nahuatl, was read aloud in Spanish translation. One could cite many other examples of the modern embrace of these historical records. Sometimes colonial officials also gave official recognition to such accounts, especially during the title verification programs of the early eighteenth century, when the payment of a fee or an absence of counterclaims could win the day.

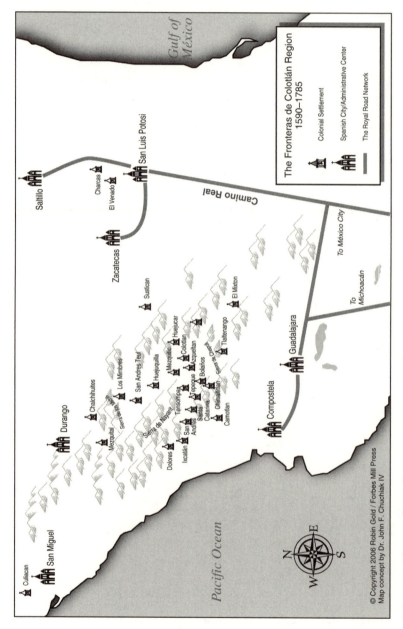

Map 12. The northern frontier of Nueva Galicia

The Fronteras de Colotlán Region
1590–1785

⌂ Colonial Settlement

Spanish City/Administrative Center

The Royal Road Network

Gulf of México

Pacific Ocean

Saltillo

Charcas
El Venado

San Luis Potosí

Zacatecas

Camino Real

To Mexico City

To Michoacán

To

Sustican

El Mixton

Guadalajara

Compostela

Tlaltenango

Huejucar
Colotlan
Azqueltan
Bolaños
Santa Catarina
Chimaltitlan
Camotlan

Mezquitic
Huejuquilla
Tepeque
San Andrés
Ixcatlan
Dolores

Sierra de Nayarit

San Andres Teul

Los Mimbres

Chalchihuites

Mezquital

Sierra del Meye

Durango

San Miguel

Culiacan

N
W   E
S

© Copyright 2006 Robin Gold / Forbes Mill Press
Map concept by Dr. John F. Chuchiak IV

288

CHAPTER NINE

"By the Force of Their Lives and the Spilling of Blood"

Flechero Service and Political Leverage on a Nueva Galicia Frontier

BRET BLOSSER

T he Spanish Crown relied upon Indian troops known as *flecheros* for
the provision of military force on the Nueva Galicia frontier located
north of Guadalajara from 1590 until the final years of the colonial
period. In contrast to the Indian auxiliaries recruited from the central highlands for earlier campaigns on the northern frontier, these soldiers were
drawn from local communities.[1] Their military service fulfilled the require-
ment that Indian pueblos provide goods or labor to the Crown or to designated colonists.[2] The Crown rewarded flechero pueblos by privileging
their petitions for land, forest, and water resources. Flechero muscle, while
serving as the backbone of Spanish control in the region, enabled approximately twenty-five Indian communities to attain an unusual degree of
political autonomy and territorial integrity for the duration of the colonial
period. In this chapter I explore the variety of military operations in which
flecheros took part, the Indian experience—as the record permits—of these
operations, and the several ways in which Indians employed flechero experience and military force in the defense of pueblo interests.

The flechero system took shape during Crown efforts to terminate a prolonged conflict that had interfered with a crucial source of wealth: the mining districts discovered in the central desert of the colony's northern reaches.
For four decades, beginning in the early 1550s, the Crown waged a contin-

uous military campaign against thinly dispersed groups of Indians resident on the northern plateau. These diverse groups, termed "Chichimecos" by Spaniards and their Indian allies, threatened the silver mines of the Zacatecas region, the farms and ranches provisioning those mines, and the transportation routes linking mineral production zones with the core of the colony.[3] Most of the troops engaged against the Chichimeca were Mexica, Tarascans, and Otomí—recruited elsewhere in the realm—and "pacified" Chichimeca. A typical expeditionary force comprised thirty to forty Spaniards and four to five hundred Indians. By the 1570s the Crown had begun to exempt pueblos that regularly provided troops for this war from tribute and labor exactions.[4] *Presidios* (forts) garrisoned with veteran Spanish frontier fighters, supplemented with Spanish colonists recruited for particular campaigns, were established to protect the mines and transportation corridors.[5] In 1587 Viceroy Marqués de Villamanrique determined that the interminable conflict was being prolonged by presidio soldiers' slave-raiding practices. These frontiersmen were supplementing meager salaries by capturing and selling Chichimeca as slaves. Since only belligerent Indians could be enslaved legally, presidio soldiers attacked peaceful groups to provoke retaliation, thus creating slave-taking opportunities. The viceroy ended these provocations by limiting military activity and curtailing the presidio system. Beginning in 1588 he sent experienced frontier captains, such as Francisco de Urdiñola and Miguel Caldera, to offer food, clothing, land, livestock, agricultural implements, training in agriculture and animal husbandry, and religious instruction as inducements for Chichimeca to settle in peace. This strategy brought the Chichimeco War to a close by 1590.[6]

To maintain military capacity on an unstable frontier while decommissioning the presidio system, Viceroy Luis de Velasco (the younger) established a special military district southwest of the city of Zacatecas in 1590. This jurisdiction, known as Fronteras de Colotlán, was administered by a military governor, the *capitán protector*, who answered directly to the viceroy and exercised military, political, and judicial authority over the district's Indian population. Although responsible for military affairs within Fronteras de Colotlán and for occasional expeditions beyond the district, the capitán protector neither commanded a garrison nor was authorized to recruit Spanish colonists for military operations. Assisted by two or three lieutenants, he relied entirely upon flecheros drawn from local Indian communities for military force.[7]

Fronteras de Colotlán comprised a vast region that embraced the southern terminus of the rugged Sierra Madre Occidental, known as Sierra de

Tepeque, and a zone of broad valleys and rolling hills drained by the Rio Bolaños and Rio Chapalagana, located between the Sierra and the city of Zacatecas. The languages spoken at contact included Zacateco, Guachichil, Cazcan, Tepehuan, and Huichol. At least two groups of Nahuatl-speaking immigrants from the core of the colony settled in the region during the second half of the sixteenth century. A group of Mexica military auxiliaries established the pueblo of Huejucar midway between the Sierra and Zacatecas in 1561.[8] A group of Tlaxcalteca immigrants established a colony at the pueblo of Colotlán in 1591 as part of a Crown scheme to stabilize the frontier by introducing Indian settlers considered to be loyal and relatively "civilized."[9]

In the second half of the sixteenth century Spanish military officers occasionally recruited troops from Indian communities located in the region later designated as Fronteras de Colotlán. For example, in 1561 four pueblos— Colotlán, Tlaltenango, Huejucar, and Susticacan—provided soldiers for Spanish expeditions against the Guachichil and Zacateca, two Chichimeca groups reported to have launched a broad rebellion.[10] By 1608 Spanish officials had assigned five pueblos in the region with responsibility for the provision of troops for military campaigns and relieved these pueblos from the burdens of tribute and labor exactions.[11] The Crown eventually required all Fronteras de Colotlán pueblos to supply soldiers for military operations undertaken by the capitán protector or his superior, the chief military officer of the Zacatecas region.[12] These pueblos were relieved from tribute and labor obligations, and the flecheros were rewarded with a uniform set of privileges. Fronteras de Colotlán pueblos retained their military role, exemptions, and privileges until the final years of the colonial period.

Exemption from tribute payments and labor drafts would have been a significant relief for Fronteras de Colotlán communities. Indians resident in neighboring districts sometimes found these burdens so great that they fled beyond the orbit of Spanish dominion. For example, in 1649 Fray Miguel de Molino sent a message to a group of two hundred "apostate" Indians who had established a settlement in the Sierra Nayarita, an unconquered zone immediately north of the Sierra de Tepeque, requesting their return. These refugees replied with a demand for a royal order "such that the *alcaldes mayores* did not bother them or compel them to go to work in the mines, mills, or sugar plantations" and for relief from tribute debt.[13] Prominent among the privileges extended to flecheros were the rights to bear arms and to ride horses. Although these rights were given to Fronteras de Colotlán flecheros to augment their military capacity, one supposes that they would have exercised the privileges on occasions other than military expeditions. From the perspective of Spanish colonial society, such displays would have marked flecheros as members of an exclusive and prestigious category, otherwise restricted to Spaniards and their Tlaxcalteca allies.[14] Flecheros were also accorded the *fuero militar* (military privilege), which guaranteed that civil and criminal charges would be heard in military courts, a right in principle enjoyed by all Crown soldiers.[15] Flechero pueblos were exempt from sales taxes (*alcabala*), a significant benefit for the several communities that produced foodstuffs, livestock, charcoal, lumber, and other goods for sale in mining centers.[16]

The capitán protector might call upon all of the district's pueblos to supply troops for a particular campaign or request troops from specific pueblos. Capitanes protectores cited proximity to the strategic object of the operation, knowledge of the enemy's language, familiarity with terrain, tracking skills, military prowess, or superior loyalty as reasons for mustering troops from particular pueblos. Each pueblo's cohort operated as a distinct unit with a command structure consisting of at least a *capitán de la guerra*, a second-in-command known as *cabo* (lieutenant) or *sargento*, and regular soldiers. An expeditionary force usually comprised the capitán protector, one or two of his lieutenants, and several units of flecheros. Spanish troops mustered in mining towns occasionally served alongside flecheros. For example, Spanish recruits participated in the response to a raid on livestock ranches in 1657, responses to "uprisings" (*sublevaciones*) by Fronteras de Colotlán pueblos in 1658 and 1705, and the invasion of the Sierra Nayarita in 1721.[17] At first most flecheros were foot soldiers, but by 1718 four companies of flecheros undertook a lengthy expedition on horseback.[18] Flecheros, as the term implies, were usually armed with bow and arrow, but by 1724 some had substituted their own harquebuses.[19] The Crown provided munitions for *harquebuseros*, but flechero communities were expected to stockpile and provide arrows. Flecheros generally supplied their own food. Stints of service lasted from a few days to three months. On longer expeditions, apparently launched with a minimum of logistical preparation, soldiers often suffered shortages of food and munitions.

FLECHERO OPERATIONS

Fronteras de Colotlán Indian soldiers participated in a variety of military operations over the course of the colonial period. These included campaigns mounted against Indians residing in regions outside of Spanish control, such as the Chichimeca of the desert frontier or the Cora and Tecualme of the Sierra Nayarita; against groups that had raided Spanish ranches or Indian pueblos; and against Indian "uprisings," both within and beyond Fronteras de Colotlán. In the late sixteenth century and again in 1644 flecheros marched or rode against Chichimeca groups located in the central desert, between three and five hundred kilometers distant from their pueblos.[20] In 1561, 1657, 1659, and 1718, they pursued groups of raiders from other regions who had attacked Indian or Spanish settlements within Fronteras de Colotlán.[21] In 1634, 1689, 1705, and 1749, flecheros from one or two pueblos helped to suppress "uprisings" by other Fronteras de Colotlán pueblos.[22] In 1734, 1749, 1760, and 1771 flecheros helped to quell uprisings by pueblos outside of the district.[23] Between 1721 and 1780 flecheros participated in the invasion and occupation of Cora and Tecualme territory in the Sierra Nayarita.[24] The following passages illustrate this range of operations and shed light on Indian soldiers' experience of frontier warfare.

The earliest record of local Indians' participation in a Spanish military project in the region is a report regarding four Indian pueblos—Colotlán, Tlaltenango, Huejucar, and Susticacan—sent by Captain Pedro Davalos Montiel to Viceroy Luis de Velasco (the elder) in 1561: "All have helped against the rebels, who have retreated into the backcountry mountain ranges, there being among these heathens a pernicious nation called the Guachichiles. And these make a lot of war on those pueblos of Christian Indians. . . . Their number in the four pueblos, [including] some who live apart, amounts to 4300 not counting the old men and boys, and all are enlisted against the heathens, and they are always armed."[25] Captain Davalos implied that the "Christian" Indians' willing service against the "rebels" was inspired by loyalty to the Crown and a need for defense against aggressive Guachichil and other "rebel" Indians. He intimated that the enemy's retreat to the backcountry had resulted in large measure from flechero efforts and noted that all able-bodied men were enlisted and constantly prepared for war.

Accounts of Huichol flecheros' participation in six military campaigns are recorded in a manuscript produced by Sierra de Tepeque Indians in 1664 for presentation before Crown officials in support of land claims by two Huichol pueblos.[26] The document purports to quote two prominent Spanish military officers' praise for the pueblos' roles in expeditions, which can be assigned, based on internal evidence, to the period 1585 to 1597.[27]

While the Indian author or authors could well have exaggerated, borrowed, or invented their claims, such embellishments would have been based upon local understandings of frontier warfare and thus do not detract from the value of the text as a reflection of Indian perspectives on late-sixteenth-century flechero service. The following passage from the final page of the manuscript suggests that the document was produced to support the pueblos' land claims: "And our captains Don Miguel Caldera and Don Pedro Salasar told us: 'Thus, my sons, you staked out your lands such that this realm is yours.'[28] And thus they [the captains] emphatically recommended to the Lords, his Majesty's Judges, not to harm, nor worry, nor disturb them, or cause them grief, these soldiers, in anything . . . saying to us 'My son, all of this land is to be yours, since wherever you like you can take possession, since you earned it with your work and sweat, since you were loyal conquistadors, in our company, everywhere.'"[29] According to this manuscript, the Huichols of Santa Catarina de Cuescomatitan received Captain Salazar "with much love and good will . . . they fed him and they guided him." Huichol troops from Santa Catarina and San Andrés Coamiata "went with him . . . conquering with the Señor Capitán everywhere, where some hijos were in the cliffs."[30] In a later campaign, a contingent of soldiers from the Huichol pueblos of Santa Catarina, San Andrés, and Tensompa and from the Tecualme pueblo of Ixcatan entered the Tepehuan pueblo of Mesquitiqui to put down a revolt.[31] The flecheros did the fighting, while their Spanish companions looked on. According to another passage, soldiers from five Huichol pueblos joined an expedition led by General Urdiñola and Captain Salazar against Guachichil defending a fortified position at El Venado on the central plateau. The Guachichil surrendered after a four-month campaign. After the conclusion of hostilities, a Spanish officer accompanied Huichol troops to their pueblos. According to another passage, Huichol troops descended from the Sierra pueblo of Camotlán to the pueblo of Tepeque in the canyon of the Rio Bolaños, where they engaged resident Southern Tepehuan, or "Tepecano," Indians. Five Huichol pueblos were called upon and sent reinforcements. The flechero victory concluded with the foundation of three pueblos, one in the canyon and two in high country east of the canyon.[32] The flecheros then traveled northwest towards Mesquitiqui. Along the way they quelled a revolt by Sierra Nayarita Indians without a fight. They continued on to meet Captain Miguel Caldera. According to the sixth passage, an unidentified Spanish military leader recruited forty Sierra Huichol soldiers under three Huichol leaders to help end Chichimeca hostilities in the Saltillo region of the central desert. The flecheros displayed enthusiasm upon their return.

These accounts of sixteenth-century military operations involving troops drawn from Fronteras de Colotlán Indian pueblos suggest the following general patterns. Flecheros were regularly recruited from a number of Sierra de Tepeque pueblos for expeditions mounted against local groups such as Tepecan and Cora and against distant groups such as the Tepehuan of Mesquitiqui, the Guachichil of El Venado, and the Chichimeca of El Saltillo. Some conflicts were concluded with a show of flechero force, while others required flecheros to engage in combat. Some operations were brief, but the El Venado expedition was reported to have lasted four months, and the El Saltillo expedition, a 1,050-kilometer round trip, would have required at least two months. Flecheros expected Crown support for community land claims in reward for military service.

PURSUING RAIDERS

Fronteras de Colotlán flecheros participated in two expeditions against "rebellious Indians" led by General Juan Hurtado de Mendoza, the chief military officer of the Zacatecas district. In 1657 the capitán protector Juan de Soto brought twenty "friendly Indian flecheros" and ten "harquebus soldiers" from the multiethnic pueblo of Huejuquilla to join a group of seventy-four soldiers armed with harquebuses whom General Mendoza had recruited in Zacatecas. The force pursued a group of Indians reported to have killed thirty-six persons, captured four women, and stolen livestock and clothing.[33] In 1659 Indians attacked a convoy of lime carts on the Zacatecas road and raided three nearby ranches, killing fifteen people, "young and old, men and women." The raiders turned back a contingent of twenty harquebus soldiers that pursued them, killing one and wounding the sergeant. General Mendoza assembled a force consisting of the harquebus soldiers, forty-seven mounted soldiers recruited in Zacatecas, a "brotherhood" of rural Spanish vigilantes, and "Capitán Francisco Lopez, Protector of Colotlán, who helped Your Mercy with 24 friendly Indian flecheros." However, "after having traversed some canyons and mountain ranges in search of said enemies, whom they could not find, the señor general returned to this city with those who helped him."[34]

In 1718 General Mathias Blanco de Velasco, chief military officer for the Zacatecas region, assembled an army of flecheros from the three barrios of Colotlán and the adjacent pueblo of Santa Maria to pursue a group of Indians that had raided frontier settlements. Unable to lead the army due to illness, General Blanco composed a comprehensive set of instructions, amounting to five pages of compact script, for the conduct of the campaign. These he entrusted to Bernabe Lozano, a Tlaxcalteca scribe and military leader, instructing Lozano to read the document before the assembled army on every day of the campaign. General Blanco's "orders" provide an unusually rich account of the circumstances of an eighteenth-century flechero expedition.[35] General Blanco directed his troops to follow an explicit itinerary. He apparently judged that the raiders had not retreated into the Sierra de Tepeque or Sierra Nayarita but instead were bound for the extensive canyon country northwest of the Rio Mezquital. To reach that region without passing through open country near Chalchihuites, the raiders would have had to cross the one-hundred-kilometer-long crest of the Sierra de los Michis. The general seems to have reasoned that the flecheros might cut the raiders' tracks as they traversed the crest. The army entered Santa Maria de la Paz y Nueva Tlaxcala, adjacent to Chalchihuites, six days after leaving Mezquitic and departed two days later. They reported to General Blanco ten days after leaving Chalchihuites and eighteen days after departing from Mezquitic, having covered considerably more than 330 kilometers. They had not encountered the raiders.

The lack of Spanish military personnel on this expedition is striking. Although the raid represented a crisis requiring the attention of the region's senior military officer, General Blanco did not muster a single non-Indian. This suggests that military expeditions composed entirely of flecheros under the leadership of one or two Spanish officers were standard on the Nueva Galicia frontier in the early eighteenth century. Furthermore, General Blanco was apparently confident that the flecheros were competent to undertake this complex operation in his absence. The force that gathered in Mezquitic was composed of troops from the three barrios of Colotlán—Tlaxcala, Tochopa, and Soyatitlan—and from the nearby settlement of Santa Maria, each led by a local captain. General Blanco held the Tlaxcalteca captain, Bernabe Lozano, in high regard, lauding his "loyalty, valor, and ability" and assigning him special responsibilities. Although the general deliberately refrained from elevating Lozano or any other cohort captain to the position of expedition leader, the war captain of Santa Maria de la Paz perceived Captain Lozano as such upon the army's arrival in his pueblo. He described the flecheros as "the company of the Señor Capitán Don Bernabe Lozano

. . . who came to patrol the sierras of their districts by order of the Señor General Don Mathias Blanco de Velasco."[36] The Tlaxcalteca cohort was led by six officers—a capitán, an *alférez*, a *sargento*, two *cavos*, and an *alguasil de la guerra*—while the other troops were led by captains with at most one subordinate officer.[37] Each captain was responsible for the "government" and discipline of his troop. The size of the company was not recorded but was greater than thirty-seven.[38] The soldiers were mounted on horses and armed with bow and arrow or musket. They provided their horses, weapons, and supplies. The document offers little information on the "enemy." General Blanco states that the raiders had killed people, were beleaguering the frontier settlements, and were probably hiding in the Sierra de Chapultepec or Sierra de los Michis. The raiders must have been mounted, since sentinels were instructed to be alert for "the bustle of horse-men" and "neighs of horses." These raiders, or similar groups whom the general had previously encountered, must have been bold and strategic fighters, rather than simply armed thieves, since Blanco directed the flecheros to guard against night or dawn attack. Considering that horses and mules were probably the only form of wealth found in the Fronteras de Colotlán countryside that could have been quickly removed by a raid-ing party, it seems likely that the attackers were a band of mobile, wide-ranging, experienced, and audacious horse thieves.[39]

The Sierra Nayarita, an extensive canyon and mesa territory inhabited by Cora and Tecualme Indians, escaped African slaves, and other fugitives, remained free of Spanish control into the early eighteenth century.[40] Between September of 1721 and January of 1722 a Crown army composed of one hundred Spanish recruits from Zacatecas and several contingents of Fronteras de Colotlán flecheros invaded the Sierra Nayarita, defeated an alliance of Sierra Indians, and established mesa-top presidios.[41] Spanish observers judged these victories to mark the conquest of Sierra Nayarita, although most Cora and Tecualme continued to reside in steep canyons beyond the orbit of Spanish control for the remainder of the eighteenth century.[42] Padre Jose de Ortega's account, *Maravillosa reducción, y conquista de la provincia de San Joseph del Gran Nayar, nuevo reino de Toledo*, although obviously constructed to glorify the invasion, provides details that enable us to imagine how flecheros might have experienced an assault on a cliff-lined stronghold.[43] He records that flecheros were endangered during the assault by "stormy discharges of arrows, of rocks thrown from the heights, and of huge boulders that, uprooted with levers, they released to roll down from the summit."[44] His description of a Huichol war captain's accurate arrow-strike on a swiftly descending Cora attacker suggests that the flecheros' bow and arrow weaponry served as an effective complement to the Spaniards' firearms.

In 1724, two years after Commander Juan Flores de San Pedro had completed his "conquest" of the Sierra Nayarita and been appointed governor of the new province of Nayarit, Cora and Tecualme revolted against the occupation. According to Padre Ortega's account, several Cora pueblos were abandoned, two churches were burned, and a Cora collaborator was assassinated.[45] Flecheros took part in all phases of the military response to this uprising. The day after the revolt began, Governor Flores wrote to the capitán protector of Colotlán with a request for flechero troops: "This is getting worse every day because now they are so bold that they attacked 30 soldiers and killed one, wounding eight, although many heathens were killed . . . the provisions are running out and the horses are few, almost none. . . . Your Mercy send me right away those [flecheros] of Santa Maria, and the Hernandez, and all the rest that you can, sending an urgent letter to the pueblo of San Sebastian, and to those of Santa Catarina, San Andres Coamiata, and the pueblo of Azqueltan."[46] "The Hernandez" seem to have been a Tlaxcalteca lineage based in Colotlán and nearby Santa Maria.[47] Governor Flores apparently requested the assistance of those flecheros whom "the Hernandez" could muster, presumably contingents from the three barrios of Colotlán and from the pueblo of Santa Maria, as well as flechero contingents from Huichol and Tepehuan sierra pueblos. By mid-January, Governor Flores was pursuing Cora refugees at the head of a force of 550 flecheros, seventeen presidio soldiers, twenty "servants," eighty-five recruits from various jurisdictions who supplied their own firearms, a Spanish captain, and a Jesuit priest.[48] He instructed a separate force composed of flecheros from Sierra de Tepeque, a few Spanish soldiers, and two Spanish captains to apprehend the "rebellious Indians who are taking refuge in . . . the canyons named El Coionqui." On January 21 Captain Juan Hernandez wrote to Flores reporting that he had apprehended "a large troop of Nayarita Indians, and among them, different Indians from the pueblo of San Francisco del Mezquital" in El Coionqui.[49] Considering that Captain Hernandez did not report combat or casualties, it seems likely that the captured "troop" comprised refugee families rather than armed rebels. On March 3 Flores learned of the death of 2nd Lieutenant Juan Hernandez in El Coionqui:

I questioned the Indians who said that a lot of rebel heathen Indians who had taken refuge in the canyon known as El Coionqui made war for an entire day, from sunup to sundown, on Capitán Agustin Hernandez, who with eleven soldiers had descended into that canyon where the death of the Alférez [second lieutenant] occurred and that the Capitán and another seven soldiers had escaped very badly wounded. And furthermore, they told me that if Salvador Gonzales, a soldier of Your Majesty, with another 50 men, had not arrived that night reconnoitering the canyon, none of Hernandez' company would survived the night since they were in such a tight spot that they had killed their mounts [horses or mules] to make a sort of barricade with which to defend themselves. And they also told me that some other Indian allies, reconnoitering the canyons in search of the heathens, found them [the heathens], and that these, being numerous, hurt the Indian allies badly, and finding themselves so afflicted, they abandoned their mounts and fled from the heathens, escaping towards the lowlands.[50]

These reports indicate that Fronteras de Colotlán flechero troops placed themselves in extreme danger by engaging rebel Cora and Tecualme in their rugged canyon territory. The passage describing skirmishes in El Coionqui suggests that although horses or mules might have provided a tactical advantage for flechero troops on long-distance campaigns, mounts restricted flecheros' mobility and increased their vulnerability in precipitous sierra canyons.

In 1758 Francisco Xavier de Ocampo, parish priest of Huejuquilla, produced a document for the pueblo of Santa Maria to certify that Santa Maria's "banner and companies of frontier soldiers" had joined troops from other Fronteras de Colotlán pueblos in Huejuquilla to serve under Commander Antonio Serratos, the chief military officer of Sierra Nayarita. The priest noted that "their number, combined with [that of] the rest of the troops from the other Colotlán frontiers assembled for this purpose, exceeded (in my opinion) 1300 men armed with bow and arrow, and some musketeers, all at their own expense."[51] Captain Serratos had marshaled this impressive army to destroy Cora residences in the location known to Crown officials as Dolores, no doubt because this place was perceived as a center of resistance to Spanish control. Captain Serratos certified "that Isidoro Caldera, War Captain of the Pueblo and Frontier of San Diego de Huejuquilla . . . with his company of

Indian auxiliaries . . . aided in the imprisonment of the Tonati [a Cora leader] and the rest of the ringleaders."[52] This contingent of flecheros then conveyed the captive Cora leader to Mexico City.[53] The size of the army assembled to destroy Dolores indicates that the Cora continued to pose a military threat some thirty-seven years after the "conquest." Despite the destruction of their village in 1758, the Coras of Dolores continued to resist Spanish occupation for decades. In 1769 Commander Vicente Canaveral complained that Dolores was the "inevitable, permanent scene of their idolatry."[54] In 1780 Fray Josef Navarro, director of Sierra Nayarita missions, complained that Indians had fled from Dolores to locations beyond his control, where "being in those pueblos, many fugitives abandon their own wives and take others', and others adhere to idolatry, witchcraft, and other superstitions, which has been impossible to remedy, nor to bring to them the knowledge of the Truth and abandonment of their heathen rites."[55] Fray Navarro reported that a contingent of flecheros had been unable to repatriate the fugitives: "The Commander of this Province having sent some Indian auxiliary soldiers for the fugitives from the pueblo or barrio of Dolores, pertaining to the Mission of Santa Teresa of this Province, not only did they [the fugitives' hosts] not turn over the fugitives, but they disarmed the auxiliary soldiers and imprisoned them, saying that if he wanted them [the fugitives], the Commander himself should come for them, so that they might do the same to him."[56]

In 1749 the capitán protector Juan Antonio Romualdo Fernandez de Cordova chronicled a fruitless flechero expedition mounted "for the purpose of cleaning the Sierra de Chapultepec of rebel Indians who had intimidated the surrounding territories."[57] His immediate superior had directed him to "encircle, pursue, punish, and apprehend the Indians of the Pueblo of San Andrés de Teul . . . who have rebelled and taken refuge in the Sierra Madre de Chapultepec."[58] The capitán protector eventually determined that the disturbance arose from a long-standing dispute between a group of Indians and a Spanish *hacendado* (hacienda owner) over the ownership of a tract of land known as Rio de Medina.[59] His record of malnutrition and fatal illness among the troops indicates that the hardship and danger intrinsic to such operations increased during the episodes of drought, crop failure, and epidemic disease that periodically afflicted Nueva Galicia.

MILITARY SERVICE AND POLITICAL LEVERAGE

Fronteras de Colotlán pueblos, like Indian communities throughout the colony, regularly brought petitions regarding land and other community resources before Crown officials or courts. Fronteras de Colotlán pueblos requested titles for communal land holdings, replacement of title documents destroyed by enemies, or the return of documents submitted in support of earlier petitions. They sought protection from expropriation of communal land or timber by Spanish colonists and hacendados. During the eighteenth century they requested additional farmland to support larger populations and additional rangeland for expanding herds of cattle, horses, and mules. Fronteras de Colotlán pueblos invariably accompanied petitions with documents produced by Crown or Church officials to certify their pueblos' provision of flechero troops for particular military operations. Certification documents were compiled and guarded in pueblo archives, often for centuries, as proof of the community's right to privileged consideration from Crown authorities. Court records demonstrate that authorities took note of these documents and were favorably influenced in many instances.[60] In this section I present examples of the production and deployment of certification documents.

In 1561 Captain Pedro Davalos Montiel concluded his report to Viceroy Velasco with a prediction that the Indians of Colotlán, Tlaltenango, Huejucar, and Susticacan would continue to make advances against the Guachichiles. The captain recommended that the viceroy reward these crucial allies with approval of their land petitions: "And thus if these Indians present themselves before Your Excellency to ask for some grant of lands or other thing that you [might] offer to them, Your Excellency can grant these."[61] The captain seems to have provided each of the four pueblos with a copy of his letter to the viceroy as documentation of their military service. The Mexica immigrants of Huejucar put their copy of the letter to immediate use in support of their request for title to the lands upon which they had recently settled and for official status as a pueblo, both of which were granted in 1562. Nine years later, when Spanish colonists attempted to expropriate Huejucar lands, the Indians presented their title document, no doubt accompanied by their copy of the captain's letter, before the Audiencia de Guadalajara. The invaders "were immediately thrown out."[62] Huejucar flecheros continued to serve the Crown, and Huejucar leaders continued to deploy certification documents in support of petitions regarding the pueblo's territorial integrity for the remainder of the colonial period. For example, in 1734 the pueblo petitioned the viceroy for intervention against a hacendado who had seized a tract of pueblo land. The viceroy's advisors examined the pueblo's record of almost two hundred years of military service, including participation in the suppression of the Fronteras de Colotlán revolt of 1705, the "conquest" of the Sierra Nayarita in 1722, and the suppression of the Sierra Nayarita revolt of 1724. The advisors determined that "the petitioners are *fronterizos* [frontiersmen] of Tepeque who have served as *fronterizos* with their arms and horses at their own expense on the occasions in which the enemy Indians have offered uprisings, especially in the year of 1705, when 21 pueblos from that district revolted."[63] The viceroy proclaimed that Huejucar Indians were *militares* (soldiers) and fronterizos, ordered district officials not to bother them, and instructed the Spanish *corregidor* in charge of the Zacatecas district to compel the hacendado to vacate their land.

Although the manuscript produced by Sierra de Tepeque Indians in 1664 to document the participation of Huichol pueblos in early flechero campaigns was intended for presentation before Crown officials, the document would surely have been discounted since it violated genre canons and employed transparently spurious dates. The Indian authors claimed to quote and summarize well-known Spanish officers' promises and assertions regarding the pueblos' flechero service:

San Andrés Coamiata, Santa Catarina de Cuescomatitan, Tensompa, Oxtoc, and Camotlán. "All of that land is called Galicia. And all of that land all of you will take, my sons, since you earned it with your work and sweat." They told that to all of the hijos soldiers of the King, because they helped the Christians, and went fighting everywhere, by the force of their lives and the spilling of blood. And they received the Christian Doctrine. And therefore, now I have recommended to Don Pedro Salasar, that he always regard them with mercy, as loyal soldiers. "And to the Señores judges of Your Majesty, I request and entreat them a lot, that you will do as I have recommended, by the King our Señor, that God keep you many years.[64] You will regard them as our sons, because they always helped us and did us a lot of good. Ever since we entered this land, they have loved us well and we thank them a lot." That is how they spoke to the hijos soldiers and that is how the Señor Captain ordered.[65]

The authors apparently believed that a pueblo with a record of flechero service, acceptance of Christian doctrine, and amicable relations with representatives of the Spanish Crown would be rewarded with titles to ample tracts of land and preferential treatment by "the Señores judges of Your Majesty."

Following a stint of flechero service during the suppression of the Sierra Nayarita revolt of 1724, the Tepehuan pueblo of Mezquitic submitted a compilation of certification documents in support of a request for additional land. The compilation included a document produced by a Crown inspector certifying that Mezquitic had remained loyal during the Fronteras de Colotlán revolt of 1702, a document certifying that two officers and ten flecheros had served in the suppression of the San Andrés de Teul revolt of 1716 and on an expedition into the Sierra Nayarita in the same year, and ten more documents produced between 1721 and 1724 certifying that the pueblo had provided flecheros for the "conquest" of the Sierra Nayarita and the suppression of the subsequent revolt. This last set of documents certified that Mezquitic flecheros had served loyally, fought well, and supplied their own arms, including a few harquebuses. They had fended off an ambush, assaulted a key Cora stronghold, delivered messages, convoyed munitions, built a fortress, pursued and captured rebels, and guarded captives. Three Mezquitic soldiers had been seriously injured. When the Spanish captain who led Mezquitic forces during the Cora revolt was slow to produce a requested certification document, Mezquitic leaders wrote to his superior in Zacatecas asking that the captain be compelled to provide the document, with the desired results. Two months after obtaining the delayed document, emissaries from Mezquitic were in Mexico City with their stack of certification documents, petitioning the viceroy for additional farm and ranch land to support their growing population. Four months later the land surrounding the pueblo, plus an additional seven thousand hectares of range land, had been surveyed, marked, and titled.[66]

Fronteras de Colotlán flecheros and their pueblos were rewarded by the Crown for military service with certification documents for use in colonial courts, relief from tribute exactions and labor drafts, and privileges that marked flecheros as members of an exclusive social category. Flecheros also found informal and unsanctioned ways to deploy military experience and capacity on behalf of their communities. During the course of prolonged military operations directed by Spanish officers, flecheros must occasionally have formed or strengthened personal connections with those officials. Relationships of trust and respect between prominent Crown officers and flechero leaders, as between General Blanco and the Tlaxcalteca captain Bernabe Lozano, are likely to have provided Indian leadership with

vital political leverage within the centralized hierarchy of regional governance. The potential value of such relationships is documented in a promise that General Mathias Blanco de Velasco inscribed in the certification
document that he inscribed for members of his 1718 expedition. At the start
of that operation he had promised "in the name of the king to bear them
in mind in order to reward them in every way possible." General Blanco
wrote that one of the ways that he would "bear them in mind" was that
he, rather than the capitán protector, would hear criminal or civil charges
brought against the flecheros.[67] The promised arrangement would have
diminished the capitán protector's capacity to coerce or exploit Colotlán
and Santa Maria Indians. This promise was of particular significance since,
as General Blanco noted, he appointed the capitán protector. The tenor of
the promise suggests that requests for intervention by the general might
have been favorably received in the event that their pueblos encountered
difficulties in their relations with the capitán protector.

The capitán protector of Colotlán was usually assisted by one or two
Spanish lieutenants (tenientes) posted to outlying pueblos. However, in 1741
an Indian from the pueblo of Chimaltitlán, Juan de los Santos Renteria, held
the position of "teniente de capitán protector y justicia mayor," posted in
Chimaltitlán.[68] In that year Santos sent a petition to the viceroy, supported
by documents certifying twenty years of military service, in which he
requested intervention in a conflict between himself and a powerful mine
owner from the adjacent district of Bolaños. Lieutenant Santos's documents
provide a unique record of the career of an Indian professional soldier. In
1721, at the age of twenty-two, he had enlisted in Zacatecas with a troop
recruited for an expedition into the Sierra Nayarita. After eight months in
the Sierra, he was promoted to the rank of sergeant, with responsibility for
command and training of troops. From 1733 to 1738 he served as lieutenant
to the commander of the Sierra Nayarita presidios. In this position he would
have commanded *mestizo* and Spanish soldiers. In 1738 he was removed by
the viceroy for harsh punishment of disobedient soldiers, but the capitán
protector of Colotlán immediately appointed him to serve as his lieutenant
in Chimaltitlán. In his petition, Lieutenant Santos charged that the mine
owner, Phelippe Pastor, had him beaten, stabbed, and imprisoned for interceding on behalf of eight Indian men from Chimaltitlan whom Pastor had
imprisoned and forced to work in his mine.[69] Lieutenant Santos wrote, "And
the reason that Don Phelippe Pastor, principal miner of the aforementioned
mining town, became inflamed against me was that, having seized eight

fronterizo Indians of my pueblo from me after Easter, who are strong soldiers of your Majesty of the sort who serve loyally and resist any heathen invasion, and shut them up in his mine to do forced labor, civil messages not sufficing to cause him to remit them to me, I had to send two captains to bring them to their pueblo, and they did that."[70] Lieutenant Santos's position within Fronteras de Colotlán military government enabled him to intercede successfully on behalf of Indians from his pueblo against one of the most powerful Spaniards in the region. This example demonstrates that military service afforded Fronteras de Colotlán Indian men the opportunity to attain posts that enabled them to protect pueblo interests.[71]

THE THREAT OF REBELLION

The political leverage afforded by the Indian population's notable military capacity was not overlooked by Indian leaders in their negotiations with Crown authorities regarding land conflicts or the removal of troublesome officials. For most of the colonial period, flechero troops constituted the only military force within Fronteras de Colotlán and adjacent jurisdictions. Spaniards were occasionally recruited in Spanish towns for particular expeditions, but after the close of the Chichimeco War, troops of professional soldiers were not maintained in the region. Soldiers garrisoned in the presidios established in Sierra Nayarita in 1722 did not venture beyond that Sierra. Although dispersed among approximately twenty-five communities, flechero cohorts were capable of rapidly assembling as sizable and effective armies. The number of "enlisted" flecheros was reported as 4,300 in 1561, 3,000 in 1785, and 1,894 in 1790. In 1758, 1,300 flecheros were mustered on short notice to destroy the Cora settlement of Dolores.[72] General Blanco's 1718 campaign demonstrated that Colotlán flecheros were capable of mounting a complex cavalry campaign without the active participation of a single Spanish officer.

The use of flechero military capacity as a bargaining point is evident in the record of a 1617 meeting between the viceroy's emissary, General Francisco de Urdiñola, and Fronteras de Colotlán Indian leaders at the onset of the Tepehuan rebellion. The Indian leaders assured General Urdiñola of their pueblos' loyalty and then, in an orchestrated maneuver, presented the general with several written petitions denouncing a variety of abuses by the capitán protector, demanding his removal, and requesting the appointment of a specified Spaniard whom they knew and trusted. General

Urdiñola immediately replaced the capitán protector with the man whom the Indians had selected.[73] The Indian leaders had evidently recognized and employed the political advantage afforded them by the viceroy's urgent concern that the Fronteras de Colotlán pueblos' considerable military capacity not be joined to that of the Tepehuan rebels.

In 1658 Fronteras de Colotlán Indians signaled their capacity for armed rebellion during an unusual negotiation with a Crown official. On Holy Saturday of Easter week in that year, three hundred Indians from the pueblo of Colotlán, armed with bows and arrows, "naked" and painted for war, surprised the district's Spanish colonists in the central pueblo of Colotlán and forced the Spaniards into confinement in the municipal building and church. Although the celebrants were taken by surprise, the attackers did not harm a single person. The rebels then sent for representatives from the remaining Fronteras de Colotlán communities. Eighteen pueblos, almost all of the remaining communities, responded with substantial numbers of unarmed and "unpainted" observers. The rebels held the Spaniards in confinement for four days until General Juan Hurtado de Mendoza arrived from Zacatecas with a force of fifty *harquebuseros* and a few flecheros. Rather than initiate hostilities, General Mendoza soon distributed gifts of money, corn, calves, harquebuses, swords, and horses to the rebels and the unarmed representatives from the other pueblos, thus resolving the dispute without conflict or punishment.

Considering that the rebels had attacked at a moment during Easter week when the district's entire Spanish population would have been concentrated at the Colotlán church, we can be certain that the operation was planned to achieve strategic objectives. Since the rebels did not kill or injure a single Spaniard, they must have planned not to harm the celebrants. Considering that they held the Spaniards in confinement until General Mendoza arrived, it seems apparent that their objectives included summoning the general to Colotlán, dramatizing the gravity of their grievances, and demonstrating their military capacity. Since substantial numbers of representatives from eighteen pueblos responded to the rebels' call, their grievances must have been widely shared. The audacity of the attack and the presence of substantial numbers of men from the other pueblos apparently convinced General Mendoza of the potential for coordinated rebellion by a majority of the district's Indian population. The document upon which my reading of the event is based was a request for reimbursement of expenses in which the general did not provide an account of the rebels' grievances. However, at some point during the ensuing nineteen months (when a capitán protector's name next appears in the documentary record), General Mendoza appointed a new capitán protector.[74] It is reasonable to suppose that the attack was staged to persuade General Mendoza to remove an abusive capitán protector. The general apparently ended the crisis by replacing the offending official as well as by distributing gifts.

In 1702 an alliance of Sierra de Tepeque pueblos rid themselves of an abusive capitán protector with a less politic maneuver. The rebels descended into Colotlán, seized the capitán protector Matheo de Silva, attached him to a cross on a hill above town, and shot him full of arrows. They also killed an Indian governor allied with Silva, repossessed extensive tracts of land expropriated by Spanish settlers, and absconded with the colonists' livestock. The Crown officials who investigated Silva's assassination simply declared a general pardon on condition that the pueblos publicly declare their loyalty to the Crown. The officials justified this unusual response with the observation "that this action was taken in common, and that it is not just to proceed against a general population."[75] This assessment implied that the pueblos had acted en masse and without culpable leaders, although the operation had obviously been strategically coordinated since it involved the simultaneous entry of troops from several pueblos into Colotlán. Despite this indication of strategic action, and although five Colotlán Indians were later identified as the "prime movers" of the uprising, not a single Indian was ever punished for the deaths, loss of colonists' land-holdings, or livestock theft. Such leniency was at odds with the Crown's usual postrevolt procedure in which purported leaders were captured and punished, offending pueblos were forced to perform public rituals of obedience, and threats of severe reprisal for renewed resistance were issued. Furthermore, although some livestock was eventually returned, the repossessed land remained in Indian hands despite the Spanish colonists' persistent complaints. Fronteras de Colotlán Indians flaunted the memory of this event in a political ritual maintained for at least eighty years. Whenever a newly appointed capitán protector arrived in Colotlán, they took the cross upon which Captain Silva had been executed down from the hill and carried it in procession to the municipal building for the edification of the incoming official. In the years immediately following the revolt, Audiencia de México ministers proposed canceling military privileges, disarming the flecheros, installing a dozen Spanish families in Colotlán, creating a *villa* (Spanish town) of forty Spanish families near Colotlán, and imposing tribute obligations. None of these plans were effected.[76] The most likely explanation for the lack of punishment, lack of support for colonists' land claims, and continuation of flechero privileges is that the Crown was not willing to risk precipitating a broad rebellion. Plans to eliminate Fronteras de Colotlán Indians' military capacity were regularly entertained by the Audiencia de México between 1702 and the close of the colonial period but never enacted.[77] The following determination by seven ministers (*oidores*) of the Audiencia de México in 1785 indicates that flechero military capacity was a key factor in the continuation of Fronteras de Colotlán Indians' exemptions and privileges during the late colonial period. The oidores advised the viceroy:

> For now do not make changes with the Indians of the Fronteras de Colotlán with regard to their liberty from tribute, arms, and privileges because experience has excessively demonstrated the unfortunate consequences that we experience with them . . . in which the State is suffering damages that exceed all exaggeration. And for these strong considerations, and [for] the [consideration] that the Coloteco Indians, disgusted [and] in such great numbers, being 3,000 armed, and unarmed more than 7,000, can unite and stir up the Nayaritas, Tarahumaras, and their other neighbors . . . and it is evident in the proceedings formed by the General Command [that] to alter their present situation is to be greatly feared.[78]

The documentary evidence cited in this section demonstrates that Fronteras de Colotlán flecheros occasionally deployed their military experience on behalf of pueblo interests and that the Crown, fearing broad rebellion, was inhibited from imposing stringent control. This pattern, in evidence from 1617 to 1785, indicates that one of the benefits to the pueblos of flechero service—certainly unintended by the architects of the flechero system—was the maintenance of a militia whose formidable power was key factor in negotiations of the terms of the colonial contract in Fronteras de Colotlán.

CONCLUSION

From the final decades of the sixteenth century to the end of the colonial period, Fronteras de Colotlán pueblos employed privileged access to Crown officials and courts—awarded in recognition of military service—

to secure ample tracts of land, defend communal territory from invasion by Spanish colonists, and, on at least one occasion, influence the removal and appointment of Spanish officials. Fear that Fronteras de Colotlán pueblos—perhaps in alliance with Cora, Tecualme, or Tepehuan rebels—might turn their proven military capacity against Spanish dominion haunted viceroys and their advisors, causing them to refrain from applying the usual harsh sanctions against Indian offenses and to defer indefinitely plans to end the flechero system, disarm the pueblos, insert a Spanish colony, and impose tribute and labor obligations. Fronteras de Colotlán Indian leaders strategically deployed the leverage afforded by their pueblos' histories of military service and by the Crown's fear of rebellion to open, expand, and defend a relatively extensive and autonomous space for Indian cultural and political life for most of the course of the colonial period.

NOTES

1. Indian interpreters, scouts, load-bearers, and troops played crucial roles in all major Spanish military campaigns in Nueva Galicia during the sixteenth century. Antonio Tello reported that Nuño de Guzmán enlisted five hundred Spaniards and between fifteen and twenty thousand Indians from Mexico City, Oaxaca, Guatemala, and Michoacan for his 1529 expedition to explore and conquer the region that became known as Nueva Galicia. See Tello, *Cronica miscelanea*, 1:91. Viceroy Antonio de Mendoza took a large force of auxiliary Indian troops along with Spanish troops on his expedition to extinguish the 1541 Mixton rebellion in Nueva Galicia. See Weigand and Weigand, *Tenamaxtli y Guaxicar*, 138. Among these were troops from Chalco led by the *cacique* of Chalco, Francisco de Sandoval Acazitli. Acazitli's scribe recorded that the force was composed of Chalca, Tlaxcalteca, Huexotzinga, Quauhquecholteca, "Mexicanos," Xilotepeca, Aculhua, and Indians from Michoacan and Mextitlan. See León-Portilla, *La flecha en el blanco*, 86.

2. The term "pueblo" denoted an Indian district governed by a central town, the *cabecera*. The district and cabecera shared a toponym. The term "pueblo" also connoted a district's resident population. Subordinate towns within the district were termed *sujetos*. Spanish observers lamented that the populations of several Fronteras de Colotlán pueblos included many blacks and mulattos and a few "disreputable" Spaniards.

3. This term is rendered as "Chichimeco" in accordance with the usual usage in colonial texts from the northern frontier. The correct Nahuatl and usual modern usage is "Chichimeca." Spaniards and their Indian allies bundled the diverse Indian groups of the central desert under this rubric.

4. The extension of privileges as a reward for military service was a long-standing and practical tradition on the Iberian peninsula. This institution took form within the crucible of seven hundred years of intermittent warfare during which

the Moors were driven from the peninsula. See Gibson, *Tlaxcala*, 161–62. E.g., all Basque families resident in two provinces and half of the Basque families in two other provinces were granted the privileges attendant upon nobility for military service during the reconquest. See Burkholder, "Honor and Honors," 19.

5. Powell, *Soldiers, Indians, and Silver*, 92, 141–58, 165, 263n56, 249n8.

6. See Powell, *Mexico's Miguel Caldera*, 186–203. Robert Shadow argues that the Chichimeca understood these gifts, which in many cases continued for decades, as tribute from vanquished Spaniards to Chichimeca victors. See Shadow, "Conquista y gobierno español," 51.

7. In 1590 a presidio was constructed near Colotlán for the protection of one of the routes between Zacatecas and Guadalajara. See Powell, *Mexico's Miguel Caldera*, 148. This presidio did not figure in any military operation chronicled in the surviving documentary record and was probably decommissioned as Chichimeco War hostilities drew to a close.

8. Biblioteca Publica de Jalisco (hereafter, BPEJ), Ramo Civil, caja 90, exp. 19, ff. 1–13. It is reasonable to suppose that the founders of the pueblo of Huejucar first entered the region as participants in Captain Pedro de Ahumada Sámano's campaign against an alliance of Guachichil and Zacateca in 1561. See Powell, *Soldiers, Indians, and Silver*, 73–89. The immigrants were granted title to lands upon which they established their settlement in 1562. In a deposition during a land dispute with a neighboring hacienda in 1782, Huejucar's lawyer wrote that the pueblo had been founded primarily "to contain within their proper boundaries the barbarous nation of Nayarit and many other pagan, insolent Indians" ("contener en sus devidos terminos a la barabara nacion de Nayarith, y otras muchas de Ynfieles, insolentes Yndios"). BPEJ, Ramo Civil, Caja 173, exp. 2.

9. In 1585 Viceroy Pedro Moya de Contreras became the third viceroy to convoke a council to discuss strategies for the resolution of the interminable Chichimeco War. The council proposed founding colonies composed of Indian allies and Spaniards to secure the territory and provide "pacified" Chichimecos with examples of civilized life. In 1591 four hundred Tlaxcalteca families migrated to the Chichimeco region and founded five colonies, including a colony at San Luis de Colotlán. See Sego, *Aliados y adversarios*, 37, 47–66.

10. BPEJ, Ramo Civil, caja 90, exp. 19, ff. 3v–4v. See Powell, *Soldiers, Indians, and Silver*, 73–89.

11. In 1608 an inspector (*visitador*) from the Audiencia de Guadalajara, Gaspar de la Fuente, reported that the Colotlán and Tlaltenango region contained one Spanish settlement and seventeen pueblos of "peaceful Indians" (*indios de paz*). The visitador wrote that "of those, five pueblos, although they are peaceful, do not pay tribute because they are [located] on a war frontier and have served on those occasions of war that have occurred." The remaining twelve pueblos paid tribute either to the Crown or to Spanish colonists designated by the Crown (*encomenderos*). Gaspar de la Fuente noted that thirteen pueblos of Chichimeca, located in the remote Sierra de Tepeque, were subject to neither tribute payments nor labor drafts. Archivo General de Indias (hereafter, AGI), Contaduría 874.

12. The provision of flecheros by all Fronteras de Colotlán pueblos, with corresponding privileges, is not documented until the eighteenth century, but is likely to have begun in the early or mid-seventeenth century, a poorly documented period. It is reasonable to suppose that the massive, coordinated, strategic, and sustained Tepehuan Revolt of 1616–17, based in the Sierra Madre Occidental not far north of Fronteras de Colotlán, moved the Crown to augment regional military forces by dedicating more pueblos to the provision of troops. See Gradie, *Tepehuan Revolt*.

13. AGI Guadalajara 10, documento 19, April 13, 1649. I consulted microfilm at Instituto Davila Garibi, Guadalajara.

14. The right of Tlaxcalteca immigrants to bear arms, ride horses, "and use saddle and bridle," was confirmed in 1591. See Sego, *Aliados y Adversarios*, 52–53, 266. I presume that these rights were originally restricted to men. It seems likely that the prohibition against Nueva Galicia's nonflechero Indians riding horses was eventually relaxed. One indication that this might be the case can be found in the absence of comment on Cora and Tecualme horse-riding by the chroniclers of the Spanish occupation of Sierra Nayarita, although Cora and Tecualme, having avoided Spanish control for almost two hundred years, were undoubtedly competent horsemen. See, e.g., Archivo General de la Nación (hereafter, AGN), Provincias Internas 244, 93v–417 (1724); AGN, Provincias Internas 127, exp. 8, 163–75 (1769).

15. AGN, Provincias Internas 130, f. 68v. Since the Fronteras de Colotlán Indian population was under military jurisdiction, all Indian residents' cases were heard in military court.

16. AGN, Provincias Internas 129, f. 192v. In 1593 exemption from the sales tax was confirmed for Tlaxcalteca and Chichimeca residents of Chalchihuites, and presumably also for those of Colotlán, as a condition of settlement rather than as a reward for military service. AGN, Provincias Internas 129, ff. 159r–59v). In 1792 Colotlán Indians complained that such sales taxes were improperly charged on their foodstuffs brought for sale to Zacatecas and Bolaños. AGN, Provincias Internas 210, ff. 98–99.

17. Insitituto Technologico y de Estudios Superiores de Monterrey, Campus Zacatecas archive (hereafter, AHITESMCZ), unfiled (1657); AHITESMCZ, caja 43 (1658); BPEJ, Ramo Civil, caja 48, exp. 8, ff. 1–2 (1705); AGN, Indios 44, ff. 163v–66 (1721). I place "uprisings" in quotation marks to indicate that Spanish observers glossed a variety of modes of resistance within the broad category of *sublevación*.

18. AGN, Provincias Internas, ff. 166–68v.

19. AGN, Provincias Internas 129, exp. 11, ff. 252–55. The harquebus was a matchlock gun with a heavy barrel, supported on a tripod.

20. Archivo Historico de Zapopan (hereafter, AHZ), Caja Documentos Importantes, 1; BPEJ, Ramo Civil, caja 23, exp. 7. Huejuquilla flecheros claim to have attacked Tobosos. The Tobosos were a central desert group, located in what are today the states of Coahuila and Chihuahua, known for violent resistance to the advance of Spanish control. The Toboso band was wiped out by 1653, but the term "Tobosos" continued as a generic label for "belligerent, unconquered Indians from the central desert." See Griffen, *Culture Change*, 167.

21. William Merrill describes a multiethnic raiding band based northwest of Durango in 1773. See Merrill, "Cultural Creativity." Some of the raiding bands that pillaged the Fronteras de Colotlán region are likely to have included Spanish, black, and mulatto, as well as Indian, members. BPEJ, Ramo Civil, caja 90, exp. 19, ff. 1–13; AHITESMCZ, unfiled; AHITESMCZ, caja 43; AGN, Provincias Internas 129, ff. 155–70.

22. AGN, Provincias Internas 129, ff. 392–400; BPEJ, Ramo Civil, caja 90, exp. 19, ff. 1–13; BPEJ, Ramo Civil, caja 173, exp. 2, f. 4v; AGN, Indios 94, ff. 77–82v.

23. AGN, Provincias Internas 129, ff. 189–90v; AGN, Provincias Internas 130, ff. 66–72v.

24. AGN, Indios 44, ff. 163v–66; Archivo Histórico del Estado de Zacatecas (hereafter, AHEZ), Fondo Ayuntamiento, Indios, caja 1, legajo 1722; AGN, Provincias Internas 129, exp. 11, ff. 191–94v; AGN, Provincias Internas 244, parte 2, ff. 1–362; AGN, Provincias Internas 129, exp. 11, ff. 195–328v; AGN, Provincias Internas 129, exp. 11, ff. 421–27v.

25. BPEJ, Ramo Civil, caja 90, exp. 19, ff. 3v–4v. In 1779 the pueblo of Huejucar had official copies made of this and several other certification documents from the pueblo's archive that had begun to deteriorate due to age. These official copies later were submitted to a Crown court in Guadalajara as supporting evidence during a land dispute.

26. AHZ, Caja Documentos Importantes 1. This one of the few seventeenth-century documents found in the Archivo Historico de Zapopan.

27. Several of the dates recorded in the manuscript are spurious. Without relying on those dates, the military campaigns described in the text can be tentatively assigned to the period during which Captain Miguel Caldera, a key figure in these accounts, was active in the Sierra de Tepeque. Caldera held the rank of captain during the Chichimec War from at least 1582. He began a series of military and diplomatic visits to the Sierra de Tepeque and Sierra Nayarita in 1585. He exercised considerable responsibility for the peace process and the congregation of "pacified" Chichimeca, with the title of chief justice of all the new settlements of Chichimecos from 1590 until his death in 1597. See Powell, *Mexico's Miguel Caldera*, 103–106, 243; Tello, *Crónica miscelanea*, book 2, 3:303; Ortega, *Maravillosa reducción*, 10. However, considering that the authors were not confined by the strictures of Spanish scribal canons and might have mixed accounts from several time periods, this approach to dating events recorded in the manuscript is not secure.

28. Pedro de Salazar appears in the official documentary record in 1616 as alcalde mayor of San Luis Potosi, in the central plateau. He arrived in the New World some years earlier as an experienced soldier and thus is likely to have served as a military leader on the Nueva Galicia frontier, as suggested by the current document, before becoming alcalde mayor. See Borah, "La defensa fronteriza," 17; Sego, *Aliados y Adversarios*, 214. Colonial officials commonly used the term *hijos* (sons) to refer to Indians. The term implied both Spanish paternal responsibility and Indian subordination and dependency.

29. AHZ, caja Documentos Importantes 1, f. 8v.

30. Guadiana was a common name for the Spanish town of Durango during the early colonial period. Guazamota was a Tepehuan pueblo in the Sierra Madre Occidental south of Durango. See Gerhard, *North Frontier*, 202, 212. Santa Catarina Cuexcomatitlan is a Huichol pueblo in the Sierra de Tepeque. San Andrés Cohamiata is a Huichol pueblo in the Sierra de Tepeque. AHZ, caja Documentos Importantes 1, f. 3v.

31. The toponym Mesquitiqui probably referred to San Francisco Mesquital, a major Tepehuan congregation south of Durango in the late sixteenth century. Tensompa was a Huichol pueblo at the base of the eastern flank of the Sierra de Tepeque. Ixcatan, in the Rio San Pedro Mezquital canyon of the Sierra Nayarita, was a Tecualme pueblo. See Gerhard, *North Frontier*.

32. In 1561 and for many years thereafter, a large group of "hostile" Indians known as the Chapuli Tepeque were reported to reside in the Sierra de Chapuli, located between the Tlaltenango and Bolaños valleys, above the Rio Bolaños settlement of Tepeque, about seventy kilometers southwest of Colotlán. The Chapuli Tepeque were reported to have sent four hundred warriors to join a Chichimeca force threatening Spaniards near Durango in 1561. See Powell, *Soldiers, Indians, and Silver*, 77. The Huichol pueblos' assertion of participation in the foundation of three pueblos in Chapuli Tepeque territory amounts to a claim for a major role in the suppression of this threat to Spanish control of the Nueva Galicia frontier.

33. AHITESMCZ, uncataloged document, "Junio de 1657, Alzamiento de Indios Chichimecos."

34. AHITESMCZ, uncataloged document, "Junio de 1657, Alzamiento de Indios Chichimecos," ff. 3r–4r.

35. AGN, Provincias Internas 129, ff. 166–68v.

36. AGN, Provincias Internas 129, f. 169r.

37. *Alférez* corresponds to "second lieutenant"; *cavo* corresponds to "corporal"; *alguasil de la guerra* glosses as "war sheriff."

38. General Blanco mentioned thirty-seven soldiers by name in a document certifying the flecheros' service but noted that he had not recorded all of the soldiers' names.

39. General Blanco wrote that the "enemy" had "caused many deaths." Perhaps the raiders method was to chase off or kill the inhabitants of livestock ranches and make off with the ranches' horses and mules, trained pack animals, tack, and dry corn supply. The corn supply, carried on stolen pack animals, would have speeded the removal of the herd from Fronteras de Colotlán by eliminating the need to pause for pasturage.

40. The Sierra Nayarita was reported to be a refuge for African slaves, "apostates," and others fleeing Spanish control by Fray Antonio Margil in 1711; by the bishop of Guadalajara, Juan Ruiz Colmenero, in 1649; and by Fray Miguel de Molino in 1649. Our Lady of the Lake University, Old Spanish Missions Collection, microfilm roll 1:2365–2403; AGI Guadalajara 56, April 20, 1649, part 2, microfilm at Instituto Davila Garibi, Guadalajara; AGI Guadalajara 10, doc. 19, April 13, 1649, microfilm at Instituto Davila Garibi, Guadalajara.

41. Flecheros were recruited from the Fronteras de Colotlán pueblos of Huejuquilla, Mezquitic, Tensompa, San Christoval, and Santa Catarina as well as from Guazamota, a Tepehuan pueblo located north of the district. Huejuquilla was of mixed ethnicity. Mezquitic (by the early eighteenth century) and Guazamota were Tepehua. Tensompa, San Christoval, and Santa Catarina were Huichol. See Ortega, *Maravillosa reducción*, 127, 132, 164; Gerhard, *North Frontier*, 73–78.

42. Evidence for incomplete Spanish control of Sierra Nayarita during the remainder of the eighteenth century is found in the following documents: Commander Vicente Canaveral's 1769 recommendation for a much larger military force for the effective control of the Cora and Huichol Sierras: AGN, Provincias Internas 127, exp. 8, 163–75; Fray Antonio Navarro's 1783 complaint that only 18 Cora families reside in the seven missions and his request for more soldiers: AGN, Provincias Internas 85, 313–15v); and Fray Ysidro Cerezo's 1805 complaint that the Coras and Tecualmes ignore the priests and his request for military force to compel obedience: AGN, Misiones 2, ff. 202–203v). Richard Warner emphasizes that "the Coras were not fully conquered" during this period of Cora history. See Warner, "Ethnohistory of the Coras," 122–54.

43. Padre Jose de Ortega was a Jesuit missionary who began twenty-six years of service in the Sierra Nayarita in late 1727, six years after the "conquest." His *Maravillosa reducción, y conquista de la provincia de San Joseph del Gran Nayar, nuevo reino de Toledo* comprises one of three sections in a volume that documents and glorifies Jesuit evangelical accomplishments in New Spain. Ortega's account of the "conquest" of Nayarit is recorded on pp. 74–189.

44. Ortega, *Maravillosa reducción*, 162, my translation.

45. Ibid., 205–17, my translation.

46. AHEZ, Ayuntamiento, caja 2, Carpeta 1724, ff. 10–10v. The Sierra de Tepeque pueblos of San Sebastian, Santa Catarina, and San Andrés Coamiata are Huichol, while Azqueltan is Tepecano.

47. In 1710 the governor of Colotlán was Christoval Hernandes. AGN, Indios 95, f. 316. In 1724 the leaders of a contingent of Sierra de Tepeque flecheros were Captain Augustin Hernandez and Alférez Juan Hernandez, both from Santa Maria. AGN, Provincias Internas 244, parte 2, ff. 96v, 183; AGN, Provincias Internas 129, f. 192v. In 1730 the governor of Colotlán and also of the barrio of Tlascala was Juan Hernandez. AHEZ, Ayuntamiento-Indios, caja 2, 1731, f. 37v. The Hernandez therefore must have been a prominent Tlaxcalteca lineage residing in the contiguous pueblos of Santa Maria and Colotlán.

48. AGN, Provincias Internas 244, parte 2, f. 87.

49. In a later report Flores states that Juan Hernandez held the rank of alférez. The captain was Augustin Hernandez. Both were Tlaxcalteca. AGN, Provincias Internas 244, part 2, f. 183. San Francisco del Mezquital was a Tepehuan pueblo.

50. Alférez Juan Hernandez was a resident of the Indian pueblo of Santa Maria. AGN, Provincias Internas 129, f. 192v. Quote from AGN, Provincias Internas 244, part 2, ff. 183r–183v.

51. AGN, Provincias Internas 129, ff. 194r–194v.

52. Isidoro Caldera was probably one of the three Caldera brothers lauded for exceptional valor during the invasion of the Sierra Nayarita in 1721, thirty-seven years before the destruction of Dolores. See Ortega, *Maravillosa reducción*, 133, my translation.

53. AGN, Provincias Internas 129, exp. 11, ff. 299v–300v.

54. AGN, Provincias Internas 127, exp. 8, f. 167.

55. AGN, Provincias Internas 129, exp. 15, f. 424v.

56. AGN, Provincias Internas 129, exp. 15, f. 425.

57. AGN, Indios 94, f. 77.

58. AGN, Indios 94, f. 77. This region was north of Huejuquilla, in the upper drainage of the Rio Chapalagana, near the mining district of Chalchihuites. See Gerhard, *North Frontier*, 77.

59. AGN, Indios 94, f. 81; AHEZ, Ayuntamiento, caja 2, 1749, ff. 1–2.

60. Indigenous communities throughout Mesoamerica produced documents to support resource protection efforts within colonial judicial forums. See, e.g., Wood, "Cosmic Conquest."

61. BPEJ, Ramo Civil, caja 90, exp. 19, ff. 3v–4v (1561).

62. BPEJ, Ramo Civil, caja 173, exp. 2, ff. 3–5.

63. BPEJ Ramo Civil, caja 48, exp. 8

64. This phrase was often attached to any mention of the king in official documents. The phrase was typically enclosed within parentheses, but in this document the scribe employed only one bracket, placing it within the phrase "que Dios guarde muchos Años." This anomaly demonstrates that the scribe was not schooled in the canons appropriate to the production of official documents.

65. AHZ, caja Documentos Importantes 1, ff. 3v–5r.

66. AGN, Provincias Internas 129, exp. 11, ff. 245–67; AGN, Indios 50, ff. 216r–18v; AGN, Indios 50, ff. 220–21; AGN, Indios 50, ff. 314v–15r.

67. AGN, Provincias Internas 129, f. 170r.

68. Santos's ethnicity is not explicitly recorded in the available documents. He almost certainly considered himself to be Indian since he refers to Chimaltitlán, an Indian pueblo, as "mi pueblo" in his petition. An invective used against him by a group of mulattos employed by the Bolaños miner suggests that he was perceived as Indian. Santos reports that as the miner's men struck and stabbed him, one of them said, "muera esse perro." AGN, Indios 94, ff. 17v–18v. Other Fronteras de Colotlán documents that record the use of the invective "dog" against Indians include one from 1716 in which a Tlaxcalteca scribe complained about a Franciscan priest: "diciendonos que somos perros alzados." AGN, Indios 40, ff. 99–102v.

69. AGN, Indios 94, ff. 3–5, 14, 17v, 16–19v. Santos's certification documents were never returned to him from Mexico City.

70. AGN, Indios 94, ff. 17v–18r.

71. Records documenting the existence of professional soldiers identified as Indians in Fronteras de Colotlán are rare. However, in 1783 an Indian lieutenant was posted in Mezquitic. See Velázquez, *Colotlán*, 114, 116.

72. BPEJ, Ramo Civil, caja 90, exp. 19, f. 4; BPEJ, Ramo Civil, caja 173, exp. 2, f. 11; Archivo de Simancas, Guerra Moderna 7014, ff. 1–107; AGN, Provincias Internas 129, exp. 15, f. 425.

73. AGN, Tierras 2686, f. 154–82v.

74. AHITESMCZ, "Junio de 1657, Alzamiento de Indios Chichimecos," unfiled.

75. AHEZ, Fondo Ayuntamiento—Indios, caja 1, carpeta 1702.

76. AGN, Indios 95, ff. 96–112; AGN, Indios 95, ff. 56–64v; Velázquez, *Colotlán*, 36, 58.

77. Prominent among the many late colonial period proposals to eliminate the flechero system were recommendations made in 1790 by Felix Calleja (later a leading Spanish general during the War of Independence and one of the last viceroys), who inspected Fronteras de Colotlán for the viceroy, reviewing flechero troops in each pueblo. BPEJ, Ramo Civil, caja 174, exp. 5; Archivo de Simancas, Guerra Moderna 7014, 1–107. Nine companies of *dragones* composed of Spaniards, "clean" mestizos, or (as a last resort) "well-behaved" blacks ("pardos de buena disposicion y costumbres") were established in the region by 1792, but Fronteras de Colotlán pueblos continued to resist the termination of the flechero system in 1794. AGN, Bandas 16, ff. 201r–202v, 212; AGN, Correspondencia de Virreyes: Marques de Casafuerte 178, f. 145.

78. BPEJ, Ramo Civil, caja 173, exp. 2, f. 11.

Conclusion

LAURA E. MATTHEW AND MICHEL R. OUDIJK

In colonial-era documents describing the conquest of Mesoamerica, both indigenous and Spanish participants argue that "if it had not been for us, the conquest would not have taken place." The juxtaposition of these seemingly contradictory claims—and the surprising force with which indigenous conquistadors made theirs—inspired us to produce this book. It is not a question of who is telling the truth and who is lying. In history, everybody tells the truth and everybody lies, at least in some way. These are, rather, the same ethnohistorical questions that have led others to talk about the "people without history": What if there is another side of the coin? What if our view on history is distorted by the accounts of those who have the upper hand?

We have come a long way since Francisco López de Gómara ascribed the conquest of Mexico to the genius of Hernando Cortés. The classic early modern and nineteenth-century narratives of desperate, triumphal Spanish conquest have been interrogated many times before and replaced with new explanations for the Spaniards' success. If the Christian God was not responsible for the conquest, then it was the return of a Mesoamerican one, Quetzalcoatl, that turned the cards in favor of the handful of Spanish soldiers. If the superiority of European guns and cannons did not make the crucial difference, then it was European germs that weakened and broke indigenous resistance. And if none of these work, we simply mix them together and argue that all of them were responsible for the seemingly impossible feat of the conquest of Mesoamerica.

But a big part of the story—the meaning and events of the conquest as understood from a Mesoamerican historical perspective—is still missing. Many of the sources used in the chapters of this volume have been known for some time, but they have been considered "curious" or "strange," laments for a losing side, and non- or ahistorical. The *lienzos, probanzas,* and other indigenous-authored documents that recount a Mesoamerican view of the conquest are, of course, as one-sided, in their own way, as the Spanish accounts. They tell stories not of poor Indians standing by while a supposed Quetzalcoatl takes hold of his rightful throne nor of overwhelming Spanish military superiority but of their own active participation in conquest-era military campaigns, the mutual adoption of different Mesoamerican and European military technologies, and the incorporation into the native world of European status symbols like horses, coats of arms, and swords. Our contention is that these alternative narratives of conquest have not been sufficiently listened to, nor have the implications of their testimonies been given full consideration.

This book, then, is a joint effort to come to terms with what it means to look at the other side. It is difficult even to imagine the consequences of such an exercise, and all the authors have struggled with this uphill battle. Five hundred years of history weigh enormously on our shoulders. Cortés looms large, while Matzatzin of Tepexi de la Seda is still an insignificant historical figure. We are neither the first nor the only scholars to have attempted a deconstruction of this "official" conquest history.[1] But here we have tried to go further, to turn the story upside down. Where traditionally Cortés decides to go south, in our history an indigenous lord or guide provides both the suggestion and the resources to make such an expedition happen. Where traditionally Cortés and his men fought their way out of Tenochtitlan during the Noche Triste, in our view warriors from Tlacopan, Azcapotzalco, and other indigenous towns saved the Spaniards and paid with their own lives. Where traditionally the Spanish conquistadors and priests claimed to have saved millions of indigenous souls from purgatory, in our view millions of indigenous people embraced a new god and incorporated it into their religious view of the world.

Indigenous histories tell us that the conquest of Mesoamerica could and did happen because of the continuation of prehispanic patterns and the overwhelming presence and participation of the indigenous peoples themselves. It is not an account of traitors, of complaints, or of people feeling sorry for themselves. On the contrary, it is an account of pride, of bravery, and of people believing in the process in which they have been involved. But in the end, it is also an account of disillusionment, of great suffering, and of people who fought very hard and who gave their lives in order to receive what according to their rules was rightfully theirs, only to find out that their rules no longer applied.

A major goal of this volume is to complicate the term "Indian conquistador." The Tlaxcalteca are, without doubt, the most famous Mesoamerican allies of the Spanish. But as the chapters in this volume make clear, the Tlaxcalteca did not act alone. From central Mexico, tens of thousands of other Nahuatl speakers from various *altepetl*—among them Tlatelolca Mexica, Xochimilca, Cholulteca, Huexotzinga, Texcoca, Quauhquecholteca, and the defeated Tenochca Mexica themselves—supplied tactical guidance, troops, and weapons to their Spanish partners. Elsewhere, we encounter alliances with Chontal, Popoluca, Kaqchikel, K'iche', Achi, and Huichol, among others. Unduly emphasizing the Tlaxcalteca has created an aura of exceptionality around them, fueling a secondary narrative of conquest that highlights native collaboration (in the most negative sense) and Spanish manipulation of Mesoamerican politics. The Spanish have the agency, and the Tlaxcalteca are seen as a bewildering enigma: how could they—and by extension, any native group that assisted the Spanish—have been so short-sighted as to enable the very power that wanted to subjugate them? Our bewilderment, at least when looking at things from this European perspective, is only deepened by the acknowledgment that the Tlaxcalteca were not so exceptional after all. Before and after the fall of Tenochtitlan in 1521, many thousands of Mesoamericans allied not only with the Spanish but also with one another to carry out multiple conquests throughout the viceroyalty of New Spain that extended into the eighteenth century. The sheer numbers of indigenous conquistadors, the extent to which they outnumbered Spanish actors, and the variety of their mutual alliances throughout the region cannot be explained merely by Spanish exploitation of native rivalries.

What might have inspired so many Mesoamericans to join in costly, difficult, and protracted military expeditions or to leave home to settle permanently as military colonists in the most far-flung regions? That not all indigenous participants in the conquest wars did so willingly pushes the question further still. Many Mesoamericans were forced to support military conquest, either by their own native lords or, increasingly, by Spanish *encomenderos* and colonial officials. Others were refugees from devastated areas with few other options or possibilities to escape conscription. The Honduran Lenca and Jicaque; Oaxacan Zapotec, Mixtec, and Mixe; and Tabascan slaves documented in the conquest of Yucatan did not receive any privileges for their service, nor did they remain as settlers. We might question whether they, or the women, children, and nonmilitary colonists who traveled with conquest armies, deserve the nomenclature "conquistador" at all. But the role of these and other noncombatants like translators and messengers was militarily crucial. They carried supplies, forged paths, prepared food, and acted as diplomats. Relationships between Mesoamerican women and Spanish conquistadors cemented alliances, literally and symbolically. Later colonists helped establish a secure presence in conquered regions. As the Spanish themselves fully recognized, the invasions of Central America, the Yucatan, the Gulf Coast, Michoacán, Nueva Galicia, and many other campaigns could not have succeeded without these essential actors.

The vast numbers of native participants, their profound importance at every level of military organization, and their geographic and temporal spread across Mesoamerica calls into question whether we can rightfully label them auxiliaries in a Spanish conquest rather than primary agents and conquistadors in their own right. The chapters in this volume suggest an especial role for the Nahuatl-speaking peoples of central Mexico, who advised the Spanish in the earliest conquests and fanned out across Mesoamerica as warriors and colonists throughout the colonial era. Nahua-European chroniclers like Domingo de San Antón Muñon Chimalpahin, Diego Muñoz Camargo, and Fernando de Alva Ixtlitlxochitl all cast the early conquests as native rather than Spanish victories.[2] So did many leaders of the Nahua conquistador diaspora. Nahua pictorials of the conquest portray willing alliances of equals between altepetl lords and the Spanish; a joint gathering of forces; and the conquest of barbaric peoples. Nahua and Spanish conquistadors in Guatemala and Chiapas supported one another's petitions to the Crown for the booty of war. In Yucatan, the vast majority of native combatants came from central Mexico, while Central American natives appear more often as slaves and porters. And in the Sierra Norte of Oaxaca and the northern frontier, we see the particular reputation of the Tlaxcalteca unfolding in colonial Mesoamerica. While they did not act alone in any of these conquests (with the possible exception of the Sierra Norte), the Tlaxcalteca appear to have enjoyed even more Spanish "name recognition" than the other Nahua conquistadors.

What is typically considered a Spanish conquest thus begins to look, from another perspective, like a political reshuffling in central Mexico to fill the power vacuum following the fall of Tenochtitlan. In this view the Tlaxcalteca appear not as traitors or enigmas but as the example par excellence of a political and military scramble for preeminence. We do not believe this is too far of a stretch and submit that a full understanding of the conquest period must place it squarely within the flow of Mesoamerican as well as European history. Mesoamerican understandings of political confederation, warfare, alliance-building, and colonization are all evident in the Spanish conquest. The gathering of troops, the use of messengers, the prominent display of altepetl insignia in battle, the following of established trade routes, the diplomatic role of women, and the organization of colonists all echo Mesoamerican norms recognizable in the postclassic period and even earlier. We need more studies that go beyond the acknowledged enmity between the Tenochca Mexica and the Tlaxcalteca. We also need more studies of regional conquests, for it may be that the emphasis on Nahua peoples reflected in this volume is itself a distortion produced by the dominance of the Nahua in Mesoamerica at the time of the conquest, in colonial-era documentation, and in the recent historiography.

The essays in this volume also suggest new questions about the implementation of Spanish colonialism in Mesoamerica. To what extent and for how long did conquest and colonization continue to depend on violence? How did the ongoing need to recruit and reward indigenous militaries affect Spanish-native relations in different places? In Nueva Galicia, the tactics and responses of the indios amigos affected the implementation of Spanish power in the region, both militarily and politically. In the Sierra Norte of Oaxaca, Nahua conquistadors and settlers had to continuously earn their privileges in order to preserve them. Rather than being recognized as conquistadors by local colonial officials, they were labeled free migrant Indians, or *naborías*. The Indian conquistadors living in Ciudad Vieja, Guatemala, by contrast, ceased their military adventures earlier but enjoyed a higher status than their counterparts in Oaxaca. They too fought hard to maintain their privileges, but a significant sector of colonial-era

Spaniards accepted their pretensions as conquistadors and supported their claims. In yet another geographic and social setting, the *fronterizos* in Nueva Galicia safeguarded their privileges through continued military service, which they then leveraged in threats of violence against the colonial government itself.

Throughout the indigenous conquistador diaspora we see native Mesoamericans weaving their own conquest narratives but rarely as tales of subjugation. Many native Mesoamericans remembered their roles in the conquest with pride as late as the nineteenth century, long after it should have been clear (from a traditional European perspective) that they themselves had been colonized. Even more surprising, native narratives of conquest were deployed not only by the indigenous conquistadors themselves but also by local elites who did not participate in the conquest campaigns. The Lienzo de Quauhquechollan, the Lienzo de Analco, and the Mapa de Cuauhtlantzinco all indicate new sources of elite authority based on both prehispanic tradition and the power of European symbols like the Hapsburg eagle, the Christian cross, the Spanish conquistador on his horse or his chair, and the Virgen de los Remedios. Some of this clearly had to do with gaining and safeguarding colonial-era privileges. But beyond their political utility, these narratives represented a Mesoamerican melding of historical traditions and symbols that linked past, present, and future for their storytellers. They should be discussed alongside other indigenous narratives—theatrical and performative as well as written—that interpret the Spanish conquest not as the beginning of the story but as a middle point in a much longer narrative of Mesoamerican history.[3]

Susan Schroeder leaves us with a fitting question to ponder at volume's end: who were the winners and who were the losers of the so-called Spanish conquest? If we admit the extensive participation of Mesoamericans in the conquest and the imprint of Mesoamerican history and culture on both the events and remembrances of the period, does the victor/vanquished dichotomy continue to make sense? The chapters in this volume do not diminish the tremendous historical implications resonant in the meeting of two worlds in 1519: the fall of Tenochtitlan, the beginnings of Spanish empire, the precipitous loss of Mesoamerican life, the introduction of Christianity, the threats to native political autonomy. They do bring us closer, we hope, to a fuller account of the conquest's place in Mesoamerican as well as European history, in which the actors are not simply Europeans and Mesoamericans nor even Spaniards, Nahua, and Maya but Mixe,

Tzutuhil, Tlaltelolca, Tarahumara, Mexica, Tlaxcalteca, Tzotzil, and all the many other Mesoamerican peoples whose lives and histories were brought to bear on the conquest of the region.

NOTES

1. See, e.g., Lockhart, *We People Here*; Graulich, *Montezuma*; Schwartz, *Victors and Vanquished*; and Restall, *Seven Myths*.

2. See, e.g., Schroeder, "Looking Back"; Miller, "Covert Mestizaje"; and Voight, "Peregrine Peregrinations."

3. E.g., as analyzed by Bricker, *Indian Christ*; Horcasitas, *El teatro náhuatl*; and Harris, *Aztecs, Moors, and Christians*.

GLOSSARY

adelantado (Spanish): Captain general

alcalde mayor (Spanish): Spanish official in charge of a district

altepetl (Nahuatl): City-state

cabildo (Spanish): Municipal council

cacique (Arawak): Indigenous nobleman

cédula (Spanish): Royal order or decree

encomendero (Spanish): Holder of an encomienda

encomienda (Spanish): Grant of an indigenous town, with rights to tribute and labor

entrada (Spanish): Military invasion

fiscal (Spanish): Court officer; treasurer; low–ranking indigenous ecclesiastical official

flechero (Spanish): Archer or bowman

hidalgo (Spanish): Spanish nobleman

lienzo (Spanish): Pictorial texts

mapa (Spanish): Map

mayordomo (Spanish): Estate manager; ecclesiastical custodian

mestizo (Spanish): Of mixed native and European descent

naborías (Spanish): (1) Individuals or groups of natives who were separated from home communities and formed lasting associations with Spaniards; (2) nontributary Indians; (3) native day laborers.

principal (Spanish): Prominent indigenous person and/or office-holder

probanza (Spanish): Legal document proving merit or services, usually in petition for reward

tameme (Nahuatl): Porters or carriers

tlacuiloque (Nahuatl): Scribes

vecino (Spanish): Citizen or permanent resident

BIBLIOGRAPHY

Acacictli, Francisco de Sandoval. *Conquista y pacificación de los indios chichimecas.* Ed. José María Muría. Zapopan, Jalisco: Colegio de Jaliso, 1996.

―――. [Francisco de Sandoval Acazitli]. "Relación de la jornada que hizo d. Francisco de Sandoval Acazitli, cacique y señor natural que fué del pueblo de Tlalmanalco." 1541. In *Colección de documentos para la historia de México,* ed. Joaquín García Icazbalceta, 2:307–32. México: Editorial Porrúa, 1980.

Acuña, René, ed. *Relaciónes geográficas del siglo XVI: Tlaxcala.* 2 vols. México: Universidad Nacional Autónoma de México, 1984.

Adorno, Roleno. "Arms, Letters, and the Native Historian in Early Colonial Mexico." In *1492–1992: Re/discovering Colonial Writing.* Hispanic Issues 4, ed. René Jara and Nicholars Spadaccini, 201–24. Minneapolis: Prisma Institute, 1989.

―――."Discourses on Colonialism: Bernal Díaz, Las Casas, and the Twentieth-Century Reader." *MLN* 103 (1988): 239–58.

―――. "The Discursive Encounter of Spain and America: The Authority of Eyewitness Testimony in the Writing of History." *The William and Mary Quarterly* 49.2 (1992): 210–28.

Aguirre Beltran, Hilda Judith. "El Códice: Lienzo de Quauhquechollac / Manuscrito pictográfico indígena tradicional azteca-nahuatl." Ph.D. diss., Universidad Nacional Autónoma de México, México, 1999.

Alcina Franch, José. *Calendario y religión entre los zapotecos.* México: Universidad Nacional Autónoma de México, 1993.

Alessio Robles, Vito. *Francisco de Urdiñola y el norte de la Nueva España.* 2nd ed. México: Editorial Porrúa, 1981.

Altman, Ida. "Spanish Society in Mexico City after the Conquest." *Hispanic American Historical Review* 71.3 (1991): 413–45.

Alvarado, Pedro de. *An Account of the Conquest of Guatemala in 1524.* 1525. Ed. Sedley J. Mackie. New York: The Cortés Society, 1924.

Alvarado Tezozomoc, Fernando. *Crónica mexicana.* 1878. Ed. Manuel Orozco y Berra. México: Editorial Porrúa, 1987.

———. *Crónica mexicayotl.* Trans. Adrián León. México: Universidad Nacional Autónoma de México, 1992.

Alvarez-Lobos Villatoro, Carlos Alfredo, and Ricardo Toledo Palomo, eds. *Libro de los parecers de la Real Audiencia de Guatemala, 1571–1655.* Guatemala: Academia de Geografía e Historia de Guatemala "Bilbioteca Goathemala," vol. 32, 1996.

Anawalt, Patricia Rieff. "A Comparative Analysis of the Costumes and Accoutrements of the Codex Mendoza." In *The Codex Mendoza,* ed. Frances E. Berdan and Patricia Anawalt, 103–50. Berkeley: University of California Press, 1992.

———. *Indian Clothing before Cortés: Mesoamerican Costumes from the Codices.* Norman: University of Oklahoma Press, 1981.

Andrén, A. *Between Artifacts and Texts: Historical Archaeology in Global Perspectives.* New York: Plenum Press, 1998.

Anguiano, Marina. *Nayarit: Costa y altiplanicie en el momento del contacto.* México: Universidad Nacional Autónoma de México, 1992.

Aparicio y Aparicio, Edgar Juan. *Conquistadores de Guatemala y fundadores de familias guatemaltecas.* México: Tipográfica Guadalajara, 1961.

Asselbergs, Florine G. L. *Conquered Conquistadors: The Lienzo de Quauhquechollan: A Nahua Vision of the Conquest of Guatemala.* Leiden: CNWS, 2004.

———. "La conquista de Guatemala: Nuevas perspectivas del Lienzo de Quauhquecholan en Puebla, México." *Mesoamérica* 44 (2002): 1–53.

Ayeta, Francisco de. *Ultimo recurso de la provincia de San Joseph de Yucathan.* Madrid: S.n., 1693.

Ballesteros-Gaibrois, Manuel. "El Lienzo de Tlaxcalla de la Casa de Colon de Valladolid." *Cuadernos prehispánicos* vol. 5, Seminario Americanista de la Universidad Casa de Colón, Valladolid (1977): 5–16 + láminas.

Bandelier, Adolph F. *Report of an Archaeological Tour in Mexico, in 1881.* Millwood: Kraus Reprint, 1976.

Barón Castro, Rodolfo. *Reseña histórica de la villa de San Salvador.* Madrid: Ediciones Cultura Hispanica, 1950.

Baumann, Roland. "Tlaxcaltecan Expression of Autonomy and Religious Drama in the Sixteenth Century." *Journal of Latin American Lore* 13 (1987): 139–53.

Beltrami, Giacomo Costantino. *Le Mexique.* Vol. 2. Paris: Crevot, 1830.

Berdan, Frances E. *The Aztecs of Central Mexico: An Imperial Society.* Orlando: Harcourt Brace College Publishers, 1982.

Berdan, Frances E., and Patricia Anawalt. *The Essential Codex Mendoza.* Berkeley: University of California Press, 1997.

Berdan, Frances E., et al. *Aztec Imperial Strategies*. Washington D.C.: Dumbarton Oaks Research Library and Collection, 1996.

Berthe, Jean-Pierre, Thomas Calvo, and Agueda Jiménez Pelayo, eds. *Sociedades en construcción: La Nueva Galicia según las visitas de oidores, 1606–1616*. Guadalajara: Universidad de Guadalajara, CEMCA, 2000.

Blom, Frans. "El Lienzo de Analco, Oaxaca." *Cuadernos Americanos*, 4.24 (1945): 125–36.

Borah, Woodrow. "La defensa fronteriza durante la gran rebelión tepehuana." *Historia mexicana* 16 (1966): 15–29.

Brand, Donald D. "Ethnohistoric Synthesis of Western Mexico." In *Handbook of Middle American Indians*, ed. Robert Wauchope, vol. 11, *Archaeology of Northern Mesoamerica*, pt. 2, ed. Gordon F. Eckholm and Ignacio Bernal, 632–56. Austin: University of Texas Press, 1971.

Bricker, Victoria Reifler. *The Indian Christ, the Indian King: The Historical Substrate of Maya Myth and Ritual*. Austin: University of Texas Press, 1981.

Brugge, David. "Pueblo Factionalism and External Relations." *Ethnohistory* 16.2 (1969): 191–200.

Buenaventura Zapata y Mendoza, Juan. *Historia cronológica de la Noble Ciudad de Tlaxcala*. Ed. and trans. Luis Reyes García and Andrea Martínez Baracs. Tlaxcala: Universidad Autónoma de Tlaxcala, 1995.

Burgoa, Francisco de. *Geográfica descripción: De la parte septentrional del polo ártico de la América y, Nueva Iglesia de las Indias Occidentales, y sitio astronómico de esta provincia de predicadores de Antequera, Valle de Oaxaca*. 1674. 2 vols. México: Editorial Porrúa, 1989.

Burkhart, Louise M. *Holy Wednesday: A Nahua Drama from Early Colonial Mexico*. Philadelphia: University of Pennsylvania Press, 1996.

———. *The Slippery Earth: Nahua-Christian Moral Dialogue in Sixteenth-Century Mexico*. Tucson: University of Arizona Press, 1989.

Burkholder, Mark. "Honor and Honors in Colonial Spanish America." In *The Faces of Honor: Sex, Shame, and Violence in Colonial Latin America*, ed. Lyman L. Johnson and Sonya Lipsett-Rivera, 18–44. Albuquerque: University of New Mexico Press, 1998.

Burns, Kathryn. "Gender and the Politics of Mestizaje: The Convent of Santa Clara in Cuzco, Peru." *Hispanic American Historical Review* 78.1 (1998): 5–44.

Bustamante, Carlos María de. *Historia de las conquistas de Hernán Cortés, escrita en español por Francisco López de Gómara, traducida al mexicano y aprobada por verdadera por D. Juan Bautista de San Antón Muñón Chimalpaín Quauhtlehuanitzin, indio mexicano*. 2 vols. Mexico: Ontiveros, 1826.

———. *Necesidad de la unión de todos los mexicanos contra las asechañzas de la nación española y liga Europa comprobada con la historia de la antigua república de Tlaxcallan*. México: Imprenta del Aguila, 1826.

Butzer, Elisabeth K. "Caretsías y epidemias. Su impacto demográfico." In *Constructores de la nación: La migración tlaxcalteca en el norte de la Nueva España,*

ed. Israel Cavazos Garza, 35–50. San Luis Potosí: El Colegio de San Luis,
Gobierno de Tlaxcala,1999.

Butzer, Karl W. "Tecnología de irrigación tlaxcalteca: ¿Mito o realidad?" In
Constructores de la nación: La migración tlaxcalteca en el norte de la Nueva España,
ed. Israel Cavazos Garza, 135–40. San Luis Potosí: El Colegio de San Luis,
Gobierno de Tlaxcala, 1999.

Cahill, David. "Colour by Numbers: Racial and Ethnic Categories in the Viceroyalty
of Peru, 1532–1824." *Journal of Latin American Studies* 25.2 (1994): 325–46.

Cañizares-Esguerra, Jorge. *How to Write the History of the New World: Historiographies,
Epistemologies, and Identities in the Eighteenth-Century Atlantic World*. Stanford:
Stanford University Press, 2001.

Carmack, Robert. *Quichean Civilization: The Ethnohistoric, Ethnographic, and
Archaeological Sources*. Berkeley: University of California Press, 1973.

Carmack, Robert M., and James L. Mondloch, eds. *El título de Totonicapán*. México:
Universidad Nacional Autónoma de México, 1983.

———. *El título de Yax y otros documentos Quichés de Totonicapán, Guatemala*. México:
Universidad Nacional Autónoma de México, 1989.

Carrasco, David, and Scott Sessions, eds. *The Cave, the City and the Eagle's Nest: An
Interpretive Journey through the Mapa de Cuahtinchan #2*. Albuquerque: University
of New Mexico Press, 2006.

Carrasco, Pedro. "Indian-Spanish Marriages in the First Century of the Colony."
In *Indian Women of Early Mexico*, ed. Susan Schroeder, Stephanie Wood, and
Robert Haskett, 87–104. Norman: University of Oklahoma Press, 1997.

———. *The Tenochca Empire of Ancient Mexico: The Triple Alliance of Tenochtitlan,
Tetzcoco, and Tlacopan*. Norman: University of Oklahoma Press, 1999.

Carrera Stampa, Manuel. *Nuño de Guzmán*. México: Editorial Jus, 1960.

Casaus Arzú, Marta. *Guatemala: Linaje y Racismo*. San José: FLASCO, 1992.

Castañeda de la Paz, María. "De Aztlan a Tenochtitlan: Historia de una peregrinación." *Latin American Indian Literatures Journal* 18.2 (2002): 163–212.

———. "El largo periplo de un documento colonial: La pintura de la peregrinación
de los culhuas-mexitin (El Mapa de Sigüenza)" *Anuario de Estudios Americanos*
59.1 (2002): 613–41.

Castillo, Cristóbal del. *Historia de la venida de los mexicanos y otros pueblos e historia
de la conquista*. Ed. and trans. Federico Navarrete Linares. México: Instituto
Nacional de Antropología e Historia, 1991.

Cavazos Garza, Israel. "Los tlaxcaltecas en la colonización de Nuevo León." In
Constructores de la nación: La migración tlaxcalteca en el norte de la Nueva España,
ed. Israel Cavazos Garza, 7–16. San Luis Potosí: El Colegio de San Luis, Gobierno
de Tlaxcala, 1999.

Celestino Solis, Eustaquio, Armando Valencia R., and Constantino Medina Lima,
eds. *Actas de Cabildo de Tlaxcala, 1547–1567*. México: Archivo de la Nación, 1984.

Cervantes de Salazar, Francisco. *México en 1554, tres diálogos latinos traducidos por
Joaquín García Icazbalceta*. México: Universidad Nacional Autónoma de México,
1952.

Chamberlain, Robert. *The Conquest and Colonization of Honduras, 1502–1550*. New York: Octagon Books, 1966.

———. *The Conquest and Colonization of Yucatan, 1517–1550*, New York: Octagon Books, 1966.

———. *The Governorship of the Adelantado Francisco de Montejo in Chiapas, 1539–1544*. Washington: Carnegie Institution of Washington, Publication #574:3, 1948.

———. "Probanza de meritos y servicios de Blas Gonzalez, Conquistador of Yucatan." *Hispanic American Historical Review*. 28.4 (1948): 526–36.

Chance, John K. *Conquest of the Sierra: Spaniards and Indians in Colonial Oaxaca*. Norman: University of Oklahoma Press, 1989.

———. "On The Mexican Mestizo." *Latin American Research Review* 14.3 (1979): 153–68.

Charlton, Thomas H. "Archaeology, Ethnohistory, and Ethnology: Interpretive Interfaces." In *Advances in Archaeological Method and Theory*, vol. 4, ed. Michael B. Schiffer, 129–76. New York: Academic Press, 1981–82.

Chavero, Alfredo. *Antigüedades mexicanas: Publicadas por la Junta Colombina en el cuarto centario del descubriemiento de América*. 2 vols. México: Oficina tipográfica de la Secretaria de Formento, 1892.

Chimalpahin Quauhtlehuanitzin, Domingo de San Antón Muñón. *Codex Chimalpahin*. Vols. 1 and 2, *Society and Politics in Mexico Tenochtitlan, Tlatelolco, Texcoco, Culhuacan, and Other Nahua Altepetl in Central Mexico*, ed. and trans. Arthur J. O. Anderson and Susan Schroeder. Norman: University of Oklahoma Press, 1997.

———. *Codex Chimalpahin*. Vol. 3, *Annals of His Time*, ed. and trans. James Lockhart, Susan Schroeder, and Doris Namala. Norman: University of Oklahoma Press, 2005.

———. *Codex Chimalpahin*. Vol. 6, *Chimalpahin and the Conquest of Mexico as Written by Francisco López de Gómara*, ed. and trans. Anne J. Cruz, Cristián Roa-de-la-Carrera, Susan Schroeder, and David Távarez. Norman: University of Oklahoma Press, forthcoming.

———. *Memorial Breve acerca de la fundación de la ciudad de Culhuacan*. Trans. Victor M. Castillo Farreras. México: Universidad Nacional Autónoma de México, 1991.

Chipman, Donald. "Isabel Moctezuma: Pioneer of Mestizaje." In *Struggle and Survival in Colonial America*, ed. David G. Sweet and Gary B. Nash, 176–86. Berkeley: University of California Press, 1981.

———. *Moctezuma's Children: Aztec Royalty under Spanish Rule, 1520–1700*. Austin: University of Texas Press, 2005.

———. *Nuño de Guzmán and the Province of Pánuco in New Spain, 1518–1533*. Glendale: A. H. Clark, 1967.

Chuchiak, John F. "'Ca numiae, lay u cal caxtlan patan lae': El tributo colonial y la nutrición de los Mayas, 1542–1812: Un estudio sobre los efectos de la conquista y el colonialismo en los Mayas de Yucatan." In *Iglesia y sociedad en América Latina colonial*, ed. Juan Manuel de la Serna and Richard E. Greenleaf, 107–218. México:

Centro Coordinador y Difusor de Estudios Latinoamericanos, Universidad Nacional Autónoma de México, 1998.

Cieza de León, Pedro de. *The Discovery and Conquest of Peru*. Ed. A. P. Cook and N. D. Cook. Durham: Duke University Press, 1998.

Clavijero, Francisco Javier. *Historia Antigua de Mexico*. 4 vols. Ed. P. Mariano Cuevas. México: Editorial Porrúa, 1958–59.

Cline, Howard. "Native Pictorial Documents of Eastern Oaxaca, Mexico." In *Summa Anthropológica en Homenage a Roberto J. Weitlaner*, 110–30. México: Instituto Nacional de Antropología e Historia, 1966.

Colección de documentos inéditos relativos al descubrimiento, conquista y organización de las antiguas posesiones españolas de América y Oceania. 24 vols. Madrid: Archivo General de Indias, 1864–84.

Cook, Sherburne F., and Woodrow Borah, *Essays in Population History: Mexico and the Caribbean*. 2 vols. Berkeley: University of California Press, 1974.

Cortés, [Hernando]. *Cartas de Relación*. 17th ed. Ed. Manuel Alcalá. México: Editorial Porrúa, 1993.

———. *Letters from Mexico*. Ed. and trans. Anthony Pagden. New Haven: Yale University Press, 1986.

Council of Huexotzingo. "Letter of the Council of Huexotzingo to the King, 1560." In *Beyond the Codices: The Nahua View of Colonial Mexico*, ed. and trans. Arthur J. O. Anderson, Frances Berdan, and James Lockhart, 176–90. Los Angeles: UCLA Latin American Center Publications, 1976.

Davies, Keith A. *Landowners in Colonial Peru*. Austin: University of Texas Press, 1984.

Davis, Andrew McFarland. "The Employment of Indian Auxiliaries in the American War." *The English Historical Review* 2.8 (1887): 709–28.

Desbarats, Cathedrine M. "The Cost of Canada's Native Alliances: Reality and Scarcity's Rhetoric." *The William and Mary Quarterly* 52.4 (1995): 609–30.

Díaz del Castillo, Bernal. *The Conquest of New Spain*. Trans. J. M. Cohen. Baltimore: Penguin Books, 1963.

———. *The Discovery and Conquest of Mexico*. Trans. A. P. Maudslay. New York: Farrar, Straus, and Giroux, 1970.

———. *Historia verdadera de la conquista de Nueva España*. México: Alianza Editorial, 1997. First printed in 1632; first Alianza edition printed in 1991.

———. *Historia verdadera de la conquista de la Nueva España*. Ed. Carmelo Sáenz de Santa María. Madrid: Instituto "Gonzalo Fernández de Oviedo" Consejo Superior de Investigaciones Científicas, 1982.

———. *Historia verdadera de la conquista de Nueva España*. Ed. Joaquín Ramírez Cabañas. México: Editorial Porrúa, 1955.

Díaz-Polanco, Hector, ed. *El fuego de la inobediencia: autonomía y rebelión india en el obsipado de Oaxaca*. México: CIESAS, 1992.

Dibble, Charles, ed. *Códice Xolotl*. México: Universidad Nacional Autónoma de México, 1996.

Doesburg, Bas van, and Olivier van Buren. "The prehispanic history of the Valley of Coixtlahuaca, Oaxaca." In *Códices, Caciques, y Comunidades*, ed. Maarten Jansen and Luis Reyes Garcia, 103–60. Ridderkerk: Asociación de Historiadores Latinoamericanistas Europeas, 1997.

Durán, Diego. *The History of the Indies of New Spain*. Ed. Doris Heyden. Norman: University of Oklahoma Press, 1994.

———. *Historia de las indias de Nueva España e Islas de Tierra Firme*, 2 vols. Ed. Rosa Camelo and José Rubén Romero. México: Consejo Nacional para la Cultura y las Artes, 1995.

Dyckerhoff, Ursula. "Dos títulos de tierras procedentes del pueblo de Huaquilpan, Estado de Hidalgo." In *De tlacuilos y escribanos: estudios sobre documentos indígenas coloniales del centro de México*, ed. Xavier Noguez and Stephanie Wood, 99–135. Michoacán: El Colegio de Michoacán and El Colegio Mexiquense, 1998.

Escalante Arce, Pedro, ed. *Cartas de relación y otros documentos*. San Salvador: Consejo Nacional para la Cultura y el Arte, 2000.

———. *Los tlaxcaltecas en Centro América*. San Salvador: Dirección de Publicaciones e Impresos, Consejo Nacional para la Cultura y el Arte, 2001.

Falla, Juan José. *Extractos de Escrituras Publicas*. 3 vols. Guatemala: Editorial Amigos del País, 1994.

Farriss, Nancy. *Maya Society under Colonial Rule: The Collective Enterprise of Survival*. Princeton: Princeton University Press, 1984.

Fernández, Rodolfo, and José Francisco Román. "Presencia tlaxcalteca en Nueva Galicia." In *Constructores de la nación: La migración tlaxcalteca en el norte de la Nueva España*, ed. Israel Cavazos Garza, 17–34. San Luis Potosí: El Colegio de San Luis, Gobierno de Tlaxcala,1999.

Fernandez Tejeda, Isabel. *La comunidad indígena Maya de Yucatan, Siglos XVI y XVII*. México: Instituto Nacional de Antropología e Historia, 1990.

Fidalgo, Ana Marín. *El Real Alcázar de Sevilla / Guía de visita*. Sevilla: Aldeasa, 1995.

Flagler, Edward K. "Defensive Policy and Indian Relations in New Mexico during the Tenure of Governor Francisco Cuervo y Valdés, 1705–1707." *Revista Española de Antropologia Americana* 22 (1992): 89–104.

Fortanelli Martínez, Javier, Fernando Carlín Castelán, and Jéssica Grétel Loza León. "Sistemas agrícolas de regadío de origen tlaxcalteca en San Luis Potosí." In *Constructores de la nación: La migración tlaxcalteca en el norte de la Nueva España*, ed. Israel Cavazos Garza, 105–34. San Luis Potosí: El Colegio de San Luis, Gobierno de Tlaxcala, 1999.

Foster, Michael S., and Phil C. Weigand, eds, *The Archaeology of West and Northwest Mesoamerica*. Boulder: Westview Press, 1985.

Fowler, William R. *The Cultural Evolution of Ancient Nahua Civilizations: The Pipil-Nicarao of Central America*. Norman: University of Oklahoma Press, 1989.

Frye, David. *Indians into Mexicans: History and Identity in a Mexican Town*. Austin: University of Texas Press, 1996.

Fuentes y Guzmán, Francisco Antonio. *Historia de Guatemala o recordación florida*. Guatemala: Sociedad de Geografía e Historia, 1932–33.

Galaviz de Capdevielle, María Elena. *Rebeliones indígenas en el norte del reino de la Nueva España, XVI–XVII*. México: Editorial Campesina, 1967.

Gall, Francis. *Diccionario geográfico de Guatemala*. 4 vols. Guatemala: Instituto Geográfico Nacional, 1976–83.

García Bernal, Manuela Cristina. "Indios y encomenderos en el Yucatan español: Evolución demográfica y relaciones interraciales." *Revista de la Universidad de Yucatan* 20.116 (1978): 16–38.

———. *Los servicios personales en el Yucatan durante el siglo XVI*. Valladolid: Universidad de Valladolid, Seminario de Historia de América, 1976.

———. *Yucatan: Población y encomienda bajo los Austrias*. Sevilla: Escuela Hispano-Americanos, 1978.

García Icazbalceta, Joaquín ed. *Colección de documentos para la historia de México*. 1858–66. 2 vols. México: Editorial Porrúa, 1980.

García Martínez, Bernardo. "The Conquest of Mexico Revisited." Keynote address, New Worlds, First Nations: Native Peoples of Mesoamerica and the Andes under Colonial Rule Conference, Sydney, Australia, October 1, 2002.

García Peláez, Francisco de Paula. *Memorias para la Historia del Antiguo Reyno de Guatemala*. 3 vols. Ed. Francis Gall. Guatemala: Sociedad de Geografía e Historia de Guatemala, 1968–73.

Gasco, Janine. "The Polities of Xoconochco." In *The Postclassic Mesoamerican World*, ed. Michael E. Smith and Frances F. Berdan, 50–54. Salt Lake City: University of Utah Press, 2003.

———. "Una visión conjunta de la historia demográfica y económica del Soconusco colonial." *Mesoamérica* 18 (1989): 372–99.

Gasco, Janine, and Frances F. Berdan, "International Trade Centers." In *The Postclassic Mesoamerican World*, ed. Michael E. Smith and Frances F. Berdan, 109–16. Salt Lake City: University of Utah Press, 2003.

Gerhard, Peter. *Geografía histórica de la Nueva España, 1519–1821*. México: Universidad Nacional Autónoma de México, 1986.

———. *A Historical Geography of New Spain*. Revised ed. Norman: University of Oklahoma Press, 1993.

———. *The North Frontier of New Spain*. Norman: University of Oklahoma Press, 1993.

Gibson, Charles. "Conquest, Capitulation, and Indian Treaties." *American Historical Review* 83.1 (1978): 1–15.

———. "Significación de la historia tlaxcalteca en el siglo XVI." *Historia Mexicana* 3.4 (1964): 592–99.

———. *Tlaxcala in the Sixteenth Century*. New Haven: Yale University Press, 1952.

Gillespie, Jeanne Lou. "Saints and Warriors: The Lienzo de Tlaxcala and the Conquest of Tenochtitlan." Ph.D. diss., Arizona State University, 1994.

Gillespie, Susan D. *The Aztec Kings*. Tucson: University of Arizona Press, 1989.

Gillow, Eulogio. *Apuntes históricos sobre la idolatría e introducción del cristianismo en Oaxaca*. 1889. México: Ediciones Toledo, 1990.

Glass, John B. and Donald Robertson. "A Census of Native Middle American Pictorial Manuscripts." In *Handbook of Middle American Indians*, gen. ed. Robert Wauchope, vol. 14: *Guide to Ethnohistorical Sources*, pt. 3, ed. Howard Cline,

Charles Gibson and H. B. Nicholson, 81–252. Austin: University of Texas Press, 1975.

Gonzales, Osmar. "Tlaxcaltecas y jesuitas. Fe y formación del sentimiento nacional, siglos XVI–XVIII." In *Constructores de la nación: La migración tlaxcalteca en el norte de la Nueva España*, ed. Israel Cavazos Garza, 51–78. San Luis Potosí: El Colegio de San Luis, Gobierno de Tlaxcala, 1999.

González-Hermosillo A., Francisco, and Luis Reyes García, eds. *El códice de Cholula: La exaltación testimonial de un linaje indio*. México: Instituto Nacional de Antropología e Historia, 2002.

Gorriz, Natalia. *Luisa Xicoténcatl, Princesa de Tlaxcala*. Guatemala City: El Liberal Progresista, 1943.

Gradie, Charlotte M. *The Tepehuan Revolt of 1616*. Salt Lake City: University of Utah Press, 2000.

Graulich, Michel. *Montezuma, ou, l'Apogee et la chute de l'empire aztèque*. Lille: Fayard, 1994.

Griffen, William. *Culture Change and Shifting Populations in Central Northern Mexico*. Tucson: University of Arizona, 1969.

Grunberg, Bernard. "The Origins of the Conquistadores of Mexico City." *Hispanic American Historical Review* 74.2 (1994): 259–83.

Gruzinski, Serge. *The Conquest of Mexico: The Incorporation of Indian Societies into the Western World, 16th–18th Centuries*. Cambridge: Polity Press, 1993. First published in French as *La colonisation de l'imaginaire*. Paris: Editions Gallimard, 1988.

Gutiérrez, Ramón A. *When Jesus Came, the Corn Mothers Went Away: Marriage, Sexuality, and Power in New Mexico, 1500–1846*. Stanford: Stanford University Press, 1991.

Gutiérrez Mendoza, Gerardo, et al. "Least Cost Path Analysis: An Estimation of the Most Efficient Communication Route between the Valley of Oaxaca and the Gulf Coast Plain of Mexico." *Antropología y Técnica* no. 6, Nueva Época (2000): 11–20.

Hansen, Mogens Herman, ed. *A Comparative Study of Six City-State Cultures*. Copenhagen: Historisk-filosofiske Skrifter 27, The Royal Danish Academy of Sciences and Letters, 2002.

———. *A Comparative Study of Thirty City-State Cultures*. Copenhagen: Historisk-filosofiske Skrifter 21, The Royal Danish Academy of Sciences and Letters, 2000.

The Harkness Collection in the Library of Congress. Manuscripts Concerning Mexico. Washington D.C.: Library of Congress, 1974.

Harris, Max. *Aztecs, Moors, and Christians: Festivals of Reconquest in Mexico and Spain*. Austin: University of Texas Press, 2000.

Haskett, Robert. *Indigenous Rulers: An Ethnohistory of Town Government in Colonial Cuernavaca*. Albuquerque: University of New Mexico Press, 1991.

Hassig, Ross. *Aztec Warfare: Imperial Expansion and Political Contact*. Norman: University of Oklahoma Press, 1988.

Herren, Ricardo. *Doña Marina, la Malinche*. Barcelona: Editorial Planeta, 1992.

Herrera, Robinson. "Concubines and Wives: Re-Interpreting Native–Spanish Intimate Unions in Sixteenth-Century Guatemala." Paper presented at the Annual Meeting of the Southern Historical Association, November 2002, Baltimore, Maryland.

———. *Natives, Europeans, and Africans in Sixteenth-Century Santiago de Guatemala.* Austin: University of Texas Press, 2003.

Himmerich y Valencia, Robert. *The Encomenderos of New Spain, 1521–1555.* Austin: University of Texas Press, 1991.

Horcasitas, Fernando. *El teatro náhuatl: épocas novohispana y moderna.* 2 vols. México: UNAM, 1974–75.

Hvidtfeldt, Arild. *Teotl and Ixiptlatli: Some Central Conceptions in Ancient Mexican religion.* Copenhagen: Munksgaard, 1958.

Icaza, Francisco A. de. *Conquistadores y pobladores de Nueva España, Diccionario autobiográfico sacado de los textos originales, volumen I.* Madrid: El Adelantado de Segovia, 1923.

Israel, J. I. *Race, Class, and Politics in Colonial Mexico, 1610–1670.* Oxford: Oxford University Press, 1975.

Ixtlilxochitl, Fernando de Alva. *Obras históricas.* 2 vols. Ed. Edmundo O'Gorman. México: Universidad Nacional Autónoma de México, 1975–77.

———. *Obras históricas de Don Fernando Alva Ixtlilxochitl, Tomo 1, Relaciones.* Ed. Alfredo Chavero. México: Oficina Tip. de la Secretaria de Fomento, 1891.

Izquierdo, Ana Luisa. *Acalán y la Chontalpa en el siglo XVI.* México: Universidad Nacional Autónoma de México, 1997.

Jackson, Margaret A., and Rebecca P. Brienen, eds. *Visions of Empire: Picturing the Conquest in Colonial Mexico.* Coral Gables, Fla.: Lowe Art Museum, 2003.

Jäcklein, Klaus. *Los popolocas de Tepexi (Puebla): Un estudio etnohistórico.* Wiesbaden: Franz Steiner Verlag, 1978.

Johnson, Richard. "The Search for a Usable Indian: An Aspect of the Defense of Colonial New England." *Journal of American History* 64.3 (1977): 623–51.

Jones, Grant. *Maya Resistance to Spanish Rule: Time and History on a Colonial Frontier.* Albuquerque: University of New Mexico Press, 1989.

Jones, Oakah. "Pueblo Indian Auxiliaries and the Reconquest of New Mexico." *Journal of the West* 2:3 (1963): 257–80.

———. *Pueblo Warriors and Spanish Conquest.* Norman: University of Oklahoma Press, 1966.

Karttunen, Frances. *Between Worlds: Interpreters, Guides, and Survivors.* New Brunswick: Rutgers University Press, 1994.

———. "Interpreters Snatched from the Shore: The Successful and the Others." In *The Language Encounter in the Americas, 1492–1800,* ed. Edward G. Gray and Norman Fiering, 215–29. New York: Berghahn, 2000.

———. "Rethinking Malinche." In *Indian Women in Early Mexico,* ed. Susan Schroeder, Stephanie Wood, and Robert Haskett, 290–312. Norman: University of Oklahoma Press, 1997.

Katzew, Ilona. *Casta Painting: Images of Race in Eighteenth-Century Mexico.* New Haven: Yale University Press, 2004.

Kellogg, Susan. *Law and the Transformation of Aztec Culture, 1500–1700*. Norman: University of Oklahoma Press, 1995.

Kidwell, Clara Sue. "Indian Women as Cultural Mediators." *Ethnohistory* 39.2 (1992): 97–107.

Kirchhoff, Paul, Lina Odena Güemes, and Luis Reyes García. eds. *Historia tolteca-chichimeca*. México: CIESAS, 1989.

König, Viola. *Die Schlacht bei Sieben Blume: Konquistadoren, Kaziken und Konflikte auf alten Landkarten der Indianer Südmexikos*. Bremen: Edition Temmen, 1993.

Kramer, Wendy. *Encomienda Politics in Early Colonial Guatemala, 1524–1544: Dividing the Spoils*. Boulder: Westview Press, 1994.

Kramer, Wendy, W. George Lovell, and Christopher Lutz. "La conquista española de centroamérica." In *Historia general de Centroamérica*, vol. 2, ed. Julio César Pinto Soria, 21–91. Madrid: Ediciones Siruela, S.A., 1993.

Kranz, Travis Barton. "The Tlaxcalan Conquest Pictorials: The Role of Images in Influencing Colonial Policy in Sixteenth-Century Mexico." Ph.D. diss., University of California at Los Angeles, 2001.

Kuznesof, Elizabeth Anne. "Ethnic and Gender Influences on 'Spanish' Creole Society in Colonial Spanish America." *Colonial Latin America Review* 4.1 (1995): 153–76.

Las Casas, Bartolomé de. *Brevissima relación de la destrucción de las indias*. Sevilla: Sebatian Trujillo, 1552.

———. *In Defense of the Indians: The Defense of the Most Reverend Lord, Don Fray Bartolomé de las Casas, of the Order of Preachers, Late Bishop of Chiapa, against the Persecutors and Slanderers of the Peoples of the New World Discovered across the Seas*. 1552. Trans. Stafford Poole. DeKalb: Northern Illinois Press, 1974.

———. *Obras escogidas de fray Bartolomé de las Casas*. Ed. Juan Pérez de Tudela y Bueso. 5 vols. "Biblioteca de autores españoles" tomos 95–96, 105–106, 110. Madrid: Real Academia Española / Colección Rivadeneira, 1957–58.

Lee, Thomas A., Jr., and Carlos Navarrete, eds. *Mesoamerican Communication Routes and Cultural Contacts*. Provo: New World Archaeological Foundation, 1978.

Leibsohn, Dana. "Primers for Memory: Cartographic Histories and Nahua Identity." In *Writing without Words*, ed. E. H. Boone and W. D. Mignolo, 161–87. Durham: Duke University Press, 1994.

Leonard, Irving. "Conquerors and Amazons in Mexico." *Hispanic American Historical Review* 24 (1944): 562–79.

León-Portilla, Miguel. *La flecha en el blanco: Francisco Tenamaztle y Bartolomé de las Casas en lucha por los derechos de los indígenas, 1541–1556*. México: Editorial Diana, 1995.

Lima, Constantino Medina, ed. *Libro de los guardianes y gobernadores de Cuauhtinchan, 1519–1640*. México: CIESAS, 1995.

Lipsett-Rivera, Sonya. "A Slap in the Face of Honor." In *The Faces of Honor: Sex, Shame, and Violence in Colonial Latin America*, ed. Lyman L. Johnson and Sonya Lipsett-Rivera, 179–200. Albuquerque: University of New Mexico Press, 1998.

Lizana, Bernardo de. *Historia de Yucatan: Devocionario de Nuestra Señora de Izamal y conquista espiritual*. México: Imprenta del Museo Nacional, 1893.

Lockhart, James. *The Men of Cajamarca: A Social and Biographical Study of the First Conquerors of Peru*. Austin: University of Texas Press, 1972.

———. *The Nahuas after the Conquest: A Social and Cultural History of the Indians of Central Mexico, Sixteenth through Eighteenth Centuries*. Stanford: Stanford University Press, 1992.

———. *Spanish Peru, 1532–1560: A Social History*. 2nd ed. Madison: University of Wisconsin Press, 1994.

———. "Trunk Lines and Feeder Lines: The Spanish Reaction to American Resources." In *Transatlantic Encounters: Europeans and Andeans in the Sixteenth Century*, ed. Kenneth J. Andrien and Rolena Adorno, 90–120. Berkeley: University of California Press, 1991.

———. *We People Here: Nahuatl Accounts of the Conquest of Mexico*. Berkeley: University of California Press, 1998.

Lockhart, James, Frances F. Berdan, and Arthur J. O. Anderson, eds. *The Tlaxcalan Actas: A Compendium of the Records of the Cabildo of Tlaxcala (1545–1627)*. Salt Lake City: University of Utah Press, 1986.

Lockhart, James, and Stuart B. Schwartz. *Early Latin America: A History of Colonial Spanish America and Brazil*. Cambridge: Cambridge University Press, 1983.

Lokken, Paul T. "From Black to Ladino: People of African Descent, *Mestizaje*, and Racial Hierarchy in Rural Colonial Guatemala, 1600–1730." Ph.D. diss., University of Florida, 2000.

López Austin, Alfredo. *Los Mitos del Tlacuache*. México: Universidad Nacional Autónoma de México, 1998 [1990].

———. "Aztec." In *The Oxford Encyclopedia of Mesoamercian Cultures / The civilizations of Mexico and Central America*. 3 vols. Ed. David Carrasco, 1:68–72. Oxford: Oxford University Press, 2001.

López de Cogollado, Diego. *Los tres siglos de la dominación española en Yucatan, o historia de esta provincia*. 2 vols. Graz: ADEVA, 1971.

López de Gómara, Francisco. *La conquista de México*. Ed. José Luis de Rojas. Madrid: Dastin, Crónicas de América, 2000.

———. *Cortés: The Life of the Conqueror by His Secretary, Francisco López de Gómara*. Trans. Lesley Byrd Simpson. Berkeley: University of California Press, 1964.

———. *Historia de las Indias*. 2 vols. Zaragoza: Agustín Millán, 1552.

Lutz, Christopher H. *Santiago de Guatemala, 1541–1773: City, Caste, and the Colonial Experience*. Norman: University of Oklahoma Press, 1994.

MacLeod, Murdo. *Spanish Central America: A Socio-Economic History, 1520–1720*. Berkeley: University of California Press, 1973.

MacLeod, Peter. "Microbes and Muskets: Smallpox and the Participation of Amerindian Allies of New France in the Seven Years War." *Ethnohistory* 39.1 (1992): 42–64.

MacNutt, Francis Augustus. *Bartholomew de las Casas: His Life, His Apostolate, and His Writings*. 1909. New York: AMS Press, 1972.

Malina, J., and Z. Vasicek. *Archaeology Yesterday and Today: The Development of Archaeology in the Sciences and Humanities*. Cambridge: Cambridge University Press, 1990.

Markman, Sydney D. *Architecture and Urbanization of Colonial Central America*. Vol. 1, *Selected Primary Documentary and Literary Sources*. Tempe: Center for Latin American Studies, Arizona State University, 1993.

Marshall, C. E. "The Birth of The Mestizo in New Spain." *Hispanic American Historical Review* 19.2 (1939): 166–67.

Martín, Luis. *Daughters of the Conquistadors, Women of the Viceroyalty of Peru*. Albuquerque: University of New Mexico, 1983.

Martínez, María Elena. "Limpieza de Sangre." In *Encyclopedia of Mexico*, ed. Michael Werner, 6:749–52. Chicago: Fitzroy Dearborn Publishers, 1997.

———. "Space, Order, and Group Identities in a Spanish Colonial Town: Puebla de Los Angeles." In *The Collective and the Public in Latin America: Cultural Identities and Political Order*, ed. Luis Roniger and Tamar Herzog, 13–36. Portland: Sussex Academic Press, 2000.

Martínez Baracs, Andrea. "Colonizaciones tlaxcaltecas." *Historia Mexicana* 18.2 (1993): 195–250.

Martínez Baracs, Andrea, and Carlos Sempat Assadourian, eds. *Tlaxcala: Textos de su historia*. Vol. 6. Tlaxcala: Gobierno del Estado de Tlaxcala, 1991.

Martínez Peláez, Severo. *La patria del Criollo: Ensayo de interpretacón de la realidad colonial guatemalteca*. 11th ed. Guatemala: Talleres de Ediciones en Marcha, 1990 [1973].

Martínez Saldaña, Tomás. *La diáspora tlaxcalteca: Colonización agrícola del norte mexicano*. Tlaxcala: Ediciones del Gobierno del Estado de Tlaxcala, 1998.

Matthew, Laura E. "Marching as a Group Apart: The Mexicano Militias of Colonial Guatemala." Paper presented at the Annual Meeting of the Southern Historical Association, November 8, 2002, Baltimore, Maryland.

———. "Neither and Both: The Mexican Indian Conquistadors of Colonial Guatemala." Ph.D. diss., University of Pennsylvania, 2004.

Mazihcatzin, Nicolás Faustino. "Descripción del Lienzo de Tlaxcala." *Revista Mexicana de Estudios Históricos* 1 (1927): 59–90.

Meade de Angulo, Mercedes. *Doña Luisa Teohquilhuastzin, mujer del capitán Pedro de Alvarado*. Puebla: Gobierno del Estado de Puebla, Comisión Puebla V Centenario, 1992.

Merrill, William L. "Cultural Creativity and Raiding Bands in Eighteenth-Century Northern New Spain." In *Violence, Resistance, and Survival in the Americas: Native Americans and the Legacy of Conquest*, ed. William B. Taylor and Franklin Pease G. Y. 124–52. Washington: Smithsonian Institution Press, 1994.

Milla, José. *Historia de la América Central*. Guatemala City: Centro Editorial "José de Pineda Ibarra," 1963.

Miller, Marilyn. "Covert Mestizaje and the Strategy of 'Passing' in Diego Muñoz Camargo's *Historia de Tlaxcala*." *Colonial Latin American Review* 6.1 (1997): 41–58.

Mills, Kenneth. *Idolatry and Its Enemies: Colonial Andean Religion and Extirpation, 1640–1750*. Princeton: Princeton University Press, 1997.

Montejano y Aguiñaga, Rafael. "La evolución de los tlaxcaltecas en San Luis Potosí." In *Constructores de la nación: La migración tlaxcalteca en el norte de la Nueva España,* ed. Israel Cavazos Garza, 79–88. San Luis Potosí: El Colegio de San Luis, Gobierno de Tlaxcala, 1999.

Moreland, John. *Archaeology and Text*. London: Duckworth, 2001.

Mörner, Magnus. *Race Mixture in the History of Latin America*. Boston: Little, Brown, 1967.

Motolinía, Toribio. *History of the Indians of New Spain*. 1541. Trans. Elizabeth Andros Foster. Westport, Conn.: Greenwood Press, 1977.

Mundy, Barbara. "Lienzos." In *The Oxford Encyclopedia* of Mesoamercian Cultures: The Civilizations of Mexico and Central America, 3 vols., ed. David Carrasco, 2:121. Oxford: Oxford University Press, 2001.

———. *The Mapping of New Spain / Indigenous Cartography and the Maps of the Relaciones Geográfica*. Chicago: The University of Chicago Press, 1996.

Muñoz Camargo, Diego. *Descripción de la ciudad y provincia de Tlaxcala de la Nueva España y las Indias y del mar océano para el buen gobierno y ennoblecimiento dellas*. Ed. René Acuña. México: Universidad Nacional Autónoma de México, 1981.

———. *Historia de Tlaxcala*. Ed. Germán Vásquez. Madrid: Historia 16, Crónicas de Amércia 26, 1986.

———. *Historia de Tlaxcala: MS 210 de la Biblioteca Nacional de Paris*. Ed. Luis Reyes García and Javier Lira Toledo. Tlaxcala: Universidad Autónoma de Tlaxcala, 1998.

———. *Suma y epíloga de toda la descripción de Tlaxcala*. Ed. Andrea Martínez Baracs and Carlos Sempat Assadourian. Tlaxcala: Universidad Autónoma de Tlaxcala, 1994.

Navarrete, Carlos. "Elementos arqueológicos de mexicanización en las tierras altas mayas." In *Temas mesoamericanos*, ed. Sonia Lombardo and Enrique Nalda, 305–52. México: Instituto Nacional de Antropología e Historia, 1996.

Navarro, Marysa, and Virginia Sánchez Korrol. *Women in Latin America and the Caribbean, Restoring Women to History*. Bloomington: Indiana University Press, 1999.

Newson, Linda. *The Cost of Conquest: Indian Decline in Honduras under Spanish Rule*. Boulder: Westview Press, 1986.

Nicholson, H. B., and Eloise Quiñones Keber, eds. *Mixteca Puebla: Discoveries and Research in Mesoamerican Art and Archaeology*. Culver City: Labyrinthos, 1994.

Núñez Becerra, Fernanda. *La Malinche: De la historia al mito*. México: Instituto Nacional de Antropología e Historia, 1996.

Núñez Cabeza de Vaca, Alvar. *Castaways*. Ed. Enrique Pupo-Walker. Trans. Frances M. López-Morillas. Berkeley: University of California Press, 1993.

Ortega, José de. "Maravillosa Reduccion, y Conquista de la Provincia de San Joseph del Gran Nayar, Nuevo Reino de Toledo." In *Apostólicos Afanes de la Compañía de Jesús en su Provincia de México* [1754], ed. Francisco Javier Fluviá, 1–223. México: CEMCA, 1996.

Otzoy C., Simon, trans. *Memorial de Sololá*. Guatemala: Comisión Interuniversitaria Guatemalteca de Conmemoración del Quinto Centenario del Descubrimiento de América, 1999.

Oudijk, Michel R. *Historiography of the Bènizàa: The Late Postclassic and Early Colonial Periods (A.D. 1000–1600)*. Leiden: Research School CNWS, 2000.

———. "La Toma de Posesión: Un tema mesoamericano para le legitimación del poder." *Relaciones* 91 (2002): 95–131.

———. "The Zapotec City-State." In *A Comparative Study of Six City-State Cultures*, ed. Mogens Herman Hansen, 73–90. Copenhagen: C. A. Reitzels Forlag, 2002.

Paredes Martínez, Carlos Salvador. *La región de Atlixco, Huaquechula, y Tochimilco: La sociedad y la agricultura en el siglo XVI*. México: CIESAS, 1991.

Paredes Rangel, Beatriz, and Angel García Cook, eds. *Tlaxcala: Textos de su historia: Una historia compartida*. 16 vols. México: Consejo para la Cultura y las Artes; Tlaxcala: Gobierno del Estado de Tlaxcala, 1991.

Parker, Geoffrey. *The Military Revolution: Military Innovation and the Rise of the West, 1500–1800*. 2nd ed. Cambridge: Cambridge University Press, 1996.

Paso y Troncoso, Francisco del. *Catálogo de los objetos que presenta la república de México en la exposición histórico-americana de Madrid*. México/Madrid, 1892–93.

———. *Epistolario de Nueva España*. 16 vols. Ed. Silvio Arturo Zavala. México: Antigua Librería Robredo, de J. Porrúa e hijos, 1939.

Pérez-Rocha, Emma. *Privilegios en lucha*. México: Instituto Nacional de Antropología e Historia, 1998.

Pérez-Rocha, Emma, and Rafael Tena. *La nobleza indígena del centro de México después de la conquista*. México: Instituto Nacional de Antropología e Historia, 2000.

Pineda, Juan de. "Descripción de la Provincia de Guatemala, Año 1594." In *Relaciones Históricas y Geográficas de América Central*, ed. Manuel Serrano y Sanz. Madrid: Librería General del Victoriano Suárez, 1908.

Piña Chan, Román. "Commerce in the Yucatan Peninsula: The Conquest and Colonial Period." In *Mesoamerican Communication Routes and Cultural Contacts*, ed. Thomas A. Lee, Jr., and Carlos Navarrete, 37–48. Provo: New World Archaeological Foundation, 1978.

Pohl, John. "Royal Marriage and Confederacy Building among the Eastern Nahuas, Mixtecs, and Zapotecs." In *The Postclassic Mesoamerican World*, ed. Michael E. Smith and Frances F. Berdan, 243–48. Salt Lake City: University of Utah Press, 2003.

Powell, Philip Wayne. *La guerra chichimeca (1550–1600)*. México: Fondo de Cultura Económica, 1977.

———. *Mexico's Miguel Caldera: The Taming of America's First Frontier (1548–1597)*. Tucson: University of Arizona Press, 1977.

———. *Soldiers, Indians, and Silver: North America's First Frontier War*. Tempe: Arizona State University, 1975.

Prescott, William Hickling. *History of the Conquest of Mexico*. 1843. Ed. James Lockhart. New York: Modern Library, 2001.

"Probanza de meritos y servicios de Diego de Usagre y Francisco Castellón." *Anales de la Sociedad de Geografia y Historia* 185, vol. 41 (1968): 141–234.

"Provanca del Adelantado D. Pedro de Alvarado y Doña Leonor de Alvarado su hija." *Anales de la Sociedad de Geografia e Historia* 13.4 (1937): 475–87.

Quezada, Sergio. "Encomienda, cabildo y gubernatura indígena en Yucatan, 1541–1583." *Historia Mexicana* 34.4 (1985): 662–84.

Raluy Poudevida, Antonio. *Diccionario porrúa de la lengua española*. México: Editorial Porrúa, 1998.

Recinos, Adrián. *Cronicas indígenas de Guatemala*. Guatemala: Editorial Universitaria, 1957.

———. *Pedro de Alvarado: Conquistador de México y Guatemala*. México: Fondo de Cultura Económica, 1952. Reprint, Guatemala: José de Pineda Ibarra, 1986.

Recinos, Adrián, and Dionisio José Chonay, trans. *Memorial de Sololá, Anales de los Cakchiqueles: Título de los señores de Totonicapán*. México: Fondo de Cultura Económica, 1980 [1950]. Reprint, Guatemala: Piedra Santa, 2001.

Recinos, Adrián, Delia Goetz, and Dionisio José Chonay, trans. *The Annals of the Cakchiquels: Title of the Lords of Totonicapan*. Norman: University of Oklahoma Press, 1974.

Remesal, Antonio de. *Historia general de las Indias occidentales y particular de la gobernación de Chiapa y Guatemala*. 1617. Ed. Carmelo Sáenz de Santa María. "Biblioteca de autores españoles," tomos 175, 189. Madrid: Ediciones Atlas, 1964.

Restall, Matthew, ed. *Beyond Black and Red: African-Native Relations in Colonial Latin America*. Albuquerque: University of New Mexico Press, 2005.

———. "Black Conquistadors: Armed Africans in Early Spanish America." *The Americas* 57.2 (2000): 171–205.

———. "Gaspar Antonio Chi: Bridging the Conquest, of Yucatan." In *The Human Tradition in Colonial Latin America*, ed. Kenneth J. Andrien, 6–21. Wilmington: Scholarly Resources, 2001.

———."Heirs to the Hieroglyphs: Indigenous Literacy in Colonial Mesoamerica." *The Americas* 54.2 (1997): 239–67.

———. *Maya Conquistador*. Boston: Beacon Press, 1998.

———. *The Maya World: Yucatec Culture and Society*. Stanford: Stanford University Press, 1997.

———. *Seven Myths of the Spanish Conquest*. New York: Oxford University Press, 2003.

Reyes García, Luis. *La escritura pictografica en Tlaxcala / Dos mil años de experiencia Mesoamericana*. México: CIESAS-UAT, 1993.

Ricard, Robert. *La conquista espiritual de México*. Trans. Angel María Garibay. México: Editorial Jus, 1947.

———. *The Spiritual Conquest of Mexico: An Essay on the Apostolate and the Evangelizing Methods of the Mendicant Orders in New Spain, 1523–1572*. 1933. Berkeley: University of California Press, 1966.

Riley, Carroll L. "Mesoamerican Indians in the Early Southwest." *Ethnohistory*, 21.1 (1974): 25–36.

Rivera Villanueva, José Antonio. "La influencia Tlaxcalteca en la vida politica de los pueblos indios de San Luis Potosi en (1590–1620)." In *Constructores de la nación: La migración tlaxcalteca en el norte de la Nueva España*, ed. Israel Cavazos Garza, 89–104. San Luis Potosí: El Colegio de San Luis, Gobierno de Tlaxcala, 1999.

Rodríguez Becerra, Salvador. *Encomienda y conquista: Los inicios de la colonización en Guatemala.* Seville: Publicaciones de la Universidad de Sevilla, 1977.

Rodríguez Losa, Salvador. "La encomienda, el indio y la tierra en el Yucatan colonial." *Revista de la Universidad de Yucatan* 20.115 (1978): 50–79.

Romero Frizzi, María de los Angeles. *El sol y la cruz: Los pueblos indios de Oaxaca colonial.* México: CIESAS, 1996.

Roskamp, Hans. "La heráldica novohispana del siglo XVI." In *Esplendor y ocaso de la cultura simbólico,* ed. Herón Pérez Martínez and Bárbara Skinfill, 227–68. Zamora: El Colegio de Michoacán/CONACYT, 2002.

Rostworowski de Diez Canseco, María. *Doña Francisca Pizzaro, una lustre mestiza, 1534–1598.* Lima: Instituto de Estudios Peruanos, 1989.

Ruiz de Alarcón, Hernando. *Treatise on the Heathen Superstitions that Today Live among the Indians Native to This New Spain.* 1629. Ed. Ross Hassig. Trans. J. Richard Andrews. Norman: University of Oklahoma Press, 1987.

Rújula y de Ochotorneo, José de, and Antonio del Solar y Tabaola. *Francisco de Montejo y las adelantados de Yucatán: Notas y documentos biográficos,* Badajoz: Ediciones Arqueros, 1931.

Ruz, Mario Humberto, ed. *El magnífico Señor Alonso López, alcalde de Santa Maria de la Victoria y aperreados de Indios (Tabasco).* 1541. México: Universidad Nacional Autónoma de México, 2000.

———. *Un rostro encubierto: Los indios del Tabasco colonial.* Mexico: CIESAS, 1994.

Sahagún, Bernardino de. *Florentine Codex: General History of the Things of New Spain.* Ed. and trans. Arthur J. O. Anderson and Charles E. Dibble. 12 vols. Salt Lake City: University of Utah Press, 1950–82. Originally written 1575–77 or 1578–80.

———. *Historia general de las cosas de Nueva España.* Ed. Alfredo López Austin and Josefina García Quintana. México: Conaculta/Cién de México, 2000.

———. *Historia general de las cosas de Nueva España.* Ed. Angel María Garibay. México: Editorial Porrúa, 1979.

———. *The War of Conquest: How It Was Waged Here in Mexico: The Aztec's Own Story as Given to Fr. Bernardino de Sahagún.* Trans. Arthur J. O. Anderson and Charles E. Dibble. Salt Lake City: University Press of Utah, 1978.

Sanchíz Ochoa, Pilar. *Los hidalgos de Guatemala: Realidad y apariencia en un sistema de valores.* Seville: Publicaciones Universidad de Sevilla, 1976.

Schroeder, Susan. *Chimalpahin and the Kingdoms of Chalco.* Tucson: University of Arizona Press, 1991.

———. "Looking Back at the Conquest: Nahua Perceptions of Early Encounters from the Annals of Chimalpahin." In *Chipping Away on Earth: Studies in Prehispanic and Colonial Mexico in Honor of Arthur J.O. Anderson and Charles E. Dibble,* ed. Eloise Quiñones Keber, 89–94. Lancaster: Labyrinthos, 1994.

———. "Loser History, or the Conquest of Mexico as a Nonevent." Fellows paper, Newberry Library, May 2000.

Stuart Schwartz. *Victors and Vanquished: Spanish and Nahua Views of the Conquest of Mexico* Boston: Bedford/St. Martin's, 2000.

Seed. Patricia. *Ceremonies of Possession in Europe's Conquest of the New World, 1492–1640.* Cambridge: Cambridge University Press, 1995.

————. "Social Dimensions of Race: Mexico City, 1753." *Hispanic American Historical Review* 62.4 (1982): 569–606.

Sego, Eugene. *Aliados y adversarios: Los colonos tlaxcaltecas en la frontera septentrional de Nueva España*. San Luis Potosí: El Colegio de San Luis Gobierno del Estado de Tlaxcala Centro de Investigaciones Históricas de San Luis Potosí, 1998.

Shadow, Robert. "Conquista y gobierno español en la frontera norte de la Nueva Galicia: El caso de Colotlán." *Relaciones* 32 (1987): 40–75.

Sheridan Prieto, Cecilia. "'Indios madrineros': Colonizadores tlaxcaltecas en el noreste novohispano." *Estudios de Historia Novohispana* 24 (January / June 2001): 15–51.

Sherman, William. *Forced Native Labor in Sixteenth-Century Central America*. Lincoln: University of Nebraska Press, 1979.

————. "Tlaxcalans in Post-conquest Guatemala." *Tlalocan* 6 (1970): 124–39.

Silverblatt, Irene. *Moon, Sun, and Witches: Gender Ideologies and Class in Inca and Colonial Peru*. Princeton: Princeton University Press, 1987.

Simmons, Marc. "Tlascalans in the Spanish Borderlands." *New Mexico Historical Review* 39 (January 1964): 101–10.

Simpson, Leslie Byrd. *The Encomienda in New Spain*. Berkeley: University of California Press, 1966 [1950].

Small, David B. ed. *Methods in the Mediterranean: Historical and Archaeological Views on Texts and Archaeology*. Leiden: E. J. Brill, 1995.

Smith, Michael E. "The Expansion of the Aztec Empire: A Case Study in the Correlation of Diachronic Archaeological and Ethnohistorical Data." *American Antiquity* 51 (1987): 37–54.

Smith, Michael E., and Francis F. Berdan, eds. *The Postclassic Mesoamerican World*. Salt Lake City: University of Utah Press, 2003.

————. "Spatial Structure of the Mesoamerican World System." In *The Postclassic Mesoamerican World*, ed. Michael E. Smith and Francis F. Berdan, 21–31. Salt Lake City: University of Utah Press, 2003.

Socolow, Susan. *The Women of Colonial Latin America*. Cambridge: Cambridge University Press, 2000.

Solís y Ribadenyra [Rivadeneira], Antonio de. *Historia de la conquista de México*. 1684. Ed. Edmundo O'Goman and José Valero Silva. México: Editorial Porrúa, 1990.

————. *The History of the Conquest of Mexico by the Spaniards*. Trans. Thomas Townsend. London: Woodward, Hookes, and Peele, 1724.

Sousa, Lisa M., and Kevin Terraciano. "The Original Conquest of Oaxaca: Nahua and Mixtec Accounts of the Spanish Conquest." *Ethnohistory* 50.2 (2003): 349–400.

Spalding, Karen. *Huarochirí: An Andean Society under Inca and Spanish Rule*. Stanford: Stanford University Press, 1984.

Starr, Frederick. *The Mapa de Cuauhtlantzinco or Códice Campos*. Chicago: The University of Chicago Press, 1898.

Stern, Steve J. "Paradigms of Conquest: History, Historiography, and Politics." *Journal of Latin American Studies, The Colonial and Post-Colonial Experience: Five*

Centuries of Spanish and Portuguese America 20 (Quincentenary Supplement, 1992): 1–34.

———. *Peru's Indian Peoples and the Challenge of Spanish Conquest: Huamanga to 1640.* Madison: University of Wisconsin Press, 1982.

———. "The Rise and Fall of Indian-White Alliances: A Regional View of 'Conquest History'" *Hispanic American Historical Review* 61.3 (1981): 461–91.

———. *The Secret History of Gender: Women, Men, and Power in Late Colonial Mexico.* Chapel Hill: University of North Carolina Press, 1993.

Szewczyk, David M. "New Elements in the Society of Tlaxcala, 1519–1618." In *Provinces of Early Mexico: Variants of Spanish American Regional Evolution,* ed. Ida Altman and James Lockhart, 137–54. Los Angeles: UCLA Latin American Center Publications, 1976.

Tavárez, David. "Invisible Wars: Idolatry Extirpation Projects and Native Responses in Nahua and Zapotec Communities, 1536–1728." Ph.D. diss., University of Chicago, 2000.

Taylor, William B. *Magistrates of the Sacred: Priests and Parishioners in Eighteenth-Century Mexico.* Stanford: Stanford University Press, 1996.

Tello, Antonio. *Cronica Miscelanea de la Sancta Provincia de Jalisco.* 1652. 5 vols. Guadalajara: Instituto Jalisciense de Antropología, 1968–84.

Terraciano, Kevin. "The Colonial Mixtec Community." *Hispanic American Historical Review* 80.1 (2000): 1–42.

Thompson, Philip. *Tekanto: A Maya Town in Yucatán.* New Orleans: MARI, 2000.

Torquemada, Juan de. *Los veynte y un libros rituales y monarchia yndiana.* Seville: Mathias Clauijo, 1615.

Torre, Mario de la. *El lienzo de Tlaxcala.* México: Cartón y Papel de Mexico, 1983.

Toulet Abasolo, Lucina M. *Tlaxcala en la conquista de México: El mito de la traición.* Tlaxcala: Tlaxcallan, Ediciones del Patronato Estatal de Promotores Voluntarios en Tlaxcala, 1996.

Townsend, Camilla. "Story without Words: Women and the Creation of a Mestizo People in Guayaquil, 1820–1835." *Latin American Perspectives* 24.4 (1997): 50–68.

Trexler, Richard C. "We Think, They Act: Clerical Readings of Missionary Theatre in 16th-Century New Spain." In *Understanding Popular Culture: Europe from the Middle Ages to the Nineteenth Century,* ed. Stephen L. Kaplan, 189–227. Berlin: Mouton, 1984.

Trigger, B. *A History of Archaeological Thought.* Cambridge: Cambridge University Press, 1989.

van der Sleen, W. G. N. *Mexico: Geschiedenis, land en volk.* Tilburg: Nederland's Boekhuis, n.d.

Varner, John Grier, and Jeannette Johnson Varner. *Dogs of the Conquest.* Norman: University of Oaklahoma Press, 1983.

Velázquez, María del Carmen. *Colotlán: Doble frontera contra los bárbaros, Cuadernos del Instituto de Historia.* México: Universidad Nacional Autónoma de México, 1961.

Vinson, Ben, III, and Matthew Restall. "Black Soldiers, Native Soldiers: Meanings of Military Service in the Spanish American Colonies." In *Beyond Black and Red:*

African-Native Relations in Colonial Latin America, ed. Matthew Restall, 15–52. Albuquerque: University of New Mexico Press, 2005.

Voight, Lisa. "Peregrine Peregrinations: Rewriting Travel and Discovery in Mestizo Chronicles of New Spain." *Revista de Estudios Hispánicos* 40 (2006): 3–24.

Voorhies, Barbara, ed. *Ancient Trade and Tribute. Economies of the Socomusco Region of Mesoamerica.* Salt Lake City: University of Utah Press, 1989.

Warner, Richard R. "An Ethnohistory of the Coras of the Sierra del Nayar, 1600–1830." Ph.D. diss., University of California at Santa Cruz, 1998.

Warren, J. Benedict. *The Conquest of Michoacan: The Spanish Domination of the Tarascan Kingdom in Western Mexico, 1521–1530.* Norman: University of Oklahoma Press, 1985.

Wasserstrom, Robert. "Spaniards and Indians in Colonial Chiapas, 1528–1790." In *Spaniards and Indians in Southeastern Mesoamerica: Essays on the History of Ethnic Relations,* ed. Murdo J. MacLeod and Robert Wasserstrom, 92–106. Lincoln: University of Nebraska, 1983.

Weigand, Phil, and Acelia G. de Weigand. *Tenamaxtli y Guaxicar: Las raíces profundas de la rebelión de Nueva Galicia.* Zamora: El Colegio de Michoacán, 1996.

Wood, Stephanie. "The Cosmic Conquest: Late-Colonial Views of the Sword and Cross in Central Mexican Titulos." *Ethnohistory* 38.2 : 176–95.

———. *Transcending Conquest: Nahua Views of Spanish Colonial Mexico.* Norman: University of Oklahoma Press, 2003.

Ximenez, Francisco. *Historia de la provincia de San Vicente de Chiapa y Guatemala de la Orden de Predicadores.* Ed. Carmelo Sáenz de Santa María. Guatemala: Sociedad de Geografía e Historia de Guatemala, 1977.

Yannakakis, Yanna. "Indios Ladinos: Indigenous Intermediaries and the Negotiation of Local Rule in Colonial Oaxaca, 1660–1769." Ph.D. diss., University of Pennsylvania, 2003.

Yoneda, Keiko. "Los mapas de Cuauhtinchan." *Arqueología Mexicana* 7.38 (1999): 18–24.

———. "Los mapas de Cuauhtinchan y la historia cartográfica prehispánica, un análisis estilíco." Ph.D. diss., Universidad Nacional Autónoma de México, 1978. Published by the Archivo General de la Nación, 1981.

Zaragoza, José Luis Razo, ed. *Crónicas de la conquista del reino de Nueva Galicia.* Guadalajara: Ayuntamiento de la Ciudad de Guadalajara, Instituto Jalisciense de Antropología e Historia, 1963.

Závala, Silvio. *La encomienda indiana.* Madrid: Imprenta Helénica, 1935.

———. *Los esclavos indios en Nueva España.* México: Colegio Nacional, 1967.

———. *La filosofía política en la conquista de América.* México: Fondo de Cultura Económica, 1947.

Závala, Silvio, and María Castelo, *Fuentes para la historia del trabajo en Nueva España.* Mexico: Fondo de Cultura Económica, 1939.

Zeitlin, Judith Francis. *Cultural Politics in Colonial Tehuantepec: Community and State among the Isthmus Zapotec, 1500–1750.* Stanford: Stanford University Press, 2005.

CONTRIBUTORS

Ida Altman received her Ph.D. in history from the Johns Hopkins University and was a university research professor at the University of New Orleans, where she taught from 1982 to 2006. She joined the University of Florida's history department in August 2006. She is the author of *Emigrants and Society: Extremadura and Spanish America in the Sixteenth Century* (University of California Press, 1989) and of *Transatlantic Ties in the Spanish Empire: Brihuega, Spain, and Puebla, Mexico, 1560–1620* (Stanford University Press, 2000) and coauthor, with Sarah Cline and Juan Javier Pescador, of *The Early History of Greater Mexico* (Prentice Hall, 2003). Her current research interests include the conquest and settlement of New Galicia (western Mexico) and interethnic relations in the early Spanish Caribbean.

Florine G. L. Asselbergs received her Ph.D. in ethnohistory at Leiden University, the Netherlands, specializing in the study of Mesoamerican pictorial manuscripts and history. She is the author of *Conquered Conquistadors: The Lienzo de Quauhquechollan: A Nahua Vision of the Conquest of Guatemala* (CNWS, 2004) and has published articles in the journal *Mesoamerica*. She has taught at Leiden University and conducted archaeological, ethnological, and archival research in Mexico, Guatemala, Belize, Nicaragua, Puerto Rico, Guadeloupe, and Spain. Currently, she is working on the Mapa de Cuauhtinchan project directed by David Carrasco and on several collections of primary source material from Guatemala.

Bret Blosser, an instructor for Sierra Institute, Humboldt State University, received his Ph.D. in anthropology from Tulane University. Recent publications include "Music, massage, sweeping, and Peyote: Two Curanderos' Methods and Disease Concepts in Eighteenth-Century New Spain," in *Acta Americana*. He is currently engaged in a project on the body and landscape in the Borgia Group codices.

John F. Chuchiak IV is an associate professor of history at Missouri State University and received his Ph.D. from Tulane University. His interests include the ecclesiastical history of colonial Mexico and Yucatan and colonial Maya ethnohistory. He is the author of *The Holy Office of the Inquisition in New Spain: A Documentary History* (Forbes Mills Press, 2007) and recent articles in *Iglesia y Sociedad en América Latina Colonial, Saastun: Revista de Cultura Maya, Journal of Early Modern History, Ethnohistory, Americas*, and *Current Anthropology*. He is currently working on a book about extirpations of idolatry in colonial Yucatan.

Robinson A. Herrera received his Ph.D. in history at the University of California at Los Angeles. He is an associate professor of history at Florida State University. His book *Natives, Europeans, and Spaniards in Sixteenth-Century Santiago de Guatemala* (University of Texas Press, 2003) treats the social, economic, and cultural life of the colonial Central American capital. His current research deals with the cultural life of Guatemala in the modern period and visual representations of Latin America in U.S. culture. He has published articles in the journals *Americas* and *Anales de la Academia de Geografía e Historia*.

Laura E. Matthew received her Ph.D. in history from the University of Pennsylvania and is an assistant professor of Latin American history at Marquette University. She specializes in the history of Central America, with a particular interest in the interactions between Mesoamerican peoples over time. Her articles on Nahuatl and Nahuas in colonial Guatemala have appeared in the journals *Mesoamerica* and the *Journal of Colonialism and Colonial History*. She is currently working on a book-length study of the Nahua colony of Ciudad Vieja, Guatemala.

Michel R. Oudijk received his Ph.D. from Leiden University in the Netherlands and is a researcher at the Instituto de Investigaciones Filológicas at the Universidad Nacional Autónoma in Mexico City, where he is currently working on the translation and analysis of Zapotec colonial texts. He has published extensively on Zapotec history and Meso-american pictographic documents, including *Historiography of the Benizaa* (CNWS, 2000) but shows a growing interest in the interaction between indigenous and Spanish colonial societies.

Matthew Restall received his Ph.D. in history from the University of Califonia at Los Angeles. He is a professor of Latin American history, director of Latin American Studies, and director of Graduate Studies in History at the Pennsylvania State University. He is the author of over half a dozen books on the history of colonial Spanish America, including *The Maya World* (Stanford University Press, 1997), *Maya Conquistador* (Beacon Press, 1998), and *Seven Myths of the Spanish Conquest* (Oxford University Press, 2003).

Susan Schroeder, France Vinton Scholes Professor of Colonial Latin American History at Tulane University, received her Ph.D. in history from the University of California at Los Angeles. Her research interests are Nahua Mesoamerica and Nahuatl philology. She is the author of numerous works on indigenous perceptions of the conquest, the Jesuits, Nahuas as marginal intellectuals, resistance, religion, and women and is the general editor, coeditor and cotranslator of the two-volume *Codex Chimalpahin* (University of Oklahoma Press, 1997) and *Annals of His Time* (Stanford University Press, 2006).

Stephanie Wood, an historian, is the associate director of the Wired Humanities Project and a senior research associate at the Center for the Study of Women in Society at the University of Oregon. She received her Ph.D. from the University of California at Los Angeles. Her most recent book is *Transcending Conquest: Nahua Views of Spanish Colonial Mexico* (University of Oklahoma Press, 2003). She is also editing the online Mapas Project, Early Nahuatl Virtual Library Project, and the Virtual Mesoamerican Archive.

Yanna Yannakakis is an assistant professor of history at Montana State University. She received her Ph.D. from the University of Pennsylvania. She specializes in ethnohistory, cultural, political, and legal history, and the regional history of Oaxaca. She has published articles in *Historia Mexicana* and *Latin American Research Review*. Her book *The Art of Being In-Between: Native Intermediaries and The Politics of Indigenous Identity in Colonial Oaxaca, 1660–1810* is forthcoming from Duke University Press.